THE FIRST FR[EEDOMS]

8 20

THE FIRST FREEDOMS

Church and State in America
to the Passage
of the First Amendment

THOMAS J. CURRY

OXFORD UNIVERSITY PRESS
New York   Oxford

Oxford University Press

Oxford   New York   Toronto
Delhi   Bombay   Calcutta   Madras   Karachi
Petaling Jaya   Singapore   Hong Kong   Tokyo
Nairobi   Dar es Salaam   Cape Town
Melbourne   Auckland

and associated companies in
Beirut   Berlin   Ibadan   Nicosia

Copyright © 1986 by Thomas J. Curry

First published in 1986 by Oxford University Press, Inc.,
200 Madison Avenue, New York, New York 10016

First issued as an Oxford University Press paperback, 1987

Oxford is a registered trademark of Oxford University Press

Library of Congress Cataloging in Publication Data
Curry, Thomas J.
The first freedoms.
Bibliography: p.   Includes index.
1. Church and state—United States—History—18th century.
2. Church and state—United States—History—19th century.
3. United States—Church history—Colonial period, ca. 1600-1775.
4. United States—Church history—19th century.   I. Title.
BR516.C94   1986   322'.1'0973   85-13693
ISBN 0-19-503661-1
ISBN 0-19-505181-5 ppbk.

2 4 6 8 10 9 7 5 3 1
Printed in the United States of America

To the memory of my father and mother,
Thomas and Mary Curry

Preface

The continuing dispute over the meaning of the statement "Congress shall pass no law respecting the establishment of religion or prohibiting the free exercise thereof" began with the Supreme Court's *Everson v. Board of Education* decision in 1947. There the Court construed the "establishment clause" to mean that government might not aid one religion exclusively or all religions equally. Critics from then until now have argued that the religion clauses were intended to ban exclusive aid to one religion, i.e. the creation of a state religion, but not to forbid evenhanded government aid to all religions.

The opposing sides have tangled in heated engagements, but have now settled into a kind of trench warfare. The Court's defenders rely on Madison's and Jefferson's clearly enunciated predilections for Church and State. They especially cite the evidence surrounding the controversy over a general assessment in Virginia in the 1780s, wherein that state, after a widespread public debate, refused to approve a plan to grant non-exclusive state assistance to religion. On the other hand, the Court's critics cite the terminology used by those connected with the passage of the Amendment. This repeatedly called for a ban on "articles of faith" or for the prohibition of an establishment of a "national" religion or "any one" sect or religion in "preference" to others. They also point to the fact that both before and after the Amendment's enactment, state and federal governments maintained numerous contacts with religion and assisted it in multifarious ways.

A study of the modern literature on the meaning of the religious clauses of the First Amendment might well lead one to the conclusion that opposing scholars had checkmated each other, and that history had nothing more to offer by way of clarification. One scholar concluded: "The search for original meaning and historical purpose underlying the language [of the First Amendment religion clauses] has yielded inconclusive results, and it would not be profitable to explore the matter in detail. In the end the Supreme Court is free to give this language the meaning it chooses."* Judgment as to the wisdom of my disregarding that advice will have to rest with the reader.

Most of the studies on both sides of the argument have relied principally on the events immediately surrounding the passage of the Bill of Rights. The present work attempts to elucidate the intentions underlying the First Amendment's religion clauses by framing the concepts embodied in them within the overall picture of colonial and revolutionary America, and it has proceeded primarily as an exercise in tracing ideas on Church and State.

In contrast to many other Church-State commentators, I have avoided using the term "separation of Church and State." That phrase provides a handy summation of the First Amendment religion clauses and will doubtlessly perdure in common usage. For purposes of analysis, however, it obscures rather than clarifies the issue. Treating the First Amendment in terms of "a wall of separation" only moves the subject from the sphere of the legal and concrete to the realm of metaphor and symbol.

This study has emerged from an examination of public colonial and state documents, but principally from a systematic combing of Evans's *Early American Imprints* and relevant newspapers. As the references will show, I have also been guided by the work of many preceding scholars. Even a brief perusal of the notes will indicate my indebtedness to the work of William G. McLoughlin, especially his splendid *New England Dissent.*

Over the several years this work has been in preparation, I have run up a considerable debt of gratitude. I am grateful to the Haynes and MacNeel Pierce Foundations for providing financial support while I was researching the original dissertation. To Cardinal Timothy Manning, who provided the opportunity for me to do this study, I am deeply beholden. I consider myself singularly fortunate to have studied with Professor Leonard W. Levy at the Claremont Graduate School. He suggested the topic and guided me at every stage. In the giving of his time, knowledge, and resources, he has been to me the model teacher and enviable mentor. For the unfailing assistance of Lois B. Marquez at each phase of the work's progress, I can only offer an inadequate but most sincere thanks.

Los Angeles   T.J.C.
April 1985

*Paul Kauper, *Religion and the Constitution*, Baton Rouge, 1964.

Contents

THE FIRST FREEDOMS

I

The New England Way in Church and State to 1691

When Henry VIII separated England from the papacy, he retained intact the substance of the Roman Church. His daughter Elizabeth saw no reason to do otherwise, much to the vexation of a growing body of Puritans, English Calvinists who wanted to regenerate the English Church until it conformed—especially in liturgy and government—to what they believed the Word of God, i.e. the Bible, dictated:

> The Doctrine Condemns and cashieres at once all the Ceremonies, and whatever other Inventions of men have been introduced into the worship of God by the Spirit of AntiChrist, and reteined, and continued by some reforming Magistrates, who have made but incomplete and imperfect Reformations. As who knows not, that almost all the Ordinances of Christ have been polluted and corrupted by them. The Gospel might not be preached without a Surplice, nor Baptisme administered without the sign of the Cross, So likewise kneeling at the Sacrament, bowing to the Altar, and to the name of Jesus, Popish holy days, holiness of places, Organs and Cathedral Musick, The Books of Common prayer, Prelacy or Church Government by Bishops . . . They are nothing else but reliques of Popery, and remnants of Baal, and therefore when the Kingdome of Christ is come, they shall perish from off the Earth, and from under these Heavens.[1]

Upon Elizabeth's death in 1603, the accession to the English throne of the Scottish and Presbyterian James I seemed the answer to a Puritan prayer, but not for long. James proved disappointing. His famous statement "No Bishop, no King" summarized his apprehension that Puritan inspiration might not be limited to purely religious affairs, and he did not choose to test the validity of his suspicion.[2]

James's successor, Charles I, by his reliance on Archbishop Laud and predilection for "popish" ceremonies, disillusioned Puritans even more. In 1630, despairing of changing the Church at home, numbers of them decided to abandon the struggle and instead try to build the Church of God in the wilderness of the New World. Hardly had they secured a foothold on the shores of New England, when the opposition to both Church and government of their brethren in England pushed that country into civil war between king and Puritan-supported Parliament. The resulting defeat of Charles cleared the way for the long-awaited religious reform.

In the aftermath of this Puritan success, what had appeared to be a unified religious movement in the Mother Country disintegrated into a multiplicity of competing groups. In 1660 England's victorious reformers, unable to agree among themselves, finally resorted to restoring the monarchy by recalling the king's son, Charles II, from exile. High hopes for uniformity of belief and practice had to give way before the realization that religious toleration might be the only path to national stability.

The desire for religious homogeneity died hard, however. Not until the Revolution of 1688 removed another king from the throne and replaced him with the Dutch William of Orange, did England finally come to accept Protestant diversity, whose legitimacy the government officially proclaimed in the Act of Toleration of 1689. By that time, more than half a century had passed since the founding of the New England settlements, years during which American Puritans had enforced uniformity far more successfully than their English counterparts. Yet successive religious and political developments in England reverberated through the colonies across the Atlantic as constant warnings that they would ultimately have to adapt to a larger world.

Until they came to power in England in the 1640s, antipathy toward a common foe, Anglo-Catholicism, served to hold Puritans together in an apparent unity. Bishops who wanted to retain Catholic forms of worship and government topped their list of enemies. Contemporary English politicians admitted the usefulness of a solid opposition. In 1641, in a moment of zeal, the members of Parliament declared they would maintain and defend "the true reformed religion expressed in the doctrine of the Church of England"; but a week later, they explained that "whereas some doubts have been raised by several persons, out of this House, concerning the meaning of the . . .

Protestation," they intended only to specify the doctrine of the Church of England "so far as it is opposite to Popery, and Popish innovations."[3]

Before deep divisions fragmented English Puritans, numbers of them had uprooted themselves and their families from English soil to construct, thousands of miles to the west, a pure church and a godly society that could be a model for the old corrupted world.[4] Among the four settlements founded for this purpose, the Massachusetts Bay colony assumed primary importance in working out the experiment, defining its objectives, waging its battles, and recording its progress. Originally formed as the Massachusetts Bay Company, a trading association, it transformed itself into a body politic in 1630, when its members emigrated and carried their charter with them. Massachusetts drew to itself a majority of the important Puritan clerical and lay leaders who came to America, as well as most of the attention and comment, both sympathetic and hostile, of those who remained in England.[5]

Massachusetts was not the first Puritan colony, however. Plymouth had preceded it by ten years. The Pilgrims who settled there were Puritans who, to avoid persecution, had earlier fled England for Holland, from where they subsequently embarked on their journey to the New World. Poorer than their Massachusetts brethren and possessed of little social or intellectual distinction, the Pilgrims entertained less grandiose notions of mission. They wished simply to enjoy pure worship and simultaneously preserve their English heritage for their children. For most of the years of its existence as an individual colony, until its merger with Massachusetts in 1690, Plymouth sheltered in the lee of its famous neighbor. The Pilgrims, however, although they unquestionably shared the beliefs and opinions of their fellow Puritans, tended to temper their religious zeal with a moderation born partly of poverty and partly of loose organization.[6]

The two other Puritan colonies, Connecticut and New Haven, came into being in the late 1630s, both founded by settlers who had left the Massachusetts Bay community. Situated just south of Massachusetts, Connecticut experienced less local dissension than the former and, as a result, attracted less attention from abroad.[7] West of Connecticut, the rigorous spirit of the Reverend John Davenport permeated tiny New Haven. Under his leadership, this colony adopted the least flexible attitude of the four in attempting to establish a Bible commonwealth. In limiting the franchise to church members, New Haven followed the pattern of Massachusetts; but it tended to be even stricter than the Bay colony in its discipline and more intransigent in dealing with dissent.[8]

Regardless of variations in atmosphere and degree of conformity,

Plymouth, Massachusetts, Connecticut, and New Haven shared a common determination to enjoy, as John Cotton, teacher at Boston and New England's most distinguished minister, phrased it, "liberty, not of some ordinances of God, but of all, and all in purity."⁹ The inhabitants of all four settlements adhered to a basic and optimistic belief that the Bible, liberated from "popish superstition" and read correctly, would prove a clear and infallible guide to the constitution of both Church and State, and no one who refused to follow the canons of Scripture was to be tolerated.¹⁰ Believers thought that the clarity of the scriptural message manifested itself especially in fundamental truths, as distinct from inessentials or things indifferent; but by refraining from drawing a hard and fast line between these two categories, they allowed themselves room for maneuvering and adapting to changing realities both within and without the movement.

Puritan writers did not, of course, claim that the Bible answered every question directly. Nor did all passages of Scripture carry equal weight. Old Testament law dealing with morals was far more important than that covering matters judicial or ceremonial.¹¹ Moreover, one had to make use of reason in construing the Word of God. Cotton affirmed that "whatsoever is drawn out of the Scripture by just consequence and deduction is as well the word of God as that which is an express Commandment."¹² Richard Mather, minister at Dorchester, Massachusetts, acknowledged that many of the principal terms of Puritan theology were not to be found in the Bible, but reasoned that they could be used "because the thing meant there can be found." Though they denied to any church the kind of authority Catholicism claimed in interpreting the Bible, Puritans did recommend the beliefs and practices of "the best reformed churches" as a guide to the meaning of passages of Scripture.¹³

In commenting on the Puritan colonies, historians have ranged from portraying them as theocracies ruled by dour Protestant clergy to describing them as practicing a separation of Church and State. The terms "theocracy" and "separation of Church and State" are of little use in attempting to understand seventeenth-century New England. Theocracy, now a word of opprobrium, expressed for Puritans the optimum form of government, "to make the Lord God our Governor." Separation of Church and State, now considered laudable, would for them have represented an unthinkable arrangement.¹⁴

Taken at face value, numerous statements by New England Puritan writers would prove that they accepted the modern idea of freedom of conscience—that a person should be allowed peaceably to believe and practice, or not believe or practice, any religion—and that they clearly demarcated the roles of Church and State. On the other hand, again taken at face value, divers other statements by those same writers rejected both ideas. To interpret these as discrepancies is historically misleading. One can combine both sets of propositions into a coherent picture of New England thinking on freedom of worship and on the connection between religion and government by fitting them into the framework of Puritan assumptions and presuppositions about truth, conscience, the Bible, and the power of the magistrate. This done, they cease to be contradictory.

In England the majority of Puritans never rejected the authority of the civil power in religious affairs. They were content to wait until the Lord put them in control.[15] The emigrants to America, however, having suffered at the hands of church authorities in the Mother Country, avoided imitating what they regarded as the worst features of the English arrangement. Thus the New England clergy limited themselves to religious affairs. They created no ecclesiastical courts to enforce marriage laws, probate wills, or assign fines for moral lapses. New England clerics, although on request they could and did give advice to the secular governments, could not hold civil offices, as the English bishops did. Nor did excommunication in New England deprive a person of secular rights and subject him to social ostracism. In Massachusetts, where all attended church but only the elect were church members, excommunication merely took away membership, not civil prerogatives already acquired.[16]

By divesting religious bodies of temporal power and confining them to spiritual matters, Puritan New England began rearranging the components of Church-State relations into their future American pattern. The model hidden in this new taxonomy, however, would not begin to assume visible shape and substance until it had emerged from the context of the seventeenth century. Indeed, at the time of their founding, the colonies' most radical departure from English religious practice was their failure to form a church. None of them set up a religious organization comparable to the Church of England; rather, local congregations formed churches subject to no central religious authority.[17]

The English Puritans who moved to the New World presupposed that truth existed, and that they possessed it more fully than any other people, a conviction common to seventeenth-century religious groups. Moreover, they were certain that their colonies, in order to prosper, must be united in that truth. When dissenters later began to point out that those who had traveled across the ocean in search of freedom of religion were attempting to impose on others' consciences, they vehemently denied the accusation, insisting that they forced belief on no one. This assertion on their part was true. What they did unequivocally demand—again like other English religious bodies of the time—was external conformity to the truth as they saw it. John Winthrop, the leading light and first governor of Massachusetts, warned his followers while they were still on the seas that "the only way to avoyde this ship-wracke and to provide for our posterity is . . . walk humbly with our God, for this end, we must be knitt together in this worke as one man." Emphasizing the exclusivity of the venture, both he and later writers described Massachusetts in terms of a family.[18]

Magistrates and ministers agreed on the need for religious con-formity; yet in the absence of a central church government to define and enforce orthodoxy, the semi-independent congregations were undoubtedly apt to degenerate rapidly into religious pluralism, a con-dition Puritans considered synonymous with anarchy. Consequently, in their efforts to maintain and promote uniform religious practice, Puritan governments gradually began to assume roles reminiscent of those of English ecclesiastical authorities. In 1636 the Massachusetts legislature, the General Court, issued an order forbidding the forma-tion of any new churches without the permission of the magistrates and the majority of the Elders. At first, the General Court merely invited congregations to send representatives to church synods; later, it ordered them to do so.[19]

New England divines insisted repeatedly that demand for uni-formity of religious practice in no way violated liberty of conscience. They contended that there were two types of liberty—natural (or corrupted) liberty and the "liberty wherewith Christ hath made us free." Liberty to practice error came under the former heading and was not really liberty at all, but license, the "liberty for men to destroy themselves."[20]

Nor could the plea of conscience justify the toleration of error. Puritans defined conscience in William Ames's terms, as "a man's judgment of himself according to the judgment of God of him." Only God could bind conscience; but the essential truths of God's plan for humanity were self-evident from Scripture. Thus one who refused to accept them would not be acting according to his conscience.[21] John Cotton reiterated:

> That Fundamentals are so cleare, that a man cannot but be convinced in Conscience of the Truth of them after two or three Admonitions: and that therefore such a Person as still continues obstinate, is con-demned of himself: and if He then be punished, He is not punished for his Conscience, but for sinning against his owne Conscience.[22]

When Puritans spoke of conscience, then, they referred solely to "a good conscience enlightened by the Spirit of God"; similarly, when they spoke of relying on reason, they meant "spiritual" reason, as distinguished from "carnal" reason.[23]

The numerous churches were happy to leave the task of ensuring consistency of religious practice to the magistrates. Ministers agreed that secular authority could correct erring congregations and even synods.[24] No explicit platform of carefully formulated doctrines, however, provided the basis for this mutual trust between clergy and magistracy. Indeed, much of the strength of New England Puritanism resulted from its reluctance to be tied down to precise doctrinal definitions, especially in disputed areas.

Consensus among the leaders of both spheres stemmed from the broad framework of Calvinist theology, a general espousal of a congregational form of church government, and common seventeenth-century morality. Because of their shared perceptions, experiences, and overall outlook, they could communicate with each other comfortably in the language of Puritanism, e.g. what was or was not "according to the Word," confident that they would easily recognize any belief or practice that was at odds with fundamentals, and so they did not need to spell out specific underlying tenets.

Such a climate of civil and religious accord did not exclude occasional arguments. Much of Winthrop's *History of New England* dealt with the working out, over Massachusetts's first two decades, of such matters as the right of magistrates to interfere in the regulation of church meetings, and to what extent the government could use ministers as messengers.[25] Furthermore, the records left by those who were very much a part of this ruling consensus are flavored with indications that the general populace sometimes viewed its efforts with something less than maximum respect, as when one Samuel Norman remarked—and was whipped for it—that "if any minister which come will but raile against England some would receive him"; or when the common people were delighted with the minister at Weymouth, Massachusetts, who, following English practice, allowed all baptized persons to receive communion (before the General Court caught him).[26] Nevertheless, there is no evidence to prove that the cooperation between churches and governments in the New England colonies lacked an extensive popular base. Whatever the depth or formality of their arrangements, clerics and public officials continued to work together to preserve the orthodoxy they considered absolutely necessary to the success of the Puritan experiment.

A definite demarcation existed beyond which the nonconformist could not venture without incurring civil punishment, as well as ecclesiastical retribution. Cotton wrote that "men may discover such hypocrisie as may make them unfit for the Church, but yet they may not altogether be unfit for the Commonwealth." However, if the "hypocrisie" involved a belief or practice likely to spread to others, the government would soon add its own penalty to the church's excommunication of the offender, thereby confirming Cotton's further premise that "it is a great beauty for church and state to both purge the whole country from corruption in Religion."[27]

Despite this admixture of Church and State, Puritans did not consider the powers of the two confounded as long as magistrates did not meddle in things "merely inward" or assume the power of excommunication, and as long as ministers did not interfere with temporal authority. Moreover, since magistrates were expected to determine their actions in accordance with the Word, Puritans did not think that allotting them power to punish "Idolatry, Blasphemy, Heresy, or venting corrupt & pernicious opinions" constituted an Erastian policy, i.e. state supremacy in ecclesiastical affairs.[28]

Critics of the New England way, such as Roger Williams and the Quakers, wrote about religious freedom in the abstract and in a universal context. By contrast, most seventeenth-century New England writers addressed the topic solely in the context of their own circumstances. Preoccupied with the task of constructing a wholly new society from blueprints of biblical truth, they frequently found it difficult to hide their irritation at being deterred from the work at hand by those who demanded answers to hypothetical questions, censured their policies, or questioned their methods.

For example, when Williams and others pointed out that universal application of the New England principle of endowing magistrates with power in religious matters would give pagan magistrates power over Christian subjects, Cotton replied that magistrates were to be judges in matters so fundamental that none who was studious in religion or had any spiritual discernment could act amiss, and that pagans had been able to distinguish between innocent Christians and turbulent Seducers. He and Thomas Cobbett allowed, however, that pagan magistrates ought to forbear punishing in matters of religion until they had such knowledge of the truth as would enable them to perceive the fundamentals, and also that their subjects could communicate light to them.[29]

Such a contrived answer on the part of the Massachusetts ministers can most likely be read as a feeble attempt to come up with a plausible response to a matter in which they took little or no interest, because they could not see how it was of any consequence to New England.

One should continuously bear in mind, in arriving at an assessment of the many explanations and responses penned by Puritan writers in reaction to comments and criticism regarding the New England way, that they saw themselves, above all, as a "peculiar" people, a people who had completely escaped the corruptions of the Old World and were providentially at work in the New World translating God's plan for humanity into a visible social reality for the entire world to imitate. Forging new precedents almost daily, they had little stomach for arguing about what seemed to them irrelevant issues that the true Church of God, once completed, would obviate. Nevertheless, they did confront and attempt to overcome objections, insofar as they could do so without compromising the essential nature of their mission, and in order not to imperil their efforts by provoking the wrath of English authorities.

At first they felt no need to address the universal, because they believed themselves to be its harbinger: all the world would be New England. Later, when that dream began to fade, they averted their eyes from the rest of the world and, until the American Revolution and beyond, convinced themselves that the sufferings of their ancestors in leaving England and building a colony in the wilderness justified their being left alone to follow their "peculiar" way. The world was, after all, big enough for those who disagreed with them to go elsewhere. This attitude explained the wounded tone that Puritan writers adopted to describe the hardships, even persecution, they endured at the hands of those outsiders who had the indecency to intrude upon the family affairs of Puritan New England.[30]

If New England Puritans were visionaries, intent upon building "a citty upon a hill" for all the world to see, they were neither unrealistic idealists nor "giddy professors" (as they would later term their adversaries) determined to achieve their goals regardless of the consequences.[31] On the contrary, theirs was an extremely practical mentality, ready to work within the possibilities of the age. The first half-century of their experiment made it clear that they would shrink from giving unnecessary offense, but that if all else failed, they were prepared to stand firm for their beliefs. They cajoled their friends, equivocated with their critics—a technique they were not slow to dismiss as "quibbling" when others used it against them—and, when pressed by their enemies, showed remarkable gall in offering completely implausible explanations with apparent ingenuousness.

Even before the Massachusetts Bay Company moved with its charter to Massachusetts, it had laid down a basic policy warning its ministers not to render unnecessary offense by giving the impression of a rigid separation from the Church of England. In 1629 it instructed its agent John Endecott, in Salem, Massachusetts, that despite the company's best efforts to screen prospective settlers, some libertines would get through. These he was to corral with a firm hand, adhering as much as possible to the laws of England. Should that prove insufficient, he was "to proceed according to the power you have."[32]

The leaders of the Massachusetts colony had no time for dissidents and said so. Although such hardliners as John Davenport in New Haven and John Hull, merchant and mintmaster in Boston, regretted the failure of the authorities to rid the world of any heretics within reach, Massachusetts simply wanted dissenters to stay away. Jesuits, the supreme enemy, could enter the colony only at the risk of their lives; still, the law took care to make an exception for priests cast ashore by shipwreck. Furthermore, Massachusetts officials would leave heretics alone as long as these had sense enough to keep their opinions to themselves.[33]

The Puritan emigrants never did gain the privacy they hoped for and needed to proceed tranquilly with their task of building a society according to the Word. Not even New England's dense forests could shade the New World from the hostile scrutiny of the Old. Adverse publicity in England began early, for when the Massachusetts Bay Company instructed Endecott to use the power available to him to suppress dissidents, he did exactly that and shipped home two of the first settlers, the Browne brothers, because they wanted to worship according to the *Book of Common Prayer*. As a result of the furor they stirred up in the Mother Country, an embarrassed company found itself warning the undiplomatic Endecott against introducing laws distasteful to the home government, "to which (as we ought) we must and will have an obsequious eye." Other dissenters returning to England found a ready audience there for their tales of the strictness of the Massachusetts authorities, and critics exposed the doings of Puritans in America, to the delight of the emigrants' enemies and the discomfort of their friends.[34]

The Brownes had proved that the *Book of Common Prayer* was not acceptable in New England. Thomas Morton, a rambunctious settler and trader, who tangled with Plymouth and Massachusetts and was sent packing by both, made fun of the whole enterprise and raised anew accusations of schism and of persecution and domination by the Puritan clergy. These slurs deeply disturbed the colonists; but the constitutional crisis under way in England occupied the authorities there and left them little time for New England affairs.[35]

The first serious challenge to the Massachusetts undertaking took place within the colony itself, in the form of the Antinomian Controversy—a dispute arising out of Puritan theology and centering on the extent to which saving grace freed one from the law.[36] Anne Hutchinson, the principal figure in this dispute, had emigrated to Massachusetts from England in 1634 and soon gained wide popularity among the women of Boston because of her skill as a midwife and also her activity as a spiritual adviser. Crowds began to flock to her home to discuss the weekly sermons. These meetings put her into competition with the clergy, whom she further alienated by accusing them of preaching a "covenant of works" instead of a "covenant of grace." In so doing, she was clearly violating the norms of acceptable conduct, which (as the Massachusetts Bay Company had reminded Endecott in 1629) demanded deference to the clergy.

Anne Hutchinson's trial before the Massachusetts General Court in 1637 exemplified the difficulty the colony could encounter in forcing its arrangements on an able and quick-witted opponent, operating as it did in the area of religious uniformity according to implicit and unspecified agreement among its leaders. The authorities could not allow such a radical to undermine the infant colony; but neither would they suppress her out of hand or without discussion. Only when she overreached herself by claiming an immediate revelation from God could the General Court find a clear basis on which to condemn her. By declaring herself recipient of private revelations, she placed herself outside the bounds of a society organized according to the Word, which saw in Scripture sufficient answers to all religious problems. The Court frankly admitted that "such bottomless revelations, . . . being above reason and Scripture, they are not subject to control."

With regard to Mrs. Hutchinson herself, the Court commented: "Whereas the opinions . . . of Mrs. Hutchinson have seduced & led into dangerous errors many of the people . . . there is just cause for suspition that they, as others in Germany, in former times, may, upon some revelation, make some suddaine irruption upon those that differ from them in judgment."[37]

The term "others in Germany" referred to the Anabaptists of Munster, whose aberrations a hundred years earlier had become a mighty symbol to the world of the dangers of uncontrolled religion. Its use by New England Puritans extended to the New World a favourite technique of dealing with non-conformists, i.e. damning them by associating them with Anabaptists or stressing that the acceptance of their present practice would amount to acceptance of the most deviant behavior of the times. Perry Miller has written that orthodox Protestants anywhere would have rejected Anne Hutchinson's revelations; in

Massachusetts, particularly, conscience could not excuse. As Winthrop told her: "Your conscience you must keep or it must be kept for you."[38]

Another challenge to Puritan religious harmony arose out of a division within the movement between Presbyterians, who understood the true Church of God as possessed of a centralized government—albeit without bishops—embracing the entire nation, and those who thought it should consist of more or less autonomous congregations, gatherings of individuals who had a sense of their own salvation. In England, members of the latter group called themselves Independents; in New England they referred to themselves as Congregationalists. These two differing images constituted the major disjunction within Puritanism, a separation English Puritans in their earlier phases could and did submerge in their common opposition to the Catholic proclivities of the Church of England. In the early 1640s, however, hard on the heels of their victory over Charles I, the division resurfaced and proved irreparable.[39]

New England Puritans determined not to allow such a breach to nullify their own efforts to erect the true Church of God; but their setting up of strictly Congregational commonwealths aroused the suspicions of English Presbyterians, who began to write questioning letters on the subject. New England ministers responded to these in the most conciliatory fashion they could manage. Richard Mather, of Dorchester, tried to lull the accurate misgivings of Presbyterians that they would not be welcome in Massachusetts by assuring them that "we are persuaded if you were here, you would set up and practice the very same that we do."[40] From England sympathizers with the New England Puritans also sent advice and criticism. John White asked New Englanders not to bind all to tenets that upon examination might be found indifferent. After the Antinomian crisis, when the General Court issued an order that strangers were not to remain in Massachusetts longer than three weeks, Henry Vane, a former governor of the colony who had returned to England, pointed out the danger of giving the magistrates unlimited power. In reply Winthrop defended the decree by resorting again to his concept of the commonwealth as a great family.[41]

Regardless of transatlantic censure, Massachusetts determined to exclude dissenters from its household. Among these, Baptists proved most troublesome. Although they agreed with Congregationalists that church membership should be conferred only on those who had undergone the experience of conversion, Baptists insisted that even baptism itself should be reserved to such persons, while Congregationalists excluded non-members only from admission to communion.

That the Baptists' position represented a logical extension of the general Puritan practice of limiting church membership was a theory Congregationalists collectively refused to accept either then or later.[42]

In 1644 the General Court passed a law banishing Anabaptists, as it insisted on referring to Baptists. The statute provoked controversy both at home and abroad. A petition from "divers merchants and others" at home entreated against it on the ground that it caused offense to friends in England. The General Court refused either to alter or to justify the law, but it could not suppress such adverse comment.[43] Winthrop's own son Steven confirmed from England the unfavorable reaction there. Independents, who had become proponents of toleration, wrote to say that the Massachusetts example was injuring their cause. Henry Vane again warned that by extirpating dissenters in New England, Massachusetts was teaching Presbyterian opponents of Independents to do the same in Old England.[44] Meanwhile, English Presbyterian critics turned every situation to their own advantage. On the one hand, they cited the incidence of Antinomianism in New England to prove the ineffectiveness of Congregationalism in suppressing heresy. On the other, they used Massachusetts's restraint of dissent as evidence that English Independents' professions of toleration were probably fraudulent.[45]

To pleas for moderation, New England spokesmen responded with increasingly harsh denials. In uncommonly blunt tones, Nathaniel Ward, lawyer and minister at Ipswich, asserted that conscience was free insofar as it was free from error, and that all heretics had full liberty to stay away from New England.[46] Thomas Shepard's sermon of 1645, "New England's Lamentation for Old England's Errors," left no doubt as to the Puritan ministers' opinions of England's growing toleration. Shepard, minister at Cambridge, Massachusetts, wrote to Hugh Peters, an Independent minister who had returned to England: "I feare greater sorrows attend England if they do not seasonably suppress and beare publike witness agaynst such delusions which fill the land like locusts . . . and will certainly (if suffered) eat up the greene grasse of the land."[47]

Richard Saltonstall, one of the colony's founders, wrote from England of how grieved he was at Massachusetts's behavior, arguing that persecution only turned men into hypocrites. Cotton replied by denying that the authorities persecuted anyone, maintaining that they only punished disturbers of the peace. In his answer to the argument about hypocrisy, though, Cotton struck a new chord: "Better hypocrites than profane persons. Hypocrites give God his due in an outward form at least." There, indeed, was food for thought—a New

England divine hinting that, given the difficulties of building a commonwealth according to the Word of God, mere exterior conformity might have to suffice.[48]

Despite their refusal either to be swayed by their English friends or to accept criticism from their English enemies, New England Puritans nonetheless did worry about their image in the Mother Country and took pains to publish their side of the story. They were especially anxious that two critics in particular, Robert Child and Samuel Gorton, not be left unanswered.

Robert Child was a Puritan of the Presbyterian variety who, together with several other Massachusetts residents, petitioned in 1646 to have the limitations on both church membership and the franchise abolished. The petition purported to be a request for religious freedom, but was in fact an attempt to establish Presbyterianism in New England. The General Court not only rejected it, but summarily arrested Child and confiscated his papers, which contained an appeal to the English Parliament. Nevertheless, Child managed to get to England, where his brother published an account of the proceedings against the petitioners in Massachusetts.[49]

Samuel Gorton had come to Massachusetts in 1635 and pursued a stormy career, which included expulsion from Plymouth and a whipping for disturbing the peace at Newport (in the colony of Rhode Island, founded by Roger Williams after his expulsion from Massachusetts). In 1642 he and his followers settled a little south of Providence, Rhode Island. Gorton's troubles stemmed partly from his incorrigible personality and partly from his mystical religious beliefs, which Puritans labeled Familism—another common term of opprobrium in seventeenth-century religious controversies. On the pretext of a boundary dispute, the Massachusetts authorities arrested Gorton and tried him for his life on a charge of blasphemy. Narrowly escaping capital conviction, he was sentenced to prison, but soon banished. Subsequently, in London, he, too, broadcast a recital of the injustices he had suffered.[50]

To rebut both Child and Gorton, Massachusetts employed Edward Winslow, Plymouth's agent in England. Winslow did his best to make a case for the colony, contending that Presbyterians there enjoyed liberty of religion, and that New England punished only for turbulence and not for religion. In turn Child denied these assertions and accused Winslow of seeking credibility by playing up the notoriety of Gorton.[51] However, this flurry of pamphlets and New England's obvious concern for its image in no way weakened Massachusetts's determination to maintain uniformity.

When John Clark, Obediah Holmes, and several other Baptists visited friends in Lynn and held a meeting there, the authorities arrested and fined them. Clark's friends paid his fine; but Holmes refused to have his paid and was whipped. To the familiar argument that he was sentenced not for conscience but for practice, Clark replied that there could be no such thing as freedom of conscience without freedom to act. He traveled to England as the agent for Rhode Island and there published *Ill News from New England*, an account of his recent mistreatment in Massachusetts and indictment of the colony's attitude toward Baptists. Thomas Cobbett, the minister at Lynn, responded in defense of Massachusetts. The issues hashed out in this controversy were the same as those debated in the much better known dispute between John Cotton and New England's most famous dissident, Roger Williams.[52]

Williams first arrived in New England in 1631. During the next four years, as minister at Salem and, later, at Plymouth, he became involved in several altercations. Finally, in 1635, Massachusetts banished him because he insisted that the natives, rather than the king, were the true owners of the land; that unsaved persons should not swear oaths, this being part of the worship of God; that it was not lawful to attend services of the Church of England; and that the magistrate could punish only secular offenses.[53]

Since his own time, historians have portrayed Williams as a modern radical, a democrat, a prophet, or—as the Puritans saw him—a man with an overheated brain.[54] More recent scholars, especially Perry Miller and Edmund Morgan, have depicted him as every inch a seventeenth-century Puritan.[55] Indeed, religious issues did absorb him as passionately as they did other Puritans, even if he and they reached conflicting conclusions. Both before and after his banishment from Massachusetts, he searched unceasingly and unsuccessfully for the true Church, and all his writings on religious freedom subserved this quest. But having fixed Williams firmly in the seventeenth century as a man primarily interested in Puritan religious issues, one cannot restrict him completely to that context. Although he had little impact on the development of religious freedom in either his own or subsequent generations, he continues—more than three centuries later—to draw readers to himself because of his modernity.

Williams composed most of his works on religious freedom during visits to England in the 1640s and 1650s, nearly all of them written as part of an extended debate with John Cotton. For the modern reader, Williams's and Cotton's opposing arguments carry different weight; not simply because time has proved Williams right or Cotton wrong, but because Williams was arguing passionately the questions that preoccupied him throughout his life, while Cotton—absorbed in justifying and explaining Congregational theology and church government—was reacting to the issue of religious freedom only as to a persistent nuisance that diverted him from his true interest.

Puritans believed that accomplishment of their goal, the achievement of truth according to the Word of God, would render discussion of toleration redundant. Expenditure of time and effort on that topic, therefore, represented at best a retrogressive activity and at worst a denial of their own vision. When New England ministers did write about freedom of religion, they were less concerned with debating a substantive issue than with trying to keep an irrelevant one from interrupting their lives and work. Although Cotton must surely have viewed Roger Williams's questions about liberty of conscience as emanating from the lunatic fringe, he nevertheless had to address himself to them in the interest of improving New England's reputation in England. Williams himself recognized this fact and in 1652 accused Cotton of writing in order to put the best face on New England's persecuting ways, so as to avoid embarrassment to Massachusetts's English Independent allies. However, even if the running dispute with Williams struck Cotton primarily as a bother, he did set forth in its course the main elements of Church-State policy that Puritan New England would follow, in diluted form, until after the American Revolution.

The basic incompatibility between the two disputants lay in their respective attitudes about the accessibility of truth. In a different context, Cotton wrote that "unless Faith go before, which maketh hidden things (as all spiritual matters be) evident, knowledge will not be able to give a true discernment of them." Consequently, by discerning a providence in events, Cotton's faith opened up to him the meaning of life, allowing him to fit all history into a sensible pattern. By contrast Williams, although he also believed in a divine plan for the world, could not discern its unfolding, but rather looked at history and was puzzled.[56]

Both disagreed on the nature of the evidence. At one stroke, Williams dismissed the great source book of Puritan history and precedent, the Old Testament. For him the institutions of Israel had served as types or shadows of Christ, not models for the future. The Mosaic law, except those parts that dealt with morality, was a prefiguration that vanished with the coming of Christ, thus eliminating, for instance, the precedent of the practice of the kings of Israel as a justification for punishing heretics.[57]

The thrust of Cotton's argument was that toleration had not resulted in prosperity for either Church or society; rather, condoning heresy had made the world anti-Christian. He agreed that errors had been made in the past; but the want of complete enlightenment failed to justify permitting blasphemy to go unpunished. History proved that punishing heretics was never disastrous, as the burning of Servetus in Geneva and the execution of Catholic priests by Elizabeth had made plain.[58] Thus Cotton believed, as did the Puritan clergy who followed him, that the magistrate was to be what the prophet Isaiah had called a "nursing father," protecting the people against corruption in worship that in its turn corrupted the state. Otherwise, on a people in covenant with God, His wrath would surely fall first on the people and later on church officers.[59]

Whereas Cotton was confident that after centuries of darkness, the true Church was finally emerging, Williams came to believe that the Church had been utterly destroyed by anti-Christ, the pope. Where Cotton perceived fundamental and self-evident truths, Williams reasoned that

> ... the experience of our Fathers errors, our owne mistakes and ignorance, the sense of our own weakness and blindness ... and the great professed expectation of light to come which we are not now able to comprehend, may abate the edge, yea sheath up the sword of persecution.[60]

Truth was not easy to find, but persecutors had used punishment to justify their actions throughout the ages. He asked: "What religion is ordinarily distrustful of its own strength?" Further, he noted that conscientious conviction, even at the hazard of life and limb, was not easily changed, and that both Catholics and Protestants had witnessed with equal bravery to their respective causes. Williams's perception of the vagaries of human nature left him without optimistic hopes for the future.[61]

In addition to disputing the certainty of truth and the true Church, removing the Old Testament as a model for New England, and arguing the tenacity of conscience, Williams also used history to fortify his point of view. England's recent example of switching religions showed the absurdity of forcing people's consciences. Constantine hurt the Church more than Nero did. Toleration had led not to the wrath of God, but to the prosperity of Holland.[62]

All Williams's arguments pointed toward his main concern, the discovery and preservation of the true Church or, as he referred to it, "the Garden of the Church," in contrast to the "Wilderness of the World."

Any breach in the wall separating the two would not result in the extension of the garden into the world, but would rather allow the wilderness
to engulf the garden. If the magistrate possessed power to punish error,
it followed that he also had the power to define the true Church. From
this Williams drew the inescapable conclusion that the magistrate had
no power whatsoever over the First Table, i.e. the first four Commandments, dealing with religious belief and worship.[63] Moreoever, he
carried his reasoning to its logical end—farther than most English
radicals did—and voiced the opinion that all persons, even Catholics,
should be tolerated, provided they obeyed the civil laws.[64]

Williams harried Cotton with a relentless persistence, but his arguments made no dent in New England's convictions. To protect their
own system, the New England ministers discredited the theory that the
magistrate should have no power over religion. Cotton's answer made
capital out of the discrepancy between Williams's solicitude for the true
Church and his conviction that the same Church had been utterly
destroyed and would not be restored again until Christ commissioned
new apostles to evangelize the world.[65]

Defenders of the New England way seized on the effective argument
that if the magistrate could not punish offenses against the First Table,
then he could not punish offenses against the Second Table. If
vengeance upon heretics belonged to God, was one to leave murderers
alone until the Last Day? This rebuttal to Williams derived its strength
from its solid foundation in a very real problem, which Williams was
unable to tackle and which still has not been solved: how to distinguish
between those areas that belong only to religion or conscience and
those that belong to the law. In other words, to what extent does a
claim to the free exercise of religion exempt one from the laws of the
land?[66] Williams's normal resourcefulness failed him here. The argument *ad horrendum*, that if the magistrate had no power in matters of the
First Table, then the moral legislation of the Second Table was for
naught, carried more force than any other for Williams's opponents
and became their primary approach to dismissing his and others'
suggestions that the magistrate had no power in religion.[67]

Ideas about toleration sweeping England spread to the colonies by
way of books like Williams's and the minds and tongues of newly
arriving immigrants. Some of them obviously took root.[68] In 1645
Edward Winslow of Plymouth wrote to John Winthrop describing how
the majority of deputies in the Plymouth General Court wanted

> . . . To allow and maintaine full and free tollerance of religion to all
> men that would preserve the civill peace and submit unto government;

and there was no limitation or exception against Turke, Jew, Papist, Arian, Socinian, Nicholaytan, Familist, or any other, etc.

Winslow went on to report that the governor of Plymouth wisely refused to allow the motion to come to a vote because, as he noted with horrified amazement, "You would have admired to have seen how sweet this carrion relished to the pallate of most of the deputies!"[69] Although Plymouth produced no formal defense of toleration, yet a spirit of moderation persisted there—to the annoyance of neighboring Massachusetts.

In 1645 the four Puritan colonies of New Haven, Connecticut, Massachusetts, and Plymouth formed the United Colonies, for purposes of mutual defense against the Indians. Massachusetts, however, also wanted the organization to act as a united front against a perceived spread of "error and blasphemy."[70] At least in its neighbor's eyes, Plymouth had adopted far too lax a policy. In 1649 Massachusetts wrote that colony, complaining of many errors that needed correction lest they infect the surrounding region.[71] Although the commissioners from Plymouth demurred, the colony— no doubt responding to the pressure—tightened its legislation forbidding worship different from that already set up and passed laws forbidding Baptists to hold meetings from house to house. In spite of these measures and the fact that it shared a basic agreement with Massachusetts, Plymouth's atmosphere of temperateness in no way diminished. The authorities warned against those who attempted to overthrow the churches, but also cautioned allowance for minor differences of opinion in religion and counseled prudence in dealing with these.[72]

If, in the opinion of the United Colonies, Plymouth erred on the side of leniency, Rhode Island breached completely the pale of acceptability. That colony dated from Roger Williams's expulsion from Massachusetts in 1636, when he fled to what is now Providence, the first of several towns that would later join to form the Rhode Island colony. These settlements were populated by dissenters who had been expelled from Massachusetts, among them—besides Williams—the Antinomian associates and the followers of Samuel Gorton. Radicals and eccentrics in their own world, such refugees were hardly the stuff to settle down in calm cooperation, and for twenty years the different groups disputed with each other. Even Williams's procurement of a patent from Parliament for the area, in 1644, failed to quiet the quarrels. Nevertheless, from their beginnings, all these settlements did live up to Williams's hopes for Providence itself—that it would be a refuge for those who were distressed in conscience.[73]

At Portsmouth the Antinomians, under the leadership of William Coddington, decided in 1638 that "the Judge together with the Elders shall Rule and Governe according to the Generall Rule of the Word of God," and that laws were to be drawn up according to the Word. The Word proved no clearer a guide here than elsewhere; subsequently, as a result of disagreements, Coddington and his followers departed to found Newport. Later, however, both these settlements—with Portsmouth now under the leadership of Anne Hutchinson's husband, William, adopted the more tangible English law.[74] In 1639 Newport affirmed that no one should be called to account for doctrine as long as it did not interfere with the government. By 1658 all the original towns had finally reached working agreements, and in 1663 a royal charter secured their unity in their "lively experiment . . . with a full libertie in religious concernements."[75]

From their inception, the Rhode Island settlements faced menacing attitudes on the part of their neighbors, especially Massachusetts. In 1637 the latter's General Court decreed that anyone coming there from Providence should abjure the opinion that Massachusetts persecuted for religion, or else leave the jurisdiction under pain of imprisonment. Concerned that Rhode Island provided a haven for excommunicates, the Boston church sent representatives to Newport to remonstrate with Coddington, who gave them scant satisfaction.[76]

Puritan writers dismissed the legitimacy and territorial claims of Rhode Island and stereotyped it as a place inhabited only by those who opposed the necessity of civil magistracy.[77] Such was far from the case. The Rhode Island towns carefully reiterated that liberty of conscience did not exempt one from the civil law. Williams and his associates may have broken radically with Puritan Church-State orthodoxy, but they accepted the social norms drawn from the last six Commandments, i.e. the Second Table. Providence made it clear that, despite its refusal to punish for conscience, it would still punish adultery, fornication, sodomy, and witchcraft. It never did prosecute anyone for that last crime, however, and at least some of the people of Providence doubted the existence of witches.[78]

Massachusetts's disapproving and censorial attitude expanded steadily. What began as religious horror at the "Island of errors" soon turned into social condescension for the "scum" that inhabited it.[79] This scorn solidified and persisted throughout the colonial period. In 1665 the Massachusetts General Court commented knowingly that Rhode Island's rise had been known "to any discreet person in these parts."[80]

Despite such social opprobrium, Rhode Island continued on its chosen way, neither bending under external pressure nor overreacting to it. Although the colony refused to compel any person to worship, it did insist upon a respectable observance of the Sabbath.[81] Nevertheless, the stigma of its early radicalism clung, and the colony's later penchant for issuing paper money fortified its public image of irresponsibility, with the result that what was an extraordinary experiment in religious freedom turned out to be, apart from Rhode Island itself, an idea too advanced to achieve general acceptance. Ideas of freedom of religion that would later prosper and grow in colonial America would not be derived from the example of Rhode Island.[82]

With the coming of the Quakers to New England, the worst fears of godly Puritans that Rhode Island, by offering refuge to every errant heretic, would infect the region materialized. This English sect, born at the tag end of that great seventeenth-century religious revival of which Puritanism itself had been the mainstay, created a furious turbulence on both sides of the Atlantic. Quakers not only provoked and heroically endured persecution, but actively sought it. By obstreperous or shocking behavior, such as interrupting church services to testify against false worship or going naked to symbolize the condition of their opponents' spiritual state, they drove the authorities, especially in America, to paroxysms of rage that begot savage punishments.[83] Viewing Quakers as the end result of an English policy that, as a Massachusetts minister would later put it, allowed every man to "go to hell without interruption or molestation," the New England authorities determined to defend themselves from this latest contagion.[84]

Even before the first two Quakers set foot in New England, in 1656, their notoriety had preceded them. They were first imprisoned and later expelled.[85] Then, at the suggestion of Massachusetts, all four jurisdictions of the United Colonies busied themselves passing anti-Quaker legislation.

Connecticut prohibited its towns from entertaining Quakers or Ranters (an even more radical English sect), and ships' masters from bringing them to the colony. Plymouth did likewise and also ordered Quaker books seized on the ground that their doctrines tended to subvert the state. It further whipped and expelled those Quakers who did get in for a variety of crimes, ranging from assembling in private houses to interrupting public worship. New Haven banned them and fined any of its citizens who received them.[86]

Massachusetts went to great lengths to explain its actions, declaring itself to be well-warned "by our own experience as well as that of Munster" against those who destroyed the fundamentals of religion and denied the reverence due to the civil magistrate. The colony went further and, relying on biblical precedent, reasoned that if Solomon could sentence Shimei to death for breach of confinement, Massachusetts could sentence Quakers to death for breach of banishment. It acted accordingly.[87]

Between 1658 and 1661, when the English government called a halt, Massachusetts hanged four Quakers, all of whom had insisted on returning after being expelled. Although the merchant John Hull cursed "the timidity of spirit to execute the sentence of God's Holy law upon such blasphemous persons," that is, upon Quakers awaiting banishment, the colony imposed its extreme penalties with reluctance. The General Court acknowledged a desire for "their life absent rather than their death present" and commissioned John Norton, a minister in Boston, to write a justification of its actions.[88]

The work reiterated and summarized the thinking about Church and State that New Englanders had adhered to and clarified since their arrival in America. Norton began by boldly asserting an untrue proposition, that "their [Quakers'] non-acknowledgment of the magistrate as now established in all Christian states, is more than manifest," and proceeded to an examination of another that was partially true—that they fought against civil order, especially the power of magistrates in religious matters. In fact, Quakers denied civil power only insofar as it attempted to control religion. Norton held that faith of its nature produced certainty, and that to hold otherwise was to render truth and error equal.[89]

To refute the Quakers' objection that punishment for religion by the magistrate constituted persecution, Norton first distinguished between conscience and the "error of conscience," using Ames's definition that conscience is the judgment of God concerning man. Logically, then, conscience could not lie, and to plead liberty of conscience to justify error was absurd. Next, he made a distinction between "Quiet heresy" and "Heresy Turbulent." Over the first, the magistrate claimed no power; but the second, which was held publicly and tended to seduce others or disturb the commonwealth, the magistrate could prohibit as "not matter of judgment, but matter of fact." Norton concluded with a reminder that the New England people had sacrificed estates, homeland, and worldly position for the true religion, and that "it concerneth N.-E. always to remember that," as the ministers would never allow it to forget, "Originally they are a Plantation Religious, not a plantation of Trade."[90]

The Quaker crisis did indeed raise the question whether Massachusetts would sacrifice trade to religion. In 1659 the United Colonies wrote to Rhode Island pointing out that Quakers were entertained there and asking that they be removed, lest the contagion spread. Otherwise, the letter hinted, the colonies might have to take further steps for their own protection. Rhode Island interpreted this as the threat of a trade embargo and was clearly frightened by it. Its president, Benedict Arnold, replied in a conciliatory fashion, declaring that his colony wished to retain good relations with its neighbors. Arnold agreed the Quakers were obnoxious and a threat to good government. He added that the colony further intended to bring the Quaker question before its Assembly, and expressed a hope that the colony would be able, consistent with the rights of conscience, to curb the ill effects of their behavior.

Shortly thereafter, in a letter to John Clark, its agent in England, the Rhode Island Assembly revealed its real feelings. The letter acknowledged that the Quakers were indeed making themselves a nuisance to the other colonies, but that Rhode Island had no reason to charge them with breach of the civil peace. It admitted that the Assembly felt definitely pressured by the United Colonies' communication, "though covertly expressed, as their manner is"; saw in it a definite threat; and asked rhetorically, "What will men doe for their God."[91] As it turned out, the answer was almost anything short of economic sanctions, an answer that the perceptive Rhode Islanders might have gleaned from a look at the New Haven laws, which permitted Quakers to trade in the colony as long as they did not preach. The Assembly also showed the depth of Rhode Island's attachment to religious freedom, asking Clark to plead for them so that they might not be made to force consciences as their neighbors did.[92]

Previous New England dissidents had taken their cases to England. Now Quaker apologists in the Mother Country raised a howl of protest there.[93] Their pamphlets followed a standard form. They detailed at length the sufferings of their brethren in New England, especially in Massachusetts; took issue with every justification used to punish Quakers; played up the paradox of Puritans, who supposedly had gone to America to gain freedom of religion, now persecuting for conscience; and ended with apocalyptic warnings of the judgment of God, who would avenge the punishment of his Saints.[94] By the time these apologies reached the English public, the Puritan Revolution there had run its course, and Charles II had returned as king. The Quakers immediately petitioned his government for the relief of their cohorts in New England and achieved it in the form of a letter to Massachusetts that ordered that colony to cease proceedings against Quakers and send those in prison to England for trial.[95]

Meanwhile, Massachusetts Puritans had lost no time conveying their side of the story to England. They petitioned the restored Charles II for "libertie to walke in the faith of the gospell with all good conscience, according to the order of the gospell," for which their fathers had transported themselves to the wilderness.[96] The petition availed nothing. With deep foreboding that they were incurring the wrath of God, or that the plantation might collapse, Massachusetts suspended its anti-Quaker laws—although noting that if Charles were better informed, he would have made a different decision. The following year, however, with the exception of the death penalty, it revived them—but passed on the onus of whipping offenders to local authorities in the towns, whose actions would draw less attention overseas than those of the General Court.[97]

In the decades after 1660, Quakers represented only one of the multiplying problems that beset an increasingly beleaguered region. Instead of building societies according to the Word, the Puritan colonies found themselves fighting for survival. New Haven succumbed in 1662, when the English government merged it with Connecticut.[98] The remaining colonies had to contend with diverse problems, e.g. the pressure of an English government intent upon gaining favor for the Church of England and attacking the validity of colonial charters, increasing opposition from dissenters at home, lessened fervor on the part of their citizens, and disappointment that government according to the Word was not working out as anticipated in either Church or State.[99]

In 1664 Charles sent four commissioners to visit New England. Among a multitude of assignments, such as settling boundary disputes, they were to secure for Anglicans the right to use the *Book of Common Prayer*; public support for their ministers, if possible; and, in Massachusetts, the franchise—which the colony had limited to members of the Congregational churches.[100]

The commissioners enjoyed reasonable success. Connecticut was willing to allow members of the Church of England to practice their religion, as long as they continued to contribute to the support of the Congregational ministers. Plymouth's poverty rendered support of any minister largely academic. Rhode Island posed no problem at all in that regard, since it allowed its citizens to attend and support whatever religious groups they chose. Only the colonists in Massachusetts proved inflexible and incorrigible. With neither influential allies in England nor much backing from the rest of New England, they stood alone, with courage and determination, quibbling, equivocating, and stubbornly conceding as little as possible of what they felt they had sacrificed so much for.[101]

The departure of the royal commissioners afforded the colonies a breathing space from foreign pressure, but native troublemakers remained. Although Massachusetts had revived its penalties of whipping and expulsion against the Quakers, these statutes tended to be ineffective, partly because the colony was being scrutinized by the king and also because most Quakers were by that time settled natives, rather than wandering preachers. They continued to gain increasing security.[102]

In 1675 Connecticut suspended its law fining Quakers for missing Sunday worship, provided they did not assemble themselves, and in 1677 Massachusetts ceased to whip Quakers—although that same year, it empowered constables to break down doors of houses where they suspected a Quaker meeting. After 1681 the Plymouth legislature allowed Quakers to participate in town affairs.[103] The ministers, however, continued to lament the Quakers' presence, and at the Synod of 1679 allowed that Quakers had provoked the anger of God against Massachusetts by setting up false worship there.[104] From Rhode Island even Roger Williams, in his only book published in America, joined in the general condemnation of the Quakers, accusing them of insufferable and anti-social behavior.[105]

In assigning blame for the wrath of God against Massachusetts, the Synod of 1679 determined that Baptists, as divine provocateurs, gave nothing away to Quakers.[106] The Baptists predated the Friends in New England and, like them, refused to go away. By 1665 they had a strong enough community to form their first church, at Charlestown, under the leadership of Thomas Gould. Nine years later, they moved to Boston, and despite persistent attempts—ranging from penal laws and fines to boarding up their building—to close them down, the colony was unable to dislodge them. Moreover, because they were law-abiding inhabitants, who could not be dismissed as "wanton gospelers," the nature of Baptists' offense did not come across clearly to ordinary citizens not specifically concerned with theological differences. The failure of the Massachusetts authorities to suppress the Baptists indicated that the inhabitants of New England were beginning to judge others more on the basis of moral probity than theological precision. In 1668, as they were preparing to expel Gould and his associates, the Massachusetts authorities were surprised to receive a petition signed by sixty-six citizens, many of them prominent in colonial affairs, requesting toleration of the Baptists on account of their reputable moral character.[107]

New England officials also had to take increasing account of the consequences their actions might have for their brethren in England, where Baptists found acceptance and fellowship with Congregationalists.

Thus, Puritan apologists had to take Baptist arguments for toleration more seriously than those of Quakers. English Congregationalists, referred to as Dissenters since the re-establishment of the Church of England after the Restoration, were concerned lest their own pleas to a hostile English hierarchy be rendered ineffective by the intransigence of Massachusetts toward its own dissenters. New England ministers found this delicate situation somewhat trying and wished their English cohorts would cease reminding them of it.[108]

When John Russell, a Baptist shoemaker from Woburn, accused Massachusetts of persecution in a pamphlet published in England with the approval of the Baptists there, two of the colony's distinguished ministers, Increase Mather and Samuel Willard, undertook to reply in pamphlet form. Their answer added little by way of substance to the debate about religious liberty. It ridiculed the Baptists, gainsaying rather than refuting their charge, and repeated the well-worn argument that conscience could not justify error. Mather, in the Introduction, distinguished his colony from England, emphasizing the intrusion of the Baptists on the "peculiar" people of Massachusetts. This comment set the tone for Puritan dealings with Baptists for more than a century to come. They might not be dislodged, but Baptists in New England would not belong, would not gain recognition as having a part in the enterprise for which the founders had sacrificed so much. The pamphlet's title, *Ne Sutor Ultra Crepidam* (Cobbler, Stick to Your Last), emphasized that point and signaled the social disdain that Congregationalists would substitute for theological opprobrium in their dealings with the Baptists in their midst.[109]

In addition to coping with the problems caused by pressure from without and dissenters within, New England Congregationalists had to deal with an evolving crisis of their own. As Perry Miller has so happily phrased it, "The basic assumption of Congregationalism was that it would be difficult, not to get people into the churches, but to keep them out," and the struggle against "popery" and "prelacy" had been so engrossing that Puritans had hardly stopped to think that once they had overcome these obstacles, the pure biblical truth might not usher itself into plain and unobstructed view.[110] The persistence of dissension in America and the lamentable penchant of Congregationalists in England for accommodating heterodoxy exemplified and led to the crisis of the New England way that resulted in the Halfway Covenant, the name given to a religious compromise by which those unable to recount an experience of conversion, and thus ineligible for church membership, could have their children baptized nonetheless.

It represented a downward adjustment to the actuality that New Englanders did not flock to the churches.[111]

Further, the staying power of Quakers and Baptists, together with the departing fervor of the faithful—reflected in Increase Mather's rueful query of 1682, "Are not some weary of Theocracy or Government which God hath established amongst us?"—precluded doctrinal uniformity at the level originally anticipated.[112] Not all agreed, however, on the degree of change required. Those slowest to move, such as Mather, clung tenaciously to the standards of the Fathers, whose example he invoked in his Election Sermon to the General Court in 1677, wherein he excoriated its members for failing to measure up to such men as Winthrop and Endecott in suppressing false religion.[113]

Mather was out of step with reality, however. Rather, the deputies hearkened to the sentiments of William Hubbard, whose Election Sermon the previous year had provoked Mather's outburst. Hubbard also sought uniformity, but according to a higher common denominator and from a viewpoint somewhat different from Mather's. Less theological in his stated objectives than the latter, Hubbard promoted congruence of belief more for the purpose of social peace and harmony than for theological neatness. Likening dissent to sedition, he reasoned that undue harshness in the suppression of either brought only chaos to the state, and he recommended "the moderation of the civil power to a due Temperance."[114] In principle and logic, he did not disagree with the more reactionary Mather. They differed in temperament, stomach for unpleasantness, and judgment of the possible. Hubbard would simply have dragged for heretics with a coarser net.

In the 1670s, the complicated process of adjusting Puritan ideals to the existing reality gave rise to some ministerial unrest, but the availability of a common language, whose traditional terms the Fathers had not rendered impractical for the future by precise definitions, eased the storms. As a result, opposing groups did not polarize. Instead, they temporarily diverged in their estimation of the restrictions that traditional phrases implied. Thus all Puritans could head into the future believing the oft-repeated assertion that New England originated as a plantation for religion, not trade.[115] The preachers were also in accord that the civil magistrate was the custodian of both Tables—a truth witnessed to by history, which demonstrated that no reform in religion ever took place without his sponsorship.[116] All further concurred that civil and religious liberty were inextricably mixed.[117] Finally, as if in anticipation of the Act of Toleration of 1689, New England divines agreed to oppose not toleration but a "boundless toleration."[118]

The realities might have changed, but the language stayed the same. Secure in the possession of its familiar terminology, New England would proceed in affairs of Church and State guided not by a clear system of thought, but by expansion and contraction—as circumstances allowed or dictated—of the tacitly accepted scope of its traditional lexicon. Thus, despite the hazards of fortune and an ever-changing world, New Englanders would keep faith with their ancestors.

In the 1680s, England's inexorable pressure on the colonial governments resulted in the recall of all New England's charters. During the brief reign of James II, from 1686 to 1688, the region was merged with New York and New Jersey to form the Dominion of New England. This structure disintegrated when the Glorious Revolution put William of Orange on the English throne and sparked a corresponding rebellion in America that opened the way for Rhode Island and Connecticut to recover their charters and for Massachusetts and Plymouth to unite under a new one. Even though this new charter extended to Massachusetts the substance of the Act of Toleration, it did not disrupt the existing reality so accurately characterized by William McLoughlin as "toleration grudgingly connived at."[119] Puritan New Englanders continued to harbor the theory that they were a "peculiar" people in Church and State, and they had preserved the language of their forefathers intact to prove it.

2

Church and State in Seventeenth-Century Virginia and Maryland

In contrast to the origins of New England, the founding of Virginia was hardly permeated by the aura of religion. Popular imagery of the southern colony evokes neither impressions of heroic struggles for religious freedom, nor determined efforts to propagate the true faith, nor narrow-minded and bigoted clerical oppression. Both Virginia and the New England colonies were, however, products of seventeenth-century colonizing ventures that emanated from much the same religious background, and while religion may not have played as significant a role in Virginia as it did in the northern settlements, it was nevertheless a highly identifiable factor in the building of the "Old Dominion." Moreover, the earnest sentiments associated with Puritanism that nourished much early seventeenth-century religious discourse were present in the hopes, plans, and ambitions of the settlers of Virginia.[1]

At a time when ideological antipathy between Protestantism and Catholicism remained at fever pitch, Virginia's founders considered their colony an outpost of the Church of England in the New World.[2] The charter counseled diligence in propagating religion among the natives, advice both stressed and added to in subsequent charters.[3] The colony's first General Assembly, meeting in 1619, legislated against drunkenness, idleness, gaming at dice or cards, and "excess of apparell," and for frequent church attendance. Before its abolition by the crown in 1624, the Virginia Company made abundant regulation for the settlement of the Anglican Church.[4]

This close cooperation between Church and State placed the latter firmly in control, with the governor assuming such functions as the issuance of marriage licenses, probation of wills, and appointments of ministers to parishes—activities that in England would normally have been carried out by bishops or ecclesiastical courts.[5] The colony's lawmakers also carefully prescribed from the outset that all religious practice should conform to that of the Church of England. In the achievement of this conformity, the government of Virginia succeeded remarkably well both as to degree and duration. The colony would in future experience some religious dissent and turmoil, but only minor tremors as compared with the upheavals in England or even in other colonies as the 1640s and 1650s ran their course.

Anglicanism in early Virginia covered much the same spectrum as in the Mother Country, i.e. a variety of religious opinions and practices that thoroughly vexed Archbishop Laud, who sought to impose upon the Church of England a strict uniformity of practice. Under the harsh conditions of a frontier settlement and in the absence of bishops and ecclesiastical courts, such undeviating procedures were little needed and impossible to maintain in the colony. Instead of clerical supervisors, the governor, the Council, and later—and most importantly—the local vestries assumed direction and control of the Virginia Church. As a result, unhampered by any strong centralized episcopacy, those holding various Protestant attitudes were able to adjust local worship to suit their preferences. They were not, like their counterparts in England, pushed into assuming definite non-conforming stands, and the Church of England as modified by the colonial situation continued to embrace most of the colony. Until mid-eighteenth century, the primary religious controversies in Virginia had to do with the ecclesiastical problems attendant upon the emergence of a hybrid Anglicanism, rather than with the issues of toleration or religious freedom.[6]

Because the Virginia model of the Church of England continued over the course of its first century to make only relatively moderate demands in the area of worship, it provided the colony with a high degree of social uniformity. This very homogeneity served to make life difficult for such outspoken dissenters as did exist there. Beginning in the late 1630s, those who fell under that heading, finding themselves hard-pressed at home, began moving into the neighboring colony of Maryland.

Although both Virginia and Maryland entered the eighteenth century with fairly similar arrangements, i.e. relative religious harmony under an officially established church, Maryland achieved only after a stormy seventy years what Virginia had possessed from the beginning. Like that of Rhode Island, Maryland's experience in Church and State constituted an extraordinary experiment, although it contributed even less than Rhode Island's to the development of religious freedom in the American colonies. Its failure, however, demonstrated the limits of colonial Americans' understanding of freedom of religion.

Founded in 1634, Maryland owed its origin to George Calvert and his son Cecil, first and second Lords Baltimore. The elder Calvert had held the important position of Secretary of State under James I; but he supported the recommendation of a Spanish marriage for Charles, then Prince of Wales, and found himself on the losing side when the proposal fell through. He resigned his post, but James, whose favor he retained, granted him an Irish peerage. Simultaneously, Calvert announced his conversion to Catholicism, the religion his son Cecil had already embraced.[7] After an unsuccessful attempt in the 1620s to found a colony in Newfoundland, the first Lord Baltimore set about securing a charter for a settlement in a more temperate climate. Issuance of the Maryland charter was in its final stages when he died, in 1632, and the project, together with his hopes and plans for it, devolved upon Cecil Calvert, who, as second Lord Baltimore, proceeded faithfully to carry out his father's wishes.

The first Lord Baltimore had envisaged a colony comprised of both Catholics and Protestants living in harmony, free to practice their respective religions with neither enjoying any special favor from the state. The Calvert plans for religious toleration have in the past been subject to much cut-and-thrust commentary by Catholic and Protestant historians, who have tended to view the whole Maryland enterprise either as a triumph of Catholic-inspired idealism or as an undertaking in which Catholicism played only an incidental role.[8] Both Lords Baltimore, however, shared a religious outlook far distant from any seventeenth-century norm, and their motives were much too amorphous to fit neatly the needs of religious apologists.

Under the best of circumstances, the Maryland experiment in religious toleration could barely have weathered the adversities the times laid out for it. During the colony's founding years, European powers engaged each other in the Thirty Years War, the last but most terrible of the wars of religion. In England the final episodes of the battle with Catholicism would absorb much of the country's political energies throughout the century. Thus the Calverts' fanciful notion that they could combine Protestants and Catholics in a neutral setting to form a successful colony would have tested the possibilities of the seventeenth century to the limit, even if the proprietors had not yoked that plan to the equally capricious idea that they could rule such a colony as near absolute lords had ruled feudal baronies.

In an era when the English Parliament executed one king and banished another, Cecil Calvert received a grant that drew upon medieval England as a model for a future colony. The Maryland charter of 1632 conferred upon him

> . . . as ample Rights, Jurisdictions, Privileges, Prerogatives, Royalties, Liberties, Immunities, and Royal Rights, and temporal Franchises whatsoever . . . as any Bishop of Durham . . . in our Kingdom of England, ever heretofore hath.

To boot, the document designated Baltimore and his successors "absolute Lords," but paradoxically cautioned them to make laws "with the Advice, Assent, and Approbation of the Free-Men of the same Province."[9]

In attempting to regulate his colony abroad according to a feudal land policy already outmoded in England and to exercise more authority in the New World than kings did in the Old, Lord Baltimore reckoned without the pretensions of colonial freemen, whose heads had been turned by the accomplishments of their compatriots at Westminster.[10] In the resulting contest for power, the proprietor's religion rendered him vulnerable, as his enemies inevitably turned his Catholicism and even his toleration of Catholicism into a weapon to use against him. As a result, Maryland's progressive adventure in Church-State relations soon found itself hopelessly entangled in its own dishearteningly retrogressive political workings.

The efforts of both George and Cecil Calvert to combine innovative religious arrangements with medieval politics did not exhaust their puzzling qualities. Both father and son were converts to Catholicism; yet neither exhibited the fervor of the neophyte. They wanted to establish a colony in which Catholicism could operate freely but unobtrusively, yet they invited Jesuits to care for its Catholics—the priests least likely to keep a low profile and whom James I had characterized as "nothing but Puritan papists."[11] The exact thoughts and sentiments that prompted them in their colonial ventures remain obscure. However, the argument from expediency, that Cecil Calvert "adhered to . . . [his] policy for political and economic and not for religious reasons," fails to surmount the obvious objection that the most expedient course for both Baltimores would have been to remain Protestant themselves and to settle Protestant colonies.[12] Given the statutory disabilities imposed upon Catholics by Parliament in seventeenth-century England, their conversion to that faith seems prima facie evidence of religious conviction.

When George Calvert had founded his unsuccessful Newfoundland colony, he had made provisions for Catholics and Protestants there to enjoy liberty to practice their religions on equal terms, as his son would later do in the case of Maryland.[13] Unless both father and son shared a desire to make their colonial enterprises havens in some sense for their fellow English Catholics, their policy of encouraging Catholics to emigrate to those colonies, providing them with priests, and securing toleration for them—all actions that jeopardized the commercial success of the ventures—is inexplicable.[14]

Apparently, neither Calvert felt any urge to expound his views on Church and State beyond the obvious import of his actions. A few stray pointers have survived, however. In *Objections Answered Touching Mariland*, a pamphlet prepared for Cecil Calvert by the English Jesuits, the author responded to a hypothetical opponent's criticism that a refuge in America would hinder Catholics' conversion to Anglicanism by declaring that

> . . . conversion in matters of Religion, if it bee forced, should give little satisfaction to a wise State . . . for those who for worldly respects will breake their faith with God doubtlesse will doe it, upon a fit occasion much sooner with men.[15]

To his friend Thomas Wentworth, Lord Deputy of Ireland, the first Lord Baltimore wrote that "we Papists want not charity toward you Protestants, whatever the less understanding part of the world thinks of us."[16] The remark reveals a genial religious temperament; but Baltimore was doubtless overly sanguine in his assessment of his co-religionists' attitude toward Protestants, and especially so in regard to Jesuits, who would consider Protestant settlers in Maryland heretics in need of conversion.[17]

By and large, then, both Calverts approached the question of religious toleration with the attitude of the less said about it the better. They hoped that a policy of silence would banish all religious controversy from the public sphere, and that both Catholics and Protestants would be able to function peaceably together. Their preference for privacy and restraint in the religious areas of their lives anticipated a future age, but in their own time of militant and crusading religion such a policy could not be expected to attract many firm adherents, particularly when its authors were unwilling to defend it in theory or to recruit support for it. To Protestant opponents of the second Lord Baltimore, his religious course—if they grasped it at all—was unconvincing.

The Calverts' experiences in the years immediately preceding the settlement of Maryland could not have greatly encouraged their hopes of founding a society that would confine religion to private matters. In 1628 Erasmus Sturton, a Church of England minister, returned to England from Newfoundland and publicly denounced the open practice of "popery" in George Calvert's colony there. Moreover, both Catholics and Protestants in Europe were scandalized to hear that the Newfoundland colonists used a common building for Catholic and Protestant worship.[18] In 1629 George Calvert, having decided to abandon the Newfoundland enterprise, stopped in Virginia en route to England. To discourage any ideas he might have had of settling in their midst, the Virginians promptly tendered him the oaths of allegiance and supremacy. As a Catholic, he could not take them and so had to depart at once.[19]

Cecil Calvert had published *Objections* in order to scotch such rumors as the one that the new colony would give Spain a wedge with which to threaten both New England and Virginia, as well as religious horror stories about the introduction of Spanish Catholics to America.[20] Apart from trying to allay these more immediate fears, however, the pamphlet also tackled a very real moral dilemma. Throughout the seventeenth century, the religious experiments of the Calverts would collide again and again with the contention of Protestants that they could not in conscience accept the open toleration of Catholicism, since they equated such sufferance with the promotion of the anti-Christ.[21] In turn, contemporary Catholics faced the same problem in their dealings with Protestants.

To the thesis of the hypothetical objector that "such a licence will seem to be a kind of tolleration of (at least a conivance at) Popery," the Jesuit author of the pamphlet responded by extending the argument to its logical consequences—that those who held such a view would be obliged to deny Catholics the right to live in England, to prohibit foreign Catholic diplomats and traders from entering the country, and to refuse to suffer the Indian "idolators" in the colonies.[22] Beyond this one publication, however, the second Lord Baltimore made no effort to address the issue of toleration or to ground his policy in a firm theoretical or apologetic base.

The first contingent of Maryland settlers left England in 1633, under the direction of Leonard Calvert, who had been appointed governor by his brother the proprietor, and who carried careful instructions from the latter for the management of the new colony. Catholics, who formed a small but influential minority of the passengers on the two ships, were to preserve peace by offering no offense to Protestants, by refraining from all religious controversy, and by performing their religious observances in as inconspicuous a manner as possible. Like

contemporary leaders in New England, Cecil Calvert took special care
that his colonists would provide no cause for adverse comment elsewhere. In his instructions he specified that the Catholics give no cause
for complaint in England, and that the governor choose representatives
belonging to the Church of England to transact business with the
Virginia colony.[23]

From the very beginning of the Maryland settlement, Lord Baltimore's policy failed to work as he had intended. In thanksgiving for
their safe journey, the two Jesuit priests who accompanied the colonists
erected a large cross and celebrated Mass publicly.[24] The Protestant
members have left no record of their reaction. Neither have the
Catholics. However, in violating Baltimore's instructions that "all Acts
of the Romane Catholique Religion . . . be done as privately as may
be," the Jesuits do not appear to have been deliberately flaunting the
proprietor's wishes. Rather, the subtlety of his policy simply eluded
them. The next few years of Maryland's existence would demonstrate
that the Jesuits comprehended the proprietor's public policy toward
religion no better than did his later Protestant enemies. Although the
Jesuits would ultimately find Cecil Calvert's approach dismally luke-
warm and indifferent, any discordance between Lord Baltimore and
the Society of Jesus was smothered by the intricacies of English
ecclesiastical politics. Not until well after the Maryland settlement
began would differences between the Jesuits and Baltimore emerge.

The ecclesiastical provisions of the charter conferred upon the proprietor the patronage and power to license the formation and building
of churches and "of causing the same to be dedicated and consecrated
according to the Ecclesiastical Laws of our Kingdom of England."[25]
This provision, if it did not go so far as to mandate an established
church, certainly gave Baltimore permission to settle one, together with
a strong hint that he should do so.[26] The proprietor chose to ignore the
first part of the provision and to avoid the second by erecting no places
of worship.

The Jesuits, however, felt that their transfer to Maryland warranted
an alteration from their English status, as Father Thomas Copley wrote
in a letter to Lord Baltimore in 1638 suggesting that the Jesuits should
enjoy the privileges they did not in England because of the political
situation there. The privileges he had in mind were those enjoyed by
the Church in the Catholic countries of Europe, including exemption
from taxation and secular jurisdiction. In addition, Copley wanted the
Catholic Church excused from the colony's land policy, so that the
Jesuits could make independent land transfers with the Indians and
receive grants of property without Baltimore's consent.[27] In a

continuing correspondence with their English confreres, the Jesuits, rather than reflecting Baltimore's point of view, mirrored conventional seventeenth-century sentiments. Their letters were filled with Catholic versions of the providences and wonders so dear to New England Puritans.[28] Baltimore flatly rejected the Jesuits' requests for special recognition. In the dispute that ensued, the proprietor's fixed and stubborn determination to prevail showed the depth of his attachment to the order of Church and State he envisaged for his colony.

The corollary to the argument that Baltimore's religious policy proceeded from economic expediency is that had the majority of the colonists been Catholic, he would have shown them more public favor. His disagreement with the Jesuits gives not a hint that such would have been the case. Rather, the controversy confirms the fact that Baltimore's strategy proceeded from conviction and not from convenience. On Copley's letter asking for ecclesiastical privileges, the proprietor indignantly penned the comments "containing demands of very extravagant privileges" and "all their tennants as well as servants he intimates here ought to be exempted from the temporal government."[29]

Baltimore's reaction to the Jesuits affords another insight into his attitude toward Church and State. On the one hand, he demonstrated—in the face of veiled threats of excommunication—an imperious will and determination to prevail. He even had the English Statutes of Mortmain enacted in the colony in order to limit the ability of religious bodies to hold property.[30] On the other hand, he never lost sight of the religious needs of his Catholic subjects. Though he would gladly have rid himself of the Jesuit priests, he made careful plans to replace them if necessary with secular clergy. Clearly, he thought religion important; but equally clearly, he believed that it must refrain from interfering in politics and government. His attitude no doubt arose from his own experience as a member of the English Catholic gentry, who enjoyed a great deal of autonomy in religious matters and largely controlled the English Catholic Church. He would hardly surrender such influence to the clergy in his own colony.[31]

Like the Maryland religious experiment itself, the dispute between Baltimore and the Jesuits has provided much partisan history. However, apart from the merits of the case, the incident offers a clue to the nature and, ultimately, the failure of Baltimore's policy. One can agree with the view that the Jesuits harbored unrealistic expectations as to landholding and the specific nature of their role in the colony, and that from their acceptance of Baltimore's conditions for going to the colony they should have understood his intentions. Their failure to grasp what he had in mind resulted not from bad faith on their part, but from the difficulty inherent in a concept that anticipated the future and corresponded to nothing in their experience.

Like the proprietor's later Protestant opponents, the Jesuits did not reject his policy on its merits. In a sense, neither Catholic nor Protestant rejected it at all, because, as a result of Baltimore's temperament, it had never been presented with sufficient repetitiveness and force to break in upon their received opinions, beliefs, and prejudices about toleration and the relationship between Church and State.

Baltimore promoted toleration by fiat rather than by conversion. He shied away from the pamphleteering, enthusiasm, argumentativeness, and frequent public obloquy that attended his contemporaries who carried out the struggle for religious freedom and toleration in England and America. In a later age, of less religious earnestness, his taciturn approach might have succeeded. In a period charged with religious controversy, when all parties held preconceived and deep-rooted beliefs and expectations about each other, a strategy such as Baltimore's lost not by defeat but by default.

The altercation between Baltimore and the Jesuits represented an orderly and restrained dispute in a colony whose history until the last decade of the seventeenth century included rebellion, invasion, government overthrow, civil strife, and revolution—all accompanied by constant religious bickering, a habit the proprietor could not get his colonists to break. Nevertheless, his colony's government did make valiant efforts to suppress sectarian quarrels.

In 1638 William Lewis, the overseer of the Jesuit plantation of St. Inigoe, during the course of an argument with his Protestant servants, disparaged their religious books and beliefs. When the case came to court, the authorities fined Lewis heavily, even though he probably had reacted to considerable provocation, and bound him to maintain religious peace and avoid all such invective. The plan of Lewis's opponents to appeal for relief to Virginia no doubt alarmed the governor.[32] In a similar case, in 1642, the authorities punished Thomas Gerard, who tried to close Protestants out from the building both Catholics and Protestants used for worship.[33] These were doubtless some of the problems Father Andrew White had in mind when he wrote to the Jesuit Provincial in England that there were many disputes within the province, but that most of them had been allayed.[34]

Discord in Maryland, however, persisted and festered. An influential Virginian, William Claiborne, disputed a portion of Baltimore's grant known as Kent Island and used the outbreak of the English Civil War to attack him. Together with Richard Ingle, a ship's captain, and certain of the proprietor's enemies within the colony, he posed as

Parliament's champion against Maryland's "Papist devills," and the "tyrannical government of that province, ever since its first settling by recusants." Ingle seized and plundered Maryland during 1645 and, at the same time, Claiborne took over the disputed Kent Island.[35] The furor begun by Claiborne and Ingle almost cost Baltimore his charter, but England's preoccupation with her own problems and the proprietor's persistence in defense of his grant enabled him to retain it. Meanwhile, in Maryland, Leonard Calvert, assisted by Governor Berkeley of Virginia, an ardent royalist, recovered his brother's territory.

Leonard Calvert died in 1647, and the following year, responding to the accusations that had been leveled against him in England, the proprietor appointed the first Protestant governor of Maryland, William Stone, a resident of Virginia. The most important factor leading to Stone's appointment was his undertaking to bring settlers to the province.[36]

Eager to secure more colonists, the proprietor had sent to Boston in 1643 an offer of "free liberty of religion" to anyone who would move to Maryland. Massachusetts Governor John Winthrop commented dryly that none "of our people ... [had a] temptation that way."[37] Stone would prove much more successful.

In order to perpetuate and fortify Maryland's de facto religious toleration, the proprietor required the new governor and his councilors to subscribe to an oath not to disturb Christians and especially Roman Catholics in the "free exercise" of their religion. The Maryland Assembly had made only one provision for religion, declaring in 1639 that "Holy Churches within this province shall have all her rights and liberties."[38] Passed during the period of the Jesuit controversy, this statute may have exhibited a sympathy for the Jesuits on the part of Leonard Calvert or the freemen that the proprietor did not share. Although its language corresponded to Jesuit demands, the wording was vague enough to ensure its harmlessness, and it never achieved any greater stature than that of an enigmatic inclination.[39]

In 1649, however, the Assembly enacted the colony's policy of toleration into law by passing the famous Act Concerning Religion. This act, drawn up by the proprietor, has played a central role in discussions of his religious policy. Already both Catholics and Protestants could practice their religions freely, so the law changed little in fact; but it constituted the most extensive and specific pronouncement on religion made in the colony to that date.

The Act of 1649 left no doubt as to its intention:

noe person . . . professing to believe in Jesus Christ, shall from henceforth bee any waies troubled . . . for . . . his or her religion nor in the
free exercise thereof . . . nor any way [be] compelled to the beleife or
exercise of any other Religion against his or her consent.

By a curious combination of enlightenment and harshness, the Act
of 1649 attempted to continue the practice of free exercise of religion for
Christians, but decreed death or the strictest penalties for those who
exceeded the limits of Christian orthodoxy. The law's rationale that
forcing orthodoxy had only damaged those countries where it had been
tried echoed the statements in the pamphlet *Objections*, as well as much
of the wisdom of toleration emerging in contemporary England as a
result of the civil war and proliferation of sects there. Its stated objectives of providing "peaceable government" and preserving "mutual love
and amity" among the colonists also explained the practical purpose
behind it. To achieve this desired peace and quiet—for even in his most
sanguine mood, Baltimore could hardly have hoped for love—the new
law specifically proscribed, under heavy penalties, all sectarian name-
calling. The banned list reads like a short catalogue of seventeenth-
century religious invective:

. . . heretic, Scismatic, Idolator, puritan, Independent, Prespiterian,
popish priest, Jesuite, Jesuited papist, Lutheran, Calvinist, Ana-
baptist, Brownist, Antinomian, Barrowist, Roundhead, Separatist.[40]

The fluctuating temper within the Act of 1649 did not reflect a
benevolent Baltimore circumscribed by mean-spirited Puritans within
the province, as some historians have argued.[41] Rather, the proprietor
sandwiched those sections of it extending the toleration of Catholics, a
practice out of step with the times both in England and America,
between other forceful statements calling attention to Maryland's
religious conventionality and orthodoxy in other areas. Beginning with
the assumption that Maryland was a Christian commonwealth, the act
decreed death and confiscation of goods for any who blasphemed the
Trinity or denied it. Subsequent clauses addressed and prohibited
those vices that especially concerned Protestants, e.g. working on or
profaning the Sabbath, swearing, and drunkenness. Nowhere did the
law mention Catholics by name, but it fined those who used the names
of the Blessed Virgin Mary, the Apostles, and the Evangelists dis-
respectfully and granted toleration to those who believed in Jesus
Christ.

A recent commentator on the Act of 1649 has written that it was "an
admission that the original policy had failed," which indeed it was.[42] Its
language made explicit what the founder would rather have kept tacit.

It decreed by statute a policy that could only have worked through practice. To have implemented the law and punished a Protestant for calling someone a "papist" or for using "reproachful words" about the Virgin Mary would only have publicized the very subjects Baltimore wanted to avoid. His unusual choice of direct action in this case may be seen as a means of reassuring the Protestant settlers Governor Stone was attempting to attract to the province, and also as an act of frustration on his part, aimed at eliminating by legislation what he had been unable to ban by instruction and court action.

In its public and specific nature, Baltimore's Act of 1649 was at odds with his own previous policy, and also with Catholic custom in England. There, Catholics looked to an influential gentry to quietly manipulate the levers of power in order to ameliorate conditions for their co-religionists. Wedded to no strong theory of religious toleration, English Catholics remained silent on the subject. Except for the Act of 1649, Baltimore did not try to change this attitude. Nor did he make any effort after the passage of the law to gain widespread support for its contents. As events unfolded, Baltimore's scheme for toleration needed a deeper and more pervasive base than the mere presence of statutes. That same year, Governor Stone fulfilled his promise to bring settlers into the colony, though in the process the proprietor got more than he bargained for. They came, at a critical period, in the form of several hundred Puritans escaping religious harassment by Virginia's royalist Governor Berkeley.[43]

Soon after defeating and executing Charles I, Parliament moved to assert its authority over the colonies. In 1650 it provided for a commission to reduce Virginia and the West Indies to submission. Baltimore managed to have his province's name left unmentioned. However, the final instructions to the commissioners ordered them to "reduce all the plantations within the Bay of Chesopiack," a statement that left no doubt in the minds of two of them, Richard Bennett, a leader of the Puritan settlers in Maryland, and William Claiborne, Baltimore's old enemy, that Maryland was definitely included.[44] For two years after their arrival in Maryland in 1652, the commission and Governor Stone shared an uneasy partnership in the government of the province.

In 1654, when Stone tried to reassert the proprietor's sole authority, the commissioners deposed him, disfranchised Catholics, and called an Assembly that decreed that no Catholic could be protected in the Province by the Laws of England.[45] Baltimore, in another round of patient and persistent efforts in England, managed to have his plantation restored. The restoration involved pardon of past offenses for rebels and "agreement" to revive the Act Concerning Religion of 1649.[46]

In a series of pamphlets, the different parties to the disputes in Maryland aired their sides of the controversy. These writings, while shedding some light on the events themselves, also portray the attitudes of their authors toward Maryland's toleration. Oftentimes, the writers conveyed as much by what they omitted as by what they included. In no instance did Baltimore's protagonists, not all of them Catholic, advance a strong theoretical justification of religious toleration or defend its extension to Catholics as a right. Rather, they limited themselves to giving pragmatic reasons why such toleration was not harmful. They stressed the legality of Catholicism in the colonies, and anyhow, better settlements of Catholic Englishmen than of Dutch or Swedes. Furthermore, they pointed out that toleration worked, something testified to by both Catholics and Protestants alike. Moving to the offensive, they leveled charges of personal ingratitude against those who accepted refuge in the colony and then turned on their benefactor. Not conscience, but a realization of the main chance prompted Puritans to pick quarrels with Catholics in order to deprive Baltimore of his province.

Conversely, Baltimore's opponents never came to grips at all with his policy or the religious realities of the colony. In retrospect, their failure to grasp his policy was a measure of the magnitude of the task that confronted him in trying to settle a colony made up of Catholics and Protestants without government favor to either. The members of the anti-proprietary party had no interest in presenting the colony's policy on religion fairly, and indeed they did not do so. Baltimore's enemies took over the government of Maryland in their own interest and misrepresented the facts by accusing the former government of "professing an establishment of the Romish Religion onely," of making the colony a "Nursery for Jesuits," suppressing "poor Protestants," and of making the citizens swear to "countenance and uphold Antichrist, in plain words . . . The Roman Catholic Religion." They objected particularly to the oath acknowledging the "absolute dominion" of the proprietor, a demand that only confirmed what most English Protestants already believed—that "Arbitrary" and "Popish" were synonymous.

Their faulty perception now appears clearly; but in their own time, the Protestant apologists never even hinted that they had any understanding of what Baltimore was trying to accomplish. They never gave any indication that the Maryland experience had even dented the deep universal stereotype of Catholicism or the habits of mind inherited from more than a century of bitter Protestant-Catholic rivalry and mutual persecution. The anti-proprietary authors did not write about Maryland in terms of its actual operation, but rather in terms of the way all their given knowledge, presuppositions, and beliefs to that date told them a Catholic-dominated colony would operate.[47]

Baltimore's recovery of his province revived his policy of toleration, which would survive precariously for the next thirty years. The colony's shaky course contrasted sharply with the stability of its neighbor Virginia. Indeed, the latter strengthened its own religious homogeneity by so pressuring some of its dissidents that they moved to Maryland. Even under the English Commonwealth, the Church of England remained the established church in Virginia, in fact if not in law. The Restoration of 1660 brought added assurance and security, and in 1662 the Virginia Assembly further strengthened the Church by excluding all ministers who could not give proof of episcopal ordination.[48]

Against this secure establishment and the unyielding stances of both Church and State, Quakers, who first entered Virginia in 1657, could make little headway. The authorities were determined not to allow Friends to interrupt the colony's religious and social uniformity. The unflinching hostility of Governor Berkeley toward the "pestilent sect" prompted the Friends to seek refuge in Maryland, and their numbers greatly declined in the older colony, a loss to Virginia that writers in that colony would later lament.[49] Initially, Maryland authorities extended scant welcome to these newest immigrants. However, seventeenth-century Maryland's perennial need for more settlers soon served to ameliorate such a policy, and Governor Philip Calvert, the proprietor's nephew, specifically invited Virginia's badgered Quakers to come and settle.[50]

During the post-Restoration era, Virginia continued to fortify and consolidate its establishment. Maryland, on the other hand, discovered that for its experiment in religious toleration, the times were no more propitious than before. In England, rumors of Catholic plots, fears about the heir to the throne (Charles II's Catholic brother, James), and the increasing power and influence of France kept the religious issue at boiling point and nurtured a crisis that led to the Glorious Revolution of 1688, which deposed James after a short three-year reign and replaced him with his Protestant daughter Mary and her husband, William of Orange.[51]

The echoes of English troubles resounding in the colony sharpened Maryland's political disputes, already cast in a sectarian mold, and taking the form of a contest between the Assembly and the Upper House. The latter was dominated by the proprietor's mainly Catholic relatives and connections. Also, with fear of Indian attacks unsettling every colony in the New World, the presence of a substantial number of Catholics in Maryland lent a special urgency to the anxiety of those who connected French, Catholic, and Indian in a plot to overthrow the Protestant powers.

Nevertheless, according to one settler, George Alsop, the proprietor's policy of toleration appeared successful. In 1666 Alsop wrote an enthusiastic and inflated pamphlet asserting "an unanimous parallel of friendship and inseparable love" between Catholics and Protestants. Given the previous experience of the colony, Alsop rather missed the nature of religious relations, as he did the point of the Maryland undertaking, when he commented, "and truly where a Kingdom, State of Government, keeps or cuts down the weeds of destructive Opinions, there must certainly be a blessed Harmony." However, the author had already made his apology to Baltimore in the pamphlet's Introduction, wherein he explained: "If I have wrote or composed anything that's wilde and confused, it is because I am so myself."[52]

Again in 1671, Baltimore warned Maryland's governor, then his son Charles, that he and the Council were to be careful about executing policy regarding religion. Despite the proprietor's reaffirmations of it, however, belief in toleration failed to take hold. In England and America at the time, animosities between different Protestant groups were burning themselves out; but the hostility between Catholic and Protestant remained unabated. Moreover, Baltimore's policy of keeping religion out of the public eye in order to lessen sectarian friction gave rise to another difficulty, a general feeling that many in the colony were drifting away from religion altogether. This intuition of unease manifested itself in a steady trickle of petitions to England for an established church.

In 1661 the Lower House had tried to provide public financial support for ministers of the Church of England, but the proprietor had squelched the attempt. In 1666, the year of Alsop's admiring pamphlet, a Mr. Burle asked in the Lower House that a minister be settled in every county of the province.[53] A letter to the Archbishop of London from Reverend John Yeo, a minister of the Church of England, survives from 1676. Yeo's letter failed to provide an accurate picture of religion in Maryland, because its author addressed himself primarily to the lack of uniformity and the weakness of the Protestant—by which he meant Anglican—religion in the colony. Thus, in his estimation, the condition "whereby the lords day is prophaned, Religion despised, & all notorious vices committed" and the tendency of the people to fall away into "Popery, Quakerism, or Phanticisme" were both unacceptable, and he did not carefully distinguish between the two.[54]

Twelve years later, Mary Taney, "on the behalf of herself and others of his Majesty's subjects," sent a petition to the Archbishop of Canterbury asking that a maintenance be settled on a minister of the Church of England in Calvert Town. The reasons she gave for this request were the poverty of the inhabitants, which made them unable to support a minister themselves, and her fear that their children would "be condemned to infidelity and apostacy."[55] None of the foregoing efforts succeeded immediately; but they help to explain why Maryland would eventually settle an established church with relative ease.

Political reality rendered nil any chance Catholics might have had of achieving acceptance in Maryland by remaining inconspicuous. Contemporaries varied in their judgments of the size of the Catholic population. Baltimore himself estimated that Catholics were one of the smallest groups, and an estimate made in 1681 set the proportion of Protestants to Catholics as 30 to 1. More likely, Catholics amounted to about 3000 in a total population of 25,000; but they exercised influence and political power to a degree far exceeding their numbers. For a period of thirty years before the revolution in Maryland, Catholic relatives of the proprietor, or Protestants who were connected to him by marriage, dominated the Council and also occupied the principal positions in the colony's government and judicial system. Consequently, men of growing prosperity—Protestant in almost all cases—found themselves excluded from those positions of power consonant with their social and economic prominence.[56] These turned to the Assembly and assumed the leadership in a struggle against the power of the proprietor.

The conflict included economic, legal, and political issues. Overall, however, it took the form of a contest to limit Baltimore's prerogative in the name of the rights and liberties of Englishmen, a struggle that the history of the century connected with Protestantism.[57] Among those who opposed Baltimore and his supporters, Josiah Fendall and John Coode proved most effective in manipulating for their own purposes current grievances and fears. Fendall, erstwhile governor of Maryland, had turned into the implacable enemy of the proprietary party. Coode would eventually lead the revolution of 1689.[58]

In 1676, the year of Yeo's letter to the Archbishop of London and also of an unsuccessful attempt to overthrow the Maryland government, Baltimore's opponents sent to king and Parliament a petition entitled "Complaint from Heaven with a Huy and crye and a petition out of Virginia and Maryland," probably written by Fendall or his associates. Though its authors masqueraded behind a quaint and rustic style, the "Complaint" gathered up and cleverly interwove the political and religious grievances that were currently unsettling many in the colony. It skillfully blended fear of the Jesuits, as well as of the

French and the Indians, with accusations that Baltimore ruled tyranni-
cally, overtaxed the province, violated the charter, denied Englishmen
their native liberties, and arrogated to himself absolute power.[59]

As for religious toleration, the authors of the "Complaint" in effect
denied that the Maryland system was feasible. To the argument of the
proprietor's party that "the papists are no sutch people as th[e]y are
black[e]ned," they countered that Catholics "by their canon law not
beeinge bound to keep faith with protestants, the protestants are not
bound to believe their fayr outsides." Neither the laws of England nor
the colony's charter could justify turning the province to the pope's
devotion, and "Liberty of Conscience will not cover that neither."
These sentiments fitted into a larger overview purporting to show that
the Jesuits dispersed themselves over the country to set Protestants at
odds with each other, so that in the resulting confusion the pope could
"spring aloft" and gain "supremacy in America."[60]

The statements that liberty of conscience could not work because
Catholics only pretended to accept it, and that the system was not lawful because it violated English laws help explain the request that
followed that "Protestant Ministers . . . and glebe lands may be
errected and established in every County, notwithstanding liberty of
conscience and maintained by the people." Both the "Complaint" and
Yeo's communication averred that Catholics in Maryland were aided
more than Protestants. The "Complaint" asked the English bishops
why they did not match the pope's efforts in sending clergy to America.
Yeo's letter claimed that the Catholic clergy and Jesuits were
encouraged, that the Quakers took care of their own, but that the
general Protestant population was destitute of religious care.[61] The inti-
mation that Catholicism was established, implied here but later
explicitly asserted, represented, in spite of its being untrue, a Protestant
perception of the reality.

Baltimore did procure Jesuits for his province, and he demonstrated
considerable concern that Maryland Catholics be provided with
priests. The Jesuit mission in the colony evidenced an institutional,
organized, and continuous Catholic Church presence. The proprietor
also recommended and encouraged Anglican ministers, but these
functioned without any clearly visible organization. Apart from the
Quakers, most of the other settlers did not belong to religions with a
strong tradition of voluntary support of churches. Thus, contrasted
with the haphazard Protestant arrangements, the Jesuit organization
appeared very favorably, and Protestant critics, careless about making
distinctions, were quick to equate it with an establishment of religion,
the only kind of organized church they had known.

In response to the concern for the Anglican Church in Maryland—
or the lack thereof—raised by Yeo's letter, the Committee for Trade
and Plantations, of which the Bishop of London was a member,
pushed Baltimore to remedy the situation by legislation.[62] In his reply
to the Committee, Charles Calvert, who had recently succeeded his
father as the third Lord Baltimore, relied heavily on the view that
religious toleration had been granted to attract settlers to the colony.
He exaggerated when he argued that most came for that purpose, as he
did also when he claimed that there were a sufficient number of
churches and houses called Meeting Houses, and that among the
various religions in the province, Anglicans constituted one of the
smallest groups. The new proprietor also affirmed that in view of the
existing "Act for Religion," it would be difficult to compel the
inhabitants to maintain ministers of a religion other than their own and
implied that to do so would violate freedom of religion.[63]

The following year, replying to a questionnaire the same Committee had sent to all the colonies, Baltimore reaffirmed in even
stronger terms his opposition to any alteration in the Maryland
religious arrangement. To the question that dealt with a religious
census and arrangement for the support of ministers, the proprietor
again emphasized the role that toleration had played in populating
the province, and he went so far as to write that "such scruteinyes . . .
would certaynly either endanger Insurections or a General Dis-
peopleing of the Provynce." He was, however, a little out of touch
with the history of his own colony, to say nothing of the contemporary mood of its populace. He presented the Act Concerning
Religion as having arisen out of a popular demand to which his father
had agreed, and he allowed that the colonists looked on it "as that
whereon alone depends the preservation of their Peace their
Propertyes and their Libertyes."[64]

In 1681, testimony given the Committee for Trade and Plantations
by a ship's master, Captain Richard Shepherd, to the effect that he
knew of no quarrel "between the Protestants and Papists" appeared to
confirm the proprietor's sunny view of sectarian relationships in his
province. Other evidence, however, painted a grimmer picture. That
very year, in response to the Exclusion Crisis in England, brought
about by the attempt to close out the Catholic James from the throne,
Coode and Fendall tried to stir up rebellion in Maryland and spread
throughout the colony rumors of an Indian-Catholic conspiracy. They
were arrested and subsequently tried. Before the trial, Fendall
challenged each juror to state his religion. Several demurred, protesting the question; Fendall insisted, however, and rejected every

Catholic. Though Coode was acquitted, Fendall was found guilty and banished to Virginia, where he died in 1687.[65]

Reacting once again to complaints from Maryland, this time protesting the absence of Protestants from the Council, as well as partiality to Catholics, the Privy Council ordered the proprietor to redress the situation if it proved true. In his own defense, Baltimore had twenty-seven of the chief Protestants in the colony submit a testimony of the fairness and impartiality of the government, together with a list of those Protestants who held office.[66]

As news of the Glorious Revolution drifted into the colonies, both government and people reacted with considerable anxiety. Baltimore alleged that he had sent an order to proclaim William of Orange and Mary the new sovereigns, but that the messenger never reached Maryland. By well into 1689, the colony had still not heralded the new regime, and the Council's inactivity and indecision lent credence to the suspicion that the proprietor was a Jacobite. Rumors of Indian-Catholic plots now ran rampant. The governments of both Virginia and Maryland examined the circumstances giving rise to these and declared them completely groundless, but such declarations could not ease the tension brought about in Maryland by its government's failure to issue a proclamation about the new monarchs. Finally, in July 1689, John Coode and the leaders of the anti-proprietary party, calling themselves the Protestant Association, seized that government.[67]

The Maryland revolutionaries presented their uprising as an action carried out for king, liberty, and the Protestant religion. By the terms of the Articles of Surrender, no Catholic could henceforth hold office in the province. The Protestant Association then issued "The Declaration Of the reason and motive for the present appearing in arms of His Majesty's Protestant Subjects in the Province of Maryland," which again gathered up the by then standard grievances and accusations of tyranny and charges of absolutism against the proprietor and clad them in fears of Indian schemes, French designs, and Catholic plots to submerge the colony in the toils of "Slavery & Popery." After a period of uncertainty, William accepted the work of the Associators, who then managed the colony until the arrival of a royal governor. Lord Baltimore lost the government of the province, though he retained his rights as proprietor of the land.[68]

The Associators presented themselves as defenders of Protestant liberties; yet the revolution in Maryland did not simply pit Protestants against Catholics. The latter opposed it, as did Quakers for the most part. Clearly, all the Associators were Protestant; but not all Protestants supported the Association. Michael Taney, whose wife, Mary, had earlier petitioned the Archbishop of Canterbury to support a Protestant minister, was jailed for not cooperating with the revolution. Anne Arundel County, first settled by Puritans from Virginia, but by 1689 a Quaker stronghold, refused to send representatives to the revolutionary Assembly, and many Protestants wrote to England describing the "fraudulent rumors promoted by Coode and his Associates."[69] However, those Protestants who opposed Coode did not necessarily oppose a Protestant government other than the one provided by the revolution. Of the petitions sent to England, some supported Baltimore and mentioned that the Association denied the enjoyment of civil and religious liberty; but none attacked the Association on the ground that it denied religious toleration. The Lords Baltimore's sixty-year experiment died without a whimper.[70]

The royal governor, Lionel Copley, arrived in Maryland in 1692 with instructions to administer the English oaths of office and test to all officeholders. Catholics could not subscribe to an oath that denied all spiritual and temporal power to a foreign prince or abjure belief in transubstantiation. Quakers could not in conscience subscribe to any oath, so the instructions automatically excluded both groups from the legislature. Otherwise, Copley was to "permit a liberty of Conscience & of all Persons so they be contented with a quiet and peaceable Enjoyment of it, not giving offense or scandall to the Government" and to establish the Church of England in the province.[71] Although most Protestants within the colony probably welcomed the new government, they showed no alacrity in the matter of setting up a satisfactory establishment of religion. A decade elapsed—and the Privy Council disallowed three legislative acts—before the colony passed a law for the establishment of the Church of England that proved acceptable to the home government.

The vague perceptions that had existed before the revolution of the need for more Protestant ministers, as well as the definite opinions regarding the strength and favor shown to Catholics, led in the post-revolutionary period to the elimination of every public manifestation of Catholicism, rather than to the strengthening of Protestantism. That the new Assembly was more interested in forestalling any repetition of the ills associated with the proprietors than in providing for the needs of the Anglican Church appeared clearly in its determination to use the Church acts to assert the rights and liberties of Englishmen, even though such clauses caused the English government to disallow the Acts of 1692 and 1696.[72]

In 1700 Governor Nehemiah Blakiston secured passage of another establishment act. This new act omitted the offending references to political liberty that had killed the previous two, but retained a clause from the Act of 1696 demanding that the *Book of Common Prayer* and the rites according to the Church of England be read "by all and Every Minister or Reader in Every Church or other place of Public Worship within this Province."[73]

The wording reflected the Anglican disposition to equate Protestantism with the Church of England (the first two acts had referred to the Protestant religion) and also careless draftsmanship in the Assembly. That body clearly did not intend the literal interpretation, which would have carried Anglican worship into every church.[74] Nevertheless, counsel to the Committee for Trade and Plantations in England thought that the phrase could be construed to deny liberty of worship to dissenters, and so the Privy Council disallowed the law as a violation of the English Act of Toleration.[75]

Finally, the Privy Council itself drew up an act that the Maryland legislature passed the next year. This law limited Anglican worship to "every church which now is or here after shall be settled and established within this Province." It retained the provisions of the previously disallowed acts dividing the counties into parishes, providing for the erection of churches, for setting up of vestries, and for receipt of forty pounds of tobacco from each inhabitant—regardless of religion—for the support of the Anglican minister. It also extended the Act of Toleration to Maryland, as well as the law allowing Quakers to substitute a solemn affirmation for an oath.[76]

This Act of 1702 established the Church of England in Maryland, but not to the satisfaction of the clergy and governors. As far as provision of an adequate maintenance for clergy was concerned, the revolution and the subsequent acts apparently did not greatly influence the minds of most Maryland taxpayers. To rebel in the name of Protestantism was one thing; to pay for it was another. Judging from later compaints from the clergy, more colonists preferred the first to the second option. Governor Nicholson later commented that the Church of England was well received until people found themselves paying forty pounds of tobacco towards it, and then "They grew into a dislike of it and to form partys against it."[77]

Repeatedly, the governors had asked the Assembly for glebes and houses for ministers, but to no avail. In 1699, in response to the governor's instructions decreeing that "a competent Maintenance be assigned to each Church & Convenient houses, etc.," the Assembly had declined to do anything, saying that it had provided sufficiently well for ministers, and that as the colony grew in wealth, they would receive more, provided they did not "by their Cowldness Stiffen our Zeale."

Finally, in 1704, and then in only a half-hearted way, the Lower House moved in the matter of maintenance by allowing parishes without a minister to allot the tobacco collection toward a glebe.[78]

For their part, the clergy wrote to the Bishop of London complaining about the lack of glebes and parsonages, the inadequacy of their allowance, and the mean quality of the tobacco they received. Because they could not rely on the Anglican population to provide even a poor maintenance, the ministers were especially anxious that Quakers and Catholics be allowed no exemption. In turn, Quakers and Catholics joined forces to defeat and frustrate plans for the establishment.[79]

Because the Catholics did not choose to make public demonstrations of their opposition to the settlement of the Church of England, little information remains of the strategies they used. They did make a plea by way of the Spanish ambassador in London. According to this petition, the colony had been founded as a refuge for Catholics. The petitioners were concerned with mistreatment of Catholics since the revolution, but they did not mention the establishment or the tobacco tax. Elsewhere, and on more technical though tenuous legal grounds, both Catholics and Quakers argued that the colony could not reenact a law that had been previously vetoed repeatedly by the king.[80]

The Quakers showed no such reticence as the Catholics. They first reaffirmed for themselves their repugnance to "contributing towards maintaining Idollatrous priests [and] . . . their houses of worship," and then took their case to the provincial governor, writing to remind him that giving maintenance violated their consciences, and that they could not pay it even if they were to be ruined in their estates.[81] When the Assembly turned down their requests for relief from maintenance and from oaths, they took their case to England, where they enlisted their co-religionists in an unsuccessful battle against the Maryland Anglican establishment. However, as a result of the extension to the colony of the English Act of Toleration and the clause in the Act of 1700 allowing solemn affirmation in place of an oath, the Quakers found themselves somewhat better off than their Catholic allies.[82]

After 1689 the treatment of Catholics in Maryland reflected long-standing attitudes and fears, as well as contemporary events in both Europe and America. The Declaration of the Protestant Association had not only repeated previous assertions that the province favored Catholicism over Protestantism, but had gone further—to claim, or at least strongly intimate, that the Act of 1649 amounted to an establishment of the Catholic Church.[83] Another and persistent felt grievance on the part of Protestants arose out of their conviction that Catholics, and Jesuits in particular, were by fair means or foul converting the population of Maryland to Catholicism. Finally, the fear of "Irish Papists" always associated with the proprietor because of his Irish peerage became more acute in the 1690s, when events in Ireland were sending Catholics and priests into exile having "no better place of refuge in the king's Dominion upon their being banished from Ireland."[84]

The post-revolutionary penal legislation sought both to stem the growth of Catholicism and to remove its influence from every aspect of public life. Catholics had already been excluded from office, and in 1692 an act forbade them to act as attorneys. To limit Catholic numbers, a law of 1699 laid a poll tax of twenty shillings on each Irish immigrant, payable by the captain of the ship transporting him. In 1704 the Act To Prevent the Growth of Popery prohibited Catholic worship and forbade priests to make converts or to baptize children of any but Catholic parents. In response to a Catholic petition, the provincial government made temporary exception for Catholic worship in private houses—an exception that Queen Anne demanded be made permanent. In 1718 Catholics were disfranchised.[85]

By the time Maryland finally settled into its new religious arrangement, Virginia had been living with an established church for more than a century. The overall religious mood there at the time strikes one as an attachment to Anglicanism because it was the religion of the colony, a dislike of dissenters precisely because they were nonconformists, and a definite reluctance to pamper the ministers of the established church. In 1696 the Assembly bristled at the clergy's suggestion that they were inadequately paid, declaring their petition "malicious, Scandalous and an unjust reflection on the House." Similarly, the Assembly refused utterly to countenance any move towards ecclesiastical courts for the punishment of moral offenses and was ever suspicious of any move to increase the jurisdiction of the clergy or weaken local or lay control of the Church.[86] The colony kept a similarly strict eye on the activities of dissenters, declaring that "dissenters . . . shall have such liberty allowed them as the law directs Provided they use it civilly and quietly."[87]

Seventeenth-century Maryland provided a unique example of Church-State relations. Other colonies without an established church were Protestant in composition, and consequently experienced none of the religious tension or insecurity that Catholicism sparked in Maryland. Not even Rhode Island's radical experiment had to undergo the test involved in absorbing Catholics. As Cotton Mather commented, Rhode Island had "every thing in the world but Roman Catholics and real Christians."[88] Such adverse statements from without, however,

only helped cement Rhode Islanders together. Protestant Marylanders, too, felt threatened by outside dangers—French, Indians,and
the power of Rome—but instead of creating unity, these fears caused
especially severe disunity and instability, arising out of the perception
of Catholics as a fifth column in the colony's midst. That many of the
fears were baseless did nothing to lessen their urgency.

During the formative years of the colony of Maryland, the world was
not ready for its extraordinary example of Catholics and Protestants
living together in relative harmony while freely and openly practicing
their respective religions. No strong tradition of toleration upon which
the Lords Baltimore might have based their pluralistic attitudes existed
in Catholicism. Differing Protestant sects were gradually being forced
to the conclusion that even if they could not agree to equality with each
other, they would at least have to tolerate one another. Nothing, however, had evolved to weaken the determination of Protestants and
Catholics to secure each other's elimination.

For their part, the Lords Baltimore, themselves apparently disinterested in developing an ideology of religious liberty, concentrated
on the practical business of colonization and hoped to avoid religious
issues. Their silence on the topic of religious freedom only confused
their Protestant subjects, who could not see beyond the accepted
stereotype of the age, for which neither Maryland Catholics in general
nor the proprietors in particular suggested any replacement. As a
result, their decision to link progressive religious practices with a retrogressive political policy only helped confirm the colony's Protestant
settlers in their not unnatural assumption—in a world divided into two
armed camps of Catholics and Protestants—that Maryland could only
represent a back door left ajar for the enemy.

To have caused Maryland Protestants to think otherwise, the successive proprietors would have had to launch a hitherto unheard of
campaign to demonstrate both the religious and practical value of toleration. In consequence of their disinclination to engage in any such
action, an unusual and noble project fell victim to its time. Representing no rising consensus or felt need within either contemporary
Catholicism or Protestantism, Maryland's seventeenth-century toleration proved quixotic and inevitably failed to survive. England's
Glorious Revolution brought the colony into harmony with the era.
Instead of practicing their different religions with equal liberty and
maintaining their churches voluntarily, all Marylanders wound up
supporting the Church of England. Catholics there worshipped
unobtrusively, as the Baltimores had planned, but not in freedom.

In 1692 the Maryland Council rejected the colony's past policy of toleration by dismissing it as a "specious" liberty of conscience designed to depopulate Virginia.[89] This interpretation, together with the story of the failure of the Maryland experiment, serves to delineate more sharply the nature of the religious freedom and toleration that actually was acceptable to colonial Americans. The sources for the continuing development of religious liberty would be found within a Protestant America, would be nourished within that exclusvie atmosphere, and for considerable time to come would inhabit that world exclusively.

3

Church and State
in the Restoration Colonies

After the death of Oliver Cromwell in 1658, the majority of Englishmen could see no better way of avoiding anarchy than by restoring the monarchy in the person of Charles II. Presbyterians, the largest non-Anglican group, hoped that they would find some place in the new established church, and Charles's declarations on the subject encouraged their expectations. After the Restoration became a fact, however, a hostile Parliament dominated by Cavaliers and Anglicans bent on revenge enacted the draconian Clarendon Code, designed to punish, harass, and exclude Dissenters from public life.[1]

Later, in order to overthrow Charles's successor, the Catholic James II, Anglicans acceded to the Act of Toleration in 1689 in order to secure the support of Dissenters. Merely "An Act for exempting their Majesties Protestant subjects, dissenting from the Church of England, from the penalties of certain laws," the Act of Toleration only recognized the right of Dissenters to exist. They remained second-class citizens devoid of political rights in a country dominated by Anglicans.[2]

The new colonies of the Carolinas, New York, New Jersey, and Pennsylvania, founded during the Restoration period, would also experience the influence of a dominant Anglican Church. However, a triumphant Anglicanism would in America have to interact with forces, both practical and ideological, that were conspiring towards greater pluralism and toleration in religion. American dissenters, because of their numerical and geographical status, would fare much better than their brethren in England.

In the years following the Restoration, the Church of England in the colonies not only lacked those advantages that had enabled Anglicanism to triumph again in the Mother Country, but faced a whole series of problems not encountered by the same church in England. In 1671 the existing American mainland colonies could count only thirty Church of England ministers, and by the end of the century, that number had merely doubled. In the Mother Country, the established church opposed non-Conformists not so much because of differences in doctrine as because Dissenters inhibited unity and uniformity of religious practice. In America, on the other hand, the diversity of religions rendered such uniformity impossible.[3]

An eighteenth-century North Carolina planter allowed that while there were many roads to heaven, nevertheless "no gentleman would choose any but the Episcopal." That kind of social pressure, however, hardly operated in newly founded wilderness settlements, where society in the English sense barely existed, and where, as John Archdale, governor of Carolina, wrote in 1707, "Dissenters Kill Wolves and Bears, etc., as well as Church-Men; and also Fell Trees and Clear Ground for Plantations."[4]

Thus the Anglican Church, in its desire to carry its victory at home to the colonies, contended with the realities that America lacked not only bishops, but to a great extent even lower clergy; that the need to settle profitable colonies took precedence over a strict uniformity of religion; that 3000 miles separated the Anglican Church in England from its colonial counterpart; and that in the new settlements, the majority of inhabitants belonged to what in England were Dissenting churches. All these conditions shaped the pattern of Church-State relations in the Restoration colonies.

New American settlements began forming early in the reign of Charles II. In 1663 eight courtiers and Stuart supporters secured a charter for territory extending from northern Florida to the Virginia border and stretching from sea to sea. This huge province was eventually divided into North and South Carolina.[5] In their origin and development, the two Carolinas had little in common—apart from the proprietary bond.

North Carolina grew from a nucleus of immigrants from Virginia, some of them Quakers, who had taken up residence in the area of the Carolina grant even before the charter of 1663. South Carolina was populated in great part by settlers from Barbados, and the proprietors favored the southern colony and promoted its interests over those of the northern one.[6]

Like the Maryland grant, the Carolina charter conferred on the proprietors powers "in as ample manner as any bishop of Durham ... enjoyed." Clearly the charter presumed that the Church of England would be established in the new colony, but that it would be settled in accord with Charles's moderate preferences rather than with the vengeful order the Restoration Parliament had compelled the king to accept. To those who could not conform to the Anglican Church, the charter allowed "such Indulgences and Dispensations" as the proprietors "shall, in their discretion, think fit and reasonable." These generous provisions proceeded from the frankly pragmatic reasoning that because of the remoteness of Carolina, toleration would "be no breach of the unity and uniformity established in this [English] nation." Early decisions of the Proprietors granted liberty of conscience to all without exception, allowed Quakers to enter pledges in a book in lieu of swearing, and permitted each county to decide which minister it wished to support. This "full and free Liberty of Conscience," emphasized in early promotional and travel literature, helped populate the area.[7]

North Carolina developed first. Although the charter provided for the Church of England, no Anglican ministers lived there. In 1703 Henderson Walker, governor of North Carolina and an Anglican partisan, informed the Bishop of London that the area had "neither priest nor altar." Earlier, in 1676, the Quaker missionary William Edmundson had written in his journal that the Friends were well settled, and that there "was no room for priests."[8] Quakers exercised more influence than any other religious group in the colony during the seventeenth century, not because they were in the majority, but because they possessed a higher profile and were better organized. As distinct from Anglicans, or even Presbyterians or Congregationalists, the Quakers were able to exist and prosper without a professional ministry or a formal church structure.

The proprietors' policy enabling citizens to subscribe to oaths by signing their names in a book rather than swearing permitted Friends to participate in public affairs, which they did to the fullest. In 1680 some of them paid fines rather than carry arms, but the subsequent administration of Quaker governor John Archdale exempted them from even that burden. In 1696 a law guaranteed "all Christians (Papists only excepted) ... full liberty of conscience." By excluding Catholics, this provision brought North Carolina more closely into line with the English system and portended further restrictions within the colony.[9]

The colony continued to grow steadily as the eighteenth century approached. By 1700 the population numbered about 11,000, of whom Quakers, with three gatherings, constituted the only easily identifiable religious grouping. The remainder of the inhabitants, most of them nominally Anglican, showed no strong religious identity or organization. The Reverend John Blair, an Anglican missionary, visited North Carolina in 1704 and found among the inhabitants only one unifying sentiment regarding religion: "to prevent anything that will be chargeable to them, as they allege Church government will be, if once established by law."[10]

Although South Carolina for the most part experienced the same proprietary policy of toleration as North Carolina, its particular mix of inhabitants caused it to develop differently. South Carolina attracted a significant body of Anglicans from Barbados. The proprietors' promotional efforts also brought Presbyterian and Baptist settlers from England, as well as Huguenots fleeing persecution after the revocation of the Edict of Nantes in 1685. The interaction of these three groups shaped the internal affairs of the colony. They settled around Charleston, whose population by 1700 numbered roughly 8000, half of whom were black slaves.[11]

South Carolina's first law, passed in 1670, ordered proper observance of the Sabbath, but religious issues played little part in the settlement's affairs during that century. In 1698, with no recorded opposition, partly accountable for by the Huguenot tendency to gravitate to the Anglican Church, the Assembly conferred a maintenance of £50 per year on the minister of St. Philip's Episcopal Church, built in 1682 and the only church in the colony.[12] In 1697 John Granville, Earl of Bath, a strong supporter of the Church of England, became chief proprietor. His partisan stance would coincide with a renewed vigor and aggressiveness on the part of the Anglican Church.

James II's removal from the English throne banished the Church of England's fears of a Catholic ascendancy. During the final years of the seventeenth century and the opening years of the eighteenth, an invigorated and confident Anglican Church focused its attention on the colonies. It was determined to make effective the instructions for the promotion of the Church of England delivered to royal governors during the Restoration years, which for the most part had remained a dead letter. This push for a stronger Anglican Church in the New World coincided with a move on the part of authorities in England to exercise greater political and commercial control over the American settlements. In the minds of royal governors, religious and political centralization blended into a picture of the social order that must be imposed on the colonies.

On the ecclesiastical side, Bishop Henry Compton of London, who supervised colonial religious affairs, proved an eager and aggressive promoter of Anglicanism. In 1701, to supply the colonies with ministers, Thomas Bray founded the Society for the Propagation of the Gospel. Ultimately, the endeavors of royal governors and ecclesiastical authorities managed to establish the Anglican Church in both Carolinas.[13]

In 1702 Sir Nathaniel Johnson, a man determined to suppress nonconformists, arrived to take over the governorship. By calling an emergency session of the legislature and taking a vote before all the members were seated, Johnson pushed through a test act, requiring all members to conform to the Church of England, thereby excluding dissenters. The Assembly then proceeded to declare the Church of England "Settled and Established" in the colony. The law set apart six parishes, whose clergy were to be provided for from an existing import tax, but, in addition, authorized vestries to assess all the inhabitants of the parishes up to £100 per year for parochial expenses. Finally, the establishment act allowed the majority of the Church of England members in each parish to elect the minister, but set up a commission of twenty laymen empowered to remove clergy accused by the parish vestry of immoral or imprudent conduct.[14]

South Carolina's non-Anglicans reacted quickly. To several grievances already lodged with Parliament, they added complaints against the test and establishment acts. Their agents enlisted Daniel Defoe as a publicist to take their case to Parliament and the English public. Their arguments displayed no great altruism. Indeed, while they protested the exclusion of dissenters, they equally objected to "aliens, Jews, . . . and Frenchmen" exercising the franchise in South Carolina.[15]

The reasoning against the test and establishment acts stressed that the lay commission deprived the Bishop of London of ecclesiastical jurisdiction over the colonies, and that both laws militated against the best interests of colonial trade by discouraging and discriminating against dissenters.[16] The House of Lords concurred and secured the disallowance of both. On receipt of this news, the South Carolina Assembly repealed the test act and, in 1706, passed another establishment law, which would survive as the basis of the colony's established church. The new establishment act provided for ten parishes, within which parishioners could still elect their minister, whose salary, together with the cost of building a church, was to be taken from public monies. The lay commissioners remained, but no longer had power to remove clergy.[17]

A further act of 1710 declared that since the provision allowing vestries to levy additional parish charges on the inhabitants had been "found inconvenient," each parish was authorized to draw up to £40 from the public exchequer. The statute hinted at the presence of opposition to the established church by reaffirming its legal basis, since "factious persons have given out that the acts of 1706 and 1707 are not lawful."[18] With the passage of this law, South Carolina became the only one of those American colonies with provisions for a tax-supported clergy that levied the total cost of maintenance of the Church of England in the colony on the public treasury. Although dissenters' taxes would still help support the Anglican Church, individuals would not experience the sting of contributing directly to the salary of a minister whose services they did not attend.

The act of 1710 was one of a series of measures and developments which lessened tension and hostility between Anglicans and dissenters. After the death in 1707 of John Granville, the intransigent promoter of the Anglican Church, the proprietors moderated their stance on establishment. In 1712 Governor Charles Craven began his administration with a promise to protect the Church of England, but also "to show the greatest tenderness to those who are under the misfortune of dissenting from her."[19] As a result of this more tolerant policy, dissenter resistance eased. The Anglican Church also profited from the fact that Quakers, at this period the most active and vociferous opponents of Anglican or other establishments in colonial America, formed the smallest and weakest dissenting bloc in South Carolina.[20]

In 1710 the colony had eight Anglican clergymen and eight dissenting ministers, of whom Presbyterians formed the strongest group. Ten years later, the Anglicans had seven to the dissenters' eleven.[21] By that time, South Carolina dissenters had come to be accepted, if not loved, by their Anglican neighbors, although the latter did try unsuccessfully to persuade the Assembly to restrict the right of dissenting clergy to perform marriages. By the early 1720s relations among the different religious bodies in South Carolina had fallen into a pattern that would survive until the American Revolution. Like Maryland, the colony made it clear that Catholics were not welcome, and a law of 1716 prohibited the importation of Irish Catholic servants.[22]

Protestants, though, enjoyed toleration, and those who would take oaths could hold government positions. Nevertheless, the Church of England continued to be the favored church. It alone could receive public support, and its parishes formed the administrative units of government. However, because the Anglican ministers supplied to the colony by the Society for the Propagation of the Gospel had in turn to be elected to their parish appointments by local vestries, the established church was very much an adaptation of the Church of England suitable to South Carolina.[23]

North Carolina, too, established the Anglican Church; but while South Carolina finally managed to combine dissenters and Anglicans in relative harmony, each group well supplied with ministers by colonial standards, its northern neighbor achieved no such overall concord. In 1701, Henderson Walker, governor of North Carolina, pushed through the Assembly an act establishing the Anglican religion. No copy of the statute remains, but later comments on it indicate that it envisaged a number of parishes in which all inhabitants would be taxed £30 for the support of the Anglican minister. This act called forth furious opposition on the part of North Carolina dissenters. In 1703, led by Quakers, they captured a majority of the Assembly seats and vowed to repeal the law. Before they could do so, the proprietors voided it on the ground that £30 represented an inadequate maintenance for the clergy. That same year, a group of Anglicans, in a petition to the proprietors, protested their willingness to support a minister, but the Quakers had vowed to resist any establishment.[24]

The sequence of legislative events in the colony over the next few years, leading to the establishment of the Anglican Church, is unclear, because no copies of the legislation passed have survived. In 1704, shortly after another Anglican, Robert Daniel, succeeded Walker as governor, news of the English oath of allegiance prescribed at the beginning of Queen Anne's reign reached North Carolina. Daniel immediately proffered the oath, thereby disfranchising the Quakers and probably enabling the passage of another establishment act the following year, though no copies of such a law remain either.[25]

In 1711 an Anglican-controlled Assembly demanded that office-holders subscribe to oaths in accord with English law and reaffirmed the Anglican establishment, though recognizing the "laws made for granting Indulgences to Protestant dissenters" in England.[26] Quakers continued to be excluded from the political arena, where from the earliest days they had played an important role and had constituted the mainstay of opposition to an Anglican establishment.[27]

In 1715 the Assembly brought the colony's religious system into conformity with that of England. In statutes passed that year, it outlined parishes and decreed that the inhabitants of each would be liable for the support of an Anglican minister. An additional law demanded that officeholders subscribe to all oaths sworn by members of Parliament. Another section of the same ordinance permitted Quakers to substitute an affirmation for an oath, but they were still—as in

England—excluded from holding office or testifying in criminal cases.[28]

Although established in North Carolina, the Anglican Church never took root there. By 1710 the population numbered about 16,000 people, most of them Anglicans, one-tenth to one-seventh Quakers, and the rest other dissenters—predominantly Presbyterians. Because of the scarcity of ministers, the Anglican majority received little pastoral care. From 1708 on, North Carolina rarely had more than two Anglican clergymen, and in some years, it had none at all.[29] Those few clergy who did arrive were little enamored of the region. They all had the same laments: their own poverty, the backwardness and lack of religion in the province, the opposition of Quakers to the established church, and the fact that—in the absence of religious services—North Carolinians tended to flock to Quaker meetings.

Missionary John Blair had written in 1704 that North Carolina was the "most barbarous place on the continent." Another minister, John Urmstone, irascible and cynical but a colorful character, made no secret of his loathing for the place, which he described as "a hell of a hole," allowing that he would "rather be a curate of a Bear Garden than Bishop of Carolina."[30] Urmstone's jaundiced view stemmed to a great extent from his struggle to pry his salary from reluctant parishioners, who apparently resisted paying it by every means possible. Although Quakers led the opposition to maintenance of Anglican clergy, they had, from Urmstone's account, little trouble recruiting the support of Presbyterians and of those he contemptuously referred to as "anythingarians." Urmstone also reported that vestries found employing readers, whom they paid £15, a better bargain than paying a minister fifty. In 1715 he wrote the Society for the Propagation of the Gospel that the inhabitants of North Carolina "have all in general imbibed a Quaker like abhorrence of Hirelings."[31]

Other commentators, too, confirmed the influence of the Quakers, which resulted not only from their opposition to the established church, but also from their providing the only religious services and active religious leadership in the province.[32] For their part, North Carolina Friends sent a representative, John Porter, to England to argue their cause, employing the same defenses against maintenance that were used in Maryland—that they were the original settlers in the colony, and that taxing them for an established clergy would discourage settlement and damage trade. When such protests failed, they counseled their brethren to keep a strict account of the sufferings they endured in consequence of distraint for refusing to bear arms or to contribute to parish levies.[33] Beset by opponents and supported by few friends, the Anglican Church of North Carolina would represent the least stable and most opposed Anglican establishment in the American colonies.

Of all the Restoration colonies, New York presented by far the most varied array of people and religions. In 1642, while the Dutch still ruled the territory, the Jesuit missionary Isaac Jogues discovered eighteen languages among four hundred residents. During the remainder of the seventeenth century, reports sent to Europe by Dutch clerics and English governors continued to emphasize New York's multiplicity of beliefs. In 1686 Governor Thomas Dongan reported that "of all sorts of opinions there are some."[34] This diversity of population peculiarly shaped the course of Church-State relations in the province and presented a microcosm of the pluralism that would later emerge throughout the colonies.

In 1664, when hostility between England and Holland was about to boil over into war, Charles II granted the Dutch colony of New Amsterdam to his brother James. James dispatched four ships of the English navy to the colony under the command of Richard Nicholls, whom he appointed governor. They turned New Amsterdam into New York without firing a shot.[35] In reorganizing the religious laws of his new colony, James showed a far better grasp of New York's sectarian diversity than had its former Dutch rulers. The latter had established the Dutch Reformed Church, and although they tolerated the New England Puritan immigrants who settled on Long Island, Dutch governors— especially Peter Stuyvesant—had proven extremely intolerant not only of Quakers but also of Lutheran and Jewish immigrants.[36]

In 1665 the religous provisions of the legislation known as the Duke's Laws, agreed upon by the people of Long Island and designed principally to govern that section, guaranteed the free exercise of religion to all Christians. They called for the inhabitants of each town to select and contribute towards the support of a Protestant minister. Governor Francis Lovelace, who took office in 1667, supported this system, but within reason. When the Presbyterians at Southold distrained a man of a differing sect of his cattle in order to pay their own minister, he gave them a severe dressing down. Meanwhile, in Manhattan, where the Duke's Laws did not yet apply, Dutch Reformed ministers lamented their loss of their establishment and the reluctance of their congregations to pay their salaries. Subsequently, in 1674, James appointed Edmund Andros governor and instructed him to permit the free peaceable exercise of "what Religion soever."[37]

In 1683, responding to popular pressure for a voice in the government, James authorized a meeting of an Assembly. Once convened, this body enacted a Charter of Liberties, which confirmed the substance of the Duke's Laws regarding religion. The Assembly also witnessed to the popular acceptance of the system for ministerial support by extending it to the entire province, and by further defining it to state that while two-thirds of a town (rather than a simple majority) must agree on a minister, any dissenting minority would be bound by such a compact.

This arrangement persisted through James's accession to the English throne in 1685, when New York automatically changed status from a proprietary to a royal colony, and it lasted until the Glorious Revolution in 1688 altered the government of both England and America. Most religious groups seemed to live together with little friction. Not all towns provided themselves with a minister, and those that did appeared to exercise a spirit of accommodation. In some instances, different religious groups shared the same building, and at Brookhaven the minister promised not to use the *Book of Common Prayer* unless the congregation present wished it.[38]

The clergy—both English and Dutch— complained that their problems lay within their own congregations, whose members showed no enthusiasm for paying their salaries, a trend confirmed by Governor Dongan when he reported to England in 1684 that "as for the King's natural-born subjects that live on Long Island and other parts of the Government I find it a hard task to make them pay their ministers."[39] Apart from disputes about maintenance, Quakers, who in their early and fervent stages insisted on disturbing religious worship, presented New York's only real source of religious turmoil.

Critics tended to damn Quakers by calling them "Ranters," thus associating them with one of the most bizarre sects that had emerged during the period of the English Civil War.[40] They also experienced harassment at the hands of the authorities. A letter from Richard Gildersleeve, constable at Hempstead, Long Island, indicated that Governor Andros, despite the provisions of the Duke's Laws and the Charter of Liberties, had forbidden Quakers to meet—an order they ignored. They also protested fines imposed on them for performing marriages according to their own rites and pleaded, unsuccessfully, that the colonial provision for liberty of conscience exempted them from bearing arms. Nevertheless, on the eve of the Glorious Revolution, the religious atmosphere of New York appeared calm. The Dutch minister Henry Selyns noted that the troubles caused by the "fantastic Quakers" had mostly died down, and his colleague Rudulphus Varick wrote in 1688 that eight other ministers of different denominations served on Long Island, with whom he lived in harmony.[41]

The first Assembly, in 1683, had by no means satisfied New Yorkers' desire for the "liberties of english men." In 1688 James exacerbated his colonists' continuing suspicions that they were subject to tyrannical government by annexing New York, whose population then numbered about 15,000, to the Dominion of New England. Shortly thereafter, news of a rebellion in Boston against James's government touched off a similar revolt in New York, led by Jacob Leisler, a captain of the militia.[42]

Fears of a Catholic-Indian conspiracy swept New York, where Dongan and several government officials were Catholic. Leisler, who appeared to believe firmly in the existence of such a plot, and who harbored anti-Catholic sentiments second to none, contacted Coode in Maryland, as well as the rebels in Boston, with a view to promoting inter-colonial cooperation against the supposed "Popish" threat. Leisler's rebellion immediately created bitter factions within the colony. Though he prevailed temporarily, his enemies were able to bring about his downfall when, through his own naïveté and incompetence, he failed promptly to accept the new royal governor, Henry Sloughter, sent in 1691 by William of Orange, and was executed. Although Leisler paid for his blundering with his life, he left behind him a party that would continue to bedevil New York politics.[43]

Sloughter arrived with instructions designed to bring religious legislation in New York into conformity with the religious settlement in England, whose Act of Toleration was more restrictive than existing statutes in the colony. Catholics were to be excluded from "liberty of Conscience" for the first time, and New York's system whereby each town selected a minister and taxed its inhabitants for his support was to be changed into an Anglican establishment. In the few short months of his administration, Sloughter, who died within the year, tried to implement his orders from England by introducing "an Act for ministers in every town, and their Maintenance" and "A Bill for settling the Ministry, and allowing a Maintenance for them, in every Respective City and Town that Consists of forty Families and upwards." Royal governors understood "the Ministry" to mean the Anglican ministry. So, apparently, did the predominantly dissenting New York Assembly, which failed to pass either bill, but did adopt test oaths aimed at excluding Catholics from office and eliminating them from the guarantee of liberty of conscience, as well as a rule allowing Quakers testifying in civil cases to substitute an affirmation for an oath.[44]

Where Sloughter failed in promoting the interests of the Church of England, his successor, Benjamin Fletcher, succeeded. Fletcher belonged to that group of royal governors of the late seventeenth and early eighteenth century bent on advancing Anglicanism as a means of centralizing authority and extending the influence of the home government. In his opening address to the Assembly, in March 1693, he rebuked its members for neglecting to act on his previous recommendation to them for "the settling of a ministry in this Province." After some more prodding, the legislature passed a bill in September of that year for "Settling a Ministry" in four counties (New York, Westchester, Kings, and Queens)" and set up the mechanism necessary to collect tithes from all the inhabitants within them and distrain those who refused to pay.[45]

Whether the Ministry Act of 1693 established the Church of England in four New York counties became a bone of contention for colonial New Yorkers and has remained a point of discussion for historians to the present time. Because the law billed itself as "An Act for Settling a Ministry & Raising a Maintenance for them," and because the language of the act referred only to "good sufficient Protestant" ministers, dissenters in the colony immediately contended that the law did not establish the Anglican Church there at all.[46] The governor disagreed, as did New York's Anglicans. The circumstances surrounding the act, however, provided enough clues for both Governor Fletcher and the Assembly to read each other's minds and to understand that they were settling for a bill whose language was deliberately vague, but which each side hoped to interpret in its own favor.

The strongest evidence that Fletcher deceived the Assembly about the meaning of the act rests on information provided by Colonel Lewis Morris in a letter written to the Society for the Propagation of the Gospel in 1711. Morris claimed that in the early 1690s, a group of dissenters in Queens had failed to raise enough money for their proposed church and resolved to get the Assembly to help them. According to Morris, Fletcher determined to seize the occasion to help the Church of England and succeeded in getting the Ministry Act passed. From an Assembly all "but one being dissenters," the act was "the most that could be got at the time for had more been attempted the Assembly had seen thro' the artifice." Morris's evidence must be weighed against the fact that, although he remained a staunch Anglican, he thought the royal governors did a disservice to the Anglican Church by attempting to force it on the colony. Neither is Morris's claim that Fletcher seized upon a favorable opportunity to introduce an act a convincing one, since the governor had been badgering the Assembly to support "an able ministry" since 1692.[47]

If the New York Assembly thought, as its members later claimed, that with the act of 1693 it was renewing the familiar system of ministerial support and leaving the choice of ministers to the towns, a policy to which few objected, then its members proved surprisingly recalcitrant about enacting the arrangement into law. In fact, a later legislature tried in 1699 to pass a statute reviving precisely that system, but the then Governor Bellomont felt, correctly, that his instructions forbade him to accept such a bill. Neither did Governor Fletcher act with such duplicity as Morris's later comments might suggest. His instructions demanded that he promote the Church of England and gave him power to collate ministers to benefices when vacant. The Assembly specifically refused to give Fletcher collating power, knowing full well that whoever held such authority would turn the proposed act to his own advantage. It also protected its interpretation by specifying that the new act should not touch existing agreements.[48]

Moreover, Fletcher had made his intentions fully plain in 1693, when he told the Assembly: "There are none of you but what are big with the privilege of Englishmen and Magna Carta, which is your right; and the same law doth provide for the religion of the church of England."[49] Given the tendency of the Anglican Church to identify itself with Protestantism or orthodoxy, the absence of specificity as to denomination might have been more an indication of Anglican over-confidence than of duplicity. That same year, when Fletcher wrote the Committee of Trade that he had succeeded in getting provisions for "a Ministry" in New York, he undoubtedly referred to an Anglican ministry.

John Yeo, in his earlier petition from Maryland, had equated Protestantism and Anglicanism. The Maryland law of the preceding year, which had clearly established the Anglican Church in that colony, bore the title "An Act for . . . the Establishment of the Protestant Religion within this Province," and an act passed there subsequent to the one in New York came to grief in England precisely because Anglicans equated Protestantism with the Church of England. Whether the New York statute of 1693 established Anglicanism is a question that cannot be answered definitively. The governor clearly intended that it should do so, and the Assembly equally clearly intended that it should not. Each side got as much as it could enacted in a somewhat vague piece of legislation, upon which each hoped it would later be able to impose its own interpretation.[50]

In 1694 the New York Vestry voted money for a minister's maintenance and asked the Assembly if the Ministry Act permitted them to call a dissenting minister. The Assembly answered in the affirmative, whereupon Fletcher called them into the Council chambers and informed them that their function was not to interpret the law. More significantly, he noted that "there is no Protestant Church [which] admits of such officers as Church-Wardens and Vestrymen but the Church of England." The point could hardly have been lost on the law-makers, even if they had not already noticed that the act of 1693 used the Anglican terms mentioned by the governor, whereas the earlier system of providing for ministers according to the choices of the indi-vidual towns relied on "overseers."[51]

Though each side checkmated the other, the Anglicans were able to break the stalemate and elect one of their ministers for New York City in 1696 by allying with the Dutch, who, in turn, received a charter of incorporation for their own church. Fletcher then issued a charter for the Anglican Trinity Church, a document that stated it was the estab-lished church and ensured that it would remain under Anglican control. Indeed, with the exception of Lewis Morris, Anglican New Yorkers would either presume or affirm that their church was the established one of the colony.[52] But without ministers to collate to parishes, Anglican governors could do little to promote their church, and Trinity in New York City remained the sole Anglican church in the colony for the rest of the century.

In 1704 William Vesey, rector of Trinity Church, though he tried to put the best possible face on his report to the Bishop of London, could name only three Anglican ministers in the province beside himself— and of all four, only two had churches. New York's population doubled in the years between 1698 and 1723, roughly from 20,000 inhabitants to 40,000; yet as late as 1714, Caleb Heathcote, an influential Church of England member, reported that Anglicans in the colony numbered 1200, of whom only 450 were communicants.[53]

The Church of England in New York faced stiff competition from several other denominations who accounted for the majority of the inhabitants and who were relatively well supplied with ministers. Moreover, a "Bill to enable the respective towns within this Province to build and repair their meeting houses and other public buildings" passed without controversy in 1699, thereby granting the differing denominations, where they enjoyed a majority in a town, access to ‚public monies. Following enactment of this bill, Suffolk and Queens counties petitioned Governor Bellomont for the right to settle a dis-senting minister among them, a petition he ignored. Thus New York produced the anomalous system whereby a town could use public money to build a non-Anglican church, but could not levy a tax to staff it with a minister.[54] As a result of this unclear system, the different denominations, especially Dutch Reformed, French Huguenot, and

Presbyterian, became embroiled in controversies with the authorities over the extent of the government's jurisdiction in religious matters.

A complicating factor was the assumption of the governorship in 1702 by Edward Hyde, Lord Cornbury. Later in that century, the historian William Smith wrote of him that "his talents, were, perhaps not superior to the most inconsiderable of his predecessors; but in his zeal for the Church he was surpassed by none."[55] Cornbury tried not only to impose the Church of England on the province, but to arrogate to himself the role of overseer of all the religious bodies within New York.

In the same year that Cornbury took office, the Dutch church in Kings County decided as a courtesy, and over the objection of a substantial number of its congregation, to consult him before calling a minister to serve them. He reacted by refusing to accept the church's nomination and told the Dutch to send to Holland for another candidate. He chose to interpret his instructions as giving him blanket control over all clerical appointments and insisted on licensing every minister, using the language "I do hereby License & Tollerate you."[56] Successive internal divisions among the Dutch and appeals by one or another faction of them ensured Cornbury's continued interference in their ecclesiastical affairs.

For their part, the Dutch church authorities asserted that the governor's policy amounted to a deprivation of liberty of conscience, and they wrote to the Amsterdam Classis asking its members to contact the ambassador in England and through him to reassert the liberties of the Dutch Reformed churches in America. In 1707 a Dutch member of the Council, Abraham Gouverneur, reiterated the argument that the governor had no right either in law or custom to appoint Dutch Reformed ministers to their churches, although this failed to convince Cornbury.[57] Only gradually, and with the persistent advice of the Amsterdam Classis to ministers to maintain the liberty and independence of their congregations, did the problem dissolve, as more reasonable governors succeeded Cornbury and the Dutch learned to avoid taking their disputes to the civil authorities.[58] In 1723, when the first stirrings of the revival that would come to be known as the Great Awakening split one of the Dutch Reformed churches in New Jersey, the local consistory, or supervisory body of the church, cited the dissidents to appear for a hearing, but added, "you may know indeed, that we cannot cite you with the help of the Civil Power. Its influence is far from us."[59]

Civil interference in religious affairs lasted well beyond Governor Cornbury's regime. In 1724 Louis Rou, minister of the French Calvinist church in New York, was dismissed because he refused to recognize the legitimacy of the newly elected consistory of his own church. Rou and his followers appealed to the governor and Council for relief. They, in turn, ordered the consistory to show cause for Rou's dismissal.[60] In their defense, the consistory members pleaded "the free use and exercise of . . . Liberty of Conscience" and acknowledged no "jurisdiction in any Civil Court within this Province in and over the private affairs of our Church." Rou, on the other hand, presented the case as one of fairness and due process, having nothing to do with liberty of conscience.[61]

During the trial proceedings, the members of the consistory labored under the handicap of having denied the authority of secular judges over the affairs of the French church. Also, when counsel for the consistory referred to it as a court, the members of the Governor's Council bristled at the assertion and demanded to know the source of its jurisdiction. Badgered in this regard by Cadwallader Colden, the Council's chairman, the consistory pleaded that "they were no Court," but they held that the power by which they called the minister enabled them also to discharge him. This plea failed to satisfy the Council, which insisted that the consistory had no authority to dismiss Rou. It did, however, advise both parties to reach a peaceable solution.[62] Failing in this also, Rou took his case to the Court of Chancery, which apparently restored him—since he continued as minister in the church until 1750.[63]

In 1721 Nicholas Eyers, a Baptist minister who had been serving in the city for the previous five years, received the governor's permission to preach, though hardly his approval. Governor Burnett's statement referred to Eyers as "pretending to be . . . a Teacher or preacher of a Congregation of Anabaptists," thereby demonstrating the scorn and social condescension usually applied to Baptists.[64] At the same time, Burnett made it clear that he regarded Baptists and, by inference, other non-Anglicans as dissenters on the same level as Dissenters in England.

The most celebrated clashes involving Church and State in early New York history involved Presbyterians. Nourished by nearby New England Congregationalists, who varied from them only in church organization, and who generally had no objection to joining their churches in New York, Presbyterians constituted one of the principal religious bodies in the colony. In 1707 the Presbyterian missionary Francis Makemie, en route to Boston, stopped in New York, where Cornbury refused him permission to preach. When Makemie held a religious service in a private house anyway, the governor had him arrested on the ground that he had no license. Makemie argued that the Act of Toleration gave him liberty to preach.

Later, Makemie changed his approach, and at his trial, the defense attorney argued that since the English religious penal statutes did not extend to the colonies, neither did the need for toleration. In his written account of the affair, Makemie contended that "no particular Persuasion [was] established by law," and that all persuasions were "upon an equal bottom of liberty." The jury returned a verdict of "not guilty," although Cornbury reaped some revenge when the court assessed the defendant the costs of the litigation.[65]

The Makemie trial pointed up the confused and inconsistent nature of Church-State relations in New York. By attempting to control all ministers, yet simultaneously arguing that the Church of England was the only established church and, as such, the only church with an official status, the governor clearly demonstrated the illogic of his position. On the other hand, Makemie's published account of his trial shows that dissenters had no monopoly on consistency. Toward the end of the proceedings, the prosecuting attorney argued that since Anglican ministers had to receive licenses, dissenters should also, otherwise they must expect special favor. Makemie retorted:

> There is a great deal of reason, why Ministers of the Church of England should submit to License, but we are not; because it is only here Liberty which Dissenters have; but they have not only Liberty, but a considerable Maintenance also; ... and Dissenters having Liberty only without any Maintenance from the Government, are not under any obligations, neither is it required of them to take Licenses of any.

Despite this assertion, he also argued that according to the Ministry Act, every "sufficient Protestant minister" duly appointed had a right to benefit from it.[66]

The other controversy involving the Presbyterians included fewer confusing arguments, but took place over a much more extended period. New Englanders had settled the town of Jamaica and built, at public expense, a Presbyterian church and parsonage. The inhabitants also supported, although according to the records with no great alacrity, a Presbyterian minister chosen by the town. During 1703 and 1704, Governor Cornbury deprived the Presbyterians of both church and parsonage for the benefit of an Anglican minister, and they dug in for a long siege.[67]

The Presbyterians refused to collect the minister's salary. In 1710 they recovered the parsonage, installed their own minister in it, and constituting themselves a "vestry," decided that he should have the town's ministerial taxes. In 1719 a new Anglican minister, the Reverend Thomas Poyer, secured from the Chief Justice of the province a judgment in his favor in the matter of salary. Some thirty to forty of the inhabitants of Jamaica still refused to pay, however. In 1727 the Presbyterians brought suit to recover the church and won their case. The proceedings are, unfortunately, unreported, but the Anglicans attributed the victory to "sly tricks and quirks of the Common Law." In any event, the dissenters wound up in control of both church and parsonage and, according to a Church of England correspondent, were determined to deprive the Anglican minister of the salary as well. Poyer died in 1731, and the Anglicans built their own church, thus eliminating some of the sources of contention. Apparently, the town continued to pay the Anglican minister until the townspeople again balked in the late colonial period.[68]

Elsewhere, the towns arrived at pragmatic solutions. In Brookhaven a dissenting minister received a salary from the town. In 1719 two townspeople objected, but the town replied that the money raised had been spent in the best possible manner for the support of religion.[69] Presumably, most towns continued to work out an arrangement acceptable to the majority of their inhabitants.

New York continued to provide a haven for diverse groups. Though the records do not disclose whether he was successful, Rabbi Abraham DeLucena at least felt secure enough to petition the governor, in 1710, for the same exemptions, civil and military, that other ministers enjoyed. Twenty years later, the city of New York contained no fewer than seventy-five Jewish families, who were able to practice their religion in peace, and who exercised some political rights, although they could be challenged by public officials demanding subscription to test oaths.[70]

Quakers, who enjoyed religious freedom, also exercised the franchise, but in the early part of the eighteenth century could be harassed in their attempts to vote by being tendered an oath by an unsympathetic sheriff. In 1734 New York passed a law allowing them to qualify for the franchise by affirmation.[71] The very few Catholics in the colony were excluded from toleration, and in 1700 the legislature passed a law banishing priests under pain of perpetual imprisonment.[72]

Historians have described the Church-State system in colonial New York as one of "multiple establishment," i.e. a system whereby many denominations might be established, depending on the choices of the particular towns.[73] This theory, however, projects back into the colonial period an understanding that contemporaries did not have. During the Jamaica controversy, some Anglicans reported that the Presbyterians "stick not to call themselves the Established Church & us Dissenters."[74] Even at this distance in time, the note of provocation in this statement rings clear, but the assertion must be seen merely as a sortie in a war of words.

Dissenters, when subjected to Anglican pressure, made full use of the colony's imprecise legal Church-State arrangements to counter Anglican claims. They concentrated, however, on denying an Anglican establishment, and because of the preponderance of their numbers managed to devise arrangements they did not define, but which were acceptable to themselves at the local level.

When non-Anglicans disputed an Anglican establishment in the colony, they did not claim one for themselves. Neither the Duke's Laws nor the Charter of Liberties referred to the system of church support by towns as an establishment of religion, nor did the inhabitants describe it as such. The Ministry Act of 1693 nowhere mentioned an establishment, although Anglicans construed it as constituting one for their church. Francis Makemie's statement that no particular church was established in New York should not be read to mean that he understood more than one church to be established there. He allowed that many denominations could benefit from the Ministry Act, but he never claimed that by doing so they became established.

In ordinary discourse, apart from controversy, non-Anglicans assumed that the Church of England was established in the colony. The Dutch, for example, told Cornbury that his power extended only to the "Established Church." In 1720 Presbyterians asking for a charter for their church avowed they would carry out their worship by voluntary contribution "and not compulsory or otherwise, in derogation of the National Church of England, by law established." In 1725 one of the parties to a schism in the French church advised the opposition to form another congregation or join the Church of England "as by law established."[75]

New Jersey and Pennsylvania, the last two colonies formed in seventeenth-century America, shared a common outlook on the nature of the relationship between religion and government. Neither established a church, and both evolved under the dominating influence of Quaker ideas and leaders. Originally part of the grant given in 1664 to James, Duke of York, the territory that would become New Jersey was initially divided into East and West Jersey, and eventually passed into the hands of Quaker proprietors.[76] Both sections maintained a tradition of liberty of conscience, though the western one, more completely under Quaker influence, provided the broader freedom.

In East Jersey, New England Congregationalists and Scottish Presbyterians outnumbered Quakers and tended to reproduce the mores, church customs, and institutions of their former habitations.

The Fundamental Constitutions of 1683 guaranteed free exercise of religion to those who believed in God and demanded belief in Christ on the part of officeholders. Although the Constitutions promised that none should be "compelled to frequent and maintain any Religious Worship, Place or Ministry," several towns did support a minister at public expense. By 1700, however, due in great measure to the opposition of Quakers, who campaigned against "Tythes, Militia, and great Taxes," these communities had all adopted voluntary maintenance.[77] In 1697 the East Jersey Assembly defeated a move to establish a maintenance for ministers similar to the one set up earlier in New York; but two years later, it excluded Catholics from officeholding and from the provisions for religious liberty.[78]

In 1702 the crown combined both Jerseys into a single royal colony and gave the usual instructions to the governor to exclude Catholics from liberty of conscience. Subsequently, in 1722, the colony passed legislation allowing justices of the peace to tender oaths of allegiance and abjuration to any citizen, Quakers excepted. Those refusing to take the oath were to be deemed "Popish Recusant" convicts, subject to all the penal laws of England. No record indicates that any Catholic actually suffered these stringent penalties, but those Catholics who did live in New Jersey practiced their religion inconspicuously and without benefit of public buildings.[79] Because of an anticipated shortage of suitable candidates, the royal instructions for New Jersey—unlike the orders issued for other colonies—permitted Quakers to hold office on the basis of an affirmation. Much to Governor Cornbury's chagrin (New Jersey and New York shared the same governor), the Quakers took full advantage of this allowance, enacting it into a law accepted by the English government in 1718.[80]

At the time it became a royal colony, New Jersey's population, a patchwork of Protestant Christian sects, exceeded 20,000. As in neighboring New York, no single denomination could lay primary claim to the people's religious affections. The Scottish Presbyterians and New England Congregationalists formed an important bloc, since both were inclined to sink their differences in the neutral ground of a new home. Quakers, because of their sizable numbers (especially in what had been West Jersey) and because of the royal exception allowing them to participate in politics and to hold public office, exercised a good deal of influence. That they did not wield more resulted from the decision of Quaker leaders to focus their attention on the area south of New Jersey, i.e. Pennsylvania, where William Penn had determined to secure his own colony "to lay the foundations of a free colony for all mankind, more especially those of my own profession [Quakerism]."[81]

Like Roger Williams and other seventeenth-century radicals, Quakers denied the power of government over conscience, which led them to constant disavowals of the right of the civil arm to punish them for their religious beliefs and practices. In the *Apology for the True Christian Divinity*, "the Glory and Alcoran of Friends," as an Anglican minister later referred to it, published in 1676 by Robert Barclay, a Scottish Quaker and friend of Penn, the Friends found one of their most powerful defenses, including a defense of religious liberty and, later, a guide for American Quakers.[82]

Penn, too, wrote in defense of religious liberty and suffered imprisonment in its cause. From Newgate prison in 1671, he defended Quaker principles and practice, being particularly concerned to show that they did not lead to anarchy. To the argument that persecution violated not only the Scriptures but reason, too, he appended pragmatic objections to interference by the State in matters of religion. Their import was that persecution violated the nature of civil government, as well as the bonds of natural affection; that it discouraged trade; and that it encouraged the oppression of Protestants by Catholics.[83]

In subsequent pamphlets, Penn developed the theme that a ruler, rather than creating among his citizens a smouldering hostility by forcing uniformity of belief or impoverishing dissenters by fines, should bind those citizens to himself in a common interest by giving them liberty of conscience. Instead of enacting penal laws covering religious belief, rulers should promote a "practical religion" through Christian action and good works.

In 1686, during the reign of his Catholic friend James II, Penn encouraged Catholics and Protestant dissenters to recognize their common concerns, and he even pointed to the Catholic Church, with its competing religious orders all under the jurisdiction of the pope, as a model for people of different denominations co-existing under a single government.[84] Penn's friendship with James would subject the former to the accusation that he was a secret Catholic or a Catholic supporter; but that same friendship and family support of the Stuart cause helped him acquire in the 1680s, at a time when the English government was beginning to look with disfavor on proprietary provinces, a charter for a colony of his own.[85]

The difference between Penn's charter and the previous grants made for Maryland and Carolina, which gave the proprietors the expansive powers of the Bishop of Durham, reflected the tighter control the home government wished to exercise over the colonies, a trend exemplified by the setting up of the Lords of Trade in 1675. The charter issued to

Penn in 1681 did make him "the true and absolute Proprietaire" of Pennsylvania, but other provisions rendered his power less than absolute—certainly far narrower than Lord Baltimore's.

The grant carried careful and strict provisions for the implementation of the restrictive English trade laws known as the Navigation Acts, demanded that all laws be submitted to the king for approval, and reserved full right of appeal to the monarchy from the provincial courts. The only charter provision touching religion reflected the influence of the Bishop of London on the Lords of Trade. It allowed any twenty settlers to request that an Anglican minister be sent to them, and that he be permitted to live without molestation in the colony.[86]

By way of the Frame of Government he drew up for his province in 1682, later confirmed by the Pennsylvania Assembly, Penn granted liberty of belief and worship without hindrance to those who believed in God. The Charter of Privileges of 1701 demanded a belief in Christ on the part of officeholders, reflecting the pressure to conform more nearly to English practice. In a series of prohibitions that characterized the morally earnest Quaker, though they have come to be associated with Puritan restrictiveness, Penn, on the ground that "wildness and looseness of the people provoke the indignation of God," outlawed numerous actions and events. The list included swearing, drinking of healths, playing at cards and dice, stage plays, masques, and cock fights—all of which "excite the people to rudeness, cruelty, looseness, and irreligion." Pennsylvania from its beginnings, however, established perhaps the broadest religious liberty in colonial America, and its government provoked no serious charges of persecution.[87]

The colony incorporated into its laws two Quaker characteristics, an abhorrence of oaths and a refusal to provide public tax support for churches and clergy. Pennsylvania allowed its inhabitants to substitute an affirmation for an oath in all cases. In addition, Quaker judges not only refused to swear, they also refused to administer oaths. These practices provoked both comment from and friction with Anglican officials, but the Friends refused to budge from their position, arguing that they had come to the colony for liberty of conscience.[88]

The Friends remained equally adamant on the question of public support of churches. Penn had written that they could not support the practice of "an Humane Ministry," and not out of "Humour or Covetousness" did they refuse to "pay Tithes, or such-like pretended Dues," but because they had "a Testimony against" them.[89] The Frame of Government of 1682 decreed that "no person . . . shall at any time be compelled to frequent or maintain any religious worship, place or ministry whatsoever, contrary to his or her mind," a policy from which the colony never deviated. Anglican officials and ministers in the colony, however, wanted public support, at least for their own churches, and they hoped to recruit the influence of royal governors or even of Parliament to have the colony alter its policy.[90]

In 1714 Thomas Chalkley, a noted Quaker missionary, published a lengthy pamphlet reaffirming the Quakers' stance. He relied on Scripture and on people's natural abhorrence of having to support churches whose doctrines and practices they did not approve. He was careful also to indicate that he did not favor a legal maintenance from a minister's own congregation, either. All financial support should be voluntary. For Chalkley, Quaker practice did not amount to a formula for anarchy, as had been so often asserted; rather, as the history of the primitive Church demonstrated, their way led to true prosperity for religion.[91] His work represented more the determination of Pennsylvania Quakers to maintain a policy of voluntarily supported religion than a new argument in defense of that policy. For the remainder of the colonial era, periodic defenses of voluntary maintenance continued to be issued in Pennsylvania, mostly in the form of reprints from England.[92]

In 1701 the three lower counties of the colony secured their own legislature. Declaring themselves the province of Delaware, they continued to share a common governor with Pennsylvania. In spite of the fact that the majority of Delaware's inhabitants were non-Quakers, the new colony maintained policies of religious liberty and voluntary support of religion and churches similar to those of Pennsylvania.[93]

Quakers had always asserted that their ways and beliefs were not inimical to civil government, and Pennsylvania vindicated them. By 1700 its population was approaching 20,000. Some 5000 people lived in Philadelphia, a city by then equal to New York and about to surpass it as the most populous and important urban center in colonial America. A German immigrant, Justus Falckner, thought that "sects and hoardes" had overrun the province. "Hoardes" did indeed come, multiplying the population perhaps twenty times during the first half of the eighteenth century. Throughout that period, however, the irenic spirit of the Friends prevailed and made Pennsylvania the only English colony where Catholics worshipped in public.[94]

The Restoration colonies set some of the most important themes for Church-State relations in colonial America. In some of them, English civil and church authorities were able to establish Anglicanism, but unable to make the Church of England really take root. Thus they set up a structure for continuing conflict between an unpopular established church and popular causes and forces in those colonies. On the other hand, as Maryland Quakers were pointing out by the end of the seventeenth century, not only New Jersey but especially Pennsylvania offered a different example of a relationship between religion and government, one wherein churches were prospering on the basis of voluntary support and without benefit of any established religion, thus proving the workability of a system of broad religious liberty.

4

Liberty of Conscience in Eighteenth-Century Colonial America

American religious freedom sprang from several sources—from the passionate adherence to religious freedom of those who held it to be an article of faith, from the steady increase in numbers of those who believed that no article of faith commanded sufficient importance to warrant persecution on its behalf, and from the circumstances of colonial America that threw a multitude of different religions together and demanded that they get on in peace with the business of colonization.

Americans during the first three-quarters of the eighteenth century speculated about religious freedom to a far lesser extent than did their predecessors of the preceding century, when the old medieval system of religious uniformity broke down and thinkers ran the gamut from extreme reactionism to religious anarchy. By about 1700, however, a consensus had emerged within Protestantism that captivated and held most thinkers and writers on the subject of Church and State until the American Revolution. Toleration of dissenters from the dominant religion of a region or country, which in the seventeenth century some groups resisted or only grudgingly accepted, came in the eighteenth century to be commonly embraced as a matter of principle.

When colonial commentators upheld freedom of religion as a natural right and wrote in favor of "absolute liberty of conscience, and entire freedom in all religious matters," they represented broad-based agreement.[1] Such eighteenth-century comments on Church and State, though, must be read within the matrix of assumptions that supported them. They differed from contemporary opinions not so much in substance as in context. Colonial writers would not have taken kindly to the modern understanding that religious liberty includes the right not to believe. When the Reverend Moses Dickinson told the Connecticut legislature that it was "absurd, to speak of allowing atheists Liberty of Conscience," he voiced a widespread sentiment.[2] Most commentators, however, neither actively agreed with nor repudiated such a proposition; rather, they simply did not consider it, so their rejection of it has to be inferred from an overview of their thinking. Their consensus as to religious freedom was firmly embedded in a Christian and Protestant world view. Colonial writers proclaimed liberty of conscience, but they grounded that liberty in the unexamined assumption that the legal systems of the time would uphold and maintain a Christian and Protestant State.

The English Act of Toleration of 1689 fixed the basic rules for the coexistence of the Church of England with dissenting Protestant denominations. At the same time, in his *Letter on Toleration*, John Locke summarized contemporary moderate thinking on that subject and justified such coexistence to the satisfaction of most Englishmen, both at home and in the colonies.[3] The substance of the Act of Toleration was applied to America either by charter or by instructions to royal governors ordering them to allow a like toleration to all Christians except Catholics.[4]

Maryland and South Carolina discovered by experience that they could not secure royal approval of ecclesiastical statutes more exacting than those of the Mother Country. In 1702 Connecticut tried to ensure religious uniformity by a statute forbidding its citizens to entertain "any Quaker, Ranter, Adamite, or other notorious heretic," only to be informed by the English government that such laws violated the liberty of conscience granted to Dissenters in England and, by charter, to dissenters in Connecticut. The colony repealed the law, and in 1708 enacted one "for the ease of such as soberly dissent from the ways of worship and ministrie established by the . . . laws of this government."[5]

Even before passage of the Act of Toleration, Pennsylvania, New Jersey, and Rhode Island had enacted more liberal religious legislation than it demanded. Overall, dissenters in eighteenth-century America found themselves in a happier position than their brethren in England. There Dissenters received a bare toleration that still excluded them from political rights and public life.[6] In America, by contrast, all persons who would take the loyalty oath prescribed for English Dissenters were eligible to hold office, and no test or articles of subscription

kept any Protestant out of an American college. In the southern
colonies, where the Church of England was established, all were
required to contribute toward its upkeep; but the weakness of that
church in comparison to its strength in the Mother Country propor-
tionately lessened the burden. Neither did American dissenters have to
deal with ecclesiastical courts. In New England, too, although required
support of the Congregational Church proved a source of aggravation
to non-Congregationalists, dissenters on the whole fared much better
than their counterparts in England.[7]

Catholics and Jews, on the other hand, remained suspect oddities,
not only because there were few of them, but also because they existed
beyond the Protestant world view that encompassed eighteenth-
century America. Consequently, neither group exerted much influence
on the development of relationships between Church and State, either
by direct contribution or by provoking the larger society into any
attempts to embrace them.

Catholics lived for the most part in Maryland, which excluded them
from liberty of conscience, and in Pennsylvania, which did not. The
outbreak of the French and Indian War in the 1750s served only to
increase the already deep suspicion that Catholicism and America
were incompatible. Many of the colonies acted to guard against any
possible "papist" fifth column functioning on behalf of Catholic
France; and Maryland, in 1756, imposed double taxation on its
Catholic inhabitants.[8]

In Pennsylvania, where Penn's original grant gave liberty of religion
to all who believed in God, Catholics built six churches between 1732
and 1763. Although the governor, in 1734, suggested that the presence
of a Catholic church violated English penal laws, his Council declined
to pursue the issue.[9] In every American colony, however, specific test
laws or the possibility of being challenged to subscribe to a test or oath
of abjuration, with refusal leading to prosecution as a "popish
recusant," ensured the exclusion of Catholics from public life. Even
more than these statutes, a pervasive opinion that "Popery" was
synonymous with tyranny relegated Catholics to a position beyond the
realm of acceptability.[10]

Jews, too, in colonial America, lived without experiencing direct
persecution, but nevertheless on sufferance. They possessed few civil
rights, and those that they did exercise locally, such as voting,
remained subject to challenge. Jews did worship freely, however, and
by late colonial times had begun to publish religious literature, as had
Catholics also.[11]

Within the dominant Protestant consensus, individual religious groups reflected their particular historical inheritances in their approaches to Church and State. Quakers, Anglicans, Congregationalists, Baptists, and the multi-denominational combination that constituted Rhode Island all exhibited attitudes and concerns peculiar to themselves.

Quakers adhered to the clearest tradition. Although the Quaker colony of Pennsylvania required its officeholders to submit to a religious test, it otherwise proved remarkably faithful to Penn's vision of religious liberty. Because Quakers conscientiously opposed taxes for the support of ministers and churches, Pennsylvania never instituted any such system, thus precluding a source of considerable religious dispute, as witnessed by the controversies Friends provoked in those colonies that did call for ministerial maintenance.

Quakers prohibited not only fornication and drunkenness, but also "drinking Healths . . . Banquetings, and using Games, Sports, Plays, Revels, Comedies" and expected the government to enforce laws banning such activities, as well as to see to it that all kept the Sabbath holy. In Pennsylvania, however, citizens were not bound to attend church in order to observe the Sabbath correctly, but could remain at home and read Scripture instead. To most Americans of the time, Quaker or otherwise, such moral legislation did not pertain to the stuff of religious freedom. They saw it as an indispensable protection of the very fabric of society.[12]

The Friends breached the limits of the conventional morality when they refused to swear oaths or to engage in military service.[13] In the matter of oaths, they had encountered great difficulties in England. Not until 1722 did Parliament devise a wording for an affirmation that was acceptable to them. In the New World, however, the various colonies accommodated them, at least to the extent that oath taking never became a serious source of conflict with the authorities.[14]

The peculiarities of Quaker belief, their opposition to tithes, their habit of bewailing the sufferings of their ancestors—particularly at the hands of New Englanders—and the notoriety that still clung to them from the unorthodox behavior of sixteenth-century Friends made Quakerism a source of controversy throughout the colonial era.[15] The Friends reacted to discrimination and persecution by loudly publicizing accounts of their oppression and by inundating the authorities with complaints. Through their Meetings they kept each other informed of mistreatment of their members. In 1709 Governor Lovelace of New York commented on the effectiveness of Quakers due to their "intelligence from foreign parts," referring to the efficient information network they maintained with their London brethren. By such means, especially during the first years of the eighteenth century, colonial Friends consistently challenged, in a well-organized and united way, both legal and social developments they regarded as threatening their religious liberty. As the century progressed, however, so did they—both in prosperity and respectability.[16]

Anglicans, especially their clergy, had inherited no strong tradition of religious liberty and hardly concerned themselves with that topic. They assumed that the English arrangement constituted a proper order of Church and State. As representatives of the dominant and established church of the Mother Country, they felt themselves deprived, in the heterogeneous colonial environment, of their rightful position. Throughout the eighteenth century, whenever they wrote to the Society for the Propagation of the Gospel in England, Anglican clergymen, no matter what colonies they found themselves in, referred to members of other religions as "Dissenters." Their attempts to extend the influence of the Church of England, particularly their efforts to secure Anglican bishops for the colonies, precipitated a number of the most bitter Church-State disputes of the late colonial period.[17]

Of the religious traditions in eighteenth-century America, none presented a more complex approach to Church-State relations than Congregationalism, which dominated New Hampshire, Massachusetts, and Connecticut. The governments of all three of those colonies enacted copious legislation to ensure public support and protection of their churches. New Hampshire, on the periphery of the region, devised the least formal arrangements. The central government there issued orders to every town directing it to provide itself with a minister and see to his support, but provided no machinery for supervising a community's implementation of the orders or for forcing compliance. Because the colony harbored more dissenters, New Hampshire experienced less uniformity of practice than Massachusetts or Connecticut, and disputes over religion that did arise there took place at a local level.[18]

The Massachusetts Charter of 1691 demanded that there be "a liberty of Conscience allowed in the Worshipp of God to all Christians (Except Papists)," thereby precluding that uniformity the original settlers had sought. The provincial government, however, decreed that each town select and pay at public expense an "able, learned orthodox," i.e. Congregational, minister. The laws further provided that the provincial government would supervise the individual towns to see that they carried out their duties.[19]

Neighboring Connecticut devised a similar system, which also ensured Congregational dominance. In 1708 the General Court at

Hartford actually approved the Saybrook Platform, organizing Connecticut's Congregational churches according to a model much closer to Presbyterianism than the one that persisted in the Bay colony. Indeed, Connecticut Congregationalists sometimes referred to themselves as Presbyterians.[20]

The complexity of New England's Congregationalist heritage stemmed from the ever-increasing disparity between the original Puritan concept of liberty of conscience and the development of that concept in seventeenth-century England and America. No other major religious group in the colonies proved so wrong in anticipating the future of Church and State as the Puritans who settled Massachusetts and Connecticut in the 1630s. They had come to the New World with high hopes of building communities united in the "true Christian religion," whose example would reform the world they had left behind. Instead, events shattered the Old World into a multiplicity of denominations and sects, each claiming to possess the truth. In turn, these sects and opinions crossed the Atlantic to model the New World in the image of the Old.

By the Act of Toleration of 1689 England admitted that uniformity of religious belief and practice was unachievable. In imposing this decision on the American colonies, the Mother Country only validated existing conditions, even in Puritan New England. By that time, Massachusetts had in practice accepted the presence of Quaker and Baptist dissenters, and her Puritan clergy had already started adjusting their statements to accommodate that presence. However, instead of devising a new system of thought to coincide with changed realities, the ministers continued to use the old language of their forebears to describe the relationship between Church and State, while simultaneously, and without saying so, assigning to that language less strict and less precise meanings. This process, begun even before the passage of the Act of Toleration and issuance of the new charter, continued throughout the succeeding century.

Consequently, pronouncements of the New England clergy on the subject of liberty of conscience took on the dimensions of a ritual, serving less as a guide to contemporary events and more as an assurance to their hearers that New England was at one and the same time conforming to the demands of the Mother Country regarding liberty of conscience and remaining faithful to its own Puritan past. As a result of this rhetorical phenomenon, thought and action on matters of Church and State tended to separate from each other in eighteenth-century New England. The annual Election Sermons in Massachusetts and Connecticut epitomized this somewhat schizophrenic development.

In 1692 Cotton Mather, the most prolific writer in the American colonies, had heralded Massachusetts's acceptance of liberty of conscience as demanded by the new charter, declaring in his Election Sermon *Optanda*: "I would humbly put in a Bar against the Persecution of any that conscientiously dissent from Our Way." Perry Miller has commented, "Cotton Mather's brave words served mainly as a political device: they proved that New England was theoretically tolerant, but not that it actually tolerated."[21]

Neither Cotton Mather nor the ministers who followed him at the lectern before the General Court gave any indication that they wished to return to the intolerance of an earlier time. What neither he nor successive preachers of Election Sermons would do, however, was develop a rationale for the changing times. All of them continued to employ the language of the past, combining it, at times incongruously, with a rhetorical commitment to liberty of conscience. Thus, in his disavowal of compelling men to worship in ways to which they were "conscientiously indisposed," Mather passed over in silence the distinction made by his forebears that conscience could not justify adherence to false worship. The Westminster Platform had declared that to follow "out of conscience" doctrines not found in the Word "is to betray true Liberty of Conscience."[22] Similarly, in his declaration that force produced only hypocrites, he skirted the belief of his grandfather and father that hypocrites were preferable to "profane persons," since even an outward reformation prevented the judgments brought on the commonwealth by errors and heresies.[23]

Magistrates might not persecute, but for Mather there was none-theless "an Aspect of Singular Kindness Defense and Support, which Magistrates are to bear unto them that Embrace . . . the truths of God." Clearly, he had modified the old New England stance to a point where the magistrate should no longer punish those in error, but should continue to promote those who held the truth. In 1704 Jonathan Russell told the legislators that they should do all they could for "Unity and Uniformity; and Sacrifice all but a good Conscience thereunto."[24]

Roger Williams's query from the grave as to how the ruler can distinguish between truth and error remained unanswered. To the mind of Cotton Mather, the question was superfluous, and when he spoke of those who dissent from "Our Way," neither he nor his listeners harbored any doubt which way was the true one. Succeeding preachers of Election Sermons played variations on Mather's themes, sometimes of greater length, but seldom clearer.

Thundering assertions on the magistrate's role in matters religious drowned out delicate strains regarding liberty of conscience. Magistrates were to be "Nursing Fathers" to religion and were to have custody of both Tables of the Law.[25] The speakers did not advocate violation of conscience in the interest of uniformity, but they nevertheless called on rulers to promote the best interests of Christ, terrify evildoers, advance civil and religious happiness, serve as God's ministers for good, and guard public virtue and religion.[26] In his 1692 Election Sermon Cotton Mather had already specified that no "pretence of conscience" could justify living "without any worship of God, or to Blaspheme and revile his Blessed Name." His fellow ministers took up this motif with a vengeance. They declaimed against neglect of public worship, profanation of the Sabbath, using liberty "for an occasion of the flesh" or people's thinking that liberty meant doing "what is right in their own eyes."[27]

In Connecticut Gurdon Saltonstall and Solomon Stoddard warned the General Court against heretics. Samuel Estabrook intimated that the Court should prevent schisms in churches and averred that those who refused to "Acquiesce in the Judgment of the Churches . . . ought to be Compelled, which would very much Conduce to Peace and Quietness in our Churches." Stephen Hosmer told the Court that rules must discourage "bold Intruders and such as advance Damnable Doctrines," and Jonathan Marsh explained that things lawful in themselves are not to be tolerated when they are abused to the point of "Idolatry."[28]

Thus, though they hardly went beyond grand generalities in their sermons, New England election speakers left no doubt that the magistrate should both protect and promote religion. In describing how the magistrate should go about doing so, ministers had to perform a difficult balancing act. In 1722 John Hancock told his hearers that magistrates, while they possessed no power

> . . . that is *formally* and intrinsically Spiritual & Ecclesiastical, but only *objectively* so: they have not the power of *order* which gives authority to Preach, nor the power of the Keys by Ecclesiastical Censures; yet they have a power of Jurisdiction over Churches, and ought by their Laws to provide for the Worship of God, to root out Heresies, to prevent Schisms and Rents in the Church of God.

Benjamin Colman had already enumerated four religious categories for the magistrates to oversee. These were, "The Public Worship of God, both Natural and instituted," the "Peace, Order, Discipline and Government of the Church," the "Honourable Maintenance of the Ministry," and "A People's Morals."[29]

Most New England ministers, however, shied from such specificity. Samuel Whitman merely told Connecticut legislators to "do all that may be done by you, both by your Example and Authority; to Recover Religion to its Primitive Glory." Others declined to undertake "to Determine the Extent of the Civil Magistrates Power in Matters Ecclesiastical" or to "particularly mention those Laws which immediately relate to the First Table."[30]

By and large, Election Day preachers concentrated on the topics of ministerial maintenance and public morality. By urging the government to see that ministers were provided for, and by fulminating against evildoing, debauchery, and Sabbath breaking, they could emphasize the role of the magistrate in religious matters and give a wide berth to any topic wherein they might come into conflict with the religious demands of the Act of Toleration, i.e. matters pertaining to the First Table.

Here, too, Cotton Mather led the way. Having proclaimed that "Rules are not a Terror to Good Works, but unto the evil," he supported his thesis with the concrete example of the laws of England, which punished drunkenness and idleness, and "yet no Liberty of Conscience is invaded in those wholesome Laws."[31] Following in his path, Mather's ministerial brethren raised a mighty hue and cry against vice, sinning, and intoxication.[32]

Stripped to their essentials, the pronouncements of eighteenth-century New England clerics on the role of the magistrate in religious affairs might be interpreted as a precipitate temperance campaign, or as arising out of an obsessive desire to collar drunkards and Sabbath breakers, or as a great deal of sound and fury over laws that other contemporary colonies enacted with little or no fanfare. In fact, the Election Sermons represent much more. Set in the context of recollections of the original "errand" of New England's founders and of reminders that Massachusetts was a plantation for religion, rather than for trade, the ministers' references to moral reform served as shorthand communications that the civil power was still the supporter of regeneration and the New England Way.[33]

When Azariah Mather preached that magistrates "cannot Mortify, yet they can Curb & Restrain the corruption and ill-manners of a People in good measure and degree," he was settling for a uniformity of behavior that harked back to John Cotton's imperative of the preceding century. However, whereas Cotton had sought an external conformity to doctrine, the ground rules of the colony now precluded such uniformity, so the ministers had to fall back on a moralism that would unite New England in behavior, culture, and ethos.[34]

The Puritan clergy continued to use one of their ancestors' favorite concepts, that the magistrate was custodian of the First Table of the

Law. In the past, that had meant that he was to see to it that only "true worship" was observed. In the eighteenth century, however, that power over the First Table was reduced to making sure people observed the Sabbath, even if, in observing it, some citizens—in Baptist church or Quaker meeting house—engaged in what earlier Puritan divines would have dismissed as "instituted worship." Thus did they preserve the form, if not the substance, of the past.

Moreover, although New England ministers could no longer demand that the magistrates exclude dissenters from the New England Way, they could exhort them to favor the religion of their ancestors, to support such familiar institutions as "the College," i.e. Harvard, and to encourage the true religion.[35] Massachusetts clergy still considered the colony a family affair. As Benjamin Colman told the General Court, "They that chuse to come to live among us for their own worldly advantages, ought willingly to leave us in the Quiet Possession of the dear Purchase of our Fathers."[36]

The key to New England ministers' approach to Church and State lay in their preoccupation with what Cotton Mather called "Our Way." Given the standards set forth in Massachusetts's new charter, they had to acknowledge some weaknesses in the legacy of the past; but instead of judging the previous system according to an overall theory of religious freedom, they simply proclaimed that nothing in their "Way" violated liberty of conscience. In 1691 Cotton Mather declared that "New England has Renounced whatever Laws are against a Just Liberty of Conscience." The following year, he gingerly approached the same topic. Acknowledging the possibility of "a little too much Fire" on the part of his ancestors in seeking uniformity, he disassociated himself from the "Severities . . . [and] Zeal of some Eminent men" of the past.[37]

Only to that extent did the clerical spokesmen for New England reject the past. They accepted toleration as a fact, not as a new way of thinking. Foremost in their minds and hearts stood the New England tradition, and they always focused on toleration or "liberty of conscience" in the light of that tradition, rather than from the point of view that developments called for its reinterpretation. Thus the language of their Election Sermons remained formally linked to the past, even though the substance of that past had been to a great extent dissipated. Their terminology of toleration continued inward-looking and backward-looking. Even when they disassociated themselves from past actions, they did not repudiate the thinking that had given rise to those actions. For example, Benjamin Colman, in 1716, regretted the persecution of the past and rejoiced in the more tolerant spirit of his own time. He then proceeded to exalt his ancestors for not using "Liberty for an Occasion to the flesh, but standing fast in that wherewith Christ had made us free."[38]

No matter that the fathers employed the phrase "using Liberty [of conscience] for an Occasion to the Flesh" to describe Baptists and Quakers. The sons could proclaim their adherence to liberty of conscience, condemn licentiousness under such liberty, and appear to remain in harmony with their unbending religious patrimony—even if their citations, by the eighteenth century, were limited to over-imbibers and Sabbath breakers.

To argue that the ministers, captivated by their Puritan past, failed to conceive of a new system of thought to harmonize with the revisions in the meaning of "liberty of conscience" promulgated by the charter of 1691 is not to assert that they did not believe in such liberty. They did. Not one even hinted a preference for the narrow orthodoxy of the preceding century. Nevertheless, their understanding of liberty of conscience was bounded by the New England lexicon. They defined it as freedom from compulsory worship and from impositions and "popish" ceremonies. In their defense of religious liberty, they were still prosecuting their ancestors' case against Archbishop Laud.[39]

In 1693 Increase Mather assured his listeners that the charter of 1691 had delivered them from "all impositions on Conscience which not many years ago you were afraid of." Others followed affirming the sentiment and proclaiming that the charter secured the "Liberty of Conscience our Fathers fought for." In such efforts to reconcile present with past, the Massachusetts clergy managed to read into the liberty of conscience provision of the new charter a confirmation of all their ancestors had come to America for, when, in fact, the clause sealed the doom of the founders' hopes for liberty of conscience as they had interpreted it, i.e. religious unity, and mocked John Winthrop's exhortation to the earliest settlers that they should be one in mind and heart.[40]

New England Congregationalist clergy in both the seventeenth and eighteenth centuries defined liberty of conscience as liberty of what they regarded as conscience. Puritan divines and authorities could not or would not recognize that practices acceptable to them could possibly represent a violation of conscience to others and summarily dismissed arguments to that effect.

In 1695 Thomas Maule published a book upholding Quaker belief and excoriating Massachusetts for its previous treatment of Quakers. The authorities there had him arrested for publishing "divers slanders against the churches and government of this Province." At his trial Maule may have made the jurors uneasy by drawing a parallel between his prosecution and the recent witch trials, because they found him innocent and commented that the case demanded a "jury of divines." In triumph Maule returned to his themes and also added arguments about the detrimental effects for religion that proceeded from the alliance between religion and government.[41] Beginning in 1719 John Checkley, a convert to Anglicanism, published several works critical of Congregationalism. Again, Massachusetts authorities reacted by harassing him, trying him for propagating material that reflected badly on "the ministers of the Gospel Established in this Province," and fining him £50 and costs.[42]

On the question of ministerial maintenance, however, both Massachusetts and Connecticut had to be more accommodating of dissenters' opinions. Although legally the individual towns could select and pay any Protestant minister, in fact, before the Revolution, none but Congregationalists were chosen or indeed were supposed to be chosen. As a result, Baptists, Quakers, and Anglicans vigorously objected to paying taxes for the support of another minister. The first two groups objected to a tax for the support of any ministers, even those of their own religion. Anglicans had no such objection, but thought that the taxes should rightfully go to them as representatives of the established religion of the Mother Country.

Baptists, who formed a substantial element in the population of Rhode Island, were less numerous elsewhere in New England. As their name implied, adult baptism constituted their principal concern. However, they had inherited a tradition of voluntary support, although not until later would they develop strong theological arguments against tax-supported religion. In their early opposition to ministerial maintenance in New England, both they and the Quakers relied heavily on the charter grant of "liberty of conscience."

At first the Massachusetts authorities simply dismissed objections to maintenance as the work of "Quakers and other irreligious averse to the public worship of God." With more credibility, they pointed out that a grant of "liberty of conscience" did not free dissenters elsewhere, either in England or in the southern colonies, from paying toward the support of an established church. However, from 1727 on both Massachusetts and Connecticut devised systems whereby Baptists and Quakers were exempted from paying ministerial taxes and Anglicans' contributions went for the support of their own ministers. This change resulted not from theoretical arguments, but from existing realities: the fact that New England oppression of dissenters embarrassed Congregationalists before their brethren in England, who were themselves oppressed by the established Church of England, and the danger of intervention by the English government to stop Congregationalists, themselves dissenters, from taxing Anglicans.[43]

As in other Church-State disputes, Massachusetts especially insisted on having the last word. The colony would, if compelled, accommodate the peculiarities of dissenters, but it would make no concessions to their points of view. Thus the law exempting Quakers and Baptists from ministerial taxes referred to an "alleged scruple of conscience," and when, in 1743, Massachusetts finally got around to substituting an affirmation for an oath in the case of Quakers, the statute described its beneficiaries as "Quakers [who] profess to be in their consciences scrupulous of taking oaths."[44]

Completing the matrix of Church-State relations in colonial America, Rhode Island's radical pluralistic traditions bore little significance for contemporaries, who largely ignored them. During the eighteenth century, however, the colony itself came to accept some of the prevailing conventional thinking and practice of the time. Thus John Callendar, a Baptist minister who wrote a history of the colony in 1739, casually assumed that it was a Christian, i.e. Protestant, commonwealth, and in 1719 Rhode Island excluded Catholics from office, though not from toleration.[45]

Because no record remains of the actual passage of the law excluding Catholics, commentators have agreed that the exclusionary clause crept into the collection of laws by way of "interpolation" or "error." In any case, the law's practical implications for Catholics, given their scarcity in Rhode Island, were few. Arnold, in his *History of Rhode Island*, claimed that the penal laws meant nothing, that Catholics were in fact regularly naturalized, and that they worshipped peacefully in private. No evidence indicates that Catholics actually performed worship, however.

In writing about Rhode Island's admirable adherence to religious liberty, historians have taken pains to show that its treatment of Catholics in no way besmirched that shining record. At this distance, though, one might better hold that Catholics never came to the colony in numbers sufficient to test its liberality. In 1756, during the French and Indian War, a period in which fear of Catholic France permeated the American colonies, Rhode Island, like several other colonies, enacted statutes ordering oaths of allegiance and abjuration to be tendered to suspicious persons and decreed that any who refused to subscribe be proceeded against as "popish recusants and have their goods confiscated."[46]

Rhode Island's treatment of Jews, the other religious group affected by the law restricting political rights and the holding of office to

Christians, affords a clue to what might have happened to Catholics had they come to represent any significant portion of the population. From the middle of the seventeenth century on—though not continuously—Jewish merchants inhabited the colony. Between 1750 and 1756, a Jewish community varying from roughly 60 to 200 persons existed at Newport, a town whose population increased over the same period from 6000 to 9000. These Jews built a synagogue and worshipped freely, but they exercised no right to vote and held no office. On one occasion, petitions of two Jews for naturalization were denied by both the legislature and the Supreme Court of Rhode Island, but the reasons for their rejection have not survived. Thus, although Jews in the colony were free to practice their religion, they did so as second-class citizens.[47]

Even though eighteenth-century Rhode Island's attitude toward non-Protestants and laws regarding them more closely approximated what other colonies considered a respectable norm than it had earlier, the colony could not overcome, in the eyes of other New Englanders, its unsavory reputation for religious radicalism and libertinism. The reputation for "profaneness and atheism" in the "Eastern Parts of the neighboring Province," as Connecticut minister Samuel Whitman referred to Rhode Island, still clung to it.[48]

More surprising than the continuation of New England's horrified attitude toward Rhode Island was the absence of comment elsewhere on its exceptionalism. The memory of Roger Williams subsided to such an extent that no library catalogue published in the American colonies listed any of his works, not even his anti-Quaker treatise, *George Fox Digg'd Out of his Burrows*. Not until 1773, when the Baptist apologist Isaac Backus rediscovered him, did Williams's thoughts resurface. Even when, infrequently, inhabitants of other colonies commented on Rhode Island's religious arrangements, they showed a complete lack of familiarity with them. In 1707, when Presbyterian Francis Makemie was on trial for preaching unlawfully in New York, his defense attorney assumed that Rhode Island had an establishment of religion similar to that of the rest of New England, even though the colony had established no church and had decreed that all ministers be supported by voluntary contributions. Much later in the eighteenth century, New York Presbyterian William Smith, an ardent opponent of the New York Anglican establishment, made an identical assumption about Rhode Island.[49]

Apart from the different religious traditions in colonial America, the environment also played a part in the development of toleration and religious liberty. As early as 1650, the Puritan Edward Johnson had fretted that merchants, in the interest of profit, would connive at the toleration of "divers kinds of sinful opinions." Americans after him did, indeed, more and more agree on the practicality of toleration. Although it would be misleading to portray the majority of eighteenth-century Americans as anything less than fervently religious by modern standards, nevertheless, for more and more of them, concern with intricacies of doctrinal belief gradually gave way to a conviction that morality counted for more than theological correctness.

That time, too, blunted the sharp edges of sectarian dispute was manifested by statements of men of differing religions throughout the colonies. In 1711 the Pennsylvania almanac maker, Daniel Leeds, after a long and furious dispute with the Quakers, decided that it was time "to leave off writing against that which neither I nor themselves nor any man else know." His son Titan condemned zealots of all kinds, accusing them of possessing everything except charity. In Massachusetts the Mathers, Cotton and his father Increase, extended a friendly hand to Anglicans and Baptists and called for a "union in Piety." The call failed, but for social rather than doctrinal reasons— Massachusetts Congregationalists were not willing to recognize Baptists as equals, and Anglicans felt that the region was denying them their rightful position and influence.

The environment also played a part in the easing of sectarian disputes. One contemporary commented that the inhabitants "being simple and Ignorant" were soon "persuaded this way or that" for want of guides, teachers, and necessary books.[50]

Given Cotton Mather's prodigious output, one can find in his works an opinion on almost every subject of the age. In his statement of 1702 that no worse heresy existed than the one that "every man may be Saved by the Law or Sect which he professeth so that he may be diligent to frame his life according to that Law, and the Light of Nature," he succinctly framed the agenda for many of the debates on religion that engaged the energies of eighteenth-century Americans. Some of these debates proceeded from a movement that took one step beyond the contemporary opinion that no government should impose beliefs on its subjects to the position that not even churches should do so.[51]

The disputes that accompanied the growth of such rationalism in religion confined themselves to churches and did not involve questions of Church-State relations. However, they help illustrate the particular context of eighteenth-century colonial thinking. Several protagonists sounded ringing declarations of the right to private judgment in religious matters that when read in the abstract give the impression that eighteenth-century Americans were possessed of the spirit of modern times. Seen in the context of the time, however, they appear as peculiarly contemporary concerns. In contrast to Roger Williams or William Penn, no American religious figure of the eighteenth-century colonies formulated or thought through a system of Church and State. Those writings on the subject that did appear tended to be of a political rather than a philosophical order, i.e. they addressed specific rather than universal questions.

In the Presbyterian church, the alarm caused by a rising heterodoxy produced what came to be called the Subscription Controversy. The name derived from the proposal that ministers should subscribe to some doctrinal creed—specifically, the Westminster Confession—before taking office.[52] In the late 1720s, in Charleston, South Carolina, Hugh Fisher, a Presbyterian minister, preached a sermon on the necessity of adherence by clergymen to the fundamental articles of religion. A fellow minister and Harvard graduate, Josiah Smith, took offense at Fisher's statements and undertook to rebut his argument. To the modern eye, the titles of Smith's sermons, *Humane Impositions Proved Unscriptural, The Divine Right of Private Judgment*, and *The Divine Right of Private Judgment Vindicated*, appear self-explanatory. A perusal of the controversy, however, brings home to the reader that Smith's concerns were not general twentieth-century libertarian ones, but particular eighteenth-century religious ones. Both Fisher and Smith were, in fact, reacting in differing ways to perceived trends of their own times.

Fisher believed faithful ministers could determine fundamental doctrines with authority. To him, the defense of private judgment would lead to religious anarchy, to the denial of the Bible itself, or to the belief that "Arminians teach Christ's doctrines, in teaching their errors, no less than Calvinists, in teaching their doctrines." Smith, for his part, concerned himself not with Fisher's conclusions, but with the best way to propagate Christianity. He took pains to point out that he himself was not an Arminian, and that he did not reject the creed of his church, but objected only to its imposition. In his opinion, growing religious infidelity resulted not from the right of private judgment, but from the infusion of human schemes into religion. Neither was he propagating the right of individuals to deny such matters as the divinity of Christ or advocating deism; but he believed that Christians could, indeed, infallibly know what was essential to Christianity. What Smith argued for was not the right of judging contrary to Scripture, but "of bringing every Doctrine to the Test of Scripture."

In an eighteenth-century light, the Subscription Controversy manifests itself not as a conflict between modernity and obscurantism, nor between freedom and bondage, but as a conflict between diverging religious perceptions. Fisher—the pessimist—believed that the best solution to the problem of increasing infidelity was to resort to authority, reach back to traditional beliefs, and dig in. By contrast Smith adhered to an optimistic, forward-looking, dynamic, and evangelical approach. He objected to the imposition of creeds, because it smacked of "Romanism," and because it reduced religion to a static dead thing. His defense of private judgment sprang from no modern skepticism that since no belief is infallible none can be imposed, but rather out of the Reformation concept that if one put the Bible into the hands of every individual, truth would triumph.[53]

Jonathan Dickinson's role in a somewhat similar dispute in Pennsylvania revealed the peculiarly eighteenth-century nature of the Subscription Controversy and some of the assumptions involved in it. A Presbyterian minister at Elizabethtown, New Jersey, and a leading anti-subscriptionist, Dickinson insisted that the Bible alone was a sufficient guide for the churches. However, the fact that he opposed the imposition of a creed as a test of faith, not only by governments but even by churches themselves, did not mean he denigrated the importance of doctrine, as his participation in the Pennsylvania controversy would demonstrate.

In 1735 the Philadelphia Synod dismissed the Reverend Samuel Hemphill for preaching heterodoxy. The incident gained considerable attention, mostly because Benjamin Franklin, who had taken a liking to the new minister, because his sermons contained "little of the dogmatical kind, but inculcated strongly the Practice of Virtue," defended Hemphill in the *Pennsylvania Gazette* and in several pamphlets. Franklin cleverly used the anti-subscriptionists' argument to point out that the Synod, in order to dismiss Hemphill, would have to claim infallibility, and that the Presbyterians would look foolish for condemning a man who exhorted them "to be honest and charitable to one another and the rest of Mankind."

Agreeing that Hemphill had preached that Christianity was "only an Illustration and Improvement of the Law of Nature, with the addition of some few Positive Things," Franklin wrote that Hemphill denied such a statement violated the Confession of Faith. He further argued that to impose a test other than belief in the Scriptures not only violated the right of private judgment and negated the spirit of Protestantism by reverting to "Popery" but was useless, since creeds and impositions had always proved a source of schism and division, rather than of unity.

To counter Franklin's attack, Jonathan Dickinson now published a defense of the Synod. Again he affirmed his stand against imposition. He also rejected any claim to infallibility and agreed that since the time of Constantine, creeds had caused schism and heresies. Nevertheless, he lamented that he had lived to see "the danger that liberty will be abused to Licentiousness and that to escape Imposition, we shall open a Door to Infidelity." Neither could he accept that a simple declaration of a belief in the Scriptures of the kind that Hemphill had made would suffice. "Papists," after all did as much. Much of Dickinson's defense of the Synod's action hinged on his argument that the Church had the right to select its own doctrines and to exclude those who did not measure up to them. Firmly rejecting doctrinal impositions, he declared: "We are content that the cause be tried and decided by the only Standard of the Sanctuary."

The Subscription Controversy is of interest because of its demonstration that the anti-subscription position was not primarily what might be seen as a modern libertarian one, though much of the language used by its supporters conveys that impression. Franklin held that the only necessary condition for communion with a Christian church was professing a "belief [in] the Holy Scriptures" and in Christianity in general. He had, in fact, adopted the very attitude Fisher had earlier argued anti-subscriptionism would lead to. Clearly, however, when Josiah Smith and Jonathan Dickinson defended the right of private judgment, they had in mind something else altogether. Their cause was fundamentally religious—to protect the Protestant dynamic from those who, to cope with the difficulties of the age, had succumbed to what anti-subscriptionists viewed as the foolish strategies of Rome.[54]

During the Hemphill dispute, Franklin freely vented his anti-clerical sentiments ridiculing doctrines, especially that of Original Sin, as "a Bugbear set up by Priests." Nor was he by any means alone in his thinking. In 1730 the *American Mercury*, published in Philadelphia, had warned against ecclesiastical tyranny and advised that every doctrine should be brought under the test of reason. As early as 1724, the fiercely anti-clerical English work *The Independent Whig* had been reprinted in Philadelphia. Despite these instances of hostility, however, the strongest blasts against the clergy were to come not from rationalists, but from evangelicals during the Great Awakening.[55]

The religious revival known as the Great Awakening that began in the 1730s and spread throughout the American colonies had more to do with the style than the content of religion. Declaiming that the religious convictions that in the previous century had fired Englishmen to colonize the New World had degenerated into a dull and stodgy orthodoxy, itinerant preachers—mostly Calvinist—traversed the colonies berating "dead" and "unconverted" ministers, attracting swarms of people, provoking excitement that frequently rose to hysteria, and inducing in countless numbers of their hearers an experience of religion, as opposed to an intellectual adherence to doctrine. By altering attitudes and outlooks, the Awakening made a deep and abiding impact on colonial life.

The religious renewal also lessened the status and power of existing churches. It created divisions between its supporters and opponents, irrevocably splitting many congregations and giving rise to new churches. It strengthened the Presbyterian and Baptist denominations and propelled them into the southern colonies, disrupting and altering the religious balance there. Moreover, it encouraged inhabitants of the colonies to judge between "converted" and "unconverted" ministers and to rely on their own spiritual experiences, rather than on the authority of the clergy.

These attitudinal and structural changes ultimately transformed Church-State relations in America, although the transformation did not fully manifest itself until the revolutionary period. In the meantime, although the Great Awakening badly jarred and sometimes shattered existing religious patterns, it produced relatively little writing on the nature of liberty of conscience, no notable original thinking about Church-State relations, and no new synthesis of existing thought. Those discussions of freedom of religion that did emerge from the revival came out of multitudinous local conflicts provoked by the breakdown of religious arrangements.

New Jersey and Pennsylvania stood at the center of the Awakening; but because they had no established churches, the controversies that ensued from the religious revival remained isolated within individual congregations. Not so in New England, where the existence of established churches brought civil authorities into the disputes that split congregations into "New Light" supporters of the Awakening and "Old Light" opponents of it. These Church-State issues that arose in New England usually centered on the right of ministers of divided churches to financial support from disaffected members, or took the form of power struggles, either religious or political, between New Lights and Old Lights.[56]

After the evangelical preachers' initial onslaught against settled ministers whom they considered unworthy, the Old Lights launched a counterattack, accusing the evangelicals of censoriousness and un-charitable judging; of invading other ministers' pulpits; of causing schisms in existing churches; of encouraging unqualified lay exhorters; and, above all of unseemly emotional excesses.[57]

In Connecticut the Assembly convened the clergy of the colony to discuss the crisis and then, in 1742, enacted a law banning itinerant preachers. The statute forbade any minister to preach at another parish without the express permission of the minister and a majority of the parishioners there, under pain of losing his public salary. It also prohibited ministerial associations' meddling in one another's affairs and decreed that lay exhorters who preached in any parish without the permission of its minister and parishioners were to be bound to the peace on a £100 bond.

The Connecticut Assembly's effort to restrain the forces unleashed by the Great Awakening failed in its objective; but it did provoke an extended defense of liberty of conscience from Elisha Williams, a Congregationalist minister, former president of Yale, and a political opponent of the Old Lights who had enacted the law.[58] Published anonymously in 1744, Williams's pamphlet was the only eighteenth-century pamphlet—until the eve of the American Revolution—that addressed itself specifically to the question of liberty of conscience. It typified contemporary thinking on Church-State relations, in that Williams, though he used universal language, never transcended the assumptions and presuppositions of his specific situation.

Williams grounded his reasoning in the contractual theory of Locke's *Second Treatise* and asserted that the government possessed no mandate to go beyond the original purpose of its creators, "the preservation of their Persons, their Liberties and Estates, or their Property." Members of society possessed a natural right to follow their own consciences and judgments. He continued with the thought that "Every one is under an indispensable Obligation to search the Scriptures for himself." Thus did Williams begin to identify natural rights with the rights of Christians—and Protestant Christians at that.

Whereas Locke's *Letter Concerning Toleration* only implicitly excluded Catholics, Williams explicitly excluded them from toleration because their very principles made them into enemies of a "Protestant State." Moreover, while Locke could abstract himself sufficiently from the Christian scheme of things to hold that rulers could not punish idolatry and to discuss such practices as the sacrifice of animals (which he thought should be allowed), no eighteenth-century American minister would have shorn the magistrate of the power to prevent public idolatry, as the minister himself understood the term. Elisha Williams and others recognized the possibility of a non-Christian state, but none of their thought flowed from consideration of such a possibility. In fact, Williams reflected on nothing beyond the needs of Christian Connecticut. With regard to support of ministers, he wrote:

> ... the Civil Authority of a State are Obliged to take Care for the Support of Religion, or in other words, of Schools and the Gospel

Ministry, in order to their approving themselves Nursing Fathers (as, I suppose, every Body will own, and therefore I shall not spend any Time in proving it).

Limited by his own view of the standing order in Connecticut, he not only failed to look beyond it, but dismissed any objections to it on the part of those who might do so.

Elisha Williams did not question the existing establishment. He simply rejected any theoretical establishment that imposed a unity of belief on all subjects, something eighteenth-century ministers consistently denounced throughout the colonies. In fine, although he repudiated the act of 1742 as tyrannical, Williams's argument rested more on the assertion that the statute violated the Connecticut ecclesiastical constitution of 1708, the Act of Toleration, and the colony's charter. The sharpness of his logic was blunted, and his Lockeian statements about the absence of the magistrate's power in religious matters rang hollow when, elsewhere in his pamphlet, he casually accepted and referred to a "Law . . . for the Ease of such as soberly dissent from the Way of Worship and Ministry established by the Laws of Connecticut."[59]

The significance of Elisha Williams did not lie in the innovation of his thought or the persuasiveness of his contentions, but in the effectiveness of his method. Although Old and New Lights disagreed with each other over the law of 1742, they did not differ substantively on the role of government in religion. Benefiting from an ecclesiastical establishment they accepted without question, Williams and the New Lights portrayed themselves as defenders of liberty and the inviolable rights of conscience and clothed their arguments in the stirring rhetoric of the philosophy of natural rights. Old Lights worried that such rhetoric could not harmonize with the existing establishment in Connecticut and, like the earlier subscriptionists, fretted about religious anarchy.

Whereas New Light Nathaniel Eells could preach to the Connecticut Assembly in 1748 that the "Kingdom of Christ . . . is not of this world; as . . . [it] is purely spiritual" and blithely proceed to claim that rulers should "support & encourage those Institutions which Christ Himself has appointed to enlarge and build up his Kingdom," Old Lights could not rest so easily with such obvious contradictions. They concerned themselves with how government could "establish Truths which are really Divine" and preserve "Faith, Order and Unity."

Old Lights looked back to happier times, when rulers established "the true religion," upheld the pure worship of God, and supported the minister, and they lamented the "enthusiasm, rapture, and warm imagination" they identified as the source of their current troubles. All the fine talk about private judgment might be well and good, but what about its consequences: What of the person whose conscience "bade him Worship an Idol"? Did the Christian magistrate have to ignore "Swearing, Blasphemy, Sabbath-breaking, or Idolatry"?

Already, the momentum of the century, favoring reliance on Scripture alone and the right of private judgment, had enabled Elisha Williams and the anti-subscriptionists before him to place their opponents in a hopeless position. Carried on an irresistible wave of religious enthusiasm, New Lights could afford to ignore Old Lights, whose pessimistic defensive stance could not restrain the forces of change; and the collection of Connecticut laws issued in 1750 omitted the statute of 1742 prohibiting itinerant preachers, thereby demonstrating the advent to power of New Light supporters. Thereafter Church-State issues receded, and most religious disputes in Connecticut involved battles between Old Lights and New Lights at parish level, with each side trying to appoint its own candidates to ministerial positions.[60]

Elsewhere in the colonies, changes from the Great Awakening that promised enormous consequences for relationships between Church and State were taking place without much theoretical justification. The migration of Scotch-Irish during the 1730s brought large numbers of Presbyterians to the western regions of Virginia, where they were welcomed. In the 1740s, however, the Great Awakening brought them to the more settled eastern areas of the colony, where they posed a threat to Virginia's homogeneity, based on its adherence to the established Anglican Church. Additionally, fervent evangelists stirred up trouble by vilifying and condemning the colony's established Anglican clergy.

During the decade of the 1740s, therefore, Virginia authorities attempted to slow the spread of Presbyterianism in the colony by confining Presbyterian clergymen to preaching at designated places where they were registered, thereby eliminating itinerancy. Samuel Davies, a Presbyterian minister in Hanover County, assumed the leadership of Presbyterians' efforts to preach and evangelize freely throughout the colony. He centered his arguments entirely on the issue of the legal meaning of the Act of Toleration with regard to licensing of ministers. Davies did not object to licenses, but believed that he had a right to secure as many as he needed to carry out his work, whereas the authorities wanted to limit him to one. In 1751 each side in this controversy carried its case to England.[61] That same year, the Lords of Trade wrote to the Virginia Council:

... as Toleration and a Free Exercise of Religion is so valuable a branch of true liberty, and so essential to the enriching and improving of a Trading Nation, it should ever be held sacred in His Majesties Colonies. . . .[62]

Typically, Davies refused to characterize his harassment in Virginia as a persecution and declared that he had no need to make such a charge. Indeed, so little was he moved by the question of religious liberty that during his stay in England in 1755, he commented that the English Dissenting Deputies, the organization of English Dissenters that helped him with his petitions, seemed more concerned with "the cause of liberty" than with religion. By the late 1750s, the declining prestige of the Anglican Church and Virginia's wartime need for support combined to resolve the Presbyterians' difficulties. By 1760 they had established themselves as a religious force in the colony and had also lost some of their earlier evangelical fire.[63]

In New England the rhetoric of freedom sounded again from a different quarter—the Arminian clergy. Like earlier anti-subscriptionists, many liberal New England divines of the late colonial period believed that the Bible alone should be the rule of faith and opposed tests of orthodoxy. There, however, any similarity to anti-subscriptionists ended.

Where the more evangelical Presbyterians believed that vital experienced religion, not static formulas, would enliven the doctrines of the Church and give them vitality, New England liberal Arminian ministers were convinced that religion should be stripped of all unnecessary doctrinal baggage and be presented as the motive for and an encouragement to virtue and moral behavior.[64]

Although Presbyterian Jonathan Dickinson and Massachusetts liberals proclaimed the right to private judgment based on Scripture alone, the New England clerics were far closer in their thinking to Dickinson's opponent, Benjamin Franklin. The two most prominent New England liberals were Jonathan Mayhew, noted for his radical positions on both theological and political issues, and Charles Chauncy, principal literary opponent of the New Light preachers.

In 1749, in his first published work, Jonathan Mayhew set himself on the side of a rational reasonable God and against the traditional Calvinist approach to an absolute, incomprehensible, and transcendent God. Rejecting belief in the corruption of human nature, Mayhew demanded that all religion be brought to the bar of reason, that no makers of creeds should violate people's natural right to think for themselves. No more than any contemporary defenders of private judgment, however, did Mayhew develop the implications of his statements. He held that the right of private judgment did not bestow the right to deny the "true religion, let it be what it will," nor to use "liberty for an occasion of the flesh." To do so would be to "deny the God that is above, or reject and blaspheme the true religion." Similarly, no one had a right to go against "the law of God or the law & light of nature."[65]

In his Election Sermon of 1754, he suggested to the legislature that it consider whether "we have not some laws in force hardly reconcilable with that religious liberty which we profess." The overall tenor of Mayhew's works does not suggest that he wished the General Court to draw drastic conclusions from his statements. That he advocated private judgment was clear; but that he believed the common people capable of it was not.[66] Like others who defended liberty of thought or religion, Mayhew did so within the boundaries of the existing Church-State system. He countered with considerable valor the opposition from colleagues and contemporaries his religious views incited. However, his battles represented a fight for elbow room within the Congregational Church for theological liberals like himself, not an attempt to define standards of religious liberty against which to measure his own and other religions.

For Mayhew the ecclesiastical system of Massachusetts represented the voice of reason. Though he could have read Bishop Berkeley's assertion that the Catholic faith was not inconsistent with honest diligence to one's calling, he accepted completely and manipulated the conventional wisdom that Catholicism equated with superstition, idolatry, and tyranny.[67] Nor did the criticism of Baptists and other dissenters who felt imposed upon by the New England religious establishment gain his attention. The evaluation that Mayhew "stood out . . . as a pre-eminent spokesman in the colonies for everything that was new, bold, and radically non-conformist in matters of Church and State" holds true provided the judgment stops short of the New England way in Church and State.[68] As in the case of other disputes in New England, the rhetoric of liberty remained, but the word of religious freedom far outran the deed.

Mayhew's life and work typified the effects of the Enlightenment on eighteenth-century colonial America. Together with his colleague Charles Chauncy he wanted to further the cause of rational religion. Chauncy especially detested the emotionalism associated with the Great Awakening, and both of them utterly opposed the "dogmatical kind" of religion associated with evangelism. None of them saw any conflict between reason and religion. In matters of Church and State in New England, oftentimes those influenced by the Enlightenment tended to be defenders of the status quo as embodying the most extensive religious liberty. When Elisha Williams of Connecticut turned to Locke's works to uphold religious liberty, he was calling for a return to the system as it was before that colony's anti-itinerant law of 1742 violated it, not for a revision of the system itself.

After 1765 the controversies caused by the Stamp Act turned Americans' attention from religious to secular affairs. Late in that decade, however, members of one group that had emerged from the Great Awakening, the Separatist Baptists, proved an exception to this trend. They began arriving in Virginia in the full flush of a missionary evangelical fervor. These itinerant preachers refused to register with the authorities, thereby coming into direct conflict with the colonial government and suffering harassment and imprisonment as a result. Like earlier evangelists, they were more interested in conversion than in conversation about religious liberty. Their very presence, however, added another element to the religious composition of the colony, an element that would find its voice in discussions of religious freedom during the revolutionary era.[69]

The Great Awakening also increased and strengthened religious diversity in the Carolinas, as Separatist Baptists increased in number there after 1750; but the significance of this pluralism lay in the future, rather than in any immediate discussions of or demands for religious freedom. North Carolina shared with Rhode Island the stigma of infidelity and irreligion.[70] Most religious controversies in the former resulted from the continuing inability of the Anglican Church to make its legal establishment an effective reality in the face of passive—and sometimes active—resistance from a population made up largely of dissenters, who opposed contributing to the support of that church and found a major grievance in the Anglican monopoly of power to perform marriages.[71]

As the Stamp Act crisis diverted public discourse from revival to revenue, political issues predominated. Nevertheless, many questions in Church and State remained to be settled. The century to that time had seen a great deal of change in the colonies' manner of thinking about, as well as practicing, religion; but no new synthesis with regard to relations between Church and State had evolved.

While many Americans continued to use the language of old when speaking or writing about the role of government in religious affairs, the underlying assumptions, together with common acceptance of what the magistrate could do, had altered. Benjamin Colman, in 1718, told the Massachusetts magistrates that if they thought their way of worship was "near to the Rule of God's Word," they should "adhere to and support it." During the remainder of the century, other ministers used similar language, telling the legislators that they should be "Christian magistrates" and "Nursing Fathers" to the church.

This common language masked the fact that, increasingly, the same ministers could agree less and less on what constituted the "Rule of God's Word." Nevertheless, the idea that government should promote a Christian society persisted. Making little distinction between religion in general and Christianity in particular, most Americans tended to assume that the common elements of Protestantism equated with natural religion. They could still agree that magistrates should guard the Sabbath, find their exemplars in Scripture, and generally promote piety and Christian order.[72]

Few questioned the assumptions connecting society and Protestantism, although a hint to the contrary occasionally surfaced. For instance, in 1739 Chauncy approved the fact that in England even dissenters from Christianity itself were allowed to publish their sentiments. During the French and Indian War, William Smith, the Anglican provost of the College of Pennsylvania, scolded an unnamed adversary who criticized the clergy for "blowing the Trumpet of War, and declaiming against Popery, a subject so long exhausted." In 1774 one Barnabas Binney, a graduate of Brown, delivered the commencement address at that college. In a long oration he argued for religious liberty for all, "even those whom true Englishmen have most aversion to, Papists." The government had no business asking if citizens were "atheists, Deists, Pagans, Papists, Jews or Christians."[73]

That some harbored such notions is interesting; but few questioned such beliefs as that of Benjamin Gale, a dedicated opponent of those he perceived as trying to set up orthodoxy in Connecticut. Gale argued for liberty of conscience for everyone "whose religious Principles are not incompatible with a Protestant Country, or destructive to the Community." Such people he identified as "Roman Catholics, Deists, Atheists" and those of no religion at all. Jews and members of other non-Christian religions existed beyond the ken of the majority of those who commented on Church and State.[74]

The most significant developments in Church and State during pre-revolutionary eighteenth-century America were social, rather than intellectual. The Great Awakening increased an already growing diversity of sects within the colonies and, especially by promoting the rise of Baptists in the southern settlements, altered the existing balances. In its wake, no church or religious group could ever hope to achieve a dominance in doctrine and numbers. Especially significant would be the Baptists' adoption of the idea that government support of ministers violated liberty of conscience.

As the Revolution approached, developments in the political arena were about to enlarge the world view and climate of opinion that had predominated through most of the eighteenth century. Within different contexts, ministers and colonists had proclaimed the right to private judgment, and though they did not mean that people should rely on themselves instead of the clergy for religious guidance, they could not keep that from happening. While evangelists told the people they had to trust their religious experience over the word of tradition and a settled ministry, anti-evangelist ministers preached that all must trust to reason, rather than authority. Adherence to either experience or reason on the part of the people, however, would weaken the position of traditional clergy. As Quaker Herman Husbands of North Carolina wrote in 1770, if the common people came to have no rule but Scripture, then what need would there be for ministers, especially if they had to be paid?[75]

5

Establishment of Religion in Colonial America

In 1771 Thomas B. Chandler, an Anglican minister in New Jersey involved in a heated dispute with Boston Congregationalist minister Charles Chauncy, wrote that if Chauncy were going to continue to change the meaning of the word "establishment," he ought to "publish a Glossary, wherein the singularities of his Phraseology are carefully explained."[1] Given the usage of the word in colonial America, Chandler's suggestion was eminently practical. The ambiguities of "establishment" in the colonies stemmed from such peculiarly American situations as that in New York, where the minority Anglicans claimed to be the establishment, or in New England, where Congregationalists—Dissenters within the Empire—in fact constituted the established church.

In England "establishment" clearly referred to the Anglican Church, officially approved and supported by the government, which excluded non-Anglicans, who probably constituted less than 10 per cent of the population, from positions of power, privilege, and social influence. In America the constant need for more settlers made such exclusivity unachievable.

Virginia, the Carolinas, Maryland, and Georgia established the Church of England and taxed all residents for its support, but none of those colonies confined officeholding to Anglicans. Though their inhabitants expressed considerable discontent with the established church, their dissatisfaction, at least until the eve of the American

Revolution, centered on the operation of that church, not on the nature
or principle of establishment itself.

Delaware, New Jersey, Pennsylvania, and Rhode Island established
no religion, provided public support for no ministers, and admitted all
Protestants on an equal basis. As a result, the kind of contention that
would have produced discussion about the nature of "establishment"
failed to arise within their boundaries.

In Massachusetts and Connecticut, however, the question of establishment proved complicated. By laying claim to an establishment,
Congregationalists there wanted to assert their right to preeminence in
New England—especially over Anglicans—and to vindicate the work
of their forebears, who had planted the colonies at such cost. In
pressing their claims, however, again under the watchful eyes of jealous
Anglicans, they had to be careful not to give the English government
cause for acting to curb the pretensions of "Dissenters."

Moreover, while asserting an establishment of their own, they disassociated it from the type of establishment connected in their minds
with Archbishop Laud, from which their ancestors had fled and that
still oppressed their brethren in England. Consequently, their discourse presupposed at least two kinds of establishment, i.e. one good
(theirs) and one bad (England's). The equivocation they were forced to
resort to in referring to the former introduced another element of
ambiguity into the use of the term.

New Hampshire's history followed a different path. Its decentralized
system, wherein local towns handled their own religious affairs, did not
precipitate colony-wide controversies. The colony's laws never referred
to its ecclesiastical system as an establishment of religion, and its
inhabitants found no occasion to discuss "establishment." Anglicans
made few inroads there, and Quakers received an exemption from
ecclesiastical taxes. Further, not until 1784 did New Hampshire institute
the annual Election Sermon, that vehicle for ministerial discourse before
the General Court on the relationship between Church and State.[2]

Massachusetts and Connecticut, then, together with New York, the
colonies that experienced the sharpest controversies between Anglicans
and non-Anglicans, produced the most discussion of "establishment"
in its American context. Elsewhere, frequent use of the term went
unaccompanied by argument as to its definition.

Still governed under its original charter, Connecticut, as the eighteenth century opened, was more independent of the Mother Country
than Massachusetts and had less experience of English supervision.
Nor had Anglicans arrived there in numbers sufficient to challenge
dominant Congregationalists so strongly as to instill in them a constant

wariness of English reaction or the tendency to equivocate about their religious situation. Consequently, the colony acknowledged its establishment more explicitly than its neighbor to the north.

In 1702 the Connecticut General Court decreed that "wheresoever the Ministry of the Word is Established every person shall duely resort . . . thereunto." In 1708 the colony formally approved the Saybrook Platform:

> This Assembly do declare their great approbation [of Saybrook] . . . and do ordain that all the churches within this government that are or shall be thus united in doctrine, worship, and discipline, be, and for the future shall be owned and acknowledged established by law.

The legislature then passed "An Act for the Ease of Such as Soberly Dissent from the way of worship Established by the Laws."[3]

Preachers of Election Sermons in Connecticut lauded the colony's action in establishing the Congregational churches; but Anglicans were now beginning to stir up trouble, and a number of them petitioned against "paying maintenance to the established Church." At first, they acknowledged the reality that the Congregationalists—or, as they referred to them, the "Independency and Presbytery"—were established, and that they themselves were the dissenters. But after the "Yale Apostasy" of 1722, when several tutors at that college converted to Anglicanism, the Anglican Church secured a foothold in Connecticut and began to question the power of the colony to establish any religion apart from that of the Church of England.[4]

The same challenge was being mounted with more intensity in Massachusetts. But the Bay Colony, operating under a newer charter, had long since recognized the need for circumspection in dealings with England, especially in matters of religion. Thus, although both General Court and clergy held that Congregationalism was established in the colony, neither said so as explicitly as their counterparts in Connecticut.

From 1692 Massachusetts law had provided for the settlement and support of "able, learned, and orthodox" ministers, but the statute did not designate the arrangement an establishment of religion. However, when the first law proved inadequate to cover all situations in the province, the assembled ministers of Massachusetts petitioned the General Court to devise "Methods for the Establishment of the Christian Religion" in those places where it was not already settled. In his Election Sermon of 1694, Samuel Willard reminded his hearers they were to do their utmost to see that the true religion was "countenanced and established," and in 1708 Benjamin Colman, also before the General Court, affirmed that one of the functions of

legislators was "Establishment of Religion within this Government."
The laws of Massachussetts referred to "Maintaining and Propagating
Religion." In theory the description "able, learned, and orthodox"
could have embraced Anglican ministers, but the General Court had
no such thing in mind. It equated the true or Christian religion as
much with Congregationalism as Maryland Anglicans equated Protestantism with the Church of England.[5]

When Cotton Mather in 1718 referred to "Our Churches" and "the
protection, which the Best of Kings [George I] extended to them," he
probably meant that the Congregational churches of the province were
established with the permission of the king, by means of the charter. In
1724 Benjamin Colman reiterated Mather's sentiments that the king was
the "Protector of those Provinces in their legal Establishments." Despite
their assertions, however, both Mather and Colman were careful to state
that according to Massachusetts law, a minister other than a Congregationalist could indeed become the official minister of any town that chose
him. To the Bishop of Peterborough, Colman wrote:

> . . . that by our present Charter, granted by King William and Queen
> Mary, our Churches are here the Legal Establishment, and our
> Ministers both in respect of their Induction and Maintenance are the
> King's Ministers, as much as even the Church of England Ministers are
> in any of the other Provinces; . . . But when I say that our Churches and
> Ministers here are established by the King's Laws, I would pray your
> Lordship not to understand me in Opposition to the Church of
> England, for so they are not; but if any Town will chuse a Gentleman of
> the Church of England for their Pastor or Rector they are at their
> Liberty, and he is their Minister by the Laws of our Province, as much as
> any Congregational Minister among us is so. So far is our Establishment
> from excluding others from the common Rights of men and Christians.

Later in the same work, he casually—but more accurately—referred to
"we [Congregationalists] in the Province of Massachusetts, really the
Churches established by Law."[6]

The theory that other ministers could be established remained a
smokescreen to protect New England Congregationalism from
possible English interference. The laws regarding the selection of
ministers by the towns presumed a Congregational minister, and the
composition of the population of Massachusetts at the time ensured
that none other would in fact—then or for the remainder of the colonial
period—be an established minister. Chastened by encounters with
Anglican power by way of England, however, Massachusetts Congregationalists became increasingly discreet in their explanations of the
system they determinedly practiced.

Anglican ministers in Massachusetts had been writing to England since the start of the eighteenth century complaining about their parishioners' having to support Congregationalist ministers; but in the 1720s, Anglican convert John Checkley precipitated a direct confrontation between Anglicans and Puritans by his publications attacking Calvinism and defending episcopacy. Condemned by the Massachusetts Council and indicted by the Grand Jury of Suffolk County for printing "many vile & Scandalous passages ... reflecting on the ministers of the Gospel Established in this Province," Checkley initiated a dispute that by the time of the American Revolution would have reached a crescendo. To the accusation concerning his reflections on the established clergy, he countered:

> ... no Acts of Assembly in the Province, either by Right, could, or, in Fact have established any way of Worship and Ministry, whether Presbyterian or Congregational; so as to make That the Establishment, and the Episcopal churches to be Dissenters. ... Furthermore ... by the Laws of England, the Church of England, as established in England, and No Other, is positively established in all His Majesty's Plantations.[7]

Checkley maintained that the English statutes, the Common Law, and the requirement of orthodoxy in the laws of the province proved that only the Anglican Church had been established in New England. In reply the Reverend Thomas Walter insisted that "there can be no such Thing as a Dissenting Presbyterian in New England; for we are the Original Established Church of this Land."[8] Checkley's small conflagration was soon followed by others of greater consequence.

In 1725 the Massachusetts Council approved a petition of the Congregational clergy that the General Court call a synod of the churches of the province to offer advice upon "the circumstances of the day." The Anglican ministers of the colony immediately protested that such a synod would exclude them; would be prejudicial to their church; and by its very existence would violate the jurisdiction of the Bishop of London, whose ecclesiastical authority they claimed extended to the colonies. Appealed to directly, that same Bishop of London passed the problem on to the Duke of Newcastle for the English government's opinion on the matter and included the following in an accompanying letter:

> ... by the Act of Union [between England and Scotland] (6 ANN, C.5) every King and Queen at their Coronation shall take and subscribe an oath to maintain and preserve inviolably the settlement of the Church of England, and the Doctrine, Worship, and Government thereof as by law established within the Kingdoms of England and Ireland, the

dominion of Wales and the town of Berwick upon Tweed, and the territories thereunto belonging. If by this clause the Ministers ... of the Church of England in the Plantations be made the established Church within the several Governments, then all the rest are only tolerated as here in England, and if so this double ill use may be made of by permitting the Independent Ministers of New England to hold a regular Synod.

In the words "the territories thereunto belonging," American Anglicans found material with which to bedevil New England Congregationalists with the theory that Anglicanism was established throughout the empire.[9]

The English government sent the case concerning the synod to the Attorney-General and Solicitor-General for their opinion. Among the documents submitted was a report from the Reverend Samuel Myles, Anglican rector of King's Chapel in Boston, to the Bishop of London. In answer to the question, "What public Acts of Assembly have been made and confirmed relating to the Church or Clergy within that government?", Myles had answered:

... there are several laws for the Establishing of Independents, & settling Orthodox Ministers chosen by the people. The Church of England only Indulged, as the Anabaptists & Quakers for never in any of the Laws is the case supposed that the Clergy of the Church of England, should be here Supported.

Myles had no illusions about the reality of the Massachusetts establishment. The opinion of the Attorney-General and Solicitor-General handed the Anglicans a triumph. The two legal experts could not "collect that there is any regular establishment of a National or Provincial Church There." Therefore, no synod could be held without the king's permission.[10]

Victorious, the Anglican ministers decided to attack the whole ecclesiastical settlement in Massachusetts and to ask the English authorities to repeal it. In a lengthy memorial to the Privy Council, they presented a thorough description of the religious system that had been constructed in the colony since 1692. Astonishing to the modern reader in the inconsistency of its arguments, the memorial provides an insight into the confidence of the Anglican missionaries, who oftentimes failed to distinguish between boldness and arrogance, and who, in their assurance that the home government stood behind them, did not bother to iron out the logical discrepancies in their position.

The gist of the document was that, although the charter put all Protestants on an equal footing, the Congregationalists had turned the colony's government to their own purposes, thereby not only burdening the Church of England with taxes, but preventing its growth. Like Baptists and Quakers, the Anglicans in their petition equated mandatory payment of maintenance to Congregational ministers with violation of the liberty of conscience granted by the charter. Though they concentrated on Massachusetts's supposed violation of the charter by preferring "Independency," they did add also that the laws in question opposed the "Laws and Constitution of this Kingdom."

This last no doubt reflected the belief that the laws of England carried an establishment of the Church of England into the colonies, a position the Anglican ministers maintained both before and after the memorial in question. Thus they held, on the one hand, that the Anglican Church was in fact established in Massachusetts and, on the other, that the charter's grant of liberty of conscience prohibited giving preference to one sect over another. Moreover, in equating Anglican payment of maintenance to a minister of another church with a violation of liberty of conscience, they ignored the fact that in the southern colonies, where all sects were taxed for the support of the Church of England, the governors' instructions included a grant of liberty of conscience to dissenters. No Anglicans—either in England or in the colonies—agreed that such an instruction freed dissenters from payment of tithes to Anglican ministers. Indeed, the Anglican clergy in Maryland had earlier specifically denied that "liberty of conscience" relieved Quakers of the obligation to contribute to the Church of England.

Meantime, in 1727, both Massachusetts and Connecticut took steps to defuse some of the most grievous Anglican complaints by exempting members of the Church of England from taxation for the Congregational churches. The Introduction to the law noted the petition of the Anglicans to be exempted from paying towards the support of the "Established Church" in Connecticut, but its next sentence referred to the Congregational clergy of that same church as "Dissenting Ministers." Then it went on to say that it had always "been esteemed as an Hardship by those of the Profession Establish'd by this Government, to be Compelled to Contribute to the Support of the Church of England where that is the Church Establish'd by Law." Thereupon, it urged that no such thing "should be here Imposed, upon any Dissenting from the Churches here Approved and Establish'd," thus branding Congregationalists and Anglicans alike dissenters.[11]

The exempting laws of Massachusetts and Connecticut differed somewhat in their provisions, but both colonies agreed that they were exempting Anglicans from contributing to the Congregational establishment.[12] Unsatisfied, Anglican ministers still waged their claim, but despite their bravado about the establishment of the Church of

England extending to all the colonies, Anglicans were never really sure of their position in New England. In 1731 Bishop Gipson of London wrote to Governor Belcher of Massachusetts, a Congregationalist, asking "whether Independency be the Establishment of this Country." Belcher replied:

> I don't apprehend it is but that the Chh of England is as much establisht by the laws of this Province as that of the Independents, Presbyterians or Baptists, and should any town or parish in the Province elect a clergyman of The Chh of England to be their minister, and he be qualify'd as the law directs, altho 9/20 of such parish shoul'd be Dissenters, yet by the laws of the Province they woul'd be oblig'd to pay the maintenance of such a minister.[13]

Belcher repeated the theory advanced by Mather and Colman, one so distant from reality that it in no way threatened the *de facto* Congregational establishment.

In the following year, 1732, the opinion of the Solicitor-General and Attorney-General in England provided cold comfort for Anglican hopes. In response to the petitions for an annulment of Massachusetts's ecclesiastical laws, the legal experts declared, first, that the Massachusetts charter neither set up nor prohibited a "Provincial Church" establishment in the colony, and that provisions for the "Maintenance of Ministers" could not be said to be inconsistent with the grant of liberty of conscience. Finally, the attorneys stated that the laws in question had been passed long since and had received either explicit or tacit approval.[14]

By implication the by now favorite Anglican argument that the Act of Union with Scotland extended establishment of the Church of England to all the colonies was relegated to the status of no more than a taunt with which to bait Congregationalists. In private the Bishop of London admitted as much and regretted that Congregationalists had not been checked in their "first pretentions to act as an establish'd Church."[15]

Another clarification of the Congregationalists' position came out of Rhode Island, "that fertile soil of Heresy & Schism," as the New England Anglican clergy referred to it in 1727. In 1668 the proprietors of the Petaquamscut Purchase in Narragansett had granted 100 acres "for the Use of an Orthodox Person that should be obtained to preach God's Word to the Inhabitants." In 1723 the Reverend James M. McSparran, a convert to Anglicanism, brought suit in the Rhode Island courts to dispossess the Reverend James Torrey, the incumbent Congregational minister, on the ground that only an Anglican minister—in this case himself—met the requirement of orthodoxy. In

1739 the Supreme Court of Rhode Island found in favor of Congregationalist Torrey, and McSparran appealed the decision to the Privy Council. Both Anglicans and Puritans brought as many resources as possible to bear upon this critical controversy, but the decision hung fire until 1752, when the Privy Council also found in Torrey's favor, thereby denying the Anglicans' assertion that they alone could meet the requirements of orthodoxy.[16]

The McSparran decision only verified the stalemate that already existed in the rest of New England, particularly since the Privy Council's decision not to overturn the ecclesiastical system in Massachusetts or, by implication, in Connecticut. On the one hand, Congregationalists could claim an establishment; on the other, Anglicans continued to assert that they were established throughout the empire and point to the fact that Massachusetts had been forbidden to call a synod. These arguments manifested themselves for the most part within the context of a far wider religious controversy, which dealt primarily with the issues of clerical ordination and of which religious group should be considered schismatic from the true church. Both these questions were of greater import to the combatants than the question of an establishment, which played as a sideshow to the larger disputes.

John Checkley's publications of the 1720s had triggered a pamphlet war on a variety of issues that remained a printer's delight until the American Revolution. The tone of the disputes can still be heard in the Reverend James Wetmore's *Letter from a Minister of the Church of England to his Dissenting Parishioners*. Addressing Congregationalists in Connecticut, Wetmore, a minister of Rye, New York, wrote that, as true ministers, Anglican clergy should preach to those separated from the church "even if the iniquity of the schism is established by law." To reject such a minister was to reject Christ. Other Anglican ministers repeated the same theme.[17]

Even in an age inured to religious obloquy, such sentiments could still send opponents into paroxysms of frustration, and during the 1730s, Jonathan Dickinson undertook to answer some of the Anglican attacks. Dickinson, though he served as a Presbyterian minister in New Jersey, was a native of Massachusetts. Most of his works were theological, dealing primarily with the validity of Presbyterian ordination, but he made an occasional foray into the establishment question. He pointed out that according to the laws of Massachusetts, if Anglicans enjoyed a majority in any parish, then their minister would receive the parish salary, in marked contrast to the Episcopal clergy, who exacted their salary wherever they could—as in New York, Maryland, Virginia, and Carolina. The focus of Dickinson's argument here was not the nature of the Massachusetts establishment, but proof of his point that Anglicans had been guilty of greater persecution than Puritans. In response to the Reverend Samuel Johnson's insistence on calling New England Congregationalists "dissenters," Dickinson asked, "Who is it that dissent from the original and legal Establishment of the Country, they or we?"

John Graham, a Connecticut minister writing at about the same time, also took umbrage at Johnson's use of the word "dissenter," asking how the people in Connecticut could be dissenters, when they were cared for by an "established Pastor." Congregationalists could not be dissenters, as they were part of the

> ... established church. ... And it is no less absurd to call a Pres-
> byterian a Dissenter, in Connecticut (or any of the American Charter
> Governments where Presbytery is established) than it would be to call
> him so in North-Britain [Scotland].

Rather, the members of the Church of England, who despite their behavior had been treated with great tenderness by the colony, were the real dissenters. Indeed, he asserted, the fact that Anglicans accepted the same exemption as Quakers and Baptists showed them to be dissenters in New England.

In 1738 the Reverend Samuel Mather, scion of the famous Boston family, reasserted that "these [Congregational] Churches have their Religious Privileges" confirmed unto them by the Charter and added that "the Liberties of these Churches must be deem'd to be as Sacred Things as the Ecclesiastical Liberties of the National Churches of England and Scotland." The debate continued into the 1740s and brought forth several more protagonists, of whom the Reverend Noah Hobart, a minister of Fairfield, Connecticut, became the most notable and prolific on the Congregational side.[18]

In 1748 Hobart, in a piece entitled *A Serious Address to the Members of the Episcopal Separation in New England*, limited the Anglican estab-lishment to England. Referring to Connecticut, he wrote that "the Communion of our Churches is most safe, because established by prescription." Hobart no doubt meant to assert that the Congrega-tional churches were established in the colony, and he made a point of referring to Anglicans as "dissenters." However, his efforts to further his argument hardly clarified what he meant by establishment:

> ... tho' you [Anglicans] will deny our having an Establishment by
> express and positive Law; you must own we are established by Agree-
> ment and Prescription, which is all the Establishment the primitive
> Church had in the best and purest Ages of it.[19]

In response to persistent Anglican assertions that their church had been established in the colonies by the Act of Union, Hobart turned again to this constant irritant to New England Congregationalists and attempted to dispose of it. He explained—with a good deal of reason—that the Scots, before entering the English Parliament, where they would be a minority, established the Presbyterian Church in Scotland in perpetuity; whereupon the English Parliament secured the Church of England in its establishment. He also showed that many English commentators, including bishops and members of the Society for the Propagation of the Gospel, evidenced no consciousness that the Act of Union had altered the status of Americans, and he reminded his readers that the Attorney-General and Solicitor-General, when they had commented in 1725 on the proposed Massachusetts synod, had not claimed that Anglicans were established in the province.

More explicit when talking to fellow Congregationalists, Hobart noted in the Connecticut Election Sermon of 1751 that the churches of that colony had some "Title to the peculiar Protection and Favor of their Civil Rulers," whose duty bound them to see that the "Establishment of this Colony" be "supported, countenanced and encouraged by the Civil Magistrate." Later, in 1759, he flatly asserted that the Saybrook Platform made a "legal establishment" of the churches in Connecticut.[20]

Hobart's arguments made much sense to those who were inclined to listen to them, but they did not eradicate from the Act of Union the pertinent words "and the territories thereunto belonging," which could still be used by Anglicans who insisted on a literal reading of it. This reading received an affirmation from an unexpected source. William Douglass, a physician who had earlier achieved some notoriety by tangling with Cotton Mather in an argument over smallpox vaccination, published a large two-volume history of New England that contained much valuable information and an equal amount of inaccuracy.

Though no partisan of the Anglican Church, Douglass insisted that the Act of Union had established the Church of England "though only nominally in all our Colonies and Plantations." Apparently baffled as to the precise nature of the New England establishment, he wrote that the Anglican Church was established in the colonies "only as to Church Government, and that amongst the people of the Church of England." Other sects, though forbidden ecclesiastical jurisdiction, were tolerated "as if they were Churches established by Law."[21]

Douglass no doubt fell victim to the ambiguity surrounding the nature of the New England establishments, an ambiguity promoted by both Congregationalists and Anglicans for their own respective interests. Defenders of the New England way believed that Congregationalism was clearly the established religion there, and they turned the term "dissenter" against the Anglicans. Equally clearly, however, they understood that they could not push the claim to an exclusive establishment too far. In 1753 the Reverend Thomas Prince of Massachusetts wrote of the generosity of his fellow colonists, who had taken the Church of England ministers "into our Establishment," so that their people had to "contribute the same portion of rates to their own Ministers as they would otherwise be obliged to pay to ours." Thus did Prince convey the impression that Massachusetts Anglicans were well treated by being taken into the Congregational establishment, without actually saying they were part of it.[22]

Anglicans, too, caught between the needs of controversy and the recognition of reality, waffled as to the New England establishment. Sometimes they quoted the English authorities to prove that, since the New England colonies had no establishment, all religions were on an equal basis there. In other instances, they referred to their religion as the one established in England, while still complaining about the establishment set up by the Congregationalists. In 1749 members of the Church of England in Connecticut thanked the colony's Assembly for exempting them from paying taxes to the "dissenting ministers," but then asked for the same privileges as the "Society Established by Law."

In 1752 James McSparran reported that no religion was established in Rhode Island, forgetting that earlier in the same work he had repeated the usual Anglican nostrum that the Church of England was established in all the colonies. Later, in 1763, Henry Carver, an Anglican minister in Boston, wrote the Archbishop of Canterbury that while the Anglicans might have a theoretical *de jure* establishment, Congregationalists constituted the *de facto* establishment. Samuel Johnson referred to the Congregational system in Connecticut as a "kind of establishment." By contrast, Pennsylvania Anglicans, embroiled in no such controversy with their fellow colonists, saw no need to adopt the contrived theory of a universal Anglican establishment and consistently repeated that "the Church is not established in this part of the world" or that they had no "legal Establishment."[23]

Concurrently, however, Congregationalist writers, while approving and defending their own kind of establishment, also spoke of another kind, that of the Church of England, of which they heartily disapproved. Using code words they labeled this disapproved establishment "National" or "Provincial," or described it as imposing "Articles of Faith" and "particular modes of worship." Sometimes they would associate it with that of Constantine, although such linking failed to strike the same chords of disapprobation in their readers as the other allusions. In 1738 Samuel Mather of Massachusetts claimed that the Congregational churches in New England enjoyed the same status as the Anglican Church in England or the Presbyterian Church in Scotland, but he also asserted that New England Congregationalists did not approve of "National Establishments."[24]

This second meaning of the term "establishment" allowed New Englanders to disassociate themselves from and condemn the Anglican establishment in England. Cotton Mather had preached in 1718 that "Conformity to an Established Religion produced by meer External Coercion, is but an Hypocracy and an Abomination." That same year, Benjamin Colman warned the Massachusetts General Court not to impose "an Uniformity on the Churches."[25] Both statements, while delivered as part of an overall advice to the government of Massachusetts to take a very definite part in the regulation of religious affairs, designedly distanced their authors from advocating the kind of uniformity imposed in England.

In the 1730s, though, a number of New England ministers began to apply the term "establishment" in its pejorative sense to a local development that came about in reaction to the spread of what was generally referred to as Arminianism. Technically a denial of predestination, Arminianism, much bruited about by preachers in the seventeenth century, but an actual commodity in eighteenth-century America, represented a departure from Calvinism. Assailants of this trend towards rationalism or latitudinarianism proposed to shore up the existing order in the churches by demanding of ministers an adherence or "subscription" to a creed or set of beliefs. Those who opposed such a proposal, mostly clergymen themselves established by the laws of Massachusetts and Connecticut, resisted this as an "establishment of religion."

In their comments, these theologically liberal ministers who rejected the idea of subscription voiced approval of the general establishment of Congregationalism throughout New England, but disapproval of any attempt to impose hard and fast creeds or doctrinal standards. They believed that magistrates should promote religion, be "nursing fathers," and provide for the support of clergy. More concerned with morality than with a strict adherence to doctrine, however, they objected to any government imposition of articles of faith or modes of worship in order to assure religious uniformity, and they condemned such imposition as a "legal establishment," even though they themselves were in another sense "established" by the laws of the province and approved of that "establishment."[26]

Soon, however, the problems and divisions brought about by the Great Awakening overshadowed the question of subscription. In 1742 the Connecticut legislature's attempt to prohibit New Light itinerancy called forth Elisha Williams's lengthy defense of religious liberty, in which he also raised the issue of establishment.[27]

Williams saw in the law of 1742 confining ministers to their parishes something akin to the uniformity that conservative New England ministers had sought to impose by forcing subscription to combat Arminianism. He rejected the law as tyrannical, branding it an establishment of religion; but at the same time, not unlike the anti-subscriptionist clergy described above, he accepted as legitimate what he regarded as the existing establishment of the colony. He stated that the civil power had no authority to make "Articles of Faith, nor Rites and Ceremonies." Neither had it authority to "establish any Religion (i.e. any Profession of Faith, Modes of Worship, or Church Government) of a human Form and Composition, as a Rule binding to Christians." More than most writers, he clarified the different meanings of establishment:

> . . . if by the Word Establish he [the Magistrate] meant only an Approbation of certain Articles of Faith and Modes of Worship, of Government, or Recommendation of them to their Subjects; I am not arguing against it. But to carry the Notion of a religious Establishment so far as to make it a Rule binding to the Subjects, or on any Penalties whatsoever, seems to me to be oppressive of Christianity.

Williams and most eighteenth-century Congregational writers, be they Old Light or New Light, assumed that there existed a fundamental Christianity that every reasonable Christian could advocate and, consequently, that the State could promote without violating anyone's conscience. This reasonable Christianity usually took the form believed in by themselves, and they accepted its establishment in Massachusetts and Connecticut. Only when the government began to enforce positions they disagreed with did these writers become uncomfortable. Then, like Williams, they would condemn such laws as a "Humane Establishment"; as an imposition of "Articles of Faith" and "modes of Worship"; as tending to "establish a Form of Church Government by penal laws"; and as a "legal Establishment," such as the one in England, where "it is notoriously known, that the Clergy of the Church of England are bound to subscribe to the thirty nine Articles."[28]

Thus, to Williams's way of thinking, there were "establishments" and "legal establishments," and one needed to be aware of the intricacies of New England ecclesiastical life to distinguish between the good and the bad, the approved and the disapproved. For New Lights, then, the law represented an attempt to establish an "Humane Composure or Form of Church Government as a Rule" and one not flexible enough to include themselves. According to the Old Lights, the law was perfectly in accord with and merely affirmed the "ecclesiastical constitution of Connecticut."[29]

Both sides acknowledged a Congregationalist establishment in Connecticut. For Old Lights, the attempt to stop itinerancy amounted to an administrative action, a defense of the system that was in danger of breaking down, and their attempt to restore order to the system raised the hackles not only of New Light evangelicals, but equally of their arch-enemies, liberal Arminian ministers. To New Lights the anti-itinerancy law suppressed the minister of the Spirit by subjecting the truth to the convenience of the colony's ecclesiastical system. To liberal Arminians it smacked of creeds, of ministerial associations and uniformity of doctrine, of strict Calvinism, of episcopacy, and ultimately of "Popery."[30]

A minor incident in the 1750s further illustrated the complexities of the use of the word establishment. In his Election Sermon of 1749, Jonathan Todd, an Old Light supporter, stated that "there can but one Ecclesiastical Constitution enjoy the benefits of a civil Establishment." Todd's concern had been to exclude those Congregational churches that had strayed from the Saybrook Platform. However, Ashbel Woodbridge, the Election Sermon preacher in 1753, applied Todd's statement to attack Connecticut Anglicans. He allowed that the Church of England should be tolerated, but not "raised as to depress our establishment. Two establishments cannot subsist together as Mr. Todd remarked."

Woodbridge explained in a footnote to the printed version of his Sermon that he had been asked—whether by an Anglican he did not say—what he meant by "raising them [Anglicans] up." Instead of explaining his statement that two establishments could not exist side by side, he claimed that "our legislature have indulg'd them herein beyond what they could have reasonably asked," and trailed off into a rambling discussion of Anglican proselytizing that led nowhere. Woodbridge had blundered. Apparently unschooled in the niceties of ecclesiastical politics, he had crossed lines of thought most Congregational writers kept separate. Congregationalists did not believe that Anglicans could be established in New England, but they could not say so. Woodbridge did, however, and apparently—by the time he came to print his sermon—learned of his mistake.[31]

Massachusetts had no centralized system such as the one created by the Saybrook Platform. As a result, when the Great Awakening threw its churches into turmoil, most of the ensuing quarrels occurred at the parish level. In common with their Connecticut counterparts, however, Massachusetts preachers emphasized the role of the magistrate in religion. Both Old and New Lights there agreed that the government should countenance religion and provide for the support of ministers and public worship, albeit with due regard for liberty of conscience and warnings against the imposition of "Articles of Faith"—although both groups would have sharply disagreed on what constituted such articles.[32]

In 1761 Ezra Stiles, a Congregational minister in Newport, Rhode Island, published a lengthy discourse aimed at restoring unity within Congregationalism and Presbyterianism, both badly split by the Great Awakening. He hoped to soothe the internecine quarreling that in recent decades had wracked the two denominations, and help them form a united front against Anglican ambitions. A learned and irenic man, he preached tolerance and devotion to religious liberty as the basis for a common understanding.

In his survey of religious systems throughout the colonies, Stiles commented fairly extensively on establishments of religion, and proved unique among Congregational writers in his description of the system existing in New England. He stated that the laws of New Hampshire and Massachusetts "as fully established congregationalism . . . as the acts of parliament . . . establish episcopacy in South Britain." Both colonies and Connecticut enjoyed "provincial establishments." By "provincial establishments," he meant that

> . . . the legal power to tax a society for the maintenance of ministers, and other parochial charges, belongs to but one general denomination, the congregationalists, under their somewhat different forms, excepting that the episcopalians in Connecticut, under certain limitations, have power to tax themselves.

He then condemned the illiberality of the southern Anglican establishments, pointing out by contrast that "the happy policy of establishing one sect without infringing the essential rights of others is peculiar to the three New England provinces, where congregationalism is established."

Stiles proved singularly candid. Most New England apologists would have argued that if their provinces had Congregational establishments, those came about because the towns selected ministers of that persuasion. Stiles's discussion became somewhat confused when he attributed a "legislative establishment" to Rhode Island and "religious establishments" to Pennsylvania and New Jersey, describing these as "universal protestant liberty." The application of the term "establishment" to these three colonies was peculiar to him and varied from its common application in both England and the colonies. His usage of it can probably be attributed to his preoccupation with religious liberty, his desire to list civil immunities available in different colonies, and the peripheral location among his concerns of a definition of establishment.[33]

During the first half of the eighteenth century, American colonists, other than those in New York and New England, produced little discussion of establishment. In New Jersey, Pennsylvania, and Delaware, it did not arise as an issue. Benjamin Franklin could hardly have approved the argument justifying an establishment in Bishop William Warburton's *The Alliance Between Church and State*, but that did not prevent his offering it for sale. the Philadelphia Library also stocked a copy. So little did the question of establishment impinge on the consciousness of Pennsylvanians that the Friends' yearly Meeting could refer to their religion as "the Gospel Order Established among us." From Delaware, in 1733, Jacob Henderson, an Anglican minister, informed the Bishop of London that members of the Church of England in that colony were well disposed towards him, but had a fear of being brought under the "Church establishment" in neighboring Maryland. Henderson also noted that "a cry ... against the forty pounds [of tobacco] is a great engine of the Quakers to attract people to Pennsylvania's interest." Inhabitants of the Anglican colonies in the South, especially Maryland, manifested plenty of dissatisfaction with their established clergy, but this did not cause them to question establishment as such.[34]

At the middle of the century, non-Anglicans in New York resumed their earlier quarrel with the Church of England about the nature of that colony's establishment. This dispute proved the prelude to the all-out conflict between Anglicans and non-Anglicans that would sweep the colonies in the late colonial years.

Since the mid-1740s, New York had been raising money to fund a college. By the early 1750s, the legislature was ready to proceed with the venture; but the questions of which religious denomination should control the new institution and what kind of religious activities should be carried on there gave rise to a controversy that blanketed the colony in a paper storm. The controversy is of interest here primarily because opponents of an Anglican-dominated King's College presented themselves as combatting an establishment of religion. Trinity Church had offered land for the proposed school on the condition that the institution would be governed by the Church of England. Anglican writer William Smith pointed out the appropriateness of such an arrangement, inasmuch as his church enjoyed "a preference by the Constitution of the Province."[35]

Against the very definite drift of the embryo college towards Anglicanism, a young lawyer named William Livingston, a Presbyterian and graduate of Yale, set in motion in 1753 a public protest that occupied New York's attention for several years. Livingston and two associates, William Smith, Jr., and John Martin Scott, came to be known as the Triumvirate, on whose activities an Anglican historian later commented:

> Had a new government, tyrannical, arbitrary, and despotic, been erected, the popish religion established, the presbyterians burned at the stake and the Episcopalians their persecutors, more noise could not have been made, than was now excited about this charter [for the proposed college].

To heighten anti-Anglican feeling in the province, the Triumvirate republished Thomas Gordon's anti-clerical essay "The Craftsman" and Francis Makemie's narrative of his persecution by Governor Cornbury.[36]

To the modern reader, the Triumvirate's rhetoric, especially that of Livingston, appears overblown, and the warning that a college under the tutelage of the Anglican religion would prove "an execrable source of the keenest and most complicated disasters" seems exaggerated. Certainly Livingston's raising the specters of the earlier New England persecution of witches and of the persecution of Quakers seems an exercise in hyperbole. His Cassandra-like warnings, however, were all designed to raise the alarm in the province and to convince its citizens that Anglican aggrandizement jeopardized their religious liberty. Indeed, given later insights into Anglican intentions and attitudes, the members of the Triumvirate had reason to be worried. Samuel Johnson, future rector of the college, writing to the Archbishop of Canterbury in 1753, referred to the proposed school as a "Seminary of the Church though with a free and generous toleration for other denominations" and equated all opposition to such a scheme with deism and freethinking. Johnson also wrote that "for the establishment [of the Anglican Church] throughout our American dominion, there are strong motives of various kinds."[37]

Livingston bent his every effort to keeping the Church of England from gaining control over the proposed college. He represented such control as an establishment of Anglicanism there and the first step on the road to a general establishment throughout the colony. The members of the Triumvirate employed the term "establishment" in the pejorative sense used in New England, implying that it would entail religious tests to exclude all non-Anglicans from public life, and would introduce tithes and bishops. Further, they wished to prove that the statutes establishing the Church of England in the Mother Country did not extend to America, that the common law did not carry such an establishment, and that the colonial legislature had never established Anglicanism in New York.[38]

Livingston's opposition to an Anglican-dominated college was implacable. He was against it even if the college would admit students of other denominations. In fact, he even opposed the teaching of Divinity there. He declared that since the institution was to be supported by public funds, all should share equally in its benefits. The school would be a "civil Institution," not under the monopoly of any sect. Although his statements seem to anticipate the form of a modern secular college, the mental context that framed such sentiments in the middle of the eighteenth century differed drastically from that of the twentieth century. Thus Livingston would "always, for political reasons, exclude Papists." Furthermore, he allowed that he was "so far from opposing [religious worship] that I strongly recommend it."[39]

By religious worship in the college, Livingston meant

> ... that no religious Profession in particular be established in the College; but that both Officers and Scholars be at perfect Liberty to attend any Protestant Church at their Pleasure respectively: and that the Corporation be absolutely inhibited the making of any By-Laws relating to Religion, except such as compel them to attend Divine Service at some Church or other, every Sabbath, as they shall be able, lest so valuable a Liberty be abused and made a Cloak for Licentiousness. . . . that the whole College be Morning and Evening convened to attend public Prayer . . . as all Protestants can freely join in.

The authors of the passage above thought that religion would foster a sense of decorum, and, besides, twice-daily prayers provided an excellent method of taking attendance. Admitting the difficulty of finding a prayer acceptable to all, they gamely set about composing and publishing one, a process that gave rise to much hilarity among their Anglican opponents.[40]

The modern mind tends to assume that the logical corollary to the statement "no religious Profession in particular [should] be established" is that religion in general may or should be established, but that was not what the members of the Triumvirate assumed. They did not oppose a particular religion to religion in general in the sense of Protestantism, Catholicism, Judaism, or any other faith. Rather, they opposed a particular Protestant denomination to Protestantism in general, which latter they did not equate with an establishment. To them, as to most eighteenth-century Americans, the notion of prayer and worship based on the Bible that was accepted by all Protestants did not amount to a general establishment, but constituted an essential foundation of civilization. Such others as Catholics or Jews did not impinge sufficiently on their lives to challenge that assumption.

In their contention that the act of 1693 had not set up an exclusive Anglican establishment, Livingston and his associates referred to the "Ministry established by the Act" and the "Establishment Act." They did not examine the nature of the establishment in New York, although they proposed to do so in several planned but never written issues of their newspaper, *The Independent Reflector*. Approving the system "by which the majority in each town was to elect and pay their own minister," Livingston noted that the act of 1693 "restricted no particular Protestant Denomination whatsoever," and that the ministers "inducted and established" were to be the people's choice.[41] Either it did not occur to him that—according to his reasoning—the system he approved of would violate religious liberty, by taxing a dissenting minority for the support of a minister elected by the majority, or, given his desire to oppose the Anglicans, it did not suit his purpose to consider that fact.

Ultimately, the ecclesiastical system set up by the law of 1693 was of little interest to either side. The Anglicans were intent on claiming an exclusive establishment for themselves. Livingston and his associates used the ambiguous law of 1693 to counter Anglican claims, not to argue for another kind of establishment. At one stage, *The Independent Reflector* made a passing comment that Presbyterianism was "in some sort established" at Harvard and Yale, but made no effort to explore what that entailed. These authors were also sufficiently uninformed as to state that Rhode Island had established Congregationalism, a piece of misinformation that one of them, William Smith, Jr., incorporated into his *History of New York*.[42]

The King's College affair, like previous controversies, aired the question of establishment without clarifying the term. Disputants continued to use the word to suit their purposes of the moment, and all of them demonstrated a considerable degree of inconsistency. When William Smith, Jr., wrote that "the body of the people, are for an equal, universal, toleration of Protestants, and utterly averse to any kind of ecclesiastical establishment," he meant that they opposed an exclusive Anglican establishment, but not necessarily the "Act that established a ministry in this [New York] and three other counties."[43]

Within their own communion, Anglicans showed little inclination to believe their own rhetoric. Church of England ministers might hold that they enjoyed an automatic establishment throughout the colonies, but not even the most fervent Anglican protagonist ever claimed that tithes and ecclesiastical courts extended automatically to America. In 1754 an Anglican apologist admitted that the Church of England was only "in some sort established" in his province, and Samuel Johnson and Archbishop Seeker corresponded on the necessity of establishing the Anglican Church in America, thereby hardly indicating belief in Anglican argument that the Church of England establishment automatically extended to the colonies. Writing to Henry Carver, Anglican rector of Trinity Church in Boston, Archbishop Seeker asked whether the Congregational Church was established in Massachusetts, something Anglicans had held to be impossible and in violation of the king's prerogative. Seeker later plainly stated that only "in some Plantations" was the Church of England "the established church," thus recognizing a reality that the vast majority of colonists had long since perceived.[44]

The commotion caused by the Triumvirate over the form of religion to be adopted at King's College was followed by further and wider-ranging differences between Anglicans and the rest of the colonists. In 1763 East Apthorp, an Anglican minister at Cambridge, Massachusetts, wrote a defense of the practice of sending Anglican missionaries to areas already well supplied with other Protestant ministers, such as New England. His pamphlet set off a whole string of attacks and rebuttals, including a defense of Congregationalism by Jonathan Mayhew, who, almost in passing, noted that "our [Congregational] churches seem to have a proper legal establishment."[45]

Several Anglican commentators replied to Mayhew, among them Henry Carver, who fastened onto the Congregational claim to an establishment. Carver's examination of that claim constituted nothing more than the standard Anglican argument that the Church of England enjoyed an exclusive establishment throughout the colonies, but it prompted Mayhew to respond at length as to the nature of the Massachusetts establishment. Mayhew contended that if other churches were legally established in his colony, then the Anglican church could not enjoy an exclusive establishment. The colony had not established a "provincial church," but only "protestant churches of various denominations." As the kingdom of England contained two established churches, Massachusetts might have a hundred established churches if the people so chose.

Nevertheless, Mayhew went on to illustrate that the wording of the laws that referred to the "divine worship . . . Established by the laws of the Province" showed that the

> . . . legislature . . . supposed . . . that there was some particular manner of worship Established here, by way of eminence, or in preference to all others, particularly to that of the Church of England.

Next he warned that

> . . . it should be remembered . . . that the members and ministers of the Church of England are countenanced and encouraged; since it [the legislature] makes a legal provision for their maintaining the public worship of God in their own way.

Did Mayhew mean that the Church of England was also established in the province? He stated that laws made a "real and effectual establishment" that "more especially regarded protestant churches of one denomination," but provided a "legal method" for others to support their worship. The Anglican Church was not established in the colony by force of English law, but had the "support and encouragement of our provincial laws."[46]

Mayhew proved himself a true son of New England Puritanism in his ability to juggle the realities of both New England's ecclesiastical system and English power; in his skill at inferring possibilities, rather than drawing conclusions; and in his capacity for living with contradictory statements. Thus, according to his defense, all Protestant denominations could enjoy an establishment in the province; yet the Congregationalists were accorded a special position under the law. Anglicans did not have an exclusive establishment, but were "supported and encouraged." Did the privilege of collecting taxes from their own members constitute an establishment of Anglicanism in the Massachusetts sense? Mayhew might have liked English Anglicans to believe as much, but they would never be able to prove he had said so. Like his predecessors, he managed to defend Congregational preeminence without denying English prerogatives.

In the course of the controversy, Mayhew leveled against the Anglicans the accusation that the Society for the Propagation of the Gospel was really not out to convert the colonists, but rather to subject them to bishops. Within the next few years, the movement to oppose the sending of Anglican bishops to America would take the colonies by storm and contribute in no small way to the colonists' alienation from the Mother Country.

American fear of an Anglican episcopacy can be gleaned from the comments of a number of contemporaries. In 1765 the Reverend

William McGilchrist, an Anglican minister, wrote from Salem to the secretary of the Society that Americans believed that the introduction of bishops would inevitably bring ecclesiastical courts and tithes. A later comment by John Adams would corroborate McGilchrist's statement:

> If anyone supposes this [episcopal] controversy to have no influence on the great subsequent question, he is grossly ignorant. It spread an universal alarm against the authority of Parliament. It excited a general and just apprehension, that bishops and dioceses and churches and priests and tythes, were to be imposed on us by Parliament. It was known that neither the king, nor the ministry, nor archbishops, could appoint bishops in America without an Act of Parliament; and if Parliament could tax us, they could establish the Church of England here, with all creeds, articles, tests, ceremonies, and tythes, and prohibit all other churches, as conventicles and schism-shops.[47]

In 1767 John Ewer, Bishop of Llandaff, fueled the fire again in a sermon before the Society for the Propagation of the Gospel. Ewer declared that "instead of civilizing and converting barbarous Infidels, they [the Americans] became themselves Infidels and Barbarians," thereby ensuring that civility would take a back seat in the ensuing exchanges.[48] That same year, Thomas Bradbury Chandler, an Episcopal minister at Elizabethtown, New Jersey, issued, with the approval of a convention of Anglican clergy from that colony and New York, *An Appeal* to the American public, calling for and justifying Anglican bishops in the colonies.

Like other Anglican apologists, Chandler deemed that refusing Anglicans a bishop, who alone could make the full services of the Church of England available, violated the principles of religious liberty professed by his opponents. He asserted that the proposed bishops would exercise only spiritual power. No one, according to him, anticipated that tithes would be imposed to support such bishops; but he added—an egregious statement in the era of the Stamp Tax—that even if they were to be publicly supported, the tax required would amount to no more than four pence in every £100. Chandler's *Appeal* opened the final act of the long wrangle between colonial Anglicans and non-Anglicans.[49]

Whereas earlier battles had engaged Anglicans and Congregationalists, this one drew in a much wider segment of the colonists, blended with other colonial grievances against Britain, and kept Anglican clerics in conflict with the bulk of colonial opinion until the American Revolution. From 1768 to 1771, Chandler and Charles Chauncy of

Boston, in a series of pamphlets, exchanged arguments defending or attacking the *Appeal*. From New York, William Livingston joined in to support Chauncy. Writing this time as the "American Whig," Livingston touched off a voluminous newspaper controversy matched in quantity by Pennsylvania. The colonial dispute also spread to England, where it produced a separate series of controversial writings, some of which were published in America.[50]

The question of appointing bishops to the colonies impinged on the subject of establishment because colonists who opposed their appointment adamantly stated that as servants of an established church in England, bishops would bring with them more than spiritual authority. Newspaper articles especially trumpeted the belief that the introduction of bishops would be the beginning of forced religious conformity and tyranny both civil and religious. With equal fervor, Chandler continued to reiterate that they would have none but spiritual power.

In his replies to Chandler, Chauncy virtually ignored the use of the word "establishment" in its acceptable New England sense and concentrated on its pejorative connotation. In his first response, he hinted obliquely at the special status of Congregationalists in New England:

> The other denominations think they have as good a right as the Episcopalians, to the attention of those who have the management of public affairs; and in many of the Colonies, it is thought, they have in strict justice, a Peculiar right.

However, having touched so gingerly upon the New England establishment without naming it such, he went on to leave no doubt as to the kind of establishment of which he disapproved. In a statement that would be much quoted, he declared:

> We are in principle against all civil establishments in religion; and as we do not desire any such establishment in support of our own religious sentiments, or practice, we cannot reasonably be blamed if we are not disposed to encourage one in favor of Episcopal colonists.

By "civil establishments," Chauncy clearly meant establishment of a "mode of worship, government, or discipline" that he later called a "STATE ESTABLISHMENT," a term he insisted on printing in block capitals. The introduction of bishops would introduce an establishment, according to the "true idea of the word." Unfortunately, he did not concern himself with defining this true idea, and Chandler, though he expressed disbelief that Congregationalists had become opposed in principle to all establishments of religion, failed to make him do so.[51]

Heretofore, Congregationalists, intent on denying Anglican claims to predominance in New England, had insisted that they represented the establishment. As the American Revolution approached, however, "freedom" became the watchword, and "establishment" became another synonym for English tyranny. Consequently, New Englanders would begin to play down or even deny that their system amounted to an establishment at all—a trend that Chauncy's pamphlets inaugurated. Moreover, Chauncy's work associated the region firmly with the overall attack on the Anglican establishment that was also being carried out in England by Dissenters there.[52]

During the late colonial period, the Anglican Church found itself the center of dispute in several other colonies. In Anglican Virginia a proposal to petition for a bishop split the clergy into uneven groups, with those in favor of it in the minority. The House of Burgesses clearly supported the majority. Virginian Anglicans kept a jealous control over their church and resented any extension of English authority.[53] South Carolina produced no such specific controversy, but the comments of contemporaries indicated a similar opposition to bishops. Ezra Stiles heard from a dissenting minister in South Carolina that many in the province were prepared to "turn Dissenter in a Body" if an Anglican bishop came to the colony.[54] In North Carolina Governor William Tyron in 1765 secured an establishment act for the Anglican Church that attempted to put it on a more secure footing than hitherto and provide better support for the clergy. Given the colony's lack of Church of England ministers, the preponderance of dissenters, and their hostility to the Anglican Church, the act remained more an irritant to the majority of the population than a help to the Church of England.[55]

In Maryland other problems connected with the Anglican Church overshadowed the question of bishops. During the early 1770s, discontent that had been brewing, especially in the lower house of the legislature, came to a boil and resulted in legislation setting up a special court of ministers and laity to discipline offending clergy. Critics of the clergy also produced the argument that the establishment act, since it had been signed after the death of King William, was invalid, leaving the clergy with no legal claim to forty pounds of tobacco per person in the colony. Even the proponents of this argument, however, clearly stated that they approved of an established church and wanted only to revise the method of public support for the clergy, not abolish it.[56]

In New York Anglican claims still exercised the citizenry. As in the past, opponents of the Church of England remained more united in their condemnation of these than in agreement with each other. In 1769 an anonymous writer issued a broadside detailing a long list of Anglican offenses against the people of the colony, including a claim that the Episcopalians had in 1693 procured an act for "establishing episcopacy" in four counties in violation of the "fundamental articles . . . upon which the country was settled," i.e. the provision by which each town was to elect and support its own ministers. In 1772 another anonymous author referred to the Anglican claim to an establishment as a "ridiculous pretence." Both writers accepted the system whereby the majority of each town would select the minister and raise taxes for his support. Neither considered the plight of minorities under such a system, but concentrated wholly on opposing Anglican contentions. In 1774, in an ultimate reaction to the town of Jamaica's refusal to support its Anglican minister, Governor Tyron declared that "the National Church of England is established within this colony."[57]

As it had all through the colonial period, New England continued to produce by far the greatest number of statements about establishment of religion. New Englanders' thoughts about their own establishments ran on a track that did not intersect with the one that carried their opinion of an Anglican establishment. However, after Chauncy's fierce and well-publicized condemnation of any "STATE ESTABLISHMENT," New England preachers and writers, although they continued to refer to their own establishment, emphasized the dimension of freedom within it.

Identifying their own establishments with a system for promoting public morality and the support of religion, ministers lauded the magistrates for providing "so excellent an Establishment." They criticized those who would destroy such a liberal system and contended that dissenters had no more right to be exempted from church taxes than from any other tax. They contrasted the "Lordliness and Arrogance" of the Church of England and its "narrow" and "ungenerous" principles that excluded others because of "modes and ceremonies" with their own establishment based on "generous catholic principles."[58]

In 1773 the Reverend Izrahiah Wetmore, minister at Stratford, delivered before the Connecticut General Court a sermon that exemplified the ambiguity that characterized New Englanders' thought on an establishment of religion. Wetmore, however, carried that ambiguity to such lengths that his sermon bordered on incomprehensibility. He began by telling his audience that Providence intended government "chiefly and principally as a Means to promote the Church of Christ." He then proceeded to assert that the Church should "stand on her own foundation," and that "establishment will only sink her." Truth needs not the "charms of earthly Grandeur." Resorting to history, he held up as an example the early Church, which needed no "national Establishment, no royal Supports, no settled Revenues, no Civil Power to aggrandize and adorn it."

The coming of Constantine had destroyed all this pristine splendor. Wetmore concluded by quoting Chauncy's statement opposing establishments in principle.

In the Appendix to the printed version of this sermon, Wetmore noted that "some affected surprise at the above statements." By unqualifiedly condemning an establishment of religion in the English sense in the language usually reserved for outsiders, without at the same time lauding the liberty provided by the New England form of establishment, he confused his hearers. Reading the work, one might think he was taking a parting shot at the Connecticut establishment before going off to join the Baptists. The sermon represented no such thing. Wetmore was and remained a minister of the standing order.[59]

No lesser personages than Samuel and John Adams found they could not ignore the realities of the Massachusetts establishment, no matter how much they would have liked to do so. At the First Continental Congress in 1774, New England Baptists confronted the Massachusetts delegation and complained of their treatment at the hands of Congregationalist authorities. The Pennsylvania Quakers acted as hosts for the complaining Baptists and, having long memories, lost no opportunity to embarrass the delegation by citing past grievances of their own. According to Massachusetts delegate Robert Trent Paine, Pennsylvania Quaker Isaac Pemberton "bellowed loud on N. England persecution and Hanging of Quakers &c."

In theory Massachusetts had long exempted Baptists from paying towards the support of the established churches, but in fact the authorities—particularly after the increase in the number of Baptists there following the Great Awakening—found all kinds of legal loopholes through which to harass them and extract taxes from them for the support of the Congregational system. In turn, through the Grievance Committee of the Warren Association, which they formed in 1769, Massachusetts Baptists had waxed increasingly more vocal against the whole ecclesiastical arrangement in the colony. Thus the Massachusetts delegates to the Congress found themselves pushed into the limelight and forced to defend their province's record on religious freedom.

By his own account, John Adams responded that the "laws of Massachusetts were the most mild and equitable establishment of religion that was known in the world, if indeed they could be called an establishment." Isaac Backus, principal spokesman and agent for the Warren Association, remembered Adams as saying that "there is indeed an ecclesiastical establishment in our province, but a very slender one, hardly to be called an establishment."[60] Paine, however, probably more accurately recorded the sentiments of the Massachusetts delegation when he wrote disgustedly that the Baptists ignored real persecution in the South and trumpeted trifling incidents in New England, adding, "we shall not forget this work of our Brother Esau."[61]

What came through most clearly in both Adams's and Backus's records of the encounter at the Congress was the acknowledgment but simultaneous soft-pedaling of the Massachusetts establishment. In his *Diary* Backus noted the contradiction between John Adams's deprecation of that establishment on the one hand, and, on the other, his statement that "we might as well expect a change in the solar systim as to expect they would give up their establishment." Earlier, in 1773, Backus had asserted that Congregationalists maintained an establishment, and the Warren Association, though it did not mention the word "establishment" specifically, clearly asserted that the Congregational churches dominated the Baptists and robbed them of their goods for clerical support.[62]

Although Backus's most trenchant criticism of the Massachusetts ecclesiastical system would await the years following the Revolution, he had by 1775 grasped the tension between the reality and the public pose of its defenders, a tension that showed itself in such contradictory remarks and statements as those of John Adams. An historian, Backus earlier had pointed out manifestations of the same inconsistency as far back as Cotton Mather's time. He quoted the statement from Mather's *Ratio Disciplinae*, published in 1726, declaring that each town could select a minister by majority vote, but then went on to quote further from Mather to "show that they [Congregationalists] did not intend ever to have such a case here."[63]

John Adams's comments touched on the major themes of the discussions of establishment of religion in colonial New England. When he compared the devotion of Massachusetts to its establishment to the constancy of the solar system, he did indeed grasp reality. Neither did his reference to "their establishment" miss the mark. Spokesmen for New England might try to placate English authorities with the theory that any Protestant church could be established there, but Cotton Mather's "Our Way" represented the Congregationalist way. When Adams described the system as "mild and equitable," hardly an establishment at all, he put his finger on the pulse of the times.

Earlier, when Anglicans had attacked the authenticity of the Congregationalist establishment, its defenders did not doubt that it constituted a proper one, and that Puritans, whose ancestors had founded the colony, had indeed not become "dissenters in their own country." Later, when the colonies raised a hue and cry against English tyranny,

New Englanders no longer needed to defend their institutions from Anglican aggression, but rather to disassociate themselves from ecclesiastical tyranny. Therefore, they heightened a theme that had been present throughout the century, i.e. the mildness of their own establishment as distinct from "civil," "STATE," "national," or "provincial" ones.

New England authorities believed that their establishments amounted to the provision of public worship and support for clergy, the teachers of religion and morality. They dismissed out of hand the assertions of Baptists and Separatists that Massachusetts and Connecticut imposed articles of faith and modes of worship. Their mild and tolerant systems had nothing in common with the tyrannizing English establishment, the one Adams identified with "creeds, tests, ceremonies, and tithes." For colonial Americans, however, creeds referred to the Thirty-Nine Articles to which the Church of England forced adherence; tests connoted the oaths and tests that excluded English Dissenters from civil and political life; ceremonies brought to memory Archbishop Laud's attempts to impose "Popish" rites on their Puritan ancestors; and tithes brought visions of bishops living in luxury. Despite their own experiences to the contrary, Southerners also entered the Revolution thinking of an establishment of religion in similar terms.

In 1773 the Quebec Act, guaranteeing to the Catholic clergy in Quebec "their accustomed dues and rights, with respect to such persons only as shall profess the said religion," set up the same kind of ecclesiastical system there that Congregationalists had purported existed in Massachusetts and Connecticut. Nevertheless, New Englanders, right along with the rest of the colonists, reacted to the Quebec Act with frenzied accusations that it imposed tyranny and an establishment of Catholicism and endangered the entire continent.[64]

Every colonial government demanded religious tests for office, and many of them levied religious taxes, even if these were not strictly tithes. To most Americans, however, their own religious qualifications for office bore no resemblance to English tests, but rather served simply as a means of excluding atheists and enemies of civilized society. Thus, whether they had or had not supported an establishment, they could view with horror what Chauncy labeled a "STATE ESTABLISHMENT," a term that conjured up the tyranny of the English system, with its tests and modes of worship, and reject it as alien to America and a threat to American freedoms. By the end of the colonial era, that image of establishment of religion formed the dominant one in their minds and imaginations.

6

Religion and Government in Revolutionary America
Part I: The Southern States

During the Revolutionary era, every colony-turned-state altered the Church-State arrangements it had inherited from colonial times. Insofar as these developments illuminate what contemporaries took "free exercise of religion" and "establishment of religion" to mean, they cast a corresponding light on what Congress and the states understood by the clauses in the First Amendment to the United States Constitution that stipulate "Congress shall make no law respecting an establishment of religion, or prohibiting the free exercise thereof."

From the outbreak of the American Revolution to the adoption of the federal Constitution, no state surpassed Virginia in speed and extent of alterations in Church-State relations. By 1786 it had finally settled on an arrangement between Church and State that abolished test oaths for office, eliminated state restrictions on religious freedom, and put churches on a purely voluntary footing. Most other states did not soon accept the same definitive solution, especially of abandoning tests, so Virginia cannot be said to have served as a model for them; but in the nature and variety of the internal debates that led up to its ultimate decision, Virginia was a microcosm of the ferment taking place throughout the new nation.

On the eve of the Revolution, the Old Dominion was exhibiting a most illiberal attitude toward religious liberty, and Baptists, whose numbers from 1765 had increased by leaps and bounds, were with good cause raising the cry of religious persecution. Baptist ministers often fiercely attacked Anglicanism as a false religion. They either refused to apply for licenses to preach or, when they did acquire them, failed to confine their preaching to authorized locations. More galling to the Virginia power structure than their specific doctrinal stands was their lack of social conformity. Thus a Baptist apologist, David Thomas, found himself defending his fellow evangelicals against charges that they would not associate with other denominations, were schismatics, and lacked both education and refinement. Almost fifty Baptist ministers had landed in jail because of their unpopularity, some of them suffering such imprisonment as late as the start of the Revolution.[1] In attempts to redress Baptist grievances, neither Baptists themselves nor the Virginia authorities extended the idea of religious freedom beyond the bounds of the Act of Toleration of almost a century before.

In 1776, however, Virginia rejected toleration as an acceptable framework for Church and State. In the Virginia Convention's Declaration of Rights, the new state rejected the proposition that "all men should enjoy the fullest toleration in the exercise of religion" in favor of James Madison's proposed guarantee of the "free exercise of religion." Given his choice, Madison would also have had the Declaration provide that "no man or class of men ought, on account of religion to be invested with peculiar emoluments or privileges."[2]

In the same vein, Thomas Jefferson, while attending the Continental Congress in Philadelphia in 1776, worked on a projected constitution for his state that included the provision that no person "shall . . . be compelled to frequent or maintain any religious service or institution."[3] Either that statement or Madison's on "emoluments or privileges," had it been adopted, would have ended any establishment of religion in Virginia; but both were too advanced for their day. Patrick Henry, who introduced Madison's proposal before the Convention, when asked if its intent was to disestablish the Anglican Church in Virginia, "disclaimed such an object."[4]

The Virginia Convention believed that free exercise of religion could co-exist with an establishment of religion and stated plainly that the Church of England remained established in the state. Indeed, from the start of hostilities with Britain, the Convention felt itself at liberty to inform that church as to which ruler to pray for and how to conduct itself. At the fall session of 1776, it busied itself regulating the vestries' support and the property of the "Church by Law established."[5]

Virginia's lawmakers nevertheless realized that their concept of an establishment of religion would have to be altered in some respect if it were to square with the provision in the state's Declaration of Rights for free exercise of religion. An establishment entailing enforced contributions from all citizens for the support of one church would obviously violate such freedom. Thus they exempted all dissenters from payments to the Anglican Church. This, of course, created the problem of determining who was an Anglican—since by merely declaring themselves dissenters, Anglicans could escape paying their own ministers. The Convention solved this difficulty by postponing it—suspending the collection of all ministerial taxes until the following session. In fact, the legislature continued the suspension from one session to the next until 1779, when it abolished such taxes altogether.[6]

In the decade between 1776 and 1786, the question of how religion would be supported in Virginia, whether voluntarily or by a "general assessment," elicited "great varieties of Opinions."[7] The source of the term "general assessment" is obscure; but the idea constituted a minor variation of the system that supposedly existed in Massachusetts and Connecticut, and that non-Anglicans had claimed existed in four New York counties. Virginia's proposed general assessment would have taxed everyone for the support of religion, permitting each taxpayer to designate the minister to whom he wished his contribution allocated. Discussions of Church and State in Virginia soon began to revolve around the need for such a system, its feasibility, and its compatibility with free exercise of religion.

Anglican defenders of tax-supported religion concentrated on protection of the status quo. They emphasized their contractual rights and society's need for an established religion, and they pointed to a history of 150 years of mild and enlightened ministry by learned ministers in the colony.[8] From 1776 on, however, Anglican voices were submerged in a sea of protests from dissenters seeking the elimination of ecclesiastical taxes.

The petition of the Lutheran congregation at Culpeper to the Virginia Convention in October 1776 mentioned past hardships and requested that members of the congregation "may hereafter be exempted from further payment of Parochial Charges, other than sufficient to support our own Church and Poor." Other petitions, from Albemarle, Amherst, and Buckingham counties, were almost identical in content—asking that "every Religious Denomination may stand on an equal footing, be supported by themselves, independent of each other." These exhortations, seeking only specific relief from an immediate and chafing burden, might be read as favoring a general assessment, but in all probability, they did not.[9]

Certain other petitions to the Convention, however, especially from Presbyterians and Baptists, did present a comprehensive view of

Church-State relations. One from "Sundry Inhabitants of Prince Edward County," for example, advanced the gospel of individualism, asking that "every tax upon conscience and private judgment [be] abolished, and each individual left to rise or sink by his own merit."[10] Only two years earlier, in 1775, a Presbyterian petition from Bedford County, asking for incorporation for their church, had stated that the petitioners would cheerfully continue to support the Church of England. With the outbreak of the Revolution, however, Presbyterians threw off this mask of deference and helped lead the fight against state support for Anglicanism.[11]

Presbyterianism was the established religion of Scotland, and Presbyterians in the colonies had inherited no strong voluntary tradition, even though their churches in America were for the most part supported by voluntary contributions. When Jefferson in his autobiography commented with reference to them that "some of our dissenting allies, having now secured their particular object," of exemption from paying taxes toward the support of the Anglican Church, had taken up the cause of a general assessment, he was recalling a later struggle, because in the petitions they submitted to the Virginia legislature in 1776 and 1777, Presbyterians unequivocally opposed a general assessment.[12] Although they had exhibited little opposition to religious taxes during the colonial period, they now viewed any scheme for state support of religion as a cover "to revive the old establishment," and they requested that "dissenters of every denomination ... be exempted from all taxes for the support of any church whatsoever."[13] Certainly, they had valid reason to fear the old establishment. As late as 1778, Anglicans submitted a petition to the legislature proposing that although "dissenters" should be tolerated and exempt from taxes, their ministers should be strictly regulated and the "Preeminence" of the Anglican Church should be maintained and its ministers financially supported by the state.[14]

Baptists unequivocally opposed a general assessment as detrimental to religion:

> If, therefore, the State provide a Support for Preachers of the Gospel, and they receive it in Consideration of their Services, they must certainly when they Preach act as Officers of the State, and ought to be Accountable thereto for their Conduct, not only as Members of Civil Society, but also as Preachers.[15]

They linked a general assessment not to establishment, but to a violation of religious liberty: "Farewell to the last Article of the Bill of Rights! Farewell to the 'free exercise of Religion'!." Jefferson, for secular rather than religious reasons, had implied the same linkage when, in his proposed constitution for Virginia, he coupled "full and free liberty of religious opinion" with the statement that no one should "be compelled to frequent or maintain any religous institution."[16]

Although some supporters of a general assessment were doubtless simply facing reality and settling for half a loaf instead of the full one they would have preferred, i.e. the old Anglican establishment, many of them did not fall into that category. In December 1777 "sundry inhabitants of the county of Caroline" drew up a well-reasoned petition that matched in logic and persuasiveness anything that had been issued by the anti-assessment forces. They approved of exemption for all non-Anglicans from taxes for the support of the Church of England "as founded on the principle of justice and propriety, and favorable to religious liberty"; but then, citing Virginia's Declaration of Rights that "public worship is a duty we owe to the Creator and Preserver of mankind, and productive of effects the most beneficial to society," they argued that the legislature should promote such worship for the good of society, "without prescribing a mode or form of worship to any." They went on to point out that public worship cost money; that without a public levy, some would shirk their duty, causing a disproportionate burden to fall on other citizens; and that without public taxes, men of "genius and learning" would not enter the ministry.[17]

If the authors of the Declaration had used that religious language in order to allay suspicions that they were anti-religious, they would have been guilty of a practice Baptists and many other evangelicals abhorred, i.e. the use of religion to achieve political ends. On the other hand, if they had seriously meant to acknowledge the existence of a "Creator" and a "duty" due him, supporters of assessment could logically ask what right the State had to stipulate such a moral obligation if it allowed its citizens to ignore it.

Proponents of a general assessment accepted the "duty" and proposed that the State see to it that everyone fulfilled it, without forcing anyone to follow a particular way of worship. They believed that religion was absolutely necessary to sustain the moral fiber of society, and that the state should promote it as a means to that end. Evangelical opponents of a general assessment agreed on the indispensability of religion, but they viewed it primarily in terms of "conversion," rather than moral "duty." For them the cause of true religion could be furthered only by the grace of God, and State attempts to advance it would result in the creation of a bureaucratic state religion.

Although the opponents of assessment proclaimed that the State should not help religion at all, many of them simultaneously believed that society should be generally Protestant and that the State should see to it that the Sabbath was observed and the Bible respected. Because the vast majority of the populace concurred in these beliefs, they were not forced to confront the tension in their position.

In 1779 Jefferson's bill "for Establishing Religious Freedom," designed to place religion on a completely voluntary basis, came before the Virginia Assembly, but did not pass. Later that year, the Assembly considered a very different proposal—a bill providing for a general assessment. This bill monopolized public comment, although its backers often focused as much on criticizing Jefferson's proposal as on pushing their own.[18]

The process of drawing up a general assessment bill demonstrated the narrowness of its proponents' views. Having championed religion as the bulwark of a stable society, they now revealed that by religion they meant Christianity. Their bill proposed that the "Christian Religion" be the established religion of the state. Where the Virginia Declaration of Rights had guaranteed the free exercise of religion, the 1779 assessment bill allowed to be "freely tolerated" only those who acknowledged one God, a future state of reward and punishment, and the necessity for public worship. It further specified that to be recognized by the state, a church must subscribe to five articles, including a belief in the New Testament, thus excluding Jews and Deists. Finally, it provided in detail for the collection of ministerial taxes and their disbursement to the different designated Christian sects.

A writer for the *Virginia Gazette* justified the exclusion of "Jews, Mahomedans, Atheists or Deists" on the ground that Christians, as the vast majority, could define the common good for the benefit of themselves and others. If all benefited, then excluded minorities could no more complain about paying taxes for religion than they could about taxes for the support of judges, construction of bridges, etc.[19] Unpersuaded by these arguments, the legislators shelved the 1779 assessment bill.

The war against the British preempted Virginia's energy and attention until the advent of peace in 1783. Late in that year, however, a petition from Lunenburg County asked the Virginia legislature for a "general and equal contribution for the support of the clergy," in order "to promote religion and [for] the propagation of the Gospel." More petitions favoring a general assessment followed in 1784 from several areas of the state. Petitioners from Isle of Wight County affirmed that they were "thoroughly convinced that the prosperity and happiness of this country essentially depends on the progress of religion" and noted that "whatever is to conduce equally to the advantage of all should be borne equally by all."[20]

The movement for a general assessment benefited not only from such reasoned-out justifications as the inability of the republic to survive without religion, but also from a common sense traditional approach to the subject. George Washington's sentiments illustrated this. In 1785 he wrote to George Mason:

> Altho no man's sentiments are more opposed to any kind of restraint upon religious principles than mine are, yet I must confess, that I am not amongst the number of those who are so much alarmed at the thought of making people pay towards the support of that which they profess, if of the denomination of Christians or declare themselves Jews, Mahometans or otherwise, and thereby obtain proper relief.[21]

Washington held more expansive views than most assessment supporters, in that he looked beyond the confines of Christianity.

For the most part, supporters of a general assessment made few attempts to confront the difficulties inherent in their position. If religion in itself promoted civic virtue, it stood to reason that any religion would do the same. However, if only Christianity could achieve that goal, then they would have to define it, thereby legislating articles of faith. Richard Henry Lee, an advocate of assessment, saw the problem but thought that any religion should be supported in order to promote morality. For him the Declaration of Rights only took away the power to force "modes of faith" and "forms of worship," not the general ability to promote all religion.[22]

Nevertheless, most assessment supporters continued to identify religion with Christianity. So, too, did many of their opponents, who opposed State financial aid to religion, but who had divorced such aid from other types of State assistance. For instance, a law settling a long-standing grievance of non-Anglicans about the performance of marriages dealt only with "any ordained minister of the gospel in regular communion with any society of Christians." The limitation here represented less a desire to exclude Jews and non-Christians from their religious rights than the unconscious assumption of the vast majority of Virginians that religion and Christianity were synonymous.[23]

A second general assessment act, introduced in 1784 and championed by Patrick Henry, proved much simpler than the 1779 measure. Relying on the reasoning that

> . . . Christian knowledge hath a natural tendency to correct the morals of men, restrain their vices, and preserve the peace of society, which cannot be effected without a competent provision for learned teachers, . . .

it proposed that all be taxed for the Christian denomination of their choice, and that those taxes not designated for any specific denomination be allocated to education.[24] It further stated that these provisions did not violate "the liberal principle heretofore adopted" that abolished "all distinctions of preeminence amongst the different societies or communities of Christians." The authors of the 1784 bill thus "Christianized" the free exercise clause of the Virginia Declaration of Rights.

This new proposal for an assessment apparently enjoyed broad-based support throughout Virginia. Madison noted in January of 1785 that when the bill was introduced into the legislature the previous year, Presbyterian laity in the western part of the state were opposed, but "the other Sects Seemed to be passive." Washington wrote of a "respectable minority" opposed to the bill.[25]

The clergy of the Hanover Presbytery now reversed their 1776 stand and adopted a proposal mildly in favor of assessment. In the first of two petitions submitted to the legislature in 1784, they concentrated on their grievance that the state continued to favor the Episcopal Church. The memorial complained of the "monopoly of the honors or rewards of government by any one sect of Christians more than the rest" and insisted that the legislature's task was to preserve "a proper regard to every religious denomination as the common protectors of piety and virtue."[26] One might attribute that to a desire on the part of the Presbyterian clergy to spread the "honours or rewards" of government among the differing religions; but to read into this particular document any plan for the future would be to overburden it. Essentially, the memorial was retrospective. It looked to the elimination of favors awarded the Church of England, rather than to enunciation of any plan for subsequent relations between government and the various churches.

The Presbyterian ministers' next petition, submitted in October of 1784, moved considerably beyond their irritation with Anglican privileges. This second petition declared that although religion should be free of state interference, its importance for morality and the public welfare alone could justify an assessment according to the "most liberal plan." Such a plan would have to be consistent with the Declaration of Rights, refrain from supporting religion as a "spiritual system," eschew articles of faith "not essential to the preservation of society," leave religious bodies in freedom in their internal government, and not "render the ministers of religion independent of the will of the people whom they serve."[27]

Few Virginians would have disagreed with the view that government should protect "piety and virtue"; but whether this should be accomplished by supporting ministers and churches divided them sharply. Jefferson suspected the Presbyterians of jumping on a bandwagon, but their ministers' petition may have represented realism—an attempt to temper what seemed inevitable; or opportunism; or a fairly consistent continuity with their own past.[28]

The task of leading the opposition to the 1784 assessment bill fell to James Madison. By this time, the opposing arguments had become almost standardized. As early as 1776, Jefferson had summarized many of them for himself.[29] Madison's notes on the 1784 bill included several of the same points. First, he focused on its limitation to Christians only and noted that this provision would embroil the state in religious dispute, e.g. in deciding which Bible was the true Christian one, as well as which doctrines were essential to Christianity and which could be deemed not absolutely so. In short, the bill would inevitably draw the state into attempts to define orthodoxy. He then proceeded to the opposing political theory, i.e. that religion, being excluded from the social contract, was consequently outside the "purview of Civil Authority."[30]

Although a number of contemporaries held that religion was not indispensable to a healthy society, and although Jefferson, in his *Notes on Virginia*, had included the famous statement "but it does me no injury for my neighbor to say there are twenty Gods, or no God. It neither picks my pocket nor breaks my leg," few Virginians would have agreed with them.[31] Madison, apparently accepting the necessity for religion, decided that the key question was the one he had propounded in a youthful letter to William Bradford: "Is an Ecclesiastical Establishment necessary to support civil society?" He decided it was not. Examples from history, the prosperity of colonies that lacked an established religion, the vitality of primitive Christianity, and the corruption of past establishments all pointed to the conclusion that religion should be voluntarily supported. Confronted with the potent argument of the opposition that the decline of established religion had given rise to Deism and irreligion, he attributed these maladies to the war and predicted that good laws and personal example would prove far more powerful antidotes to them than would a general assessment.[32]

Unable to bring about a legislative defeat of the 1784 assessment bill, Madison and his allies resorted to the tactic of postponement. At the same time, they managed to get the principal proponent of the measure, Patrick Henry, elected governor of Virginia. Having thus removed that obstacle to their cause from the legislature, they convinced the Virginia Assembly to submit the proposed bill to the voters for their opinion, a move that dissolved the passivity Madison had commented upon earlier. The electorate submitted ninety petitions opposing assessment and eleven favoring it.[33] This extraordinary outpouring of opinion brought to light a variety of positions on Church-State relations unmatched in any other state, and the controversy provided the general citizenry of Virginia with a sound schooling in relations between religion and government.

Madison's *Memorial and Remonstrance*, circulated in the spring of 1785, contained a formal outline of his private arguments against the assessment bill and has become the most famous document engendered by the dispute. Distributed throughout Virginia, it served as a catalyst for a coalescence of major opposition to the bill that eventually swept the state.[34] Beginning with the "unalienable right" of each citizen to "render to the Creator such homage, and such only, as he believes to be acceptable to him," it continued with a pithy exposition of the contract theory of society as completely excluding religion from government ken and retaining all matters of belief and worship to the individual as a natural right. Any interference by government in matters of religion would "overlap the great barrier which defends the rights of the people" and lead to tyranny. A general assessment would be a foot in the door leading to despotism. If the State could demand support for all religions, it could also demand support for a particular religion.

Madison reiterated his conviction that passage of an assessment bill would make the magistrate the judge of religious truth and allow him to "employ religion as an engine of civil policy," and he cited the experiences of the past as proof that where Church and State did comingle, they ultimately corrupted each other. Turning to a pragmatic approach, he warned that an assessment law would deter immigration to Virginia; cause some citizens to leave the state; and exacerbate the threat of civil disturbance, the seeds of which could be seen in the existing popular divison over the proposed legislation. In conclusion he declared that the proposed bill violated the free exercise of religion guaranteed by the Declaration of Rights, and he questioned whether any fundamental rights could be considered secure if the legislature could rescind that one.

In the centuries since its compostion, the *Remonstrance*, combining as it does political and religious arguments into a balanced and resounding whole, has gained in stature. Judging by the multitude of other petitions submitted to the legislature, however, it did not in its contemporary setting enjoy the preeminence it would acquire over time. On the contrary, the form of petition most favored by opponents of

assessment appeared roughly twice as often. Although it used much
the same arguments as the *Remonstrance*, it bore a heavier religious and
evangelical emphasis.

This petition asserted first that the bill in question violated "the
Spirit of the Gospel" and the "Bill of Rights." The witness of the
ministers of early Christianity had made that religion prosper for 300
years in the face of all opposition; but Constantine had corrupted
Christianity by establishing it. To the complaints that, in the face of
rampant Deism, "Religion is taking its Flight," the petitioners
responded that such might be happening not for want of "Religious
Establishments," but for lack of good laws to punish vices and
immoralities and an absence of "pious Examples" in government. The
state needed devoted ministers, not ministers devoted to worldly
interest. That the state needed no establishment of religion was clearly
evidenced by the prosperity of Pennsylvania, where one had never
existed. Moreover, an assessment law would violate the Declaration of
Rights by making those who did "not profess the christian Religion"
pay to support it. In summary these petitioners declared that

> ... if Establishment has never been a means of prospering the Gospel:
> if no more faithful Men would be introduced into the Mnistry by it; if
> it would not revive decay'd Religion and Stop the Growth of Deism: or
> Serve the purpose of Government: and if against the Bill of Rights. ...

then the legislature should leave religion free to be supported as
citizens wished.[35]

Other counties trumpeted a variety of warnings against assessment.
Memorialists from Amelia County inquired ironically whether Deists
would come to preaching. Those from Rockingham County cautioned
the legislature: "If you can do anything in Religion by human law you
can do everything." These latter petitioners pointed approvingly not
only to the Pennsylvania voluntary system, but, unexpectedly, to
Rhode Island's.[36]

By their support of the 1784 assessment bill, the clergy of the
Hanover Presbytery had vexed Madison, who claimed those Presbyterian ministers "have remonstrated against any narrow principles,
but indirectly favor a more comprehensive establishment." Later, still
angry, he wrote James Monroe that the Presbyterian clergy were "seen
as ready to set up an establishment which is to take them in as they
were to pull down that which shut them out."[37] In August 1785,
however, the "Ministers and lay Representatives of the Presbyterian
Church in Virginia" met at Bethel and issued a memorial against
assessment. Presbyterians throughout the state appended their names

to a resolution in support of the Bethel memorial, making this form of petition one of the most popular of the whole campaign.[38]

For their part, supporters of assessment stressed "Equal Right and Equal Liberty" and argued that assessment imposed not "the smallest coercion" to contribute to the support of religion. They continued to emphasize the benefits of religion and the obligation of all to pay for what helped all. They cited the "depravity of the human heart" and the need for aids to "public duty & private morality" and warned that voluntary support of religion would benefit only the "profligate and unworthy." They also stressed the importance of ministers' being able to maintain a "decent rank."[39]

In 1779 a petition from Amherst County in favor of assessment had suggested that Catholics be given a guarded toleration, but that together with "Jews, Turks, and Infidels," they be excluded from office. Proponents of assessment in 1785 stressed the impartial treatment envisioned by the proposed system—but only for all denominations of Christians.[40] Opponents of assessment, on the other hand, were by 1785 leaving such restrictiveness behind. A majority of their petitions now complained of injustices wrought upon non-Christians. Petitioners from Chesterfield County pleaded, "Let Jews, Mehametans, and Christians of every Denomination" find their home in Virginia.[41]

One of the last petitions, from Botetourt County and probably written by Presbyterians, illustrated the rapidity with which post-Revolution Virginians had learned of and come to advocate positions unheard of in the colonies since Roger Williams's time. This petition branded assessment "a flagrant violation of the Bill of Rights" and argued that the state would be supporting churches holding mutually opposing views. To support all these contradictory beliefs would be absurd, to decide "what sect of Christians are most Orthodox" would be improper. This petition further stated that "to compel Jews by law to support the Christian religion . . . is an arbitrary & impolitic usurpation which Christians ought to be ashamed of." The petitioners considered the freedom guaranteed by the constitution "a Duty we owe to ourselves and posterity to defend . . . from the outrage even of a majority."[42]

The citizens of Amherst County also publicly abandoned their earlier support of assessment and claimed that the plan "bothered the minds and consciences of every pious people." They commented on the danger that a state given power over religion could legislate religious matters at will, and they, too, objected to taxation of non-Christians for the support of Christianity.[43] Not since Samuel Sewall repented of his part in the Salem witch trials had there been so public a change of heart on a matter of Church and State in America.

This groundswell of opposition to the assessment bill enabled Madison and his supporters to get it set aside and to reintroduce Jefferson's act "for Establishing Religious Freedom." Formerly shelved by the legislature, that Act passed in 1786 by an overwhelming majority. The new statute prohibited any connection between religious belief and officeholding, forbade government to demand that its citizens attend or maintain any religious institution whatsoever, and decreed that any reversal of its provisions would violate the "natural rights of mankind."[44] Thus, in the decade following the Declaration of Independence, Virginians debated and clarified for themselves the meaning of the free exercise of religion. The law of 1776 that exempted dissenters in Virginia from contributing to the support of the Anglican Church held that "nothing shall be construed to affect or influence the question of general assessment, or voluntary contribution, in any respect whatever."[45] Ten years later, a majority of the people construed the free exercise clause of the Declaration of Rights to mean that religion had to be supported by voluntary means, and that state support of churches was incompatible with religious liberty.

No comparable development took place in the concept of establishment, although all parties to the Church-State dispute in Virginia employed the term frequently. At the beginning of the Revolution, Virginians used the term in its traditional meaning of an exclusive state preference for one sect or Church. In 1776 the Anglican clergy implied that no other system was feasible, that if all Christian denominations were "upon a level," one would inevitably seek dominance.[46] In 1780 the Reverend James Madison, president of the College of William and Mary, wrote to Ezra Stiles that public opinion found an establishment in favor of a particular sect incompatible with religious freedom.[47]

Petitioners from Culpeper County in 1779 asked the legislators for "a mode of religious establishment as they suppose will be beneficial to the people." Other petitions later requested "an establishment adopted under certain regulations," and "that the reformed Protestant religion, including the different denominations thereof . . . be established."[48] The unsuccessful 1779 assessment bill itself declared that the "Christian Religion shall . . . be the established Religion of this Commonwealth." The assessment bill of 1784 dropped the reference to an establishment, but there is no reason to believe that the omission was deliberate. Whether a general assessment constituted an establishment of religion was never a bone of contention. Some supporters of the 1784 assessment bill petitioned that Christianity be the "established

Religion" of Virginia. Others renounced "any partial or exclusive Establishment," but thought that Christianity should not be without a "legal Provision."[49]

By far the majority of references to establishment, however, emanated from opponents of a general assessment. Madison's *Memorial and Remonstrance* labeled it an establishment of Christianity and referred to the "establishment proposed." In a letter to James Monroe, he spoke of "the Bill for establishing the Christian Religion in this State," and he prepared notes for the "Debate on Bill for Religious Establishment proposed by Mr. Henry." In his anger at the Presbyterians' 1784 memorial, he accused them of seeking a "more comprehensive establishment."[50]

As noted heretofore, the form of petition most frequently submitted against the 1784 assessment bill stated that the spread of Deism was "not for want of Religious Establishment" and cited Pennsylvania, wherein "no such Establishment hath ever taken place" as proof of the point. Another batch of petitions in opposition to assessment asserted that the legislature should not "establish modes of Religion, nor the manner of supporting its teachers." From Pittsylvania County, petitions pleaded for liberty of conscience without any "Establishment," either "under the Form of a general assessment, or by any other mode." Chesterfield County objected to "establishing the Christian religion." Orange County pointed out that if the State could "establish all," it could then "establish any one Denomination."[51]

Amherst County warned that if the state could force a citizen to contribute to "any one Establishment," it could compel him to conform to "any other Establishment," and that the "General Establishment of Christianity by our laws" might lead to another "Partial Establishment." Amelia County petitioners saw assessment as "a snake in the grass" and a "stepping stone to an Establishment."[52] Taken at face value these statements would appear to indicate that Virginians changed and broadened the meaning of establishment from an exclusive state preference for one church to one that embraced many churches or Christianity in general. Such was not the case, however. They used the concept in diverse and loose ways, without much debate or without forming in their minds a clear distinction between an exclusive and a non-exclusive establishment.

Opponents of a general assessment tended to see it as merely a covert way of aiding the Anglican Church and, consequently, were little interested in the question of establishment at all. Supporters of an assessment showed an equal lack of interest in defending it as a basically different kind of establishment. Rather, they took pains to demonstrate its liberal, equitable, and non-discriminatory nature. Whether the assessment bill violated the Declaration of Rights, not what kind of establishment it represented or even whether it represented an establishment at all, proved to be the crux of the dispute.

In other religious matters, Virginia's legislature followed an equally cloudy path. As late as 1784, the laws of the state conferred power to marry only on those ministers "settled with some Christian congregation." The same year, another Virginia statute decreed that "any person . . . found labouring" on Sunday "shall forfeit the sum of ten shillings."[53] This law would, in effect, have forced a devout Jewish merchant to close his doors for two days every week, to his economic detriment; yet the bill "for Establishing Religious Freedom" guaranteed that "no man shall be . . . molested or bothered in his body or goods . . . on account of his religious belief."

In the same sheaf of bills that contained the statute on religious freedom, Madison included one calling for the proclamation of "Days of Public Fasting and Thanksgiving," which stipulated that on such appointed days, ministers were to perform "divine service and preach a sermon . . . suited to the occasion" or forfeit £50.[54] This particular statute failed to be enacted, and there can be little doubt that Madison personally disapproved of it; but the fact that he included it in the collection was significant. Such incidents proceeded from the habits of mind and unchallenged assumptions about society of a people overwhelmingly Protestant Christian. They did not constitute deliberate contradictions of enunciated principles, but were rather a result of the absence within the new state of dissenters who might challenge Virginia's government to bring all its practices into harmony with its precepts.

Disestablishment in South Carolina came about more easily, and with less social division than in Virginia. At Charleston in 1776, the South Carolina Provincial Congress drew up a constitution for the new state that left the Anglican establishment intact. The only reference to religion in this constitution occurred in the context of a complaint against Britain for allowing "the Roman Catholic religion . . . and an absolute government [to be] established" in Quebec.[55]

At the onset of the Revolution, religious tensions in South Carolina were notably less severe than in some of the other southern states, especially Virginia. The Anglican Church establishment, supported from the colony's general taxes rather than by individual contributions, had taken firm hold. The Great Awakening had made no significant inroads on the established church; nor did it heighten there, as it did in other colonies, the contrasts between different Protestant sects.

Nevertheless, in 1777, the Association of Baptist Ministers, meeting at Charleston, expressed its hope "for the prospect of obtaining universal Religious Liberty in the State."[56]

Also in 1777, some non-Anglicans submitted to the South Carolina legislature a "Petition of Dissenters," written by the Reverend William Tennent, a Presbyterian minister in Charleston. Tennent petitioned for the abolition of the Anglican establishment and asked

> . . . That there never shall be any establishment of any one religious denomination or sect of Protestant Christians in this state by way of preference to another; that no Protestant inhabitant of this state shall by law be denied the enjoyment of any civil right merely on account of his religious principles, but that all Protestants demeaning themselves peaceably . . . shall enjoy free and equal civil and religious privileges.[57]

The petition might appear to have been a request for a more general establishment, but that was not its intention. Tennent, in an address to the House of Assembly, noted that there was a proposal "to establish all denominations by law and to pay them all equally." This he branded a mere divisive scheme and "absurd as the establishment of all religions would in effect be no establishment at all. Rather, pointing to Pennsylvania, he advocated freedom and voluntary support of all religion as conducive to the economic prosperity of the state.

Tennent suggested that a plan "to establish all denominations by law and pay them all equally" represented only a device to pacify the main sets of dissenters and declared that "every plan of establishment must operate as a plan of injustice and oppression." Apparently, he was not at this time acquainted with the general assessment concept that had already been mentioned in Virginia. In his understanding, such an establishment would operate on the basis of majority vote, with the majority compelling the minority to help support the chosen minister.

Tennent's petition is of interest for a number of reasons. His opposition to the establishment of "one religious sect" in preference to others appeared to leave open the possibility of a more comprehensive establishment, yet he specifically denied any such intention. Secondly, his dismissing the plan to establish all religions as absurd threw some light on the New England ecclesiastical system. A native of New Jersey, he had been educated at Harvard and had served as Moses Dickinson's assistant in Norwalk, Connecticut. The arrangement he condemned so strongly was precisely the one that purportedly existed in Massachusetts and Connecticut. Presumably, he had benefited from it there, and the exemptions given to Baptists, Quakers, and Anglicans negated the faults he attributed to it. That he did not know this demonstrates how purely theoretical New England's broad comprehensive establishment really was. Jonathan Mayhew had written that "a hundred churches, all of different denominations . . . might be established." Such indeed was the theoretical interpretation of the law in Massachusetts. In reality, however, the Congregational churches enjoyed a *de facto* establishment there, and the theory enunciated by Mayhew remained so far from practice that a man who had been a Congregational minister in New England did not even understand it.

In the short time between Tennent's delivery of his speech before the South Carolina legislature and its publication, he learned of another and acceptable type of establishment. He noted that he had "the pleasure to find that a general establishment of all denominations is now thought of." According to the plan, no preference was given to one sect, but "Christianity itself is the established religion of the state." Under this system, each church would still be supported by the voluntary contributions of its members.[58]

The constitution of South Carolina, passed in 1778, established Protestantism. It restricted elective office to Protestants, and it laid down certain uncontroversial and general beliefs, reminiscent of the original charter, that all Protestant churches must subscribe to if they were to be incorporated by the state. It also specified that no person would be obliged to support any religion.[59]

In early 1777, Richard Hutson, son of Charleston's Congregational minister, wrote to Isaac Hayne that while General Gadsen "warmly supported" the dissenters' position, "Messrs. Lowndes and Pickney threw off the masque and argued strongly for having the church continued upon its former footing," but with a provision that no non-Anglican be obliged to pay for its support. The justification for this position was that "provisions of the poor" and "the management of elections" were interwoven with the establishment. The supporters of the establishment lost by a vote of seventy to sixty.[60] By 1790 South Carolina's provisions for freedom of religion matched Virginia's, except for a clause barring ministers from state elective office.[61] The state's unique establishment of Protestantism amounted only to a method for incorporating churches, and no church received public tax support.

The requirements for incorporation posed no difficulty for existing Protestant churches. Baptists, who in New England looked upon state incorporation with suspicion, decided to seek it in South Carolina. Baptists, Presbyterians, Independent Calvinists, Independents, Methodists, as well as Anglicans, all qualified as "corporated and Established" churches and were "to be deemed and regarded in law" as the established religion of the state.[62]

In 1778 the Reverend Thomas Reese, a Presbyterian minister in Salem, South Carolina, proposed a general assessment. Like his counterparts in Virginia, he argued for the usefulness of Christianity and held that a demand that citizens contribute to the minister of their choice constituted no violation of conscience and could be seen as a general tax for the public welfare. Reese failed to arouse any support or agitation for this plan, however.[63]

South Carolina's second constitution of 1790 omitted both an establishment and, apart from clergy, religious restrictions on office-holding. It guaranteed the "free exercise and enjoyment of religious profession and worship, without discrimination or preference." The practical effects of that provision showed up shortly. In 1791 the state "declared to be a body corporate . . . by the name . . . of Beth Elochim or House of God" the Jewish congregation in Charleston.[64]

North Carolina settled its relations between Church and State with hardly a murmur. During the colonial period, the colony's name had, unfairly, become a byword for irreligion. With still only five ministers in 1765, the Anglican establishment represented more of an irritant than a threat to non-Anglicans. Dissenters, as well as Anglicans, were obliged to belong to vestries, with the result that the few ministers in the area encountered endless difficulties in collecting their salaries. Thus the payment of ecclesiastical taxes constituted a minimal source of discontent among non-Anglicans. Even so, until the Revolution, North Carolina Quakers kept an accounting of monies paid for "hireling priests" and reported to London on amounts that were more symbolic than substantial.[65]

Other ecclesiastical provisions in North Carolina, such as restriction to Anglican clergy of the power to perform marriages, proved a far greater irritant to dissenting colonists. The depth of popular frustration with this rule no doubt accounted for the swiftness with which the new state addressed the subject and extended the power to all ministers.[66] As a state, North Carolina withdrew all favors from the Anglican Church, in effect disestablishing it. Petitions from Mecklenburg and Orange counties, however, indicated that while the inhabitants thought that religion should be supported voluntarily, they also believed that the state should be officially Protestant and exclude other religions, whether "Pagan or Papal," from office.[67]

North Carolina's constitution of 1776 reflected these sentiments. Like South Carolina, the state excluded ministers from the legislature and limited officeholding to Protestants. It guaranteed the free exercise of religion to all and declared that there "shall be no establishment of any religious church or denomination . . . in preference to any other," and it prohibited laws compelling people to attend any church or obliging any citizen to pay for any church or ministry "contrary to what he believes right, or has voluntarily and personally engaged to perform." Only the limitation of officeholding to Protestants caused a "warm debate"; but its enactment concluded disputes over Church and State in North Carolina. The state held to this narrow and exclusionary principle until well into the nineteenth century; although in practice, apparently, neither Jews nor Catholics were excluded.[68]

Once North Carolina formed its constitution, religious beliefs ceased to be a matter of contention in Church-State relations. In 1791 the ministers of the United Baptist Association, hard pressed to make a living, wrote that the people paid so little because they associated maintenance with the old oppressive establishment. Also, some "too hot ministers," in preaching against forced maintenance, had gone to extremes and condemned all maintenance. They reminded their people of the divine right of ministers to financial support, but no evidence remains that either they or other groups in North Carolina tried to have the government collect it for them.[69]

Georgia, too, inherited an Anglican establishment from colonial times; but, as in North Carolina, the establishment proved weak because of the lack of ministers, churches, organization, and resources. Last to be formed of the thirteen colonies, the settlement had come into being in 1732, when a group of philanthropists and speculators in England secured territory in which they hoped to rehabilitate Britain's debtors and unemployed workers. The grant envisaged a special position for the Church of England in the colony, and the trustees provided for Anglican ministers; but they also assisted settlers of other religions in various ways. In 1754 the colony was reorganized as a royal province, and although the Church of England was established in 1758, Georgia had—by the time of the American Revolution—only two settled churches, whose revenues came from a tax on liquor.[70]

The Georgia legislature of 1775 also took exception to the Quebec Act, calling it "little short of a full establishment to a religion which is equally injurious to the rights of sovereign and of mankind."[71] The Georgia legislators did not explain what would constitute a full establishment. However, their purpose was to damn the British government by accusing it of advancing Catholicism, not to explicate the meaning of Church-State relations.

When Georgians drew up a state constitution in 1777, they guaranteed "the free exercise" of religion to all, provided their religion "be not repugnant to the peace and Safety of the State" and decreed that none should have to support ministers "except those of their own profession." This made possible a general assessment type of support for religion. The constitution also excluded ministers from the legislature and limited officeholding to Protestants.[72]

After several attempts in the early 1780s to implement the constitutional permission granted citizens to support their own ministers, a law to that effect passed the legislature in 1785. The preamble to this statute explained that as the Christian religion redounded to the benefit of society, "its regular establishment and support is among the most important objects of legislative determination." The law then provided that counties having more than thirty families could choose a minister and raise a tax for his support. It also guaranteed all Christian sects "free and equal Toleration."[73]

These provisions apparently never went into effect, although the state, in a new constitution of 1789 that dropped all religious discrimination for officeholding, retained the provision allowing the possibility of a tax for religion. In 1798 Georgia's third constitution guaranteed free exercise to all and closed off the possibility of a general assessment by decreeing that all support for religion should be voluntary.[74] The state has left little record of its citizens' reactions to matters of Church and State during the revolutionary period, and whether the attempt to implement a general assessment failed through opposition or through lack of interest is impossible to judge.

Maryland abandoned its Church of England establishment early in the Revolution. Abandonment, however, did not equal abolishment. No state explicitly disestablished the Anglican Church, but those states that had inherited Anglican establishments devised other, usually incompatible, Church-State arrangements. Maryland devised the least clear system, and in dealing with the Anglican Church the Maryland state legislature retained habits of thought and action characteristic of its colonial predecessor. Before the Revolution, Maryland Anglicans had exhibited considerable hostility towards the established church; but critics of the establishment did not call for its overthrow. Their thrust was Erastian, not libertarian. The legislature wanted to secure a tighter grip on religous affairs within the colony, not to separate itself from them. Thus it managed, in the course of the 1770s, to set up a spiritual court, exercise control over clerical behavior, and pass a new bill setting clerical salaries.[75]

Late in 1776, Maryland's Constitutional Convention issued a Declaration of Rights and a constitution. The articles dealing with religion amounted to a curious assortment of contradictory sentiments. They limited officeholding to Christians and, indeed, were worded exclusively in terms of Christianity. Having stated the duty of every man to worship God in a manner "he thinks most acceptable," the Declaration then extended protection in their religious liberty to "all persons professing the Christian religion." The same article specified that none would be compelled to attend or support "any particular ministry" unless bound by contract, but gave the legislature power to "lay a general and equal tax for the support of the Christian religion."

Article 33 guaranteed to the Church of England all its property and declared that all acts for its support were still valid, but prohibited the counties from collecting the revenues decreed by them. This provision left much of the Anglican establishment in place, but eliminated the machinery to keep it functioning.[76] Having thus ended state support of the Anglican Church, Maryland subsequently addressed that church's future by passing, in 1779, a vestry act that involved the legislature in the minutiae of its organization. This act specified who could or could not serve on vestries, regulated the selection of ministers, excluded ministers from vestries, and even decreed penalties for Anglicans who refused to serve on a vestry if elected to do so.[77]

Aside from omitting a provision for tax support of ministers, the vestry act of 1779 did not differ in form from similar acts for the established church passed during the colonial period. This attitude that the Church of England stood in a special relationship to the state persisted, and in 1798 the legislature passed another vestry act similar to the one of 1779.[78] So Erastian was the temper of the Maryland legislators that in 1783 they proposed, given the absence of bishops, to appoint officers who would ordain clergy for the Anglican Church. The Reverend Samuel Keene had to plead with the Assembly not to take so drastic a step.[79]

In that same year of 1783, the affinity between the Protestant Episcopal Church—as the Church of England came to be known—and the state of Maryland caused a public controversy. The Episcopalian clergy asked the Assembly for permission to draw up a bill making changes in the Prayer Book and in the organisation of the Church.[80] The Reverend Patrick Allison, a Presbyterian minister in Baltimore, took exception to the Episcopalians' petition and accused them of looking for a special relationship with the government. Allison pointed out that the laws already gave them the right to do everything they were asking permission for.

Under the name "Vindex," Allison wrote that in order to allay suspicion, the Episcopalian ministers should renounce the aid of the civil power altogether.[81] Other writers joined him in condemning the Episcopal clergy for issuing the petition and the legislature for accepting it. However, the dispute resulted in little or no change. Ten years later, when he reissued his newspaper pieces as a pamphlet, Allison complained that even though the establishment had died with the Revolution, the marriage laws of the state still referred to the ministers of the Church of England and to those "ministers dissenting from the Church."[82]

The chief importance of the dispute about relations between the Episcopal Church and Maryland was that it publicly aired accusations of Episcopal pretensions to favor at a time when the legislature was getting ready to propose a general assessment promoted chiefly by those same Episcopalians. In 1780 a convention of Episcopal clergy had agreed on an assessment proposal to be sent to the various vestries for submission by them to the Assembly. The vestries duly sent in the petition, but the legislators postponed the matter for a "time of less distress."[83]

Supporters of a general assessment felt that the end of the war ushered in that less distressful time. In 1783 Governor William Paca asked the legislature to provide for the needs of all Christian ministers. Citing the social value of religion, Paca emphasized that his plan treated all branches of Christianity with complete equality.[84] The Protestant Episcopal Church, stressing the compatibility of an assessment with Maryland's Declaration of Rights in that it called for no exclusive privilege, supported the plan.

Later, in 1784, the Speaker of the House claimed that Marylanders submitted "numerous petitions" in favor of an assessment; but a critic of the assessment plan rejected this assertion, saying that just two vestries actually submitted them.[85] The legislature agreed to draw up a bill for the general support of Christian denominations; but because the proposed act produced such division within the House, the lawmakers decided to submit it to the voters for their consideration—though with strong recommendations for its passage.[86]

The assessment act levied a tax of indeterminate amount on the inhabitants of the state, to be paid to the ministers of their choice or to the poor. To be eligible for revenue from this source, a minister had to head a church consisting of more than thirty male adults living within "a reasonable distance." The bill also specified that anyone who declared himself to be a "Jew or Mahometan, or that he does not believe in the Christian religion . . . shall not be liable to pay any tax for himself in virtue of this act." The Assembly's recommendation for passage of the bill emphasized its compatibility with the Declaration of Rights in its support of all denominations of Christians "without preference or discrimination." The legislature also affirmed its "right and duty . . . to interpose in matters of religion, as far as concerns the general peace and welfare of the community."[87]

The Maryland Assembly had expected that opponents of the plan would call it a "polltax . . . to raise one denomination of Christians above others." They did, indeed, label it a poll tax outlawed by the state's constitution and reminiscent of the old colonial maintenance for the support of the established clergy. They also claimed that inasmuch as the bill did not specify the amount of the tax, the levy could be raised indefinitely to keep the clergy in luxury at the people's expense. Further, they contended that such sects as the Quakers would refuse to pay, thus incurring the wrath of the law, and that every sect already had a responsibility to support the poor.

Other critics of the bill complained that its passage would discourage immigration and pointed to the experiences of Pennsylvania and other states to prove that public support for ministers was not necessary to the health of society. They argued that enactment of the bill would inhibit religion. One of its principal newspaper opponents dismissed its "unnecessary parade about the usefulness of morality and religion" and asserted that if it passed, the legislature would soon become the judge of acceptable religious worship. Opponents of the bill also connected it with other unpopular measures, particularly one for the creation of the University of Maryland, which they regarded as a scheme to tax them "for the education of gentlemen's children."[88]

On March 25, 1785, the *Baltimore Advertiser* printed a "Copy of a Petition, now Signing, to be presented to the Assembly." The petitioners in this instance wrote that the proposed assessment bill ran contrary to the "spirit of the Christian religion," which "needs not the power of rules to establish, but only to protect it." History proved that "establishments" had destroyed, not promoted religion. A clue to what these petitioners meant by establishment appeared shortly thereafter, when they wrote:

> In the opinion of all men of discernment, the law proposed for the support of the clergy, is intended to give one church a preeminence above others, else why are some societies to be compelled to pay for the support of the clergy, who do not desire it?[89]

They saw the bill, probably accurately, as reflecting primarily the desire of some of the Episcopalian clergy for public support.

No fierce resentment of the Episcopalians built up as a result of the assessment bill, but the persistent suspicion that it represented a covert way of helping them contributed substantially to its defeat. Presbyterian minister Patrick Allison did not object in principle to state support for religion; but he opposed this particular measure vigorously as an Anglican plot.[90] Catholics adhered to the same position. In 1785 John Carroll, soon to become the first Catholic bishop in the United States, wrote to a friend in Europe:

> Where the [assessment] law truly formed upon the principles of the Constitution, we R.C. should have no very great objection to it: but from certain clauses in it, and other circumstances, we, as well as the Presbyterians, Methodists, Quakers and Anabaptists are induced to believe, that it is calculated to create a predominant and irresistible influence in favor of the Protestant Episcopal Church.

A decade later, William Duke, an Episcopalian, confirmed Carroll's observation, when he wrote that the Church of England did not know how to cope without government support and so "laid hold of the provision in the constitution" allowing the state to pass an assessment.[91]

As a consequence of the considerable excitement the proposed assessment legislation had stirred up throughout the state, an unusually large number of delegates attended the opening of the next session of the legislature. The composition of the newly elected House destroyed all hope for the bill's passage. Quakers sent a message calling it "oppressive." A remonstrance from three counties branded the proposed tax for religion "unnecessary and impolitic" and claimed it would be injurious to religion. William Kilty, the historian of the session, deemed the petitions unneessary. The majority of the House members had been elected by anti-assessment voters, and they defeated the bill by a margin of forty-one to twenty-one votes. Kilty thought that Marylanders at large had begun "to taste the sweets of religious liberty" and had no desire to return to past mistakes.[92] A few subsequent requests for a general assessment came to nothing, and in 1810 the state repealed the provision in the Declaration of Rights that would have allowed it to collect such a tax.[93]

Maryland continued, however, to proclaim itself a Christian state and to exlude non-Christians from office. In 1787 William Vans Murray, a native of the state studying at the Middle Temple in London, published an article in England advocating universal liberty and expressing surprise that Americans, in their ardor for freedom, should violate the laws of nature and preclude non-Christians from office.[94] If Marylanders read Murray's London essay, they were unmoved by it, and they remained unopposed to religious tests and exclusions. Of the factions created by the controversy over a general tax for religion, not one expressed disagreement with the exclusionary nature of the state.

Patrick Allison defended religious liberty as an inherent right; but he thought only in terms of "every denomination of Christians."[95] Catholics, delighting in the eradication of the old system, which had discriminated against them, rested content with the new order, which included them. Charles Carroll, whose own father had earlier contemplated leaving Maryland because of its anti-Catholic atmosphere, thought only in terms of "the toleration of all sects of the Christian religion."[96] His cousin, John Carroll, similarly concerned himself only with "toleration" for Catholics.[97] Jews and other non-Christians would achieve political and civil rights only after a bitter struggle in the early nineteenth century. Indeed, Maryland retained a religious test for office until the middle of the twentieth century.[98]

7
Religion and Government in Revolutionary America
Part II: The Middle States and New England

The states of Delaware, New Jersey, and Pennsylvania established no churches and maintained few official connections between religion and government during the colonial period. Consequently, the American Revolution precipitated no movements within them calling for an extensive rearrangement of Church-State relations. Public discussions about the meaning either of freedom of religion or establishment of religion were therefore scarce. As colonies, however, all three had limited officeholding to Christians, and each carried that restriction into its initial state constitution.

Delaware, which comprised the three lower counties of the original Pennsylvania grant, secured its own legislature in 1701, although during the colonial years the two colonies continued to share a common governor. Its charter granted religious liberty to those who believed in God and allowed office to those who believed in Jesus Christ. The colony remained a stranger to religious controversy, and its state constitution of 1776 continued existing requirements that all office-holders be Trinitarian Christians.[1]

Both Delaware and New Jersey guaranteed that no one would be required to attend religious worship or be compelled to maintain any ministry. Both also specified, however, that "there shall be no establishment of any one religious sect ... in preference to another."[2] Delaware's second constitution, of 1792, decreed that religion be supported only by voluntary methods, but still declared that "no preference be given by law to any religious societies, denominations, or modes of worship."[3]

Taken at face value, these provisions seem puzzling and contra-dictory. On the one hand, the state of Delaware decreed that all reli-gion be supported voluntarily; on the other, the establishment clauses seemed to represent a carefully worded statement making it possible for the state to establish or aid all or several religions equally, provided it gave an exclusive preference to none. Modern readers tend to draw a corollary the inhabitants did not, that the prohibition of an "estab-lishment of any one religious sect" opened the way for an establishment of or aid to more than one sect.[4]

No more than William Tennent in South Carolina or the opponents of a tax for religion in Maryland did the people of Delaware or New Jersey envision an establishment as anything other than they had tradi-tionally understood it, a state preference for one sect. If, after a decade of dispute about a general assessment, Virginians continued to envision an establishment similarly, then all the more did citizens of Delaware and New Jersey, who had never experienced any Church-State controversy, adhere to the same definition. Nothing in their history either before or after the Revolution indicates that any party wanted a general assessment type of support for religion or that the legislatures had the slightest inkling that by their prohibition of an establishment of one religion they opened the way for assistance to many.

The new state of Pennsylvania, like Delaware and New Jersey, in-corporated into its constitution the substance of the Church-State arrangement it had known since colonial times. As a colony, Penn-sylvania had established no church and given no support to churches or ministers. In practice it had proved even more tolerant than its neighbors. Though it, too, had excluded Catholics from holding office, it allowed them freedom of worship. Even so, like other colonies, Penn-sylvania reacted to the Quebec Act of 1774 as an attempt by the British government to ensnare America in "Popery" and tyranny.[5]

Before the Revolution, some Pennsylvania colonists worried that Catholics from Canada might constitute a threat to their freedom; after the Revolution, others feared that non-Protestants—or at least non-Christians—would threaten the newly won liberty and order. Con-sequently, the only significant Church-State issue to arise in the new state was whether government should be limited to Christians.

Pennsylvania's constitution of 1776 guaranteed freedom of religion to all and ensured that none would be forced to attend or support any worship or ministry; but it required officeholders to acknowledge a belief in God and in both the Old and New Testaments.[6] As president of Pennsylvania's Constitutional Convention, Benjamin Franklin had hoped to avoid such a test for office; but he felt obliged to bow to popular demands for it. He did get a constitutional guarantee that no further test would ever be required. Franklin felt pressured by several ministers and writers, e.g. one who demanded, in the *Pennsylvania Evening Post*, that "Jews, Mahomedans, and other enemies of Christ" be banned from holding office.[7] In 1783 some Jewish inhabitants complained that the laws deprived them of "the most eminent rights of freemen." Whether the legislature responded specifically to this protest is uncertain; but the subsequent Pennsylvania constitution of 1790 extended the right to hold office to all who believed in God and in "a future state of rewards and punishments," thereby including Jews.[8]

New York entered the American Revolution with the least agreed upon Church-State settlement of any of the colonies. Anglicans claimed an establishment in four counties; many non-Anglicans emphatically denied the claim. They held that the disputed law of 1693 allowed towns to settle their own ministers, but whether that system constituted an establishment was of little interest to them.

The 1777 constitution of the state reflected past quarrels. It decreed that any parts of the common law and any statutes "as may be construed to establish or maintain any particular denomination of Christians or their ministers . . . are abrogated and rejected." The first draft of the constitution had specified the Church of England by name; but the more general reference to any "denomination of Christians" prevailed.[9] For those who had accepted the reasoning of New York's non-Anglicans that no "particular denomination of Christians" ever had been established by the law of the colony, this constitutional provision changed nothing. The New York legislature was "hedging its bets"—refraining from an explicit acknowledgment that the Church of England had been established, but disestablishing it anyhow.

In 1784 the legislature changed the charter of the Anglican Trinity Church in New York City to bring it into harmony with the new era in Church-State relations. Though the lawmakers were careful to refer to the "pretended" claim to an Anglican establishment, all the other terms they used tended to presume that one had existed. Thus the legislature condemned the practice by which non-Anglicans had had to support Anglican ministers as "contrary to every principle of justice and sound policy," but never so much as hinted whether the system by which all citizens of a town might be made to pay the minister chosen only by the majority—the very system some New Yorkers claimed to have existed during the colonial period—would similarly have violated justice and reason. No group, in fact, made any attempt to retrieve this system or any other type of public support of churches.[10]

The only Church-State dispute arose over the status of Catholics within the state. John Jay tenaciously led a minority party dedicated to banishing Catholics and, failing that, to curtailing their participation in public affairs to the maximum extent possible. Given the very small number of Catholics in New York at the time, Jay's determination could hardly have come from personal experience in dealing with them. Rather, he inherited a particularly virulent strain of the common belief subscribed to earlier by William Livingston, i.e. that Catholics for civil reasons could not safely be accepted on a basis of equality with other Christians.[11]

Jay did not hesitate to deny religious liberty to those who "hold and teach . . . principles incompatible and repugnant to the peace, safety, and well being of civil society," thus opening the way to test oaths more stringent and probing than those proposed by any other state, and, indeed, more radical than those of colonial times. Although the New York constitution guaranteed the "free exercise and enjoyment of religious profession and worship, without discrimination or preference," its final section nevertheless reflected at least some of Jay's demands, by excluding foreigners from naturalization unless they renounced all foreign powers "ecclesiastical as well as civil." In 1788 the New York legislature passed a test oath for all officeholders that contained similar language, thereby effectively excluding Catholics from office for the remainder of the century.[12]

A statute of 1784 took note of the duty of governments to "countenance and encourage virtue and religion."[13] Given the state's attitude toward Catholicism, the legislators could hardly have been urging the promotion of all religion. In fact New York inherited the common colonial ethos that America was a Protestant country and simply assumed that Protestantism should be encouraged in nonspecified ways. However, no party in the state ever proposed that public tax support of churches be one of the means for the promotion of religion.

New England during the revolutionary period, as it had throughout its colonial years, produced more Church-State commentary than any other section of the country—although Rhode Island, consistent with its own past, continued to represent an exception to the rule. Virtually a sovereign state under its charter, Rhode Island, even after it became a state in fact, maintained its chartered form of government well into the nineteenth century. Early in the revolutionary period, however, it abolished the law excluding Catholics from office, thereby joining Virginia as one of the two states that proscribed any religious discrimination in dealings with their citizens.[14]

The overwhelming majority of the inhabitants of Massachusetts adhered to the Congregational Church. Baptists constituted the principal dissenters in the state, and by the outbreak of the Revolution they had developed a hatred of the whole ecclesiastical system. When the colonial government decreed that all inhabitants of the new town of Ashfield, in western Massachusetts, must contribute towards building the Congregational church there, even if dissenters could later claim exemption from taxes for its minister, pent-up Baptist anger exploded. Baptists initiated a campaign of civil disobedience, in which they refused either to pay ministerial taxes or to procure certificates of exemption from such taxes. Although they carried their case to England and won, this experience, along with others, only nourished their fervent hatred of the system. In turn, the authorities were embarrassed by Baptist tactics, and Congregationalists became increasingly embittered at what they saw as an attack on the ways of their ancestors in Church and State. During the Revolution, mobs in Pepperell and Hingham even attacked local Baptists on the pretext that they were Tories.[15]

Most Congregationalists approved of some form of public financial support for religion, and the constitutions drawn up by the state reflected this. In 1778 the Massachusetts Council and House of Representatives transformed themselves into a constitution-making body and produced a document to "allow" the "free exercise" of religion to "every denomination of Protestants." It passed over the existing ecclesiastical system in silence, thereby accepting it. Presented to the individual towns for approval, however, the new constitution met with overwhelming rejection, in part because it lacked a bill of rights and a clear definition of "free exercise" of religion. The state then called a Constitutional Convention, which issued a new constitution, together with a bill of rights, in 1780.[16]

The principal sections dealing with religion, which rested in Article II and the long and somewhat complicated Article III of the bill of rights, elicited a volume of comment sufficient to render them a topic for household debate throughout the state. Article II proclaimed "the right as well as the duty of all men in society, publicly and at stated seasons, to worship the SUPREME BEING" and guaranteed the free exercise of religion to all those who did not "disturb the public peace, or obstruct others in their religious worship." Article III reasoned that because "the happiness of a people, and the good order and preservation of civil government" depended upon "piety, religion and morality," the government had the right to make provision for their support. In this regard, Article III gave the state legislature the right to ensure that the towns provided for the support of "public protestant teachers of piety, religion and morality." The method selected for the support of ministers allowed citizens to designate the minister to whom their taxes should be paid. In the absence of such a designation, the unallocated tax would go automatically to the town's selected minister.[17]

The same article further asserted the civil need for "public worship" and conferred upon the legislature the power to make citizens attend religious services at "stated times and seasons." The words "if there be anyone whose instructions they [citizens] can conscientiously and conveniently attend" softened the proviso, but who would define "conscientiously and conveniently"? Another clause of the same article appeared to provide for a more inclusive liberty than before by including every "denomination of Christians." A provision requiring officeholders to abjure all foreign powers both civil and ecclesiastical, however, effectively excluded Catholics from government.[18]

These new constitutional provisions for the support of ministers altered the existing practice in two ways. Instead of demanding that towns pay the minister appointed by the majority and giving exemptions from payment to Baptists and Quakers, Massachusetts after 1780 adopted what was, in fact, a general assessment (though never so stated), under which all had to pay ministerial taxes that would then be allocated to the various ministers according to the instructions of the taxpayers. It thus extended the colonial arrangement for Anglicans to all Protestant groups. Also, public support of ministers, which in colonial times had depended on statutory provisions, became after 1780 embedded in the fundamental law of the commonwealth. There it remained, with some modifications, until 1833.

Almost every town in Massachusetts contributed its opinions and observations on the constitution's religious stipulations, thereby providing one of the most voluminous collections in existence of contemporary commentary on religion and government in the early American states. For the most part, this body of observations can be divided between those who supported the Massachusetts religious system enthusiastically, or at least in principle, and the Baptists, who regarded it as a violation of religious freedom. Occasional responses from outside these two groups demonstrated either a desire on the part of their authors to return to a restrictive religious system reminiscent of the seventeenth century or an opposition to the provisions of Article III in terms somewhat distinct from the pietist argument usually advanced by the Baptists.

The first paragraph of Article III most concisely and succinctly summarized the rationale of the Massachusetts Church-State system:

> ... the happiness of a people, and the good order and preservation of civil government, essentially depend upon piety, religion, and morality; and ... these cannot be generally diffused through a community but by the institution of the public worship of God, and of public instructions in piety, religion, and morality.

Supporters of this system would elongate their arguments in sermons and newspapers, but essentially such elaborations only restated the reasoning contained in that paragraph—by nature frankly Erastian, in that it justified a publicly supported religion because of its usefulness to the State. Thus the makers of the constitution of 1780 stood their Puritan ancestors on their heads. Those founders had come to America to set up a government that would guard the true religion. Members of the Massachusetts Constitutional Convention hoped to use religion to protect and sustain good government.

Repeatedly, defenders of ministerial taxes compared them to school taxes and reasoned that the abolition of either would entail detrimental consequences for civil society.[19] A certain ambivalence on their part was not lost on Isaac Backus, who had pointed out in 1773 that

> ... they [Congregationalists] cry up the great advantage of having religion established by law But when it comes to be calmly represented that religion is a voluntary obedience ... they shift the scene and tell us that religious liberty is fully allowed to us only the state have in their wisdom thought fit to tax all the inhabitants to support an order of men for the good of civil society. A little while ago it was for religion ... but now 'tis to maintain civility.[20]

Such criticism had no effect on the defenders of Article III, other than to remind them to defend it as a secular measure. Occasionally, however, when not feeling pressed by opponents, an individual would revert to an older way of thinking. The Reverend Daniel Foster, in his Election Sermon of 1790, reminded the legislators of their obligation to uphold the kingdom of Christ.[21] Most Congregational ministers probably agreed with him, and no doubt felt that Article III did help to uphold that kingdom; but they could not justify it on that ground without leaving themselves open to the charge of imposing articles of faith and modes of worship.

Proponents of Article III stated their own understanding of religious freedom and refused flatly to consider the possibility of any other approach to the subject. They defined religious liberty as the ability to practice religion according to one's conscience, so long as the government did not demand that articles of faith be believed by the citizens or make adherents of one religious denomination pay for the support of another. That the law as it stood after 1780 would require non-Protestants to pay for the support of local Protestant ministers was less than irrelevant to either supporters or opponents of Article III, who, like the overwhelming majority of the population of Massachusetts, lived within a world circumscribed by Protestantism. Insofar as Article III posed a hardship for Catholics, most citizens—if they thought of it at all—would probably have dismissed such a minor inequity. Insofar as the law harmed religious rights of non-Christians, no scrap of evidence exists to indicate that such an idea even entered the public consciousness.

Settled on their definition of religious liberty, proponents of tax-supported churches occupied themselves with restating their arguments and dismissing objections to them as unreasonable or mischievous. Before the Revolution, in 1774, John Tucker, minister at Newbury, had written that as long as no one was forced to believe, then the taking of money to support a minister whose services some could not attend might amount to "civil oppression," but did not constitute a violation of conscience. His fellow Congregationalists did not subscribe to such a radical retrogressive view, but they regarded as unreasonable any objection to the demand that one support one's own minister.[22]

The colony's laws had stated that the Baptists "allege scruple of Conscience" to paying ministerial taxes.[23] In the 1780s, the majority still believed that the "alleged" conscience scruple was simply a ruse to avoid any paying of religious taxes, and that the abolition of such levies would only indulge the most rascally element of the population in its wish to support no minister at all. At times they seized the offensive by accusing those who wanted to do away with mandatory ministerial support of promoting "irreligion" and "licentiousness" under the guise of liberty of conscience.[24] Some contented themselves with the spurious explanation of "Irenaeus" (Samuel West), who maintained that Quakers raised no objection to public support of ministers, and that the "more honest" among the Baptists approved of it.[25]

The assumption that their state was a Congregationalist preserve thoroughly permeated the popular mind of Massachusetts inhabitants and rendered ridiculous any suggestion that the existing ecclesiastical system was other than perfectly fair and reasonable. Their overwhelming numerical predominance left Congregationalists as unable to comprehend that a society dominated by them could be unfair to dissenters as their descendants would be unable to conceive that their view of America as a Protestant country could be unpalatable to others of differing religious viewpoints.

In the face of the majority's resolve to preserve its system of Church and State, Baptists dashed themselves impotently against Congregationalists' tenacious determination, ingenuity, ability to obfuscate, and capacity to adapt to circumstances without giving away a single essential of what they wanted to achieve—the very skills earlier Massachusetts authorities and ministers had honed long and well in dealing with the English government and in religious controversy with Anglicans. In the course of their history, Massachusetts Congregationalists had developed marvelously subtle methods of coping with "outsiders," be they in England or within the colony, and of preserving their own dominance in Church and State while clothing it in the most modern rhetoric of liberty.

In addition to a wondrous deviousness, Massachusetts authorities exhibited a delightful trait—delightful, at least, from the safe vantage point of modernity—that manifested itself in an inability to refrain from commenting officially on any action of theirs that might even suggest the slightest insufficiency on their part. The specific reference to an "alleged scruple of Conscience" on the part of Baptists and Quakers in the laws of the colonial period exempting them from ministerial taxes was one example. Another was a law of 1789 incorporating an Anglican church, entitled "An Act incorporating the warden and vestry of Christs Church (so called) in Boston."[26]

Samuel Eliot Morison long ago demonstrated that the necessary two-thirds of Massachusetts voters did not in fact ratify Article III, that the required percentage was attained only by adding to the votes of those who approved it the votes of those who wanted it amended. Nevertheless, the vast majority of the people of the state did accept its principle of a publicly supported ministry. Approximately twenty-four towns wanted a clarification to ensure that no one would be taxed for support of a minister of another religion than his own, and a few towns called for no exemptions at all. When these were added to the roughly 130 towns that accepted Article III, the total far outweighed the forty-five towns that rejected it. Boston, too, which had always supported its churches by voluntary contributions, approved the principle of tax-supported religion, though the city's voters were careful to specify protection for their own voluntary system.[27]

Historians have not drawn any direct correlation between the Baptist population and the towns that rejected Article III, but the Baptists certainly exercised a direct influence upon the reactions of those communities. In Bristol County, home of the longest and most

sustained opposition to the colony's ecclesiastical system, their effect
was probably decisive. Both before and after 1780, they formed the
core, as well as the bulk, of opposition to the Massachusetts Church-
State arrangement. They articulated their position most forcefully
through the Grievance Committee of their New England Warren
Association, whose agent, Isaac Backus, emerged as a most effective
spokesman.[28]

The deep and sustained alienation of Massachusetts Baptists from
the state's Congregationalist-supported Church-State system might
lead one to assume that the two denominations operated out of differing intellectual worlds, but such was not the case. Baptists fundamentally disagreed with Congregationalists on the narrow ground of
organization and support of churches. They believed that churches
should be made up only of those who had experienced conversion, that
ministers should be appointed on the basis of holiness rather than a
college degree, and that both church and minister should be supported
voluntarily. From the Baptist theological standpoint, the Massachusetts system was not only unacceptable, but downright pernicious.
By dividing the church into territorial parishes with ministers elected
by the majority of the inhabitants of the parish, the state gave "fornica-
tors, drunkards, Railers, and extortioners . . . equal votes with the best
men in the land," thus setting up as ministers worldly men and
"hirelings" to traduce the Church of Christ.[29]

Although influential New Englanders, such as Robert Trent Paine
and Ezra Stiles, dismissed their complaints as "mountains out of mole
hills," Baptists' grievances were obviously very real to themselves. An
extract from Isaac Backus's *Diary* for 1782 illustrated the hazards they
faced in Massachusetts:

> Preacht twice at Brother Daniel Lothrop's in Bridgewater; had
> special assistance granted to expose the delusion of those who hold to
> universal salvation; blessed be God. Sawing, collector for Mr. Moses
> Taft of Braintree, took a cow from David Linsfield for a tax to him, on
> April 1, and sold her on the 4th. John Howard of Easton was seized for
> a tax to Mr. Archibald Campbell the same week. Barnabas Perkins of
> Hanover in New Hampshire, informs me of a glorious work of divine
> grace.[30]

The matter-of-fact references to distraints for church taxes sandwiched
between Backus's evangelical concerns manifested the commonplace
nature of the hardships encountered by Massachusetts Baptists. At
times Backus felt devastated by the opprobrium his critics heaped upon
him, including a supposed unlimited "Thirst for slander" against

Massachusetts. He responded by mocking their rhetoric of freedom; by insisting that it amounted only to hypocrisy, given the practices of the state; and by taunting them as to "what they would do to prevent liberty if they could."[31]

For the most part, the towns that rejected Article III couched their objections in pietist language. Their returns declared that the article would have the people conferring upon the legislature a power over religion that was not theirs to bestow, i.e. that the civil power had no authority to make such provisions for the support of religion; that civil interference deprived people of liberty of religion, corrupted true religion, and brought on persecution. Responses also claimed that Article III was unclear and contradictory, in that it did—or would—subordinate one sect to another, that it was unnecessary, and that it did not follow from or that it opposed Article II.[32] The return from the town of Ashby in Middlesex County exemplified the evangelical cast of much of the opposition:

> the third Article says the people . . . have a right to invest their legeslature with power to make Laws that are binding on religious society . . . which is as much as to say we will not have Christ to reign over us . . . and that the Ark of God stands in need of Uzza's hand to keep it from falling, . . . but lett us attend sereously to this importent Truth . . . that . . . the Gates of Hell shall not prevail against it.[33]

The majority of the towns opposed to Article III focused on its provision for public support of clergy. In 1776 the members of the Warren Association had supported the Revolution partly because they hoped it would bring "full and universal liberty of conscience." They had understood that term to mean the right to worship freely, together with dismantlement of the parish ecclesiastical structure and a turn to voluntary support of clergy. They seldom thought of religious freedom apart from these particular categories, and, like their counterparts in other states, they opposed the system primarily as a violation of religious freedom, rather than as an establishment of religion.

In 1784 Moses Hemmenway preached in Boston to the legislators that they should take heed "that the right of private judgment become not an occasion of infidelity, or skepticism, or of being carried away with unsound doctrines." Further, he cautioned them that "liberty of conscience must not be abused into a pretence for neglecting religion . . . Profaning the sabbath," or for abandoning public suport of religious instruction. With the exception of that last statement, Baptists would have concurred with him. Around the same time, Backus wrote: "That Christianity is essentially necessary to the good order of civil society is a certain truth." He added, however, that so were the "showers and the shines of heaven," but who would make a law to say when the sun should shine?[34]

Earlier, in 1779, aware of some of the bad publicity Massachusetts was getting with regard to violation of liberty of conscience, the General Court had chosen Baptist minister Samuel Stillman to deliver the Election Sermon. Stillman told his bearers: "Happy are the inhabitants of that commonwealth . . . in which all are protected, but none established." He had already advised them that, consonant with the right of conscience, "there were many ways that the magistrate can encourage religion."[35] Stillman did not go on to enumerate those ways, which in any case were more assumed than examined. They included restricting officeholding to Protestants, maintaining strict Sabbath laws, and generally supporting Protestant culture—ideas shared by both Baptists and Congregationalists, but considered by both to represent the warp and woof of civilization, rather than religion as such.

As to whether the state could require attendance at church, Backus himself was ambiguous, saying in 1783 only that he had no quarrel "with our rulers about that matter."[36] His own town of Middleborough, which contained three Baptist churches, criticized and rejected Article III. Nevertheless, the town's alternate suggestion gave the legislature the right to require attendance at public worship, to guarantee liberty to worship to "all men or Denominations of Christian People," and to demand that all specify "what Denomination of Christian people they join with." If these sentiments offended Backus and the Baptist congregations, he gave no indication of it in his public or private writings.[37] Neither did he show any sign of supporting broader religious freedom for Universalists in their dealings with the Massachusetts authorities, or for any of the other groups he regarded as heretics. Moreover, he certainly approved limiting office to Protestants, and he criticized the 1780 constitution for failing specifically to exclude Catholics from office.[38]

Again, towns that disapproved of state interference in religion defined such interference primarily as mandated ministerial support. In Massachusetts, as in America generally, financial support of religion came under a different heading than vaguer, less direct or explicit kinds of assistance. For example, the town of Bellingham in Suffolk County rejected Article III and submitted an alternative article making payment of ministers purely voluntary; yet in the same response, Bellingham proposed that the legislature have power to "Prohibit Labour and unnecessary travaling and Recreations on the first Day of the Weck," as well as to change the restriction on officeholding from

Christian to Protestant.[39] Sixty-eight towns submitted a request for the more restrictive wording on officeholding; of these, fifteen rejected Article III's mandated state support for churches and ministers.[40]

In their understanding of religious freedom some Massachusetts towns varied from either the majority Congregationalist view or the opposing, generally Baptist, position. A very few returns called for much more restrictive laws. Dunstable wanted to deny "Protection to the Idolatrous worshippers of the Church of Rome," and the town would have no truck with laws giving the press freedom to "Dishonor ... God by printing herasy [sic]."[41] A number of towns criticized the constitutional provisions for religion from the more liberal standpoint of one "Philanthropos," who wrote a series of critical commentaries on Article III that appeared in the Boston papers during 1780 and 1781. To heavily pietistic arguments he added those of Locke and Milton and, as proof of the feasibility of the voluntary support of religion, cited the examples of Virginia, Pennsylvania, New York, and New Jersey.[42]

Religious rationalists in Massachusetts, such as Samuel West, Charles Chauncy, and other ministers who benefited from the state-supported religious system, remained its devoted upholders and insisted on its fairness.[43] Backus noted, however, that Article III would not benefit his denomination, because Baptist ministers could not in conscience claim money that had been collected by force; thus their congregations' taxes would automatically go to a town's minister.[44] Similarly, when he protested the law requiring ministers to possess degrees, on the basis that it violated religious freedom, such spokesmen retorted "What! Was he an advocate of ignorance?" Backus knew—or sensed—that the root of the problem lay in failure not of argument, but of imagination. In 1779 he wrote:

> If any suppose that the article [III] establishes equal religious liberty, let them only change places with us and empower another denomination to tax them ... contrary to their consciences and then tell them, if they will require the money thus unjustly gathered they may have it for their own teachers, if not those who have got it will apply it to the support of their own party.[45]

In 1782 Baptists challenged the new ecclesiastical system in the courts and claimed that for them to have to hand in certificates of exemption from taxes subordinated one sect to another, in violation of the concluding paragraph of Article II. The case in question involved one Elijah Balkcom of Attelborough, who refused to give in a certificate on the ground that the old law had lapsed, but who also refused to pay taxes for support of religion. The Bristol County Court at Taunton agreed with the Baptists in this instance, and for a brief euphoric time they thought that they had eliminated the provision for mandatory ministerial support. Other, contrary, decisions that upheld the system soon followed, however, and Article III continued to set the pattern of Church-State relations in Massachusetts for the remainder of the century.[46]

Massachusetts's voluminous discourse on Church-State matters during the revolutionary period focused almost entirely on the meaning of freedom of religion. Some towns objected to Article III because it imposed articles of faith or preferred one sect over others, but apart from these indirect references, they generally did not raise the issue of an establishment of religion. Indeed, that subject did not give rise to public debate in the state at all except for the following instance.

In the late 1770s Isaac Backus and another Baptist apologist, who used the pen name "Milton," engaged two Congregationalist opponents in a public dispute. "Milton" wrote in the *Boston Gazette*:

> It has been proved that government have established religion by law; particularly congregationalist. The truth of which I never heard disputed till Hieronymus made his appearance. Historians agree in it. The court and the people acknowledge it.[47]

The note of exasperation in "Milton"'s declaration was understandable under the circumstances. His opponents "Hieronymous" (probably Robert Trent Paine) and "Swift" in the same newspaper denied that the commonwealth of Massachusetts or the colony preceding it had supported an establishment of religion. Their assertion was particularly galling to "Milton"—not only because it violated the plain common sense of his own experience, but because it was difficult to refute.

When "Milton" tried to demonstrate the injustice of the existing establishment, "Hieronymous" refused to come to grips with him; instead, he boldly denied that Massachusetts had any establishment:

> A religious establishment by law is the establishment of a particular mode of worshipping God, with rites and ceremonies peculiar to such mode from which the people are not suffered to vary.[48]

Such a statement embodied Chauncy's definition of "civil" or "STATE" establishments, only rendering more specific what Chauncy had left vague and ominous. Preceding from this definition, "Hieronymous" concluded that the question of the justice or the injustice of an establishment had no bearing on Massachusetts.

In the face of such reactions, "Milton" thrashed about trying to prove his point. He cited seventeenth-century Massachusetts, but encountered little success with that approach. His opponent gladly conceded the existence of an establishment then; but the second charter had altered that.[49] At one stage, "Milton" apparently became confused and said that Isaac Backus had not claimed that Massachusetts had an establishment; but "Hieronymous" gleefully pointed out that Backus had claimed that Congregationalism was as much established in Massachusetts as Anglicanism in England.[50]

So, in fact, did "Milton." He pointed to the division of the state into parishes that chose an "orthodox, learned" minister and asked rhetorically if a Baptist or Anglican minister could qualify. To him the Pepperell riot and other persecutions had made it clear that only Congregationalists were orthodox.[51] In these assertions, "Milton" was both right and wrong. Since none but Congregationalist clergy became legal ministers in any of the towns during the colonial period, the statutes in fact established Congregationalism. In law and theory, however, his position was groundless, and "Hieronymous" could thus coolly reject it by pointing out that no sect was established by law, and that all Protestants received equal treatment.[52]

Backus and "Milton," however, found their most telling points in the law themselves. Backus noted that "our legislature have constantly called those laws an establishment for these eighty seven years," and "Milton" quoted the statutes that referred to the "ministers established by law."[53] With these arguments, the polemic tide changed, and their opponents in turn found themselves groping for rebuttal. "Swift" tried to deal with the language of the law by claiming that it referred to the establishment of support, not religion, and that in the phrase "for the support of divine worship in the manner established by law," the word "established" applied to the manner and not to the worship.[54] The Baptists did not find it worthwhile to contradict such frivolities. In 1778 Backus had written:

> Many talk so plausibly about religious liberty that our good friends who have not had sensible experience of a contrary practice can hardly believe that a religious establishment by human laws is so evil and dangerous as it really is.[55]

As far as Baptists were concerned, Congregationalism was established in Massachusetts, and the constitution of 1780, which appointed the ministers of the "congregational churches" overseers of Harvard, only strengthened this conviction.[56]

Opponents of Article III were probably aware that the comments of "Hieronymous" and "Swift" were merely fabricated justifications for positions already taken. For instance, according to the former's definition, no establishment had existed anywhere in the British Empire since the Act of Toleration of 1689, because he interpreted the imposition of uniformity from which none "were suffered to vary" as essential to establishment of religion. Baptists refused to become involved in such far-fetched arguments, which did not touch their own experience.

After the outbreak of the American Revolution, as Americans throughout the states condemned England for imposing a tyrannical establishment of Catholicism upon Quebec, and as the establishments in the southern states toppled, New Englanders took care not to appear less liberal than their fellow Americans.[57] Preachers to the Massachusetts General Court condemned what Chauncy had labeled a "civil establishment." They warned the legislators not to "establish particular modes of faith, and forms of worship"; declared that none could complain of a grievance when no "particular mode of public worship is established by law"; asserted that the state had no establishment of one denomination of Christians, and that a "legal provision" for ministers according to an "equal and Liberal" plan did not even approach a "political establishment" to deprive citizens of the sacred rights of conscience.[58]

Thus did the clergy condemn the type of establishment Massachusetts did not have. Their predecessors back to Cotton Mather had also discoursed against the same kind of establishments, i.e. those that imposed or demanded articles of faith. But whereas these earlier ministers had understood and acknowledged the Massachusetts system as a different kind of establishment, their successors during the Revolution remained silent on that point.

A few references to the concept did surface publicly in New England. In 1778 the town of Boothbay in Maine, commenting on the proposed constitution, asked that every useful denomination "be equally free and equally established."[59] In 1786, in a case involving the right of the Universalists to have their taxes paid to their own ministers, Massachusetts Chief Justice William Cushing referred to sects apart from "the regular establishment, if it may be so termed."[60] By and large, however, Congregationalists during the Revolution did not choose to call their ecclesiastical settlement by that name.

Did the state of Massachusetts then, especially after the passage of the constitution of 1780, maintain an establishment of religion? Historians have generally agreed that it did until 1833, and judged by modern standards, Article III certainly constituted an establishment. Its final clause mandated that "no subordination of any one sect or denomination to another shall ever be established by law," and

Congregationalists were adamant that the state's system for the support of religion never constituted such subordination. Officially, the state maintained no establishment, and neither did defenders of the ecclesiastical system describe it as such. Baptists, on the contrary, had no doubt that the state maintained an establishment. When David Ramsey, the historian of South Carolina, wrote that all establishments of religion had been destroyed by the American Revolution, Backus noted in his *History* that such may have been the case in the South, but not in New England. Although he cited with approval a Connecticut petition stating that civil rulers had been given no power even "to establish the Christian religion at large, much less one distinguished denomination," both he and other Baptists continued to understand establishment as a preference for Congregationalism.[61] To Baptists, who "owned that religion must at all times be a matter between God and individuals," the very idea of state support—even impartial state support—was by nature wrong and an imposition of the Congregational way of religion. Thus, both parties to the Church-State dispute in Massachusetts agreed that an establishment of religion signified a state preference for one denomination, even as they disagreed on whether the state actually made such a preference.

Later, in the early nineteenth century, Congregationalists themselves split into bitterly disputing factions. Trinitarians resented the election by town majorities of Unitarian ministers. This development brought the more conservative Trinitarians into conflict with the ecclesiastical design of Article III, and they, like the Baptists earlier, did not hesitate to refer to the religious system it provided for as an establishment of religion.[62]

Massachusetts in the revolutionary years made a significant contribution to the development of civil and constitutional liberties in general, but not to the furtherance of religious liberty in either thought or practice. Perhaps John Adams provided the most basic insight into the nature of the Massachusetts Church-State system when he stated at Philadelphia in 1774 (as Isaac Backus recalled it) that "we might as well expect a change in the solar systim, as to expect they would give up their establishment."[63] Certainly the system that had emerged during the colonial era had become the constant for Congregationalists. They wrote not so much to explore religious freedom as to demonstrate that their ecclesiastical way, either before or after the adoption of Article III, embodied it. Public support of ministers had become for them an article of faith.

In 1778 Charles Chauncy preached that the military defeats suffered by the patriot cause could be attributed to the state's failure to make proper provision for its ministers. Chauncy represented the rationalist avant-garde in religion, and no less likely candidate for delivering a jeremiad walked the earth; but a threat to his beloved Church-State order pushed him back into the wonder-working world of Providence of his Puritan ancestors more than a century before.[64]

Massachusetts had made its adjustments in the name of freedom and liberty of conscience early in the eighteenth century, when it had exempted dissenters from paying ministerial support. The majority Congregationalists had long since heard all the Baptists' arguments and were not prepared to change. Only a breakdown of the system from within would wreck it, a third of the way into the nineteenth century.

Against the entrenched position of the dominant religious denomination, Baptists, despite their courageous and persistent efforts, could make no headway. They failed, however, not only because of the fortified strength of the opposition, but also because of a weakness in their own position. They differed from the Congregationalists on the narrow issues of state designation of parishes and state legislation on the selection and payment of ministers; but their acceptance of all other aspects of the Massachusetts way in Church and State diluted their resistance. Congregationalists found it difficult to believe that Baptist preoccupation with ministerial maintenance was anything more than a rationalization of self-interest on the part of people who wanted to avoid spending money. Later, Chief Justice Theophilus Parsons would say that dissenters in Massachusetts appeared to "mistake a man's money for his conscience." Congregationalists had thought so all along.[65] "Swift" contended that Baptists would not give in certificates, but would take an oath demanded by the state, which to him pertained to religion much more than a certificate of exemption. He hardly demonstrated much diligence in understanding the Baptist position; but even if he had done so, he would have found some attitudes within the writings of Isaac Backus and among the majority of Baptists that were difficult to reconcile with each other.

These attitudes are best illustrated when compared to those of another Baptist minister, John Leland, who spent the years from 1775 to 1791 preaching in Virginia, and who took a far more radical stand on Church and State than his colleagues.[66] Like Roger Williams, Leland pursued his argument to its logical conclusion: If the government had no authority over religious matters, then the State had no power to provide for ministers, to enact Sabbath laws, to pay military chaplains, or to exclude from office adherents of any religion. In his estimation, the notion of a Christian commonwealth was absurd.[67]

Backus and the other opponents of Article III agreed with none of these specific applications of a basic principle except the prohibition against paying ministers. They all argued that the government had no power in matters religious, yet they perceived Massachusetts as a Christian Protestant state, approved of test oaths and Sabbath laws, and barely considered the question of religious liberty beyond the organization of churches and support of clergy. They did not, as did Leland, challenge their opponents to consider a different, new, or broader view of Church and State.

In 1789 John Carroll, the first Catholic bishop in the United States, complained of Massachusetts's hostility to Catholics in a letter to a friend. Congregationalists and Baptists were united in that hostility. In 1790 Backus criticized the 1780 constitution (incorrectly) for having opened the door to Roman Catholics' becoming lawmakers and judges.[68] Neither he nor his fellows ever confronted the problem of how a government could maintain a Christian commonwealth without interfering in matters of religion or without defining Christianity. They complained that the majority failed to consider the situation from a dissenter's point of view; but they themselves neglected to picture the plights of other groups.

Ultimately, Baptist failure in the area of religous freedom was the same as that of the Congregationalists. Both sects adhered to Church-State arrangements that were co-extensive with their own theological, religious, and societal views; both constructed a system of Church and State to suit a world made up entirely of Congregationalists or Baptists. Neither theorized about, much less fought for, causes that did not directly involve themselves. Granted that Massachusetts Baptists, caught up as they were in a very real struggle for religious liberty, could not afford the luxury of abstract speculation about it; but neither did they concern themselves with its practical implications for society. In Virginia, on the other hand, many of those who advanced theological and theoretical justifications of religious freedom also pointed out that a state that made all its inhabitants pay for Christian ministers could hardly expect Jews and other non-Christians to bring their trade and skills there.

None in Massachusetts ever wavered or changed like the Presbyterian clergy in Virginia. None ever admitted to having changed their minds, like the petitioners from Virginia's Amherst County. Unlike Virginians, the inhabitants of Massachusetts failed to envisage a society composed of people other than Protestants—and strict sabbatarian Protestants at that. In startling contrast to Virginia, Church and State in Massachusetts emerged from the revolutionary era much as they had entered it.[69]

Connecticut, the second most populous of the New England states, adhered to the same basic outlines as Massachusetts in Church and State, but projected them in clearer contours. Especially on the question of establishment, it demonstrated none of the reticence or obfuscation of the Bay State. Connecticut also produced a smaller volume of comment on religious liberty, in part because it elected to transform its charter government into its state government, thereby eliminating the rich source of comment that constitution making produced elsewhere. Particularly in Election Sermons, Connecticut's Congregationalist ministers kept up a steady barrage of advice on the significance of religion for government and the consequent importance of the state's supporting religion. Only incidentally, however, did these preachers touch on freedom of religion, which they assumed to be compatible with state support of religion.[70]

Two sermons, the first by Judah Champion in 1776, and the second by Nathan Strong in 1790, span the revolutionary period and by their similarity demonstrate how little the Revolution had influenced the thinking of the ministers of the standing order on matters of Church and State. Both ministers pointed out that there existed a definite boundary between Church and State, yet both asserted the state's need for a connection with religion. They believed that the State should avoid propagating the "non-essentials" of religion, though neither showed the slightest interest in exploring what those might be.[71] Both repudiated "Popery" and lauded the extensive religious liberty enjoyed by the state. Both were interested in tradition and its protection, rather than in freedom of religion. Like several other preachers before the Court, both stressed the importance of preserving what their "Fathers" had come to create "at the cost of great sacrifice and hardship."[72]

In 1776 Champion summed up the ecclesiastical motifs of colonial, revolutionary, and even post-revolutionary Connecticut when he told the Court:

> As our civil liberties . . . are nearly connected with . . . our religious . . . so our religious privileges are not inferior to our civil. Every one has God's word, may read and judge for himself. . . . Every ecclesiastical society may chuse its own minister, and provide for his support. Happily delivered from Romish superstition . . . and that ecclesiastical hierarchy, which neither we, nor our fathers were able to bear—we may serve God without fear. Difference of sentiment respecting the non-essentials of religion, seems to be one of the unavoidable consequences of man's dreadful apostasy. None may impose for doctrine, the commandments of men; or force others to believe with them. Surely the sacred rights of conscience, are ever to be treated with

utmost delicacy. But if any under pretence of conscience, sap the foundation of civil society . . . they are to be restrained by the civil arm. Civil rulers are God's ministers for good . . . [and] a terror to evil works. . . . In favor of virtue, to suppress immorality, and support religion, we have a system of excellent laws enacted, while different persuasions enjoy the most generous liberty and freedom. What greater civil or christian liberty can be enjoyed, or even wish'd for, than the inhabitants of this colony are indulged?[73]

Therein were stated all the themes so dear to the ministers of the standing order in Connecticut and in New England at large.

Champion preached in 1776, but he could have preached the same sermon to the Connecticut legislature with equal appropriateness at any time between its inception and the early nineteenth century. His discourse noted the necessary link between civil society and religion. It viewed religious liberty retrospectively as something that had been fought for and achieved by the Puritan triumph over Archbishop Laud. It begged the perennial questions, e.g. the definition of non-essentials, the method by which the State could determine "pretence of conscience," and the possibility of supporting religion without imposing "rites and ceremonies." It contained, too, the implied accusation that any who would find fault with such an excellent system that so "indulged" its citizens could not possibly be acting in good conscience. Champion's final question, "What greater civil or christian liberty can be enjoyed?", was rhetorical. He was no doubt aware that many in the colony were even then demanding a broader religious liberty.

The demand came mostly from those who had separated from the established churches during the Great Awakening, persons whom the state called Separates and who referred to themselves as Strict Congregationalists. Gathered into about twenty churches in 1775, these Separates were harassed by the authorities, who insisted on taxing them for the benefit of the local parish church. Although the Separates would continue to decline, they represented, before Baptist growth in the 1790s, the only significant vocal dissenting group in the state.[74]

Separates opposed the "Ecclesiastical Constitution of Connecticut" as a compound of Church and State "not found in the New Testament."[75] Like Massachusetts Baptists, they criticized those elements of the status quo that prevented them from practising what they considered the true religion, and they likewise tended to identify the cause of religious freedom with destruction of an ecclesiastical system—in this case of the Saybrook Platform—that implemented legal provisions for a publicly supported clergy. Apart from this issue, Separates accepted the prevailing attitude in such matters as Sabbath observance, exclusion of certain religious believers or non-believers from office, and the general Protestant world view of the dominant Congregationalists.[76]

In 1777, Separates from eleven churches met and drew up a petition to the Connecticut General Court based on "the two grand charters, of nature and scripture." They asked that "the liberty which the bible grants may take place through this State," and that all citizens be allowed to support religion in the "manner that they think is most agreeable to the gospel." Asserting that even while participating in the defense of their country, they were "assaulted by domestic tyranny" in the form of ministerial tax collectors, they threatened to "beg our grievance before the Honorable Continental Congress" unless the state gave them relief.[77]

The legislators took umbrage at this language and "stopt the reading" of the petition. Some even thought that the signers "ought to be sent for, to answer for it." Nevertheless, the majority acted to give the Separates relief.[78] A law of 1777 exempted Separates from taxes for the support of the "established Ministry," and for the "churches and congregations established by the laws of this State," provided that they produced certificates attesting to their patronage and support of their own churches.[79] Separate Israel Holly criticized the statute as "a device, or a piece of policy to mend and patch up the constitution, when there has been some breaks made in it" and complained that it gave relief neither to those Separates who did not live "near" one of their churches nor to those who had not found a minister for their church. However, most Separates accepted the law gracefully as an answer to their grievances.[80]

Seven years later, in 1784, as part of a general revision of the laws, Connecticut enacted an even more generous exemption, entitled "An Act for securing the Rights of Conscience in Matters of Religion, to Christians of every Denomination." The Preamble set forth the standard apology for supporting religion as promoting "the good Order of Civil Society," and it explained that as the people of Connecticut had generally "been of one Profession in Matters of Faith," they had "by Law been formed into Ecclesiastical Societies." However, "to the End that other Denominations of Christians who differ from the Worship and Ministry so established" might enjoy liberty of conscience, no Christians "who soberly and conscientiously dissent from the Worship and Ministry by Law established in the Society wherein they dwell" were to be molested for absenting themselves from such worship, provided they attended and supported their own churches.

Moreover,

... all denominations of Christians differing in their religious Sentiments from the People of the esablished Societies in this State, whether
of the Episcopal Church, ... Separates, ... or Baptists, ... or Quaker,
or any other Denomination ...

who attended and supported "the gospel ministry" could have a certificate signed by an officer of their own church and be exempted from
the support of the established ministry. The revised statute books in
which this law appeared silently dropped the Saybrook Platform.
Nevertheless, the law clearly presumed an establishment of Congregationalism and went so far as to list the other denominations within the
state as "dissenters." Although the statute appeared to include all
Christians, the final section extended equal protection to "all protestant
churches and congregations as dissent from the worship and ministry
established as aforesaid," indicating that the legislators probably
equated Christian with Protestant.[81]

This liberal certificate law produced a good deal of anxiety among
the members of the standing order about the possible decline of religion. A writer in the *Connecticut Courant* proposed a general assessment, so that none could escape paying taxes for religion, and
explained that "religion may be established on principles consistent
with perfect freedom." Shortly thereafter, the legislature passed a
resolution in favor of a "liberal establishment," consisting of a poll tax
to be levied on all citizens for the support of "ministers of the Gospel."
Nothing came of either proposal. Nevertheless, Congregationalists
continued to fret about the growth of "deism" and "infidelity," while
opponents of the establishment continued to gain confidence in their
ability to control or at least to stymie, town proceedings on ecclesiastical matters.[82]

New Salem illustrated the frustrations sometimes encountered by
the standing order. A group of Congregationalists there combined to
erect a new church for the town and to hire a minister, only to find
themselves blocked by Baptists and townspeople unenthused about
contributing taxes for the church. The Congregationalists, led by
Zebulon Waterman, complained to the General Court that "Baptists
and others" were trying to prevent them from finishing the "Meeting
House or settling a Minister agreeable to the establishment by the laws
of this State." The dispute dragged on until the legislature, in the mid-
1790s, worked out a complicated arrangement, by which the Congregationalist minority in the parish could be the established "Society,"
while allowing the majority to avoid giving in certificates.[83]

In 1791, in order to close some loopholes in the certificate law and
shore up the ecclesiastical system, the legislature passed a bill

demanding that all dissenters from the "Ecclesiastical Societies Established by law" have their exemptions signed by two officers of the "Civil Authority" in the respective towns. Since most of these officers were Congregationalist and could use the statute to harass unpopular dissenters, the law raised a storm of protests in the state.[84] The longest and best publicized of these, entitled *The Rights of Conscience Inalienable*, was written by John Leland, who very likely also wrote a lengthy newspaper article under the name "Pandor" (probably "Candor" misprinted). He used the familiar arguments to disprove the need for state-supported religion, including the experiences of New York, Pennsylvania, New Jersey, and Rhode Island. He also advanced the pragmatic reasoning from Virginia that establishments discouraged new settlers. Apart from this grasp of the practical consequences of an establishment of religion, Leland showed an ability to expand his horizons beyond the imaginative Christian or Protestant boundaries that constrained most of his New England contemporaries, be they defenders or critics of their states' ecclesiastical systems. He declared that the certificate laws were unjust, because "heathens, deists, and Jews are not indulged," and asked if a Jew should have to support the "religion of Jesus Christ, when he really believes that he was an imposter? Must the Papist be forced to pay men for preaching down the supremacy of the Pope, who they are sure is the head of the Church?"

Leland abhorred all establishments because "fallible men make their own opinions tests of orthodoxy, and use their own systems, as Procustes used his iron bedstead, to stretch and measure the consciences of all others by." On the Connecticut system, he commented:

> The certificate law supposes . . . that the legislature have power to establish a religion; this is false. Second, that they have authority to grant indulgence to non-conformists; this is also false, for a religious liberty is a right and not a favor.[85]

The plans to provide public support for religion in other states he dismissed as various attempts "to establish a religious tyranny." Virginia, he noted, "attempted a general assessment but it finally fell though."[86] Others in America at the time would have agreed with Leland's opposition to establishment of religion; but no religious figure would have transcended his contemporary cultural milieu and followed the logic of his thought to such sympathetic imaginative conclusions. Indeed, until Leland no religious thinker matched the thought on Church and State of Roger Williams of the previous century.

Connecticut Congregationalists simply could not take Leland

seriously. The tyranny he associated with an establishment appeared to them as remote as the Inquisition. How could their mild and liberal system have anything in common with bored tongues or clipped ears? Thus they dismissed all his arguments out of hand—the moderate together with the radical.

Leland's opponents claimed he was trying to destroy every law supportive of religion and conscience and to undermine the social order. They repeatedly raised the specter of Rhode Island, that "religious state," with its "enviable and blessed condition." They contended that laws for public suport of religion had nothing to do with religious belief. A critic in the *Connecticut Courant* wrote: "Let Pandor be informed, that there is not an existing law in this state which gives one Christian sect, an advantage above another." Yet the author considerably weakened his pronouncement by appending to the same piece a note that read: "Dissenters in New England are Episcopalians, Baptists, Quakers, indeed all denominations except Presbyterians [i.e Congregationalists]."[87]

The majority of Connecticut's population refused to agree to the dissenters' definition of religious freedom, but the General Court nonetheless took action to give them relief. Late in 1791 it passed a liberal law by which "those who differ in Sentiments from the worship and ministry in the ecclesiastical societies . . . constituted by law" could write their own certificates, and thereby sign off from the established churches. One writer criticized the law as unjust, because it applied only to Christians and continued taxation of non-residents, Jews, and infidels for the support of the "platform people," but his was a voice crying in the wilderness.[88]

As its pronouncements on Church and State throughout the revolutionary period exemplified, Connecticut made no bones about the fact of its Congregationalist establishment of religion. It also preserved the concept of another kind of establishment, a tyrannical "civil" or "state" establishment, which had been used throughout the colonial period as an indirect reference to the Anglican establishment in England. At the beginning of the Revolution, Joseph Perry told the General Court that through the wickedness and negligence of England, "Popery has become the established religion in Canada." Two years later, Joseph Devotion told the same body that the government should support religion, but that

> Arguments for religious establishments, should stand upon the ground of morality. This takes the plea of conscience out of the mouths of particular sects. Such as openly plead that it is against their

consciences, to support morality for the good of civil community, forfeit all claim to the benefit of law and protection.[89]

In 1785 three Connecticut newspapers carried extracts from *Observations on the Importance of the American Revolution*, by the admiring English Dissenter Richard Price. In a section dealing with religion, Price condemned "a civil establishment of a particular mode of religion" and detailed at length the evils such an arrangement introduced into Church and State. In the course of his discussion, Price noted that the new American states were "perfect strangers to such establishments."[90] Connecticut Congregationalists had no doubt that their system was utterly foreign to the one described by Price. However, after the outbreak of the American Revolution, they did not confine the word "establishment" to the sense in which Price used it, as their brethren in Massachusetts tended to do, although in the mid-1790s Zephaniah Swift took the attitude that the state possessed no establishment at all. Swift, a prominent Connecticut lawyer and politician, and a Unitarian, claimed that in 1784, by omitting the Saybrook Platform from the revision of its laws, Connecticut had abolished its establishment of religion: "No sect is invested with privileges superior to another. No creed is established, and no test excludes any" from office. He blithely asserted that Jews, Mahomedans, and others enjoyed perfect religious freedom in Connecticut, on the ground that they could practice their religion there—even if they had to pay for the support of the Christian one.[91]

On this matter, Swift was out of touch with the religious system of his state. In the same year that the statute books had dropped the Saybrook Platform, another statute had referred to the "worship and Ministry" established by law. Contemporaries all agreed that Congregationalism was established in the state. Congregationalists held that their establishment amounted to a socially useful system for the support of religion and public morality, that it was perfectly consonant with full liberty of conscience, and that it had nothing in common with a tyrannical "civil" establishment. Dissenters from the system held that any state-supported religion constituted a "civil" establishment by definition, that Connecticut's establishment fitted that definition, and that it abridged their religious liberty.

On the outskirts of New England, Vermont and New Hampshire carried on the ecclesiastical traditions of Massachusetts and Connecticut, but with several variations from the more tightly controlled systems of their two Puritan neighbors to the south. Vermont could barely claim statehood during the revolutionary period. A territory long disputed by New York, Massachusetts, and New Hampshire, it ruled itself according to its own constitution from 1777 on, but was not permitted to join the Union as a separate state until 1791.

Many of the earliest settlers of both Vermont and New Hampshire were Congregationalists from Massachusestts and Connecticut, who brought their Church-State traditions along with them; but the frontier nature of their new environment dictated that ecclesiastical arrangements would be less formal, less centralized, and more adaptable than in the colonies they had left. Nevertheless, the authorities in both, in making provisions for the settlement of churches and ministries in the towns, assumed that the majority of the population was and would continue to be Congregationalist. This envisioned majority did not always materialize, however. As a result, the theory whereby different denominations might be supported at public expense depending on the choice of individual communities—supposedly applicable in Massachusetts and Connecticut—came much closer to actual implementation in Vermont and New Hampshire.

Isaac Backus wrote in his *History* that in New Hampshire "the Congregational denominations were never exalted so high above all others" as they were in Massachusetts and Connecticut.[92] Nevertheless, from the end of the seventeenth century, New Hampshire had authorized its towns to provide a minister at public expense. However, the casual attitude of a colony unused to sharp dissent showed itself in the clause that exempted dissenters, "but only such as are Conscientiously So," a phrase the lawmakers made no attempt to explain.[93]

The colony treated Quakers, who did object in conscience to ministerial taxes, with leniency, by exempting them from paying for the support of churches and also relieving Friends elected constables from the task of collecting such taxes.[94] By 1775 Presbyterians formed the majority in about fifteen towns in New Hampshire, and though they had no objection to church taxes, they wanted to support their own ministers. In towns where disputes over ministerial support broke out between them and local Congregationalists, the General Court solved the problem by creating two parishes—each to be maintained by its respective adherents. However, by having the Presbyterians give in certificates and assuming that all others be deemed to belong to the "Congregational Society," the colony left no doubt that Presbyterians were considered a variant from the norm, rather than one among equal groups.[95]

By the time of the Revolution, Baptists had ten churches in New Hampshire. They opposed the system of tax support and refused to accept the solution, agreeable to the Presbyterians, of being set off as a separate parish obliged to pay taxes to their own minister. Their complaints in New Hampshire remained of a local nature, and Baptists there presented no such challenge to authorities of that new state as their co-religionists in Massachusetts mounted.[96]

After the outbreak of the Revolution, New Hampshire became the first state to draw up a written constitution. The Plan of Government of 1776 left the ecclesiastical system unchanged and unmentioned. So did a new proposed constitution in 1779, except that it forbade laws infringing upon the "rights of conscience" or contrary to the laws of God or "against the Protestant religion." The people of New Hampshire waited until 1784, however, before ratifying a full constitution with a bill of rights.[97]

Having guaranteed freedom of worship, the constitution ratified in 1784 proceeded to an article akin to Massachusetts's Article III, but with some differences. The New Hampshire version empowered the legislature to authorize the towns of the state to make provision for "public protestant teachers of piety, religion, and morality." It did not, however, require that all pay to some minister or attend some worship. As in earlier legislation, New Hampshire lawmakers made no effort to provide a mechanism for the system's functioning, e.g. by specifying a certificate system, but did stipulate what many Massachusetts towns had requested be made an amendment to Article III, i.e. that no person of one sect would ever be forced to pay toward the support of another.[98]

The absence from New Hampshire constitutions of detailed instructions on how to operate the ecclesiastical system reflected a lack of opposition to the Church-State arrangement, which allowed the legislators to be careless about checking for loopholes in its operation. William Plumer, who had just abandoned Baptist preaching for Unitarianism and politics, criticized the constitution for limiting the protection of the law and officeholding to Protestants. Other than that, the constitutional provisions for religion caused little stir within the state.[99] This religious calm was an inheritance from the colonial process in New Hampshire, in which individual communities made adjustments for particular groups and settled conflicts for themselves, an approach that continued and quickened during the revolutionary period.

In 1777 the town of Plymouth, New Hampshire, distrained some Baptists for the support of the Congregational minister; but in 1780 it exempted them from such support.[100] In other towns, such as Amherst, groups who lived too far from the church or did not like the minister asked to be incorporated as a poll parish.[101] In 1788 some of the inhabitants of Cornish and Plainfield wrote to the New Hampshire General Court requesting to be set off as a poll parish because of the great "diversity of Sentiments" and the "jarring opinions concerning the most suitable place for Buildings for Religious worship." Besides, the petitioners noted, the "inhabitants of Different Settlements are so intermixed" that drawing parish lines would not solve the problem. These petitioners withdrew their request, however, when Cornish declared that only those who had previously consented to ministerial taxes would be required to pay them. Apparently, this concession brought the two towns together.[102]

Other New Hampshire towns, such as Claremont, passed exemptions for dissenters. In some areas, however, Baptists combined with others to gain a majority and exempted themselves. In Hampstead, in 1782, such a consolidation merged to prevent the settlement of a new minister on the death of the former one. After several years at loggerheads, the different groups reached an agreement to exempt non-Congregationalists; but after the next few years, during which they tried supporting their own minister, the Congregationalists themselves gave up, and the town was left without a clergyman.[103]

For Baptists a more drastic development came about when one of their own clergy, Job Seamons, accepted the position of town minister of New London in 1788. To Isaac Backus's considerable relief, Seamons abandoned the position in 1795, declaring it (as Backus wrote) "to be such a bondage to be supported by tax and compulsion."[104]

In Holderness, in 1783, Episcopalians secured a majority and installed their minister as the town's publicly supported clergyman. In Langdon in 1804 and in South New Market in 1808, Methodists and Universalists respectively did likewise. Such local adjustments would seem to confirm the comment of a Baptist correspondent, in a letter to Backus written in 1783, that "there is a Great fall of Bigotry." Nevertheless, in towns where they could not secure a majority, Baptists still had to fight—sometimes unsuccessfully—for exemptions.[105]

During the 1780s, New Hampshire ministers told the General Court much the same things their counterparts in Boston or Hartford communicated to their legislatures. In 1784 Gershon Clark Lyman admitted that the propriety of public tax support for ministers was disputed by "many serious persons." In spite of that, however, he reminded the legislature of its duty to provide such support, and his fellow preachers followed suit, not only discoursing to the legislators on the temporal benefits of religion, but informing them that liberty of religion was preserved provided government imposed no articles of faith, that the law should punish blasphemy and "open contempt" of religion, and that "Infidels and deists" should not be allowed to touch the reins of government.[106]

As the eighteenth century neared its end, Baptists and other non-Congregationalists in New Hampshire became increasingly restive and, in 1819, they toppled the ecclesiastical system there. In 1790, however, most Congregational ministers agreed with historian Jeremy Belknap that the state enjoyed "as entire religious liberty . . . as any people can rationally desire." The population at large concurred, and that year voted overwhelmingly to reject an amendment to the state constitution that would have allowed the inhabitants of the towns to hand in certificates if they wished to be exempted from ministerial taxes and also an amendment that would have abolished the requirement that holders of public office be Protestant.[107]

In Vermont the rapid growth of churches marked the pace of settlement. In 1776 Baptists had two churches there, and Congregationalists had eleven. By 1790 the figures had climbed to thirty-four Baptist and fifty-eight Congregational churches. As the population continued to rise, Baptists and other non-Congregationalists increased disproportionately to Congregationalists.[108]

In 1777 Vermont drew up a constitution whose religious provisions formed a curious mixture. These provisions survived their inherent contradictions only because the people of Vermont did not try to implement them literally. Article 3 set forth an inalienable right to worship "regulated by the word of God." It declared that no man "who professes the protestant religion" could be deprived of "any civil right" because of his religion. No one could be "compelled to attend any religious worship, or maintain any minister," but "every sect or denomination . . . ought to observe the Sabbath" and "support, some sort of religious worship." Officeholders had to proclaim belief in God, both Old and New Testaments, and the Protestant religion.[109]

A lack of controversy over support of churches and ministers indicated that the different groups within the towns of Vermont reconciled their opposing views. The first law dealing with the details of church support —passed in 1783—reflected an accommodating spirit. It enabled towns to support a ministry, but to do so, at least seven persons had to petition the Town Meeting, and the motion had to be approved by two-thirds of the voters to make it legal. Lest "some . . . pretend to differ . . . only to escape Taxation," petitioners were to produce certificates signed by an officer of the church they attended. No doubt the Vermont legislators assumed that the majority of the ministers chosen would be Congregationalist, but the law specified "Ministers of the Gospel" only.[110]

In 1785 sentiment for a general assessment apparently emerged in Vermont, but after drawing some fire from Baptists, it quietly disappeared. The revised state constitution of 1786 extended the protection of the laws to all, but retained the religious test for officeholders. Article 3 left the question of public maintenance even more unclear than its predecessor by retaining the demand that every "sect or denomination" of Christians "keep up some sort of religious worship," but omitting the words "and support" from that requirement. The following year, however, in a revision of the laws, Vermont provided a hedge against conflict by granting incorporation to all religious groups that supported worship, thus eliminating possible controversy arising out of a town's questioning the legitimacy of a dissenting group.[111]

Isaac Backus included in his *History* a letter he received in 1795 from a fellow Baptist in Hartford, Vermont, giving details of distraint of a Baptist in the town. By that time, Baptists in Vermont had begun their campaign against the law for support of churches and ministers, again claiming that it violated the rights of conscience, as well as several articles of the state's constitution. Backus noted, however, that he had "failed of obtaining more accounts of . . . [Baptist] churches, and of their sufferings in Vermont" and later wrote that he had no "account of great sufferings there."[112]

Although both New Hampshire and Vermont provided for the public support of religion, neither state referred to this system as an establishment. In 1803 Chief Justice Jeremiah Smith of New Hampshire, subscribing to the view that an establishment constituted an exclusive set of doctrines, declared that the state had no establishment.[113] Baptists would not have agreed with him. Earlier, in 1792, a Baptist minister, Caleb Blood, had preached to the Vermont legislature against "religious establshment by law." He condemned what Smith later explicitly avowed, "making religion a mere engine of state policy, and setting up ministers to be supported by the civil arm," and added that he would not "be found with those who wish for religious establishments by law."[114] The following year, Baptists at Woodstock, Vermont, issued a statement condemning "all religious establishments (so-called) which bind men in acts of building meeting houses, settling ministers, etc.," and called for purely voluntary support of religion.[115]

When Baptists opposed an establishment of religion, they were opposing the legislation by which states provided for the formation and maintenance of parishes and churches and the support of ministers. Apart from these specifics, they were at one with Congregationalists, or with Congregationalists-turned-Unitarians, such as Smith, who often became the most fervent backers of tax-supported religion. Chief

Justice Smith had also declared from the bench in 1803 that "religious opinions shall in no case form any ground of civil distinction," although he lived in a state that limited officeholding and protection of the laws to Protestants, and that enforced Sabbath laws.[116]

Vermont Baptist Caleb Blood would have disagreed with Smith both on doctrine and on the support of churches, but they would have agreed on much else of a Church-State nature. Blood thought that religion was a matter between God and the individual; yet he would not "countenance those, who through fear of religious tyranny despise good order in society and reject those friendly aids to the cause of our holy religion, which may justly be expected from our political fathers." Such "aids" included laws for punishment of murder, theft, adultery, and for protection of the Sabbath. He did not list, but the statute books did, the death penalty for blasphemy of the Trinity.[117]

Blood's acceptance of government aid to religion represented a point of agreement among probably the vast majority of Americans during the revolutionary period. In 1777 the Reverend J. H. Livingston of New York noted the responsibility of government to promote religion, but added that "by providing for religion is not intended the grant of any tythes . . . but only the putting all sects upon an equal and proper footing."[118] Americans differed sharply among themselves over whether state promotion and aid included public tax support for churches, but not over whether government should enforce the sabbath and respect for the scriptures, limit office to Christians or Protestants, and generally support the Christian Protestant mores that entwined both state and society. Moreover, the world of Protestantism or Christianity bounded the horizons of most Americans even when they spoke or wrote about "all." Coming as he did from a state that would exclude Catholics from office and naturalization, Livingston could hardly have included them on an "equal footing." Still less would he or others have envisaged the promotion of Judaism, Mahometanism, or any other non-Christian religion.

Throughout the states, Americans found themselves asserting that religion was a matter between God and the individual; that government possessed no intrinsic powers over matters of religion; and that when secular powers interfered in religious affairs, they exceeded their authority, violated religious liberty, and corrupted both Church and State. However, to portray revolutionary America as implementing these principles in all instances would be to misinterpret completely their historical context. In the absence of any significant number of dissenters from the dominant Protestant culture, Americans did not bring their accepted theories of Church and State to bear on the numerous ways by which governments did exercise jurisdiction in religious matters, and they continued to maintain the Christian Protestant society inherited from colonial times.

There were, of course, exceptions and challenges of note, if not effect. Catholics, for example, complained when they were excluded from officeholding; but they argued for a Christian State that would include them, not for a secular State that would include all.[119] John Leland was able to transcend his own intellectual milieu and articulate the extent to which the law and a particular religious view had become welded together. Jefferson's Statute for Religious Liberty asserted that "our civil rights have no dependence on our religious opinions," and Marylander William Vans Murray could see that any limitation on officeholding based on religion constituted an unlawful exercise of civil power. In Virginia a considerable number of petitioners learned to envision a whole society composed of both Chistians and non-Christians. However, all of these presaged the future more than they represented prevailing American opinion.

On one Church-State topic, the support of churches, Americans during the revolutionary period engaged in extensive discussion and applied their theory that the state had no power in religious matters. In the majority of states they decided that freedom of religion applied not only to the exercise of religion, but also to its support; one could not be compelled to attend religious worship, but neither could one be forced to pay for the worship one chose to attend.

Only one state, South Carolina, officially proclaimed an establishment. However, that state's establishment, amounting in fact to a method for incorporating churches, corresponded to no previous definition of the term, caused no controversy in the state, and disappeared without comment. Connecticut continued to assume that Congregationalism was still established. Massachusetts, New Hampshire, and Vermont, though they supported religion financially, did not refer to this as an establishment of religion.

Both those who supported and those who opposed state support of religion agreed that an establishment of religion meant primarily a state preference for one religion that constituted a tyrannical intrusion of the government into religious affairs. In Virginia supporters of a general assessment had referred to their plan to aid all Christian denominations as an establishment, but neither they nor their opponents had ever clearly or consciously differentiated between two kinds of establishments, one that helped a single denomination exclusively and one that helped all equally. Concerned primarily to show that it did not violate the free exercise of religion, proponents of a general assessment showed no consciousness of a need to develop such a distinction.

Apart from Connecticut's exception for its own "mild and equitable system," New Englanders limited their definition of establishment to the classic English sense. The theory from the colonial period that many establishments could co-exist side by side, depending on the choice of the towns, disappeared from New England discourse. Opponents of state support for religion regarded such support as an establishment, but they opposed it primarily as a violation of the free exercise of religion. Consequently, the image of an establishment that continued to dominate in the minds of Americans during the revolutionary period was a traditional one modeled on the Anglican establishment in England.

8

*"Congress shall make no law
respecting an establishment of
religion, or prohibiting the free
exercise thereof . . ."*

In 1789 the First Congress of the United States, responding to demands made by several states during the process of ratification of the federal Constitution, set about drawing up a Bill of Rights. By the end of 1791, the required three-fourths of the states had ratified this Bill of Rights in the form of a series of ten amendments to the Constitution. The first of these began with the statement, "Congress shall make no law respecting an establishment of religion, or prohibiting the free exercise thereof." This double declaration embodied the aspirations of many Americans during the colonial era, as well as the general thrust of American attitudes toward Church-State relations manifested during the revolutionary period. The meaning of so emphatic a statement should presumably have been clear; yet the question of the authors' intent has generated voluminous controversy, and the debates leading up to the passage by Congress of the First Amendment continue to raise problems ranging from paradoxical to impenetrable.

In endeavoring to determine the exact significance Congress and the states attached to the opening segment of the First Amendment, one must bear in mind the overall context of its enactment and ratification. Its guarantees did not represent the triumph of one particular party or specific viewpoint over a clear or entrenched opposition, but rather a consensus of Congress and nation. As Richard Henry Lee of Virginia noted, they were statements "for ages and nations yet unborn."[1]

Americans in 1789 largely believed that issues of Church and State had been satisfactorily settled by the individual states. They agreed that the federal government had no power in such matters, but some individuals and groups wanted that fact stated explicitly. Granted, not all the states would have concurred on a single definition of religious liberty; but since they were denying power to Congress rather than giving it, differences among them on that score did not bring them into contention.

Federalist supporters of the Constitution for the most part considered amendments unnecessary, believing that the rights it would protect were already perfectly secured. Many of them, however, were willing to go along with the idea of a Bill of Rights in order to ease the minds of those who feared the powers of the national government and to neutralize accusations that the Constitution menaced religious freedom. Anti-Federalists, suspicious and frightened of fresh and untried national control, sought more definite assurances that the powers of the new government would not destroy individual freedoms. The fact that Congress was not trying to resolve concrete disputes, but merely strengthening safeguards against possible future adversity, helps explain at least some of the inattentiveness and absentmindedness attendant upon Americans' enactment of the First Amendment.[2]

When George Mason of Virginia proposed at the Constitutional Convention in Philadelphia that a federal Bill of Rights be drawn up, the delegates—voting by states—unanimously rejected the suggestion.[3] The Convention had earlier accepted a ban on religious tests for federal office, thus depriving the new government of one of the most potent weapons of religious discrimination. Federalists believed that the Constitution in no way menaced religious liberty. With this belief, Isaac Backus, one of the most informed men in America on Church-State relations, agreed. He described the new Constitution as a door opened "for securing equal liberty, as never was before opened to any people upon earth."[4] Moreover, James Madison considered a Bill of Rights a poor strategy for protecting individual rights, in that specific definition would tend unduly to limit them. Alexander Hamilton argued that a Bill of Rights would even be dangerous, in that by specifying "exceptions to powers" not granted, it "would afford colorable pretext to claim more than were granted."[5]

A considerable number of their contemporaries felt otherwise. They found in the proposed Constitution a centralizing tendency they feared would ultimately deprive them of their liberties. Some used the omission to mask a general attack on the Constitution. Patrick Henry, one of the most dramatic and skillful Anti-Federalists, drew upon his impressive oratorical powers to prey on the apprehensions aroused by the omission of specific guarantees, such as that of religious freedom.[6]

Champions of the new government easily recognized the ploy of using the lack of a Bill of Rights to assail the Constitution in its entirety. Referring to ratification of the Constitution, Edmund Pendleton wrote Madison in 1789 that "nothing was further from the wish of some, who covered their opposition to the Government under the masque of uncommon zeal for amendments." Madison himself made the same complaint to Washington, and from Pennsylvania, Federalist Tench Coxe wrote Madison that the passage of amendments would deprive the critics of the Constitution of their best arguments.[7]

Apart from those irreconcilable opponents of the Constitution, many others genuinely wanted a formal protection for religious liberty. Richard Henry Lee wrote that while contemporary America suffered little religious turmoil, a Constitution made for the ages should proclaim the right to "the free exercise of religion." From France Jefferson sent a steady stream of correspondence to Madison pointing out the need for a Bill of Rights that included protection for "freedom of religion," and in early 1788, Madison's own father informed him that Virginia's Baptists were generally opposed to the Constitution and were complaining that, among other defects, it did not provide for religious liberty.[8]

Commentators throughout the states failed to address the question of religious freedom at great length or in detail. Anti-Federalists trumpeted the need to protect religious liberty, trial by jury, and freedom of the press; but of these three, the first assumed least importance.[9] Several exhibited a combination of contradictory sentiments on Church and State not untypical in America at the time. A writer from western Massachusetts, for example, objected that the proposed Constitution provided no liberty to the people to "perform religious worship according to the dictates of their consciences," then followed that charge with the complaint that "there is a door opened for the Jews, Turks, and Heathens to enter into publick office." Another citizen of Massachusetts wrote that although the people of his state loved liberty, they had nevertheless adopted a religious test.[10]

Luther Martin of Maryland revealed that he would have offered a Bill of Rights to the Constitutional Convention had he thought it would have gained acceptance. Nevertheless, he also stated that some members of the Convention, clearly including himself, were so unfashionable as to hold that for officeholders "it would be at least decent to hold out some distinction between the professors of Christianity and downright infidelity or paganism."[11] Henry Abbot, a delegate to the

North Carolina Ratifying Convention, mentioned that some of his constituents feared the new government would deprive them of their
religious liberty; but he also worried that in the absence of a religious
test, "pagans, deists, and Mahometans might obtain offices." A
delegate to the Massachusetts Convention complained that under the
federal Constitution, a "Papist or Infidel" would be as eligible for office
"as Christians."[12]

Expressions of this nature, on the one hand upholding freedom of
religion and on the other restricting it, exemplified the fact that
Americans habitually viewed Church-State relations within the framework of a Christian or Protestant society. The protestors from Massachusetts may well have been among those who in 1780 had criticized
their own state's constitution on the ground that it violated religious
liberty by providing for the public support of ministers, but simultaneously demanded that the holding of state offices be limited to
Protestants. Massachusetts Federalists, too, manifested peculiar incon-
sistencies. Several speakers in that state's Ratifying Convention
defended the omission from the new government of a religious test for
office, while continuing to support the imposition of a similar test by
their own state government.[13]

Apart from the matter of the omission of a test oath, concerns
expressed throughout the states as to the possible impact of the new
government on religious freedom were usually vague as to detail. They
mentioned the danger that the government might use the Constitution's general welfare clause to menace religious liberty, but only in a
loose and general way. The "rights of conscience" had been a topic of
considerable dispute in Virginia, Maryland, and the New England
states since the Revolution. In those states the principal bone of contention had been whether a provision for the public support of ministers
and churches violated these rights. However, virtually none of those
who now expressed fear for the "rights of conscience" under the federal
Constitution referred to those disputes or developed what they understood by the term.

In Pennsylvania, "Centinel" held up his own state's constitution
against the federal document and pointed out that the latter failed to
ensure that "no man ought, or of right can be compelled to attend any
religious worship, or erect or support any place of worship." The Pennsylvania Convention ratified the Constitution as submitted; but a
dissenting minority proposed the inclusion of a protection for "unalienable rights," including the rights of conscience. Like "Centinel," this
minority referred to these rights in terms of the state's constitution,
asking that the United States have no power to alter state provisions for

religious liberty. In New York, "Sydney" cited New York's guarantee of the free exercise of religion and its exclusion of clergy from office as worthy of imitation.[14]

"Timoleon" of New York did speculate that by way of a tax for the general welfare, the new government, in the absence of a declaration in "favor of the rights of conscience," might be able to suppress troublesome preachers, notwithstanding the state provision for liberty of religion. Both "An Old Whig" and "Deliberator" from Pennsylvania also opined that the national government might establish a uniformity of religion throughout the land by way of the same clause. Apart from these few clarifications, commentators enunciated the need for protection for the rights of conscience without elaboration.[15]

By contrast contemporary comments on an establishment of religion, although equally brief, followed virtually a uniform style. Americans throughout the new states, when they spoke or wrote of an establishment of religion, described it in terms of an exclusive government preference for one religion. At the Virginia Ratifying Convention, Madison asked:

> Would the bill of rights, in this state, exempt the people from paying for the support of one particular sect, if such sect were exclusively established by law? . . . Fortunately for this commonwealth, a majority of the people are decidedly against any exclusive establishment.

Edmund Randolph of Virginia pointed out that the multiplicity of sects would prevent "the establishment of any one sect, in prejudice to the rest." Patrick Henry, insisting on the need for an amendment on religion, stated that "no particular sect or society ought to be favored or established, by law, in preference to others."[16]

In the South Carolina debates on the Constitution, the Reverend Francis Cummins voiced his opposition to "religious establishments; or of states giving preference to any religious denomination."[17] In the North Carolina Convention, the delegates argued the issue of establishment in similar words.[18] Maryland's minority proposal asked that "there be no National Religion established by Law."[19] In Pennsylvania "An Old Whig" wrote of the danger of the federal government's setting up a "national religion," and John Smilie expressed a fear in that state's Convention debates that "Congress may establish any religion."[20] New York submitted an amendment on religion stating that "no Religious Sect or Society ought to be favored or established by Law in preference to others."[21]

In Connecticut, Oliver Ellsworth, replying to criticisms of the Constitution, pointed out that Americans enjoyed full religious liberty unlike other countries, where "one religion" was "established by law." At his state's Convention, he stated that given the prevalence of knowledge and liberty, the United States would never "be disposed to establish one religious sect, and lay all others under legal disabilities."[22]

This description of establishment presents a paradox to the modern historian. By emphasizing the "exclusive" favoring of "one particular sect," Americans appeared to draw a careful distinction between such an exclusive establishment and a non-exclusive establishment or favoring of several or all sects. However, during the revolutionary period, the only serious Church-State conflicts had to do not with exclusive state preference for a single religion, but with proposals for non-preferential state support of many religious groups. This issue gave rise to bitter struggles in New England, in Maryland, and in Virginia where Madison led the opposition. Nevertheless, when Americans discussed the relationship between religion and the new federal government, they all—including Madison—apparently ignored this crucial question, i.e. a general assessment type of support for religion, and apparently concentrated on exclusive or preferential government aid to religion—something that did not exist in America at the time and had not a public defender in the land. This paradoxical behavior continued through Congress's discussion of a Bill of Rights and is best examined after a review of that process.

On May 4, 1789, Madison announced in the House of Representatives his intention to introduce amendments to the Constitution.[23] Just getting elected to Congress had proved difficult for him. Patrick Henry and the Virginia Anti-Federalists had bent all their efforts to securing a second constitutional convention. Failing in this, they concentrated on blocking the election of Federalists to Congress.[24] In pursuit of this strategy, they nurtured the fears of Virginia Baptists that the federal Constitution provided insufficient protection for religious freedom. Having only recently experienced persecution in Virginia, Baptists feared even the shadow of a power that might be able to limit their preaching or tax them for the support of any religion, including their own. Madison found himself having to assuage these fears.

This was not the first time Madison had reasserted the consistency of his beliefs. At the Virginia Ratifying Convention he had cited his "uniform conduct on this subject" of religious liberty. Once again he now convinced the Baptists that he was a friend to religious freedom and, with their backing, defeated his opponent James Monroe for a Congressional seat. Once elected, however, Madison made certain not to leave himself open to any charge of negligence, and on June 8 he informed the House that he considered himself "bound in honor and in duty" to present and advocate amendments.[25]

The accomplishment of this declared duty required a certain persistence on Madison's part, since the House presented some opposition to devoting precious time to amendments many of its members considered needless. Organizing the government and enacting a judiciary bill took precedence for these members. Indeed, during the entire period when the subject of a Bill of Rights was before them, Congressmen devoted more time to debating its necessity, to discussion of whether such guarantees should be incorporated into the text of the existing Constitution or listed separately, and to philosophical orations on the nature of representation and government than they did to examining the individual rights in question.[26] However, although Congress did adopt the proposed amendments in a somewhat hasty fashion, the reported debates, brief though they were, cast a modicum of light on the meaning of what would become the religion clauses of the First Amendment.

In the course of a lengthy speech on a Bill of Rights, Madison reaffirmed the plausibility of his previous objection that "enumerating particular exceptions to the grant of power, . . . [might] disparage those rights which were not placed in that enumeration." However, this danger could be guarded against, he reasoned, by a specific declaration that the amendments did not "enlarge the powers delegated by the constitution" or "diminish the just importance of other rights retained by the people." Shortly thereafter, referring to protections for individual rights both as they appeared in the state constitutions and the proposals before the federal government, Madison commented that in some instances "they do no more than state the perfect equality of mankind." Clearly, he intended that this Bill of Rights would merely make more explicit what he believed already.

In his series of amendments, Madison included two dealing with religion. The first proposed:

> The civil rights of none shall be abridged on account of religious belief or worship, nor shall any national religion be established, nor shall the full and equal rights of conscience be in any manner, or on any pretext, infringed.

The second stated that "no State shall violate the equal rights of conscience."[27]

On June 10 the House agreed to consider Madison's amendments as a committee of the whole, but six weeks later, on July 21, Madison had once again to prod his colleagues to action. The House then referred his proposed amendments, together with those submitted by the states, to a select committee composed of one member from each of the eleven states represented in Congress.[28]

Madison sat on this select committee, which one week later, on July 28, submitted its report. By August 15 the House reached the section of the report dealing with religion, and the discussion was brief enough to allow its quotation in full:

> The House again went into a Committee of the whole on the proposed amendments to the constitution, Mr. Boudinot in the chair.
>
> The fourth proposition being under consideration, as follows:
>
> Article 1. Section 9. Between paragraphs two and three insert "no religion shall be established by law, nor shall the equal rights of conscience be infringed."
>
> Mr. Sylvester had some doubts of the propriety of the mode of expression used in this paragraph. He apprehended that it was liable to a construction different from what had been made by the committee. He feared it might be thought to have a tendency to abolish religion altogether.
>
> Mr. Vining suggested the propriety of transposing the two members of the sentence.
>
> Mr. Gerry said it would read better if it was that no religious doctrine shall be established by law.
>
> Mr. Sherman thought the amendment altogether unnecessary, inasmuch as Congress had no authority whatever delegated to them by the constitution to make religious establishments; he would, therefore, move to have it struck out.
>
> Mr. Carroll.—As the rights of conscience are, in their nature, of peculiar delicacy, and will little bear the gentlest touch of governmental hand; and as many sects have concurred in opinion that they are not well secured under the present constitution, he said he was much in favour of adopting the words. He thought it would tend more towards conciliating the minds of the people to the Government than almost any other amendment he had heard proposed. He would not contend with gentlemen about the phraseology, his object was to secure the substance in such a manner as to satisfy the wishes of the honest part of the community.
>
> Mr. Madison said, he apprehended the meaning of the words to be, that Congress should not establish a religion, and enforce the legal observation of it by law, nor compel men to worship God in any manner contrary to their conscience. Whether the words are necessary or not, he did not mean to say, but they had been required by some of the State Conventions, who seemed to entertain an opinion that under the clause of the constitution, which gave power to Congress to make all laws necessary and proper to carry into execution the constitution,

and the laws under it, enabled them to make laws of such a nature as might infringe the rights of conscience, and establish a national religion; to prevent these effects he presumed the amendment was intended, and he thought it as well expressed as the nature of the language would admit.

Mr. Huntington said that he feared, with the gentleman first up on this subject, that the words might be taken in such latitude as to be extremely hurtful to the cause of religion. He understood the amendment to mean what had been expressed by the gentleman from Virginia; but others might find it convenient to put another construction upon it. The ministers of their congregations to the Eastward were maintained by the contributions of those who belonged to their society; the expense of building meeting-houses was contributed in the same manner. These things were regulated by by-laws. If an action was brought before a Federal Court on any of these cases, the person who neglected to perform his engagements could not be compelled to do it; for a support of ministers, or building of places of worship might be construed into a religious establishment.

By the charter of Rhode Island, no religion could be established by law; he could give a history of the effects of such a regulation; indeed the people were now enjoying the blessed fruits of it. He hoped, therefore, the amendment would be made in such a way as to secure the rights of conscience, and a free exercise of the rights of religion, but not to patronize those who professed no religion at all.

Mr. Madison thought, if the word national was inserted before religion, it would satisfy the minds of honorable gentlemen. He believed that the people feared one sect might obtain a pre-eminence, or two combine together, and establish a religion to which they would compel others to conform. He thought if the word national was introduced, it would point the amendment directly to the object it was intended to prevent.

Mr. Livermore was not satisfied with that amendment; but he did not wish them to dwell long on the subject. He thought it would be better if it was altered, and made to read in this manner, that Congress shall make no laws touching religion, or infringing the rights of conscience.

Mr. Gerry did not like the term national, proposed by the gentleman from Virginia, and he hoped it would not be adopted by the House. It brought to his mind some observations that had taken place in the conventions at the time they were considering the present constitution. It had been insisted upon by those who were called antifederalists, that this form of Government consolidated the Union; the honorable gentleman's motion shows that he considers it in the same light. Those who were called antifederalists at that time complained that they had injustice done them by the title, because they were in favor of a Federal Government, and the others were in favor of a national one; the federalists were for ratifying the constitution as it stood, and the others not until amendments were made. Their names then ought not to have been distinguished by federalists and antifederalists, but rats and antirats.

Mr. Madison withdrew his motion, but observed that the words "no national religion shall be established by law," did not imply that the Government was a national one; the question was then taken on Mr. Livermore's motion, and passed in the affirmative, thirty-one for, and twenty against it.[29]

With the exception of the comments by the first speaker, the debate is explicable in its contemporary context. What construction Peter Sylvester of New York feared might be given to the proposed amendment, or how it might tend to abolish religion, remains obscure. None of the parties to disputes regarding Church and State in colonial or revolutionary America had ever argued that such statements as those proposed threatened the existence of religion. Without other evidence or expressions of his intent to serve as a guide to Sylvester's sentiments, speculation as to his intention is useless.

Elbridge Gerry's first comment owed its form to his Massachusetts background. Gerry had no doubt heard or read many Election Sermons condemning imposition of "articles of faith" or "modes of worship," and he wanted to use a familiar form.[30] Roger Sherman's statement that followed projected another attitude typical of New England, i.e. that Congress had nothing whatsoever to do with religion and the amendment was unnecessary.

Like many of those who had asked for an amendment protecting religious liberty, Daniel Carroll was satisfied with a statement to that effect without subjecting it to analysis. Indeed, all Americans could accept "phraseology" protecting the "rights of conscience" or banning the imposition of "articles of faith" or the "establishment of one sect in preference to another." They disagreed, however, over the substantive meaning of such terms. A majority of Virginians, for example, had clearly demonstrated that in their view a general assessment violated the "rights of conscience," while a majority of the inhabitants of Massachusetts obviously felt it did not. Both states proclaimed equal devotion to the term "rights of conscience," but because all believed that such matters pertained to the states, and that they were making explicit the fact that the federal government had nothing to do with religion, no collision of their differing views as to what constituted a violation of "rights of conscience" took place.

Benjamin Huntington, like Sylvester, feared a general negative impact on religion; but Huntington clarified his apprehensions. He feared the amendment might give Congress power to interfere with existing arrangements in the individual states. Since Congress sat in New York, his mention of "congregations to the Eastward" referred to his home state of Connecticut. Whether he thought that the system whereby towns were taxed for the support of the local minister (always Congregational) chosen by their inhabitants constituted an establishment of religion, Huntington did not say. Congregationalists in that state, however, generally assumed that their religion was established.

Huntington's remarks on Rhode Island could be interpreted as an assertion that the Connecticut arrangement constituted an establishment. Although he was mistaken in saying that the Rhode Island charter forbade an establishment of religion, he seemed to hold that the absence of an establishment lay at the root of what most citizens of Connecticut and elsewhere in America regarded as the irresponsibility of Rhode Island. James Johnson of Georgia, earlier in the debate on the Bill of Rights, had noted the "licentiousness" of Rhode Island, and Connecticut newspapers frequently referred to it in such sarcastic terms as 'its enviable and blessed condition."[31]

When Huntington asked that the amendment not patronize those who professed no religion, he was advancing the standard New England argument that since religion was necessary to a civil society, the states should patronize and promote it, that their doing so constituted no violation of conscience provided they forced no one to pay for the support of a religion other than his own. Abolishing such a system could only patronize and favor atheists, "Nothingarians," and the irresponsible elements of society, who would take advantage of freedom to support no religion. To avoid such a state of affairs, he wanted to keep the federal government from any pronouncement that might tend to affect Connecticut's Church-State system.

Samuel Livermore's intervention clarified only that he was wedded to the wording of the amendment proposed by his own state. In substance Livermore's wording, as he intimated, did not alter Madison's original proposal or the select committee's rewording of that—other than to clarify specifically that the limitation applied to Congress. Madison's suggestion of using the word "national" had grated on the sensibilities of the Anti-Federalist Gerry, and Madison promptly withdrew it, probably surmising that omission of the word would serve to ease the ratification of the amendment by the state legislatures. Indeed, his responses in this debate betrayed an inattentiveness to the specifics of the amendment that went along with his expressed intention not to dwell on "whether the words are necessary or not," and appeared to justify the comment of Senator Pierce Butler of South Carolina:

> A few *milk-and-water* amendments have been proposed by Mr. M., such as liberty of conscience, a free press, and one or two general things already well secured. I suppose it was done to keep his promise with his constituents, ... but, if I am not greatly mistaken, he is not hearty in the cause of amendment.[32]

The House then moved on to debate other provisions of the proposed Bill of Rights. After two more days, it arrived at the next section dealing with religion, which read that "no State shall infringe the equal rights of conscience." The select committee had listed this amendment verbatim from Madison's original proposal, no doubt with some prodding on his part, as he considered it the most valuable of all. Again, the debate proved brief enough to allow its quotation:

> Article 1, section 10, between the first and second paragraph, insert "no State shall infringe the equal rights of conscience, nor the freedom of speech or of the press, nor of the right of trial by jury in criminal cases."
>
> Mr. Tucker.—This is offered, I presume, as an amendment to the constitution of the United States, but it goes only to the alteration of the constitutions of particular States. It will be much better, I apprehend, to leave the State Governments to themselves, and not to interfere with them more than we already do; and that is thought by many to be rather too much. I therefore move, sir, to strike out these words.
>
> Mr. Madison conceived this to be the most valuable amendment in the whole list. If there was any reason to restrain the Government of the United States from infringing upon these essential rights, it was equally necessary that they should be secured against the State Governments. He thought that if they provided against the one, it was as necessary to provide against the other, and was satisfied that it would be equally grateful to the people.
>
> Mr. Livermore had no great objection to the sentiment, but he thought it not well expressed. He wished to make it an affirmative proposition; "the equal rights of conscience, the freedom of speech or of the press, and the right of trial by jury in criminal cases, shall not be infringed by any State."
>
> This transposition being agreed to, and Mr. Tucker's motion being rejected, the clause was adopted.[33]

This action by the House, recommending a limitation on the actions of states, is most perplexing in that it appeared to anticipate the judicial revolution of the twentieth century, by which the Supreme Court extended the Bill of Rights to the states.[34] Thomas Tucker of South

Carolina apprehended at least vaguely the critical implication of the proposal; but, astonishingly, neither he nor anyone else developed the argument.

If this amendment had passed, would Baptists, who detested as a violation of conscience the New England states' tax support of religion, have brought their case to federal court, thus bringing to pass what Benjamin Huntington feared might happen in Connecticut? On the matter of the violation of the rights of conscience, Madison would clearly have agreed with the New England Baptists, but equally clearly he did not intend that his proposed amendments make any alteration in the relationship between the federal government and the states. Repeatedly, in his correspondence, as well as in his speeches, he asserted that he sought achievable amendments that would eschew controversy and gain ratification of three-fourths of the states, and that he would oppose any proposal that altered the Constitution.[35]

Clearly, neither he nor the members of the House detected in the proposal an invitation to the federal government to pass judgment on existing Church-State arrangements in the states. Apparently, Congressman Tucker's point made little impression at all on his colleagues. Why they did not realize the radical potential of the amendment, not only for the future but for their own times, remains a mystery.

A partial answer to this enigma lies in the almost total obliviousness on the part of the House to Church-State dissension in New England, the only real potential source of conflict between state and federal governments in the event of passage of the amendment in question. This lack of awareness extended even to the Representatives from New England itself. Although Baptists bitterly opposed the New England system of state support for churches, none of them sat in Congress. The Congregationalists dismissed out of hand assertions that their system could be unfair, and opposing views hardly registered on their consciousness. Further, few Americans outside of New England knew of the stinging Church-State disputes that took place there.

Furthermore, Congressmen believed they were making declarations and stating principles, not solving present problems. Earlier that year Tench Coxe had written Madison that a provision analogous to the guarantee of a republican form of government might be passed to protect religion. Such would have great "eclat" in Europe and refute those who argued that the Constitution did not protect it sufficiently.

Madison himself had stated earlier that bills of rights sometimes "no more than state the perfect equality of mankind," and that the real danger to religious liberty lay in the power of majorities. Nevertheless, even though a Bill of Rights constituted no more than "paper barriers" against such majorities, he thought it important that the principle and statement of the right to religious liberty be publicly stated for the future." Some members doubtless agreed with Congressman Jackson of Georgia that the amendments were not worth "a pinch of snuff; they went to secure rights never in danger." Nevertheless, given the fears expressed by Huntington and Tucker, it is impossible to understand fully why the House in general, and Madison in particular, did not grasp the radical implications inherent in the proposed amendment to prohibit the states from violating the rights of conscience.[36]

On August 19 the House took up the amendments as reported by the committee of the whole. On August 21 Fisher Ames of Massachusetts proposed that the amendment on religion read, "Congress shall make no law establishing religion, or to prevent the free exercise thereof, or to infringe the rights of conscience." The House accepted this wording without debate or explanation for the change. On August 22 this amendment and the others adopted were referred to a committee of three that was directed "to arrange [them] . . . and make report thereof." On August 24 the House received this committee's arrangement and voted to forward the amendments to the Senate.[37]

Senate reports on the debate on the Bill of Rights are even more sketchy than those of the House. Meeting in secret session, the Senate allowed no reporters to be present. On August 24 it heard the proposed amendments and rejected a motion to postpone their consideration until the next session.[38] The *Senate Journal* for September 3 reported as follows on the progress of the amendments concerning religion:

> On motion, To amend Article third, and to strike out these words, "Religion or prohibiting the free Exercise thereof," and insert, "One Religious Sect or Society in preference to others." It passed in the Negative.
>
> On Motion, For reconsideration, It passed in the affirmative.
>
> On Motion, That Article the third be stricken out, It passed, in the Negative.
>
> On Motion, To adopt the following, inlieu of the third Article, "Congress shall not make any law, infringing the rights of conscience, or establishing any Religious Sect or Society," It passed in the Negative.
>
> On Motion, To amend the third Article, to read thus—"Congress shall make no law establishing any particular denomination of religion in preference to another, or prohibiting the free exercise thereof, nor shall the rights of conscience be infringed"—It passed in the Negative.
>
> On Motion, To adopt the third Article proposed in the Resolve of

the House of Representatives, amended by striking out these words—
"Nor shall the rights of conscience be infringed"—It passed in the
Affirmative.

On September 7 the Senators rejected without comment the House
amendment prohibiting the states from violating the rights of conscience. On September 9 they agreed: ". . . To amend Article the third,
to read as follows 'Congress shall make no law establishing articles of
faith or a mode of worship, or prohibiting the free exercise of religion
. . .'"[39]

The House disagreed with several of the amendments, including the
third—on religion—as altered by the Senate and requested a conference.[40] Even before the conference took place, the Senate agreed to
"recede from their third Amendment, and do insist on all the others."
On September 24 Madison, one of the members of the joint conference
committee, reported on the conference. The following day, the House
took up this report and agreed to the Senate amendments with three
conditions. The first was that the religion clauses of the third amendment read: "Congress shall make no law respecting an establishment of
religion, or prohibiting the free exercise thereof, . . ." The Senate
agreed to this wording, and so this amendment, together with the
others agreed to by the Congress, was ready for transmission to the
states for ratification.[41]

The Senate debate appears to add some clarity to what Americans
understood by establishment of religion. On its face, the report from
the Senate reads as a clash between those who wanted a broad prohibition of government action with regard to religion and those who
wanted a narrower restriction that would prohibit government from
imposing beliefs or favoring one sect or church, but, by implication,
would allow for non-discriminatory assistance to all religions. The
modern discussion of what Congress meant is inevitably framed by the
Supreme Court's statement on the subject.

In the *Everson* decision of 1947, a majority of the justices held:

> The "establishment of religion" clause of the First Amendment
> means at least this: Neither a state nor the Federal Government can set
> up a church. Neither can pass laws which aid one religion, aid all
> religions, or prefer one religion over another.[42]

By coming down on the side of the "broad" interpretation of an establishment of religion, i.e. prohibiting government aid to all religions,
the justices raised a storm of controversy. Their opponents charged
them with falsifying history and with subverting the original meaning
of the Amendment. Relying especially on a literal interpretation of the

references to establishment used in the Senate debate and in all the discussion dealing with the Bill of Rights, and stressing the multifarious contacts between governments and religion in colonial and revolutionary America, these critics contended that the amendment was intended only to ban a state religion—an exclusive government preference for one religion. Defenders of the Court stressed Madison's and Jefferson's clear position on Church and State and the evidence of the Virginia general assessment debate. They also argued that Americans understood and had experienced establishments that extended beyond a preference for a single religion to embrace many, and that the First Amendment banned both types. Despite their differences, both critics and supporters of the Court agreed that the Senate debate represented a clash between two different viewpoints on the meaning of establishment, although they disagreed on which position won out.[43]

Interpreting the language of establishment accompanying the passage of the First Amendment as an indication of a clash between those who would allow the federal government to give no aid to religion whatsoever and those who would allow it to give only non-discriminatory aid poses several problems for the historian. The first involves identifying the party that wanted to give the new government some, albeit limited, power over religious matters. At the Virginia Ratifying Convention, Madison had stated that the federal government had not the "shadow of a right . . . to intermeddle with religion," and all Americans, Federalists and Antifederalists, agreed with him. Apart from the literalist reading of the language used in connection with establishment, not a shred of evidence exists to verify that anyone wanted the new government to have any power in matters of religion. The argument that the First Amendment conferred—or even that a group in Congress wanted to confer—on the federal government some power with regard to religion validates the fear expressed by Madison and Hamilton that specifying a total ban on government might, in fact, limit the totality of such a ban. Ironically, what was intended as a declaration of no power has been interpreted as conferring some of the very power it was intended to forbid.

In addition, to read such phrases as "exclusive establishment" or the prohibition of any "particular sect" as meaning that those who used such terminology were distinguishing between government favor or establishment of one religion and non-exclusive government aid to all religions forces certain figures involved in the discussion of the First Amendment into absurd historical positions and contradicts all available evidence about their beliefs. James Madison and Patrick Henry diametrically opposed each other on the issue of state aid to religion in Virginia. However, if one is to interpret Madison's usage of "exclusive establishment" in the Virginia Convention and "national religion" in Congress to mean that he opposed only preferential government support to religion, then he did an inexplicable about turn and was prepared to allow the federal government power over religion that he would not grant his own state.[44]

Similarly, interpreting Henry's demand that "no particular religious sect or society ought to be favored or established by law in preference to others" as furnishing "a loophole for financial support to all churches" by the federal government contradicts his most vehemently held beliefs. Henry and the Virginia Anti-Federalists feared, almost to the point of paranoia, the power of the federal government. Specifically, they feared its taxing power, something they wanted to destroy, not protect.[45]

Moreover, the literal interpretation of the language of establishment renders the Senate debate inexplicable. If this represented a clash of parties, then the proponents of a "narrow" interpretation, i.e. those who favored non-preferential government support, having failed three times, eventually succeeded—only to "recede" without a struggle and accept the House version. Finally, the "broad" and "narrow" approach to the debate casts the Massachusetts Congregationalist Fisher Ames in the doubtful historical role of originator of the supposedly sweeping House version and opposed to those senators who purportedly championed the "narrow" one.

In order to understand Americans' usage of "establishment of religion" in 1789, one has to dispense with two assumptions common to modern commentators, be they supporters or critics of the Supreme Court's definition of the Establishment clause. The first of these is that Americans during the colonial and revolutionary eras made a conscious distinction between two kinds of establishment of religion, between an exclusive state preference for one Church and a non-exclusive assistance to all churches—what historians have subsequently described as a "multiple establishment." The second is that Americans during the same periods actually experienced both kinds of establishment.

In fact, Americans both before and after the Revolution thought of establishment as an exclusive government preference for one religion. Granted, during the colonial era, non-Anglican New Yorkers and Massachusetts Congregationalists, in order to ward off Anglican power or interference, devised contrived or confusing comments about the establishments in their colonies. The Revolution, however, removed

Anglican power and with it the need to argue that individual towns could choose which church to support. The theory of establishment by town disappeared in revolutionary America. Of the new states, only South Carolina proclaimed itself as having an establishment of religion. Although this system did embrace several Christian churches, it involved no public financial support and amounted to no more than a method of incorporating churches. The system disappeared in the new state constitution without leaving any traceable influence on its own or other states.

The New England States (Rhode Island excepted) continued to provide public support for religion, and scholars commonly refer to this practice as a "multiple establishment," i.e. a system by which all denominations received state support. This term projects back into the past a concept New Englanders did not employ. Of the New England states, only Connecticut candidly acknowledged an establishment; but references in its laws and public documents all presumed this to be a Congregational one.[46] Indeed, if citizens of any other of these New England states, especially Massachusetts, gave any thought—and there is little evidence that they did—to whether they had establishments of religion, they, too, probably conceived of such in terms of Congregationalism. Certainly, they showed no awareness that their states were supporting several, i.e. "multiple," establishments.

The dominant image of establishment Americans carried with them from the colonial period on was that of an exclusive government preference for one religion. Of course, New England Congregationalists, particularly in Massachusetts, contrasted their mild and equitable system with the English tyrannical one, what John Adams described as "creeds, tests, ceremonies, and tythes." Baptists, before and after the Revolution, disagreed with this. They regarded the New England ecclesiastical arrangements as an establishment of Congregationalism and the equivalent of the religious tyranny that Congregationalists decried in England.

After the advent of the Revolution, the supporters of a general assessment introduced a new idea into Church-State relations, a scheme that was genuinely designed to convey state support to the different Christian churches as distinct from the system in colonial New England, which was merely a cover for Congregational dominance. Opponents of a general assessment referred to it as an establishment, and at times its proponents did, too. Neither side, however, attempted to show that a general assessment constituted an essentially different kind of establishment or to differentiate it from an exclusive state preference for one religion. The parties to the general assessment dispute concerned themselves with showing whether it violated or did not violate freedom of religion. For its opponents in Virginia and Maryland, the common suspicion that a general assessment amounted to no more than a ruse to aid the Anglican Church only strengthened their assumption that it represented an extension of the traditional establishment.

One will look in vain for the analytical distinctions scholars presume the generation that enacted the First Amendment made between government establishment of a particular sect and government establishment or favor to many sects. When they condemned an establishment, they had in their minds an image of tyranny, not a definition of a system. Charles Chauncy had linked the advent of bishops with a "STATE ESTABLISHMENT," and Americans generally continued in the same vein by condemning the Quebec Act as an establishment of religion. In both cases they reacted on the basis of preconceived images rather than in response to a logical or analytical understanding of the meaning of establishment. This imagery explains why Jefferson, whose actual experience of established religion had been the relatively mild Anglican Church of Virginia, conjured up the specter of coercion of "millions of innocent men, women, and children [who] since the introduction of Christianity, have been tortured, fined, imprisoned" because governments had exceeded their legitimate power and set up establishments of religion.[47]

Moreover, during the revolutionary period, when Americans, irrespective of their stance on Church and State, spoke of banning the establishment of a particular sect or church in preference to others, they were not advocating a particular party viewpoint on establishment but employing an inherited terminology. Eighteenth-century American history offers abundant examples of writers using the concept of preference, when, in fact, they were referring to a ban on all government assistance to religion.

In 1716 Rhode Island addressed the question of public support of ministers in a law so sweeping that it even forbade voluntary contracts between ministers and churches. Yet the declared intent of the statute was to prevent "every Church, Congregation and Society . . . from endeavouring for Preheminence (*sic*) or superiority over the other by making use of the civil power." Shortly thereafter, some inhabitants of that colony wrote to correspondents in Massachusetts that religious peace consisted in "not allowing [religious] societies any superiority over one another; but each society supports their own ministry."[48] In 1764 Isaac Hunt, a Philadelphia pro-Quaker Anglican, commenting on the disputes there between Quakers and Presbyterians, noted that "no one Profession in particular can be established by law without a manifest breach of the original Foundation."[49] Isaac Backus, who opposed all goverment financial support of churches, condemned the Massachusetts system because it presumed "that the civil power has a right to set one religious sect up above another."[50]

Jefferson, in 1776, drafted a resolution to strip the civil power of all authority in matters of religion, yet his wording proposed "discontinuing the establishment of the English Church by law, taking away all privileges and preeminence of one religion over another." Virginia Baptists opposed the designedly non-discriminatory general assessment with a petition asking "that all Distinctions in your laws may be done away, and no order or Denomination of Christians in this Commonwealth have any separate Privileges allowed them."[51] In South Carolina, William Tennent called for prohibition of the establishment of "one religious denomination," even as he condemned the idea of "establishing all denominations" as absurd and impossible."[52] In 1783 a Maryland writer signing himself "E" opposed a "grant of religious privileges to any particular denomination of Christians." The writer, too, was using the language of preference to oppose all government aid, because he also commented that "our legislature have no more to do with any Christian denomination . . . than they have with the internal police of China."[53]

The Massachusetts town of Petersham, which excoriated the provision in the state's 1780 constitution for non-discriminatory public support of ministers as an "Engine in the Hands of Tyrants," submitted its own amendment for the voluntary support of religion and ended it with the words that "no subordination of any one Sect or Denomination to another shall ever be established by law."[54] When Rhode Island, that "licentious" state, notorious in New England for its refusal ever to give public support to religion, belatedly got around to ratifying the Constitution, it proposed its own amendment. It asked that "no particular sect or society ought to be favored or established by law."[55] Finally, in 1794, John Leland, one of the most radical of his contemporaries on issues of Church and State, proposed an amendment to the Massachusetts constitution banning test oaths and putting support for religion on a voluntary basis. Leland proposed, however, that that legislature never "establish any religion by law, [or] give any one sect a preference to another."[56]

Thus, men unmistakably opposed to proposals for non-discriminatory government assistance to religion continued to use the concept of preference for one religion. They did so because they never changed their image of establishment. As Madison wrote in his *Memorial and Remonstrance* about a general assessment:

Distant as it may be, in its present form, from the inquisition, it differs
from it only in degree; the one is the first step, the other the last in the
career of intolerance.[57]

Neither did those who supported a general assessment type of assistance to religion change their image of establishment. The assumption
that Massachusetts, Vermont, and New Hampshire, by their constitutions, established religion tends to confuse the issue in that it posits a
distinction on their part between a forbidden "exclusive" establishment
and a non-exclusive or "multiple" establishment set up by these state
constitutions. However, although these states demanded that religion
in general be supported, no evidence sustains the viewpoint that in so
doing they saw themselves as opting for a permissible, non-exclusive
establishment. They never described themselves as designing an establishment at all.

This common image explains the discussion of establishment
surrounding the Bill of Rights. James Madison and Patrick Henry,
although they differed diametrically over the issue of government aid to
religion, used the same words to describe establishment. When
Madison spoke of prohibiting a "national" religion, he was not opening
the door to the federal government's aid to religion in general. When
Henry called for a ban on the establishment of one sect "in preference
to others," he was not proposing that the federal government have the
power to tax for a national general assessment. A purely literalist
approach to the language used by Americans in colonial and revolutionary times in connection with the establishment of religion leads
only to confusion. For instance, when Anti-Federalists in Pennsylvania
petitioned the Pennsylvania Convention that "none should be compelled contrary to their principles . . . to hear or support the clergy of
any one religion," they were certainly not implying that people could
be compelled to hear and support the clergy of several or all religions.[58]
Similarly, when those connected with the passage of the Bill of Rights
spoke or wrote of an establishment of religion as government imposition of one sect or articles of faith, they were not implying that government could favor all sects or sponsor religion short of imposing a creed
on the populace.

Given the contemporary image and understanding of establishment,
the Senate debate can be seen as a discussion about style, not substance. By omitting the redundant phrase "nor shall the rights of conscience be infringed" from the House version, and by combining the
sections dealing with freedom of religion, press, and assembly, the
Senate manifested its concern for form. This concern with composition

rather than substance also explains why that body, after a debate that—read apart from its historical context—appears as a sharp division over the content of the amendment, "receded" so easily from its own version in favor of the House wording.

A concern for style, rather than a party attempt to leave room for a federal general assessment or other non-discriminatory aid to religion, better explains the different formats raised in the Senate debate. Senators from such states as North Carolina, Delaware, or New Jersey may well have wanted to substitute the terminology of their own state constitutions banning the establishment of "any one" sect, yet all these states demanded that religion be supported voluntarily.

Those desiring a ban on "articles of faith, or a mode of worship" may well have been New Englanders. Elbridge Gerry had argued for similar language in the House, and these phrases—covert references to the Anglican establishment and repeated in numerous Election Sermons—were dear to Congregationalists. The Anti-Federalist Gerry was hardly trying to confer more power on the federal government by substituting a "narrow" definition; nor would other New England Congregationalists, who found their own Church-State arrangements quite satisfactory, want to the give the new government a share in their ordering. In any event, the "articles of faith" terminology did not identify a "narrow" Church-State party. Isaac Backus, the most dedicated opponent of the New England ecclesiastical system, mistakenly believed that the First Amendment actually read that "Congress shall make no law establishing articles of faith, or a mode of worship," but he happily accepted that wording. This language adequately represented his aspirations for Church and State, and he continued to believe that Massachusetts's provision of tax support for churches—even on a non-discriminatory basis—violated such a ban.[59]

The House, too, exhibited a concern for style. Congressman Vining wanted to reverse the clauses. The entire body spent a goodly amount of time debating whether the amendment should be presented separately or incorporated into the existing Constitution. Samuel Livermore did not like the phrasing, but did not want to spend time on further debate. Fisher Ames displayed a somewhat contemptuous attitude toward the proposed amendments, especially insofar as he perceived them as representing popular rights. However, he also wanted to save time and enact amendments "more rational and less *ad populum*" than Madison's.[60] Ames's proposal did not differ in substance from what Madison wanted or from Livermore's previously accepted one. Since it nevertheless received the assent of the majority, the House must have found his phrasing more felicitous.

Thus the debate in Congress represented not a clash between parties arguing for a "broad" or "narrow" interpretation or between those who wished to give the federal government more or less power in religious matters. It represented rather a discussion about how to state the common agreement that the new government had no authority whatsoever in religious matters.

The process of ratification of the Bill of Rights by three-fourths of the state legislatures took slightly more than a year, but threw little further light on what contemporaries thought they were enacting.[61] The first two proposed amendments failed passage, and thus the third proposal, containing the clauses on religion, became the First Amendment. Nine states ratified quickly, recording hardly a comment. Georgia adopted the attitude that the amendments were unnecessary and refused to ratify. The upper house in Connecticut apparently took the same stand, although the lower house was willing to approve. In Massachusetts both houses accepted most of the amendments, including what became the First Amendment, but the legislature never got around to making this action formal.[62]

Virginia, whose assent to the Bill of Rights late in 1791 brought the number of ratifying states to the requisite three-fourths, delayed acceptance so long not because of any specific objection to the amendments, but because of continuing Anti-Federalist opposition to the whole federal Constitution. Edmund Randolph wrote to Washington that the House in Virginia "easily agreed" to the first ten amendments.[63] However, Patrick Henry and his allies in the Virginia Senate continued to do all in their power to hinder the operation and the progress of the federal government.

In September 1789 the Anti-Federalist United States Senators from Virginia, Richard Henry Lee and William Grayson, transmitted the proposed amendments to their state's legislature with a letter explaining that they had attempted without success to secure the "radical amendments proposed by the Convention and approved by the Legislature of our Country [Virginia]." These "radical amendments"—none of which dealt with religion—attempted to further limit the federal government and had been presented to and rejected by the United States Senate. Faced with this failure and in a desperate effort to interrupt the smooth functioning of the federal government, Virginia's Anti-Federalists even attacked the proposed third article as an inadequate protection for freedom of religion.[64]

The Senators in the Virginia legislature who opposed the amendment claimed:

> The 3rd amendment recommended by Congress does not prohibit
> the rights of conscience from being violated or infringed: and although
> it goes to restrain Congress from passing laws establishing any national
> religion, they might, notwithstanding, levy taxes to any amount, for
> the support of religion or its preachers; and any particular denomina-
> tion of Christians might be so favored and supported by the General
> Government, as to give it a decided advantage over others, and in pro-
> cess of time render it as powerful and dangerous as if it were estab-
> lished as the national religion of the country.[65]

No one in or out of Congress had believed that the federal government
had power to tax for the support of religion. Therefore, this rather confused statement must be read as part of a general war upon the Constitution, in which any ammunition sufficed. Their contemporaries
recognized this fact.[66]

Madison also recognized that Henry and the Anti-Federalists would
gain nothing by resorting to the cry that religious liberty was in danger.
The Baptists, who would have been most likely to react to any possible
threat such as the one posited by Virginia's Anti-Federalist Senators,
were completely satisfied with the amendment on religion.[67] Virginia
Anti-Federalists failed in their efforts to secure a new federal convention and merely delayed the ratification of the amendments.

The passage of the First Amendment constituted a symbolic act, a
declaration for the future, an assurance to those nervous about the
federal government that it was not going to reverse any of the guarantees for religious liberty won by the revolutionary states. Because it was
making explicit the non-existence of a power, not regulating or curbing
one that existed, Congress approached the subject in a somewhat hasty
and absentminded manner. To examine the two clauses of the amendment as a carefully worded analysis of Church-State relations would be
to overburden them. Similarly, to see the two clauses as separate,
balanced, competing, or carefully worked out prohibitions designed to
meet different eventualities would be to read into the minds of the
actors far more than was there. Scholars sometimes argue, for instance,
that the "Free Exercise" clause was intended to address different
instances than the "Establishment" clause, and the Supreme Court has
repeatedly struck down government interference with religion as a
violation of the "Free Exercise" clause and government aid to religion
as a violation of the "Establishment" clause.[68]

The two clauses represented a double declaration of what Americans
wanted to assert about Church and State. Congress settled on the wording of the Amendment because it probably found the phrases the most
felicitous-sounding of those proposed; but any of the other formats

offered would have served its substantive purpose equally well. Contemporaries did not, for example, distinguish between religious oppression as falling under the ban of the "free exercise" clause and a general assessment as being prohibited by the "establishment" clause. As the debates in Virginia in the mid-1780s had shown, the opponents of tax support of religion fought it primarily as a violation of the states' free exercise guarantee and only incidentally as an establishment. Isaac Backus and the Baptists pursued the same path in New England. The belief that government assistance to religion, especially in the form of taxes, violated religious liberty had a long history. It went back to Roger Williams, to William Penn and the Quakers, and was subsequently propagated in America by evangelicals and Enlightenment rationalists. Similarly, those who espoused government support defended it primarily as fair, equitable, and compatible with religious freedom and concerned themselves very little with the issue of establishment.

The desire for a formal pronouncement of the national government's powerlessness in matters of religion co-existed with the fact that the federal government, the Continental Congress before it, and the state governments did interfere in such matters. The organization, regulation, or support of religion did not come within the purview of the Continental Congress; nevertheless, that body sprinkled its proceedings liberally with the mention of God, Jesus Christ, the Christian religion, and many other religious references. It even considered making an appropriation for an American Bible.[69]

Both houses of Congress, almost immediately after they had agreed to a Bill of Rights, passed a resolution for a 'day of public thanksgiving and prayer to be observed, . . . [for] the many signal favors of Almighty God." In the House discussion of the matter, Tucker of South Carolina argued that "this . . . is a business with which Congress have nothing to do; it is a religious matter, and, as such, is proscribed to us."[70] Congress obviously did not agree.

In 1790 the New England Warren Baptist Association joined its Congregationalist foes in a petition to Congress to see that no Bible was imported or published without its being "certified to be free from error" by a Congressional committee. The petition probably looked only to ensuring accurate renditions of the King James version; nevertheless, the Baptists of the Warren Association had long opposed the New England states' interference in religion. The Association's long-time agent, Isaac Backus, quoted with approval statements that governments had no right ever to "establish the Christian religion at large," and that "religion at all times must be a matter between God and individuals."[71]

Congress's thanksgiving and prayer resolution represented only one of its many involvements with religion, including the appointment of chaplains in the Army and in its own houses. When, during its first session, it reenacted the Northwest Ordinance, it included the provision that "Religion, morality, and knowledge being necessary to good government, . . . schools and the means of education shall forever be encouraged."[72] The contacts between the individual states and religion proved even more multifarious.

The discrepancy between the widespread conviction of late eighteenth-century Americans that government possessed no power in matters of religion and the persistent interference of government in religious affairs arose out of the cultural and social context of the time. Americans enunciated their Church-State principles within a framework wherein Protestant Christianity and American culture intertwined. After a century and a half of colonial settlement in which the overwhelming majority of citizens were Protestant, a contemporary would in many instances have been hard put to define where Protestantism ended and secular life began.

Customs like days of prayer and thanksgiving appeared not so much matters of religion as part of the common coin of civilized living. Sabbath laws enjoyed widespread support and were so little the subject of dissent that citizens never even felt challenged to think how those laws might impose a particular religious viewpoint. Nor was the symmetry between Church-State arrangements and particular religious mindsets a phenomenon limited to Protestants. The small Catholic community in the new states had no objection to government limitation of officeholding to Christians, as long as said Christians included themselves. A Jewish petitioner from Philadelphia asked only that the New Testament limitation in that state's test for office be omitted.[73]

Oliver Ellsworth of Connecticut, in defending the omission of test oaths from the federal Constitution, wrote that

> . . . civil power has a right, in some cases to interfere in matters of religion. It has a right to prohibit and punish gross immoralities and impieties because the open practice of these is of evil example and public detriment.

Ellsworth noted his approval of Connecticut's laws against "profane swearing, blasphemy, and professed atheism." Even Baptists and Congregationalists, so sharply at odds with each other on tax support for churches, shared many common attitudes about such non-disputed Church-State matters as Sabbath laws, appointment of chaplains, and designation of days of prayer.[74] Eventually, these would become subjects of controversy. In 1789, however, they caused no conflict at either the state or federal level.

A few writers, e.g. John Leland, Madison, Jefferson, had assumed or would shortly assume clearly defined positions on some or all of such topics. Leland pursued the principle that government exercised no power over religious matters to the conclusions that state payment of chaplains, Sabbath laws, and the notion that America constituted a Christian commonwealth were wrong. Madison and Jefferson reached much the same conclusions from more secular starting points.[75] Most of their contemporaries, however, held assumptions, not opinions, about these subjects.

The vast majority of Americans assumed that theirs was a Christian, i.e. Protestant, country, and they automatically expected that government would uphold the commonly agreed on Protestant ethos and morality. In many instances, they had not come to grips with the implications their belief in the powerlessness of government in religious matters held for a society in which the values, customs, and forms of Protestant Christianity thoroughly permeated civil and political life. The contradiction between their theory and their practice became evident to Americans only later, with the advent of a more religiously pluralistic society, when it became the subject of a disputation that continues into the present.

In a few specific areas, however, Americans did during the revolutionary period work out specific practical applications of their theories on Church and State. The inhabitants of all the states decided that government had no power to prohibit the free exercise of peaceable religion. All states agreed with Jefferson that civil government could interfere when "principles break out into overt acts against peace & good order"; but otherwise, citizens had a right to practice the religions of their choice, even the hated Catholicism, which had been proscribed in colonial America.

On one other question, the financial support of religion, Americans also clarified the application of their Church-State principles. The vast majority of them believed with the Continental Congress that "true religion and good morals are the only solid foundation of public liberty and happiness." Throughout the states, individuals and government bodies issued similar statements.[76] From this premise, however, they drew differing conclusions. Some legislators, such as those in Massachusetts, decided that since good government depended on morality and piety, government should inculcate those virtues by seeing that churches and ministers were financially provided for. Others, such as those in Virginia, while agreeing with the necessity of virtue and religion for civil society, reasoned that if religion were to remain healthy, it had to remain free from the interfering hand of government. This, together with the secular viewpoint that "our civil rights have no dependence on our religious opinions," undergirded the argument for voluntarism.

Between these two positions the states divided sharply, and in 1785 a hint of this division surfaced over a plan of the Continental Congress for settling the western lands. A committee of that Congress, dominated by New Englanders, proposed that lot number twenty-nine of each township be set aside for the "support of religion" or for charitable purposes, the determination to be made by the majority of the male inhabitants of each township. The full Congress voted down this provision for the support of religion, and Madison, in a letter to James Monroe, wrote of it:

> How a regulation so unjust in itself, so foreign to the authority of Congress, so hurtful to the sale of public land, and smelling so strongly of antiquated bigotry, could have received the countenance of a committee is truly a matter of astonishment.

Even so, in July 1787, while Madison was attending the Constitutional Convention, Congress approved the sale of large tracts of land to a New England land speculator, the Reverend Manasseh Cutler, with the provision that lot number twenty-nine of each township be given for the support of religion.[77]

Of the eleven states that ratified the First Amendment, nine (counting Maryland) adhered to the viewpoint that support of religion and churches should be voluntary, that any government financial assistance to religion constituted an establishment of religion and violated its free exercise.[78] Some had done so from their earliest foundations; some arrived at that stance after the American Revolution. The Maryland constitution permitted a general assessment to support religion, but Marylanders firmly rejected a proposal to enact one. Of the ratifying states, only Vermont and New Hampshire adhered to the view that states could or should provide for tax-supported religion. On a whole range of other applications, however, Americans inherited traditions of government interference in religious matters.

Modern scholars sometimes fall into the late eighteenth-century American habit of equating "religion" with Protestant Christianity. Thus Anson Phelps Stokes, writing in 1950, noted that the Continental Congress "showed its interest in religion . . . [by] references to 'God,' . . . to 'Jesus Christ,' the 'Christian Religion' . . . and the 'Free

Protestant Colonies'." He concluded that Congress "saw the importance and the need of encouraging the religious spirit in the new
nation, while at the same time avoiding favoritism to any denomination."[79] However, a country wherein eleven of thirteen states restricted
officeholding to Christians or Protestants hardly envisaged Catholicism
or Judaism, not to mention Mohammedanism or any non-Christian
group, as part of the "religion" to be promoted and encouraged either
in the states or the Northwest Territory.[80]

Throughout the colonial period, many colonists, despite the plural-
ity of sects, hoped that a common Protestant Christianity composed of
pure biblical principles and uncorrupted by human impositions could
come to be. In 1788 a commentator on the Constitution, using the pen
name "Denatus," published an address in the *Virginia Chronicle* calling
for the creation throughout the United States of academies

> . . . for the education of youth in morality; the principles of the Chris-
> tian religions without regard to sect, but pure and unadulterated as left
> by its divine author and his apostles.

To most Protestant Americans, the aspirations of "Denatus" were part
reality in his lifetime and would become stronger in subsequent
generations.[81]

In 1787 the Delaware General Assembly declared, in the Preface to a
law for the incorporation of churches, that "this General Assembly . . .
[considered] it their duty to countenance and encourage virtue and
religion by every means in their power, and in the most expeditious
manner."[82] The Assembly's statement cloaked several unstated
assumptions. Delaware required that officeholders proclaim a belief in
Trinitarian Christianity, so the statement hatched the paradox that the
state proclaimed a desire to promote religions whose adherents it
refused to allow to participate in state government. Again, one resolves
the contradiction by looking to the unspoken and often unconscious
assumptions and limitations the citizens of Delaware attached to their
concept of "religion." Further, the state decreed that public tax support
was not to be a means for the support of religion.

That Americans during the revolutionary period did not always
carry their principles into practice either in Church-State or other
matters did not negate those principles. Except in a few instances, such
as financial support of churches, they passed to subsequent generations
the task of working out the consequences of the principle that the state
had no competence in religious matters in a society wherein customs,
mores, laws, and religion intertwined and wherein the majority
equated religion with Protestantism. However, the federal Bill of Rights

prompted several states to begin to reconcile practice with principle. Between 1789 and 1792, Delaware, South Carolina, and Georgia abandoned religious tests for officeholding, and Pennsylvania modified its test to exclude only atheists.[83]

The meaning of free exercise of religion and establishment of religion in 1789 must be examined within the historical matrix that produced these concepts. Just as Puritan demands for religious liberty take on a different hue when seen against the pattern of Puritan belief, and just as the sweeping proclamations of anti-subscriptionists of the seventeenth century were not at all what they seemed on their face, so the meaning of the First Amendment must arise out of its historical context rather than from a literalist reading. It meant at least this: that each citizen had a right to the free exercise of his or her religion as long as it did not "break out into overt acts against peace and order." Further, the people of almost every state that ratified the First Amendment believed that religion should be maintained and supported voluntarily. They saw government attempts to organize and regulate such support as a usurpation of power, as a violation of liberty of conscience and free exercise of religion, and as falling within the scope of what they termed an establishment of religion.

Notes

AHR American Historical Review
HMPEC Historical Magazine of the Protestant Episcopal Church
PMHB Pennsylvania Magazine of History and Biography
VMHB Virginia Magazine of History and Biography
WMQ William and Mary Quarterly

1. The New England Way in Church and State to 1691

1. Samuel Mather, *Testimony from the Scriptures* (Cambridge, 1672), 25; Patrick Collinson, *The Elizabethan Puritan Movement* (Berkeley, 1967).
2. W. K. Jordan, *The Development of Religious Toleration in England*, 4 vols. (Cambridge, Mass., 1936; reprint ed., Gloucester, Mass., 1968), 2:20; Carl Bridenbaugh, *Vexed and Troubled Englishmen 1542–1642* (New York, 1968), 275.
3. J. P. Kenyon, ed., *The Stuart Constitution 1603–1688: Documents and Commentary* (Cambridge, 1966), 258.
4. Perry Miller, "Errand into the Wilderness," in Perry Miller, *Errand into the Wilderness* (Cambridge, Mass., 1965), 1–15. On Puritan views of the hopelessness of reform in Europe, see "General Plantations for Planting New England," in Alexander Young, ed., *Chronicles of the First Planters of Massachusetts Bay* (Boston, 1846; reprint ed., New York, 1970), 271.
5. Charles M. Andrews, *The Colonial Period in American History*, 4 vols. (New Haven, 1934), 1:344–99.
6. William Bradford, *Of Plymouth Plantation*, Samuel E. Morison, ed. (New York, 1952), 25; George D. Langdon, *Pilgrim Colony* (New Haven, 1966); John M. Bumsted, "A Well-Bounded Toleration," *Journal of Church and State* 10 (1968): 265–79.

7. Perry Miller, "Thomas Hooker and the Democracy of Connecticut," in Miller, *Errand*, 16–47; M. Louise Greene, *The Development of Religious Liberty in Connecticut* (Boston, 1905).

8. Isabel M. Calder, *The New Haven Colony* (New Haven, 1934). "The laws of God as delivered to Moses . . . shall be accounted of moral equity and generally binding all offenders and be the rule of all courts . . . till they be branded out into particulars hereafter." (C. J. Hoadly, ed., *New Haven Colonial Records*, 2 vols. (Hartford, 1857–58), 1:130.) On strictness of excommunication in New Haven, see Thomas Lechford, *Plain Dealing* (London, 1644), 13. Only those who could demonstrate an experience of saving grace were considered church members, and only they could receive communion. All were expected or obliged to attend church, however. See Edmund S. Morgan, *Visible Saints* (Ithaca, N.Y., 1965), 64–112.

9. John Cotton, "Reasons for Removal to New England," in Young, ed., *Chronicles*, 441.

10. William Ames, *Conscience with the Power and Cases thereof* (London, 1630), Bk. 4, 10, quoted in Perry Miller, *Orthodoxy in Massachusetts* (Cambridge, Mass., 1933), 165–66.

11. M. M. Knappen, *Tudor Puritanism* (Chicago, 1939), 365.

12. John Cotton, *Grounds and Ends* (London, 1647), 3; Richard Mather, *An Apology of the Churches in New-England* (London, 1643), 25.

13. Richard Mather, *Apology*, 39.

14. John Cotton, *A Discourse on Civil Government in a New Plantation* (Cambridge, 1663), 14. Horace Evans, "Was Massachusetts a Theocracy?," *Publications of the Colonial Society* 10 (1904): 151–80.

15. Jordan, *Development*, 2:207–15.

16. On excommunication, see Williston Walker, *Creeds and Platforms of Congregationalism* (New York, 1893; reprint ed., Philadelphia, 1960), 228.

17. Edmund S. Morgan, ed., *Puritan Political Ideas* (New York, 1965), xxx.

18. "Truth was hardly ever a better penniworth since the world stood, than it hath been to us; and whether ever it will be so cheap again in our days, as it hath been now for these so many years, the Lord knows." (Samuel Willard, *Heavenly Merchandise* (Cambridge, Mass., 1686), 34); John Winthrop, *Winthrop Papers*, 5 vols. (Massachusetts Historical Society, 1929–47), 2:294.

19. Nathaniel B. Shurtleff, ed., *Records of the Governor and Company of the Massachusetts Bay in New England*, 5 vols. (Boston, 1853–54), 1:168; Walker, *Creeds*, 168, 263.

20. John Winthrop, *The History of New England from 1630–1649*, James Savage, ed., 2 vols. (Boston, 1825; reprint ed., New York, 1972), 2:229–30.

21. Ames, *Conscience*, 1, 5.

22. John Cotton, *The Bloudy Tenent Washed* (London, 1647; reprint ed., New York, 1972), 9.

23. John Cotton, "Sixteen Questions of Serious and Necessary Consequence," in David Hall, ed., *The Antinomian Controversy, 1636–1638* (Middletown, Ct., 1968), 58.

24. Walker, *Creeds*, 236; Thomas Cobbett, *The Civil Magistrates Power* (London, 1654), 76.

25. Winthrop, *History*, 1:58–59, 81, 144; 2:52 and passim.

26. John Noble, ed., *Records of the Court of Assistants of the Colony of Massachusetts Bay, 1630–1692*, 3 vols. (Boston, 1904), 1:82; Winthrop, *History*, 1:288.

27. John Cotton, *Exposition Upon the Thirteenth Chapter of Revelation* (London, 1655), 283, 26.

28. Walker, *Creeds*, 190, 236–37.

29. Cotton, *Bloudy Tenent Washed*, 191–92; Cobbett, *Civil Magistrates Power*, 64.

30. John Norton, *The Heart of N-England Rent* (Cambridge, Mass., 1659), 58; William Hubbard, *A General History of New England* (Boston, 1815; reprint ed., New York, 1972), 573; Cotton Mather, *Little Flocks Guarded* (Boston, 1681), 100–103; Samuel Willard, *Ne Sutor Ultra Crepidam* (Boston, 1681); Cotton Mather, *Magnalia Christi Americana*, 2 vols. (Hartford, 1853), 2:526.

31. Winthrop, *Papers*, 2:295; Urian Oakes, *New England Pleaded With* (Boston, 1673), 18.

32. See "The Company's First General Letter of Instruction to Endecott and his Council," in Young, *Chronicles*, 158.

33. Young, *Chronicles*, 324; *Massachusetts Historical Society Collections*, 4th Series, 7:507–9; John Hull, Diary, *Archaeologica Americana*, 3:197, quoted in Jonathan M. Chu, "Madmen and Friends and the Puritan Adjustment to Religious Heterodoxy in Massachusetts Bay During the Seventeenth Century," (Ph.D. dissertation, University of Washington, 1978), 46. On Jesuits, see Max Ferrand, ed., *Laws and Liberties of Massachusetts, 1648* (Cambridge, Mass., 1929), 26. On the non-molestation for private heterodoxy, see *Massachusetts Historical Society Collections*, 3rd Series, 1:36; Norton, *Heart of N-England Rent*, 52–53.

34. "The Company's Letter to the Governor," in Young, *Chronicles*, 291; Winthrop, *History*, 1:158.

35. Young, *Chronicles*, 315; Winthrop, *History*, 1:56; Thomas Morton, *New English Canaan* (Boston, 1883; reprint ed., New York, 1967).

36. Hall, *Antinomian Controversy*, 1. See also Charles Francis Adams, *Antinomianism in the Colony of Massachusetts Bay* (Boston, 1894; reprint ed., New York, 1967).

37. Hall, *Antinomian Controversy*, 6–7; Shurtleff, ed., *Massachusetts Records*, 1:386, 205, 211.

38. Hall, *Antinomian Controversy*, 212.

39. Miller, *Orthodoxy*, 164.

40. On English Puritans, see Jordan, *Development*, Vol. 4; William Haller, *Liberty and Reformation in the Puritan Revolution* (New York, 1955); Richard Mather, *Church-Government and Church-Covenant Discussed* (London, 1643), 84.

41. Thomas Hutchinson, ed., *Collection of Original Papers Relative to the History of the Colony of Massachusetts Bay*, 2 vols. (Boston, 1865; reprint ed., New York, 1967), 1:81–91; Winthrop, *Papers*, 3:355–56.

42. William G. McLoughlin, *New England Dissent 1630–1833. The Baptists and the Separation of Church and State*, 2 vols. (Cambridge, Mass., 1971), 1:7–9.

43. Ibid., 1:23; Robert E. Wall, Jr., *The Crucial Decade* (New Haven, 1972), 149; Shurtleff, ed., *Massachusetts Records*, 2:85.

44. *Massachusetts Historical Society Collections*, 5th Series, 8:200; Perry Miller, *The New England Mind: From Colony to Province* (Cambridge, Mass., 1953), 9; Hutchinson, *Papers*, 152–53.

45. David Laing, ed., *The Letters and Journals of Robert Baillie*, 3 vols. (Edinburg (*sic*), 1841), 2:184.

46. Nathaniel Ward, *The Simple Cobbler of Aggawam*, P. M. Zall, ed. (Lincoln, Neb., 1969), 6, 11.

47. "Thomas Shepard to Hugh Peter, 1645," *AHR* 4 (1898): 105–7.

48. Hutchinson, *Papers*, 2:132.

49. G. L. Kittredge, "Dr. Robert Child the Remonstrant," *Colonial Society of Massachusetts Publications* 21 (1919): 146; Samuel E. Morison, *Builders of the Bay Colony* (Boston, 1944), 244–68.

50. Samuel Gorton, *Simplicities Defense* (London, 1646); Kenneth W. Porter, "Samuel Gorton," *New England Quarterly* 7 (1934): 405–44; Philip F. Gura, "The Radical Ideology of Samuel Gorton: New Light on the Relation of English and American Puritanism," *WMQ* 36 (1979): 78–100; Edward Winslow, *Hyprocrasie Unmasked* (London, 1646) and *New England Salamander* (London, 1647).

51. John Child, *New-Englands Jonas Cast up at London* (London, 1647), 116.

52. John Clark, *Ill News from New England*, reprinted in *Massachusetts HistoricalSociety Collections*, 4th Series, 2:34–35; Cobbett, *Civil Magristrates Power*.

53. Andrews, *The Colonial Period*, 472–75; *The Complete Works of Roger Williams*, 7 vols. (New York, 1963), 1:324–25; Winthrop, *History*, 1:52–53, 122, 170–71.

54. For the historiography of Williams, see LeRoy Moore, Jr., "Roger Williams and the Historians," *Church History* 32 (1963): 432–50; Nancy E. Pease, "Roger Williams—A Historiographical Essay," *Rhode Island History* 35 (1976): 103–33.

55. Edmund Morgan, *Roger Williams. The Church and the State* (New York, 1967); Perry Miller, *Roger Williams, His Contribution to the American Tradition* (Indianapolis, 1953).

56. Hall, *Antinomian Controversy*, 147. On Cotton's optimistic hopes for New England, see Jasper Rosenmeir, "The Teacher and the Witness: John Cotton and Roger Williams." *WMQ* 25 (1968): 408–31; Sacvan Bercovitch, "Typology in Puritan New England: The Williams-Cotton Controversy Reassessed," *American Quarterly* 19 (1967): 166–91.

57. Williams, *Works*, 2:35, 3:3. On typology see Miller, *Williams, His Contribution*, 33–38; Morgan, *Roger Williams*, 91–93; Richard M. Reintz, "Symbolism and Freedom: The Use of Biblical Typology As an Argument for Religious Toleration in Seventeenth Century America," (Ph.D. dissertation, University of Rochester, 1967), 176, 386.

58. Cotton, *Bloudy Tenent Washed*, 19, 131–32, 82.

59. John Cotton, *Pouring Out of the Seven Vials* (London, 1642), Pt. 4:14.

60. Williams, *Works*, 5:103, 7:162, 3:206; Morgan, *Roger Williams*, 162–64.

61. Williams, *Works*, 4:44, 96, 417–18, 424, 508–9.

62. Ibid., 3:184, 285. Edward Johnson, in his *Wonder-Working Providence*, provided a different Puritan view of Holland: "Yee Dutch come out of your hods-podge, the great mingle-mangle of Religion among you hath caused the Churches of Christ to increase so little with you; standing at a stay like Corne among Weeds" (*Johnson's Wonder-Working Providence*, J. Franklin Jameson, ed. (New York, 1910), 59).

63. Williams, *Works*, 1:108, 4:169–70. This argument Williams returned to again and again. See *Works*, 4:28–29, 169, 170, 194, 243, 271, 377, 399.

64. Ibid., 3:294; Don M. Wolfe, "The Limits of Miltonian Toleration," *Journal of English and German Philology* 60 (1961): 834–36; Jordan, *Development*, 3:179–94.

65. Cotton, *Bloudy Tenent Washed*, 69.

66. Ibid., 51; Cobbett, *Civil Magistrates Power*, 40.

67. See, for instance, Cotton Mather, *Things for a Distress'd People* (Boston, 1696), 43–44.

68. Hubbard, *History*, 534.

69. Hutchinson, *Papers*, 1:174.
70. For the United Colonies, see Harry M. Ward, *The United Colonies of New England—1643–1690* (New York, 1961); "Acts of the Commissioners of the United Colonies," in Nathaniel B. Shurtleff et al., *Records of New Plymouth 1620–1692*, 12 vols. (Boston, 1855–61), 9:81.
71. Shurtleff, ed., *Massachusetts Records*, 3:174.
72. Shurtleff et al., *Plymouth Records*, 9:81; 2:57, 162; 11:73.
73. Sydney V. James, *Colonial Rhode Island* (New York, 1975), 1, 48–74; J. R. Bartlett, ed., *Records of the Colony of Rhode Island and Providence Plantations in New England 1636–1792*, 10 vols. (Providence, 1856–65), 1:22.
74. James, *Rhode Island*, 53; Bartlett, ed., *Rhode Island Records*, 1:63–65; Bruce C. Daniels, "Dissent and Disorder: The Radical Impulse and Early Government in the Founding of Rhode Island," *Journal of Church and State* 24 (1982): 357–78.
75. Francis Newton Thorpe, *The Federal and State Constitutions, Colonial Charters, and Other Organic Laws of the States, Territories, and Colonies*, 7 vols. (Washington, D.C., 1909), 6:3212. On freedom of conscience in Newport, see Bartlett, ed., *Rhode Island Records*, 1:113. For agreement between towns, see James, *Rhode Island*, 64–68.
76. Winthrop, *History*, 1:256, 329.
77. Ibid., 1:293.
78. Bartlett, ed., *Rhode Island Records*, 1:159. On doubts about witches, see "Letter of William Arnold to Massachusetts Governor, 1651," in Hutchinson, *Papers*, 1:267. On Williams's social conservatism, see Robert D. Bunkow, "Love and Order in Roger Williams' Writing," *Rhode Island History*, 35 (1976): 115.
79. Hall, *Antinomian Crisis*, 218; Hutchinson, *Papers*, 1:267.
80. Shurtleff, ed., *Massachusetts Records*, 4:Pt. 2, 233.
81. Bartlett, ed., *Rhode Island Records*, 2:503.
82. McLoughlin, *New England Dissent*, 1:8.
83. Hugh Barbour, *The Quakers in Puritan England* (New Haven, 1964), 33–71.
84. Urian Oakes, *New England Pleaded With* (Boston, 1673), 18.
85. Rufus Jones, *The Quakers in the American Colonies* (London, 1923), 26–29.
86. "Letter from Massachusetts to the United Colonies," in Hutchinson, *Papers*, 1:317; J. H. Trumbull and C. J. Hoadly, eds., *Public Records of the Colony of Connecticut*, 15 vols. (Hartford, 1850–90), 1:383; C. J. Hoadly, ed., *New Haven Colonial Records—1638–1655*, 2 vols. (Hartford, 1857–58), 2:238; Shurtleff et al., *Plymouth Records*, 2:100–101, 120.
87. Shurtleff, ed., *Massachusetts Records*, 4:Pt. 1, 385. Carla Gardina Pestana, "The City Upon a Hill Under Siege: The Puritan Perception of the Quaker Threat to Massachusetts Bay, 1655–1666," *New England Quarterly* 56 (1983): 323–53.
88. Chu, "Madmen and Friends," 46, 43; John Norton, *Heart of N-England Rent*.
89. Norton, *Heart of N-England Rent*, 46–58.
90. Ibid., 56, 58.
91. Bartlett, ed., *Rhode Island Records*, 1:373–75, 397–98.
92. Ibid., 1:396; Hoadly, ed., *New Haven Records*, 1:238.
93. John Ditsky, "Hard Hearts and Gentle People: A Quaker Reply to Persecution," *Canadian Review of American Studies* 5 (1974): 47–51; Hugh Barbour and Arthur O. Roberts, eds., *Early Quaker Writings* (Grand Rapids, Mich., 1973), 116–40.
94. George Bishop, *New-England Judged* (London, 1661), Parts 1 and 2; Isaac

Pennington, *An Examination of Grounds and Causes* (London, 1660); *A Declaration of the Sad and Great Persecution and Martyrdom* (London, 1662).

95. On Quaker petition to Charles, see W. L. Grant and James Munro, eds., *Acts of the Privy Council, Colonial Series*, 6 vols. (London, 1908–12), 1:312. For Charles's order to Massachusetts, see *Massachusetts Historical Society Collections*, 5th Series, 9:26–27.

96. Hutchinson, *Papers*, 2: 44–45.

97. Shurtleff, ed., *Massachusetts Records*, 4: Pt. 2, 34 and 59; Chu, "Madmen and Friends," 86.

98. Calder, *New Haven Colony*, 299.

99. On post-Restoration New England, see Michael G. Hall, *Edward Randolph and the American Colonies 1676–1703* (Chapel Hill, 1960); Viola F. Barnes, *The Dominion of New England, A Study in British Colonial Policy* (New Haven, 1923); Miller, *From Colony to Province*, 19–121.

100. "Letter from King Charles the Second to Massachusetts," in Hutchinson, *Papers*, 2:100–104; "Private Instructions of Charles II to Nicholls Commission, 1664," in E. B. O'Callaghan, ed., *Documentary History of the State of New York*, 4 vols. (Albany, 1849–51), 3:58–60; Hall, *Edward Randolph*.

101. Hutchinson, *Papers*, 2:140–47; *Massachusetts Historical Society Collections*, 2nd Series, 8:48; Shurtleff, ed., *Massachusetts Records*, 4:Pt. 2, 220–21.

102. *Massachusetts Session Laws* (Cambridge, Mass., 1663), 3–4; *Records of the Court of Assistants*, 1:12. Chu, in "Madmen and Friends," 120–41, shows that while the colony remained hostile to the Quakers, the towns adjusted to them. Although the towns continued to fine them, these fines often resulted from a blend of reasons, e.g. not supporting the local minister, and were not usually punishment for merely holding Quaker beliefs.

103. Turnbull and Hoadly, eds., *Records of Connecticut*, 2:264; Shurtleff, ed., *Massachusetts Records*, 5:134; Thomas C. Hall, *Religious Background of American Culture* (Boston, 1930), 131; Shurtleff et al., *Plymouth Records*, 6:71.

104. Walker, *Creeds*, 428.

105. Miller, *Williams, His Contribution*, 240–46; Roger Williams, *George Fox Digg'd out of his Burrowes* (Boston, 1676).

106. Walker, *Creeds*, 428.

107. McLoughlin, *New England Dissent*, 1:49–78, 105.

108. For requests for moderation from English Dissenters to Massachusetts, see Isaac Backus, *A History of New England with Particular Reference to the Baptists*, David Weston, ed., 2 vols. (Newton, Mass., 1871; reprint ed., New York, 1969), 1:311–15. For reaction to English pleas, see *Massachusetts Historical Society Collections*, 4th Series, 8:291; Samuel Willard, *Ne Sutor Ultra Crepidam*, iv.

109. Willard, *Ne Sutor Ultra Crepidam*, 6–8, 4, 6–7, iii, 6, 4; McLoughlin, *New England Dissent*, 1:105.

110. Miller, *From Colony to Province*, 11.

111. Walker, *Creeds*, 301–39; Robert Pope, *The Half-Way Covenant: Church Membership in Puritan New England* (Princeton, 1969).

112. Urian Oakes, *A Seasonable Discourse* (Cambridge, Mass., 1682), Preface.

113. Increase Mather, *The Danger of Apostacie* (Cambridge, Mass., 1679), 76, 79–80; Miller, *From Colony to Province*, 136.

114. William Hubbard, *The Happiness of a People* (Cambridge, Mass., 1676), Introduction, 42.

115. John Higginson, *The Cause of God* (Cambridge, 1663), 11; Increase Mather, *The Day of Trouble* (Cambridge, Mass., 1674), 23; Increase Mather, *An Earnest Exhortation* (Cambridge, Mass., 1676.), 5; Oakes, *Seasonable Discourse*, 6; John Woodbridge, *Severals Relating to the Fund* (Boston, 1682), 1; Hubbard, *History*, 116; Samuel Torrey, *A Plea for the Life of Dying Religion* (Cambridge, Mass., 1683), 7; "Petition to King," in Shurtleff et al., *Plymouth Records; Brief Relation of the State of New England to 1689* (London, 1689), 3.

116. Increase Mather, *The Necessity of Reform* (Cambridge, Mass., 1679), iv; Increase Mather, *Danger of Apostacie*, 75–76; Hubbard, *History*, 608; Hubbard, *The Happiness of a People*, 6; Samuel Willard, *The Childs Portion* (Cambridge, Mass., 1684), 192; Samuel Torrey, *An Exhortation* (Cambridge, Mass., 1674), 30.

117. John Oxenbridge, *New England Freemen warned to be Free Indeed* (Cambridge, Mass., 1673), 26–27; Oakes, *New England Pleaded With*, 49.

118. Samuel Arnold, *David Serving His Generation* (Cambridge, Mass., 1674), 16; Oakes, *New England Pleaded With*, 18.

119. McLoughlin, *New England Dissent*, 1:91.

2. Church and State in Seventeenth-Century Virginia and Maryland

1. Perry Miller, "Religion and Society in the Early Literature of Virginia," in Perry Miller, *Errand into the Wilderness* (Cambridge, Mass., 1956), 99–140; Babette M. Levy, "Early Puritanism in the Southern and Island Colonies," *American Antiquarian Society Proceedings* 70 (1960): 69; William H. Seiler, "The Church of England as the Established Church in Seventeenth-Century Virginia," *Journal of Southern History* 15 (1949): 478–81; George McLaren Brydon, *Virginia's Mother Church*, 2 vols. (Richmond, 1947), 1:11–12; Spencer Ervin, "The Established Church in Virginia," *HMPEC* 26 (1957): 82; Sanford H. Cobb, *The Rise of Religious Liberty in America* (New York, 1902), 74–75; Louis B. Wright, *Religion and Empire: The Alliance Between Piety and Commercial Expansion 1558–1625* (Chapel Hill, N.C., 1943).

2. William Walter Hening, ed., *The Statutes at Large: Being a Collection of all the Laws of Virginia 1619–1792*, 13 vols. (Richmond, 1809–23), 1:97–98. Sir Thomas Dale, Acting Governor of Virginia, prayed in 1611: "Lord blesse England our sweet native countrey, save it from Popery," (Peter Force, ed., *Tracts and Other Papers Relating Principally to the Colonies in North America*, 4 vols. (Washington, D.C., 1836–48), 3:64.)

3. S. M. Kingsbury, ed., *Records of the Virginia Company of London*, 4 vols. (Washington, D.C., 1906–55), 3:14. For an account of Virginia's first decades, see Charles M. Andrews, *The Colonial Period in American History*, 4 vols. (New Haven, 1934), 1:98–140. Hening, ed., *Statutes*, 1:58, 98, 100; Seiler, "Church of England," 481.

4. H. R. McIlwaine and J. P. Kennedy, eds., *Journals of the House of Burgesses of Virginia 1619–1776*, 13 vols. (Richmond, 1905–15), 1:9–11. Much of the religious legislation gathered out of Hening, ed., *Statutes at Large*, can be found in A. R. Goodwin, "Laws Relating to the Early Colonial Church in Virginia," *HMPEC* 3 (1934): 34–37, and Brydon, *Virginia's Mother Church*, 1:411–81.

5. Ervin, "Established Church," 86; Brydon, *Virginia's Mother Church*, 1:227; Seiler, "Church of England," 507.

6. William H. Seiler, "The Anglican Parish in Virginia," in James Morton Smith, ed., *Seventeenth-Century America* (New York, 1972), 119–42, and "Church of England," 499.

7. John D. Krugler, "'The Face of a Protestant and the Heart of a Papist,' A

Reexamination of Sir George Calvert's Conversion to Roman Catholicism," *Journal of Church and State* 20 (1978): 507–31.

8. For a sample of opposing interpretations, see discussion notes in John D. Krugler, "Puritan and Papist: Politics and Religion in Massachusetts and Maryland before the Restoration of Charles II" (Ph.D. dissertation, University of Illinois, 1971), 253, and "Lord Baltimore, Roman Catholics, and Toleration: Religious Policy in Maryland During the Early Catholic Years, 1634–1649," *Catholic Historical Review* 65 (1979): 49–50. See also John D. Krugler, "'With Promise of Liberty in Religion': The Catholic Lords Baltimore and Toleration in Seventeenth-Century Maryland, 1634–1694," *Maryland Historical Magazine* 79 (1984): 21–43.

9. Francis Newton Thorpe, ed., *The Federal and State Constitutions Colonial Charters and Other Organic Laws of the States, Territories, and Colonies*, 7 vols. (Washington, D.C., 1909), 3:1679.

10. On colonial Maryland, see Andrews, *Colonial Period*, 2:275–379. For Baltimore's land policy, see Newton D. Mereness, *Maryland as a Proprietary Province* (New York, 1901; reprint ed., Cos Cob, Ct., 1968).

11. Charles Howard McIlwaine, ed., *The Political Works of James I* (Cambridge, Mass., 1918), 126.

12. John H. Latane, *The Early Relations between Maryland and Virginia* (Baltimore, 1895), 170; Alfred Pearce Dennis, "Lord Baltimore's Struggle with the Jesuits, 1634–1649," *Annual Report of the American Historical Association for the Year 1900* (Washington, D.C., 1901), 110, 112.

13. On Baltimore's colony in Newfoundland, see R. J. Lahey, "The Role of Religion in Lord Baltimore's Colonial Enterprise," *Maryland Historical Magazine* 72 (1977): 492–511.

14. For assertions of Baltimore's religious motivation, see Andrews, *Colonial Period*, 2:279; Matthew Page Andrews, "Separation of Church and State in Maryland," *Catholic Historical Review* 21 (1935): 165–76.

15. "Objections Answered Touching Mariland" (London, 1634), in Bradley T. Johnson, *The Foundation of Maryland and the Origins of the Act Concerning Religion* (Baltimore, 1883), 25; Thomas O'Brien Hanley, *Their Rights and Liberties* (Baltimore, 1959), 73.

16. Thomas Hughes, S. J., *History of the Society of Jesus in North America, Colonial and Federal*, 4 vols. (New York, 1907–17), Text 1:207.

17. Dennis, "Lord Baltimore's Struggle," 112; John Tracy Ellis, *Catholics in Colonial America* (Baltimore, 1965), 332.

18. Lahey, "Role of Religion," 506–8; Hughes, S. J., *History*, Text 1:196.

19. William Hand Browne et al., eds., *Archives of Maryland*, 72 vols. (Baltimore,1883–), 1:16; Latane, "Early Relations," 8–9; Robert Beverley, *The History of the Present State of Virginia*, Louis B. Wright, ed. (Chapel Hill, N.C., 1947; reprint ed., Chartlottesville, Va., 1968), 58.

20. Johnson, *Foundation of Maryland*, 24–30; Krugler, "Lord Baltimore, Roman Catholics," 57.

21. Clayton C. Hall, ed., *Narratives of Early Maryland, 1633–1684* (New York, 1910), 218, 235.

22. Johnson, *Foundation of Maryland*, 25.

23. *The Calvert Papers*, 3 vols. (Baltimore, 1889–99), 1:129–33.

24. Hall, ed., *Narratives*, 40; Father Andrew White, "Narrative of a Voyage to Maryland," *Fund Publication No. 7* (Baltimore, 1874), 32.

25. Thorpe, *Federal and State Constitutions*, 3:1678–79.
26. George Petrie, *Church and State in Early Maryland* (Baltimore, 1892); Cobb, *Rise of Religious Liberty*, 364; Ervin, "Established Church," 234.
27. *Calvert Papers*, 1:157–69.
28. Hall, ed., *Narratives*, 120–23, 126, 128, 137, 138.
29. *Calvert Papers*, 1:157, 166.
30. *Maryland Archives*, 3:227, 237.
31. On the quarrel between Baltimore and the Jesuits, see Hughes, S. J., *History*, Text 1:373–557; Dennis, "Lord Baltimore's Struggle"; Krugler, "Lord Baltimore, Roman Catholics," 65–73, and "Puritan and Papist," 229–52; Ellis, *Catholics in Colonial America*, 328–34.
32. *Maryland Archives*, 4:35–39; Levy, "Early Puritanism," 204; Krugler, "Lord Baltimore, Roman Catholics," 62–64. Francis Stock, ed., *Proceedings and Debates of the British Parliaments respecting North America*, 5 vols. (Washington, D.C., 1924), 1:124.
33. *Maryland Archives*, 1:119.
34. Father Andrew White, "Relation of the Colony of Lord Baltimore," in Force, *Tracts*, 4:28.
35. Andrews, *Colonial Period*, 2:302–8. *Maryland Archives*, 4:435; Bernard C. Steiner, *Maryland During the English Civil War, Part II* (Baltimore, 1907), 48–62; Stock, ed., *Proceedings and Debates*, 1:124; Andrews, *Colonial Period*, 2:398.
36. Steiner, *Maryland* , *Part II*, 64, 69–70, 102, 105.
37. John Winthrop, *The History of New England from 1630–1649*, 2 vols. (Boston, 1825; reprint ed., New York, 1972), 2:149.
38. *Maryland Archives*, 3:210, 214; 1:40. The *Maryland Archives* use the term "Holy Churches" only once. All other references to the act use "Holy Church."
39. Krugler, "Lord Baltimore, Roman Catholics," 69; *Maryland Archives*, 1:83, 40; Thomas O'Brien Hanley, "Church and State in the Maryland Ordinance of 1639," *Church History* 26 (1957): 325–41; For a reference to the act later in the century, see *Maryland Archives*, 41:144–46, 566, and Bernard C. Steiner, "Religious Freedom in Colonial Maryland," *AHR* 28 (1923): 258–59.
40. For Act Concerning Religion, see *Maryland Archives*, 1:244–47.
41. The statement that "This inhuman clause [death for denial of the Trinity and other religious doctrines] was not part of Baltimore's original text, for it was an amendment added by the Puritan-Protestant assembly in the colony to accord with the spirit of the act of the Long Parliament of May 2, 1648, punishing heresies and blasphemies," (Andrews, *Colonial Period*, 2: 310–11) was corrected by Krugler, who pointed out that Catholics dominated the Assembly that passed the act (Krugler, "Puritan and Papist," 275–76).
42. Krugler, "Lord Baltimore, Roman Catholics," 75.
43. Andrews, *Colonial Period*, 2:312; Bernard C. Steiner, *Maryland under the Commonwealth* (Baltimore, 1911), 10; Daniel R. Randall, *A Puritan Colony in Maryland* (Baltimore, 1886), 10–14, 17–20; Latane, "Early Relations," 43–49.
44. *Maryland Archives*, 3:265; Steiner, *Maryland under the Commonwealth*, 53–55.
45. *Maryland Archives*, 1:341; Steiner, *Maryland under the Commonwealth*, 56–60, 72–81.
46. *Maryland Archives*, 3:334; Steiner, *Maryland under the Commonwealth*, 112–13; Andrews, *Colonial Period*, 320–21.
47. In 1653 the proprietor's party was defended in the anonymous *Lord Baltimore's*

Case (London, 1653). Two years later, a refutation was published, also anonymously, entitled *Virginia and Maryland, Or the Lord Baltimore's Case Uncased and Answered* (London, 1655). That same year, one of the leaders of the Puritan settlers in Maryland, Leonard Strong, published a defense of the anti-proprietary party entitled *Babylon's Fall in Maryland* (London, 1655). Strong was answered by John Langford, a Maryland settler and associate of Baltimore, in *Refutation of Babylon's Fall* (London, 1655). All the above writings are in Hall, ed., *Narratives*, 167–275. In 1665 Roger Heamans restated the anti-proprietary case in *An Additional Brief Narrative of a late bloody design against the Protestants in Anne Arundel County* (London, 1665), in *Maryland Historical Magazine* 4 (1909): 140–53. John Hammond refuted Heamans in *Hammond versus Heamans* (London, n.d.), in *Maryland Historical Magazine* 4 (1909): 236–60, and *Leah and Rachel, Or The Two Fruitful Sisters Virginia and Maryland*, in Hall, *Narratives*, 281–308.

48. Hening, ed., *Statutes*, 1:363–68, 2:46–47.

49. Beverley, *History of the Present State of Virginia*, 68. For legislation against Quakers in Virginia, see Hening, ed., *Statutes*, 1:532–33, 2:165–66, 180–83; Warren M. Billings, ed., "A Quaker in Seventeenth-Century Virginia: Four Remonstrances by George Wilson," *WMQ* 33 (1976): 127–40; Rufus M. Jones, *The Quakers in the American Colonies* (London, 1923), 274, 290; Levy, "Early Puritanism," 155, 92; *Maryland Archives*, 49:193, 231; Kenneth L. Carroll, "Quakerism on the Eastern Shore," *VMHB* 74 (1966): 174–89. David W. Jordan, "'God's Candle' within Government: Quakers and Politics in Early Maryland," *WMQ* 39 (1982): 628–54.

50. Caroll, "Quakerism on the Eastern Shore," 174–75, 184; *Maryland Archives*, 54: xxiv–xxviii, 86. For Quakers in Maryland, see *Maryland Archives*, 3:347–52, 362, 435; 41:35, 104, 112, 286, 320–21, 339; 54:222, 599; 49:193, 231; 1:436–37; 2:492; 8:63; 24:91; Francis Howgill, *The Deceiver* (London, 1660), 14–15. Kenneth L. Carroll, "Maryland Quakers in the Seventeenth Century," *Maryland Historical Magazine* 47 (1952): 301; Jones, *Quakers*, 279; Levy, "Early Puritanism," 236.

51. A. A. Seaton, *The Theory of Toleration Under the Later Stuarts*, (Cambridge, 1911; reprint ed., New York, 1972), 82–236; George N. Clark, *The Later Stuarts, 1660–1714* (Oxford, 1955), 17–143; J. P. Kenyon, *The Stuart Constitution* (Cambridge, 1966), 448–74.

52. George Alsop, *A Character of the Province of Maryland* (London, 1666), in Hall, ed., *Narratives*, 349–50.

53. *Maryland Archives*, 2:86; George B. Scriven, "Religious Affiliation in Seventeenth-Century Maryland," *HMPEC* 25 (1956): 229.

54. *Maryland Archives*, 5:130–31.

55. Lawrence C. Worth, "The First Sixty Years of the Church of England in Maryland, 1632–1692," *Maryland Historical Magazine* 11 (1916): 23–25.

56. Lois Green Carr and David William Jordan, *Maryland's Revolution of Government 1689–1692* (Ithaca, N.Y., 1976), 37–40, 55; Andrews, *Colonial Period*, 2:376–78.

57. For the background to the revolution of 1689, see F. E. Sparks, *Causes of the Maryland Revolution of 1689* (Baltimore, 1896), 447–578; Michael G. Kammen, "The Causes of the Maryland Revolution of 1689," *Maryland Historical Magazine* 55 (1960): 293–333; Carr and Jordan, *Maryland's Revolution*, 1–45; Richard A. Gleissner, "Religious Causes of the Glorious Revolution in Maryland," *Maryland Historical Magazine* 64 (1969): 327–41.

58. Carr and Jordan, *Maryland's Revolution*, 245–48.

59. David S. Lovejoy, *The Glorious Revolution in America* (New York, 1970), 81–84,

suggests that Fendall was the author. "The Complaint" is printed in *Maryland Archives*, 5:134–52.

60. *Maryland Archives*, 5:147, 149.

61. Ibid., 5:149, 131; Michael Hall, Lawrence H. Leder, and Michael G. Kammen, eds., *The Glorious Revolution in America. Documents on the Colonial Crisis of 1689* (Chapel Hill, N.C., 1964), 152.

62. *Maryland Archives*, 5:260–61, 252–54. For Baltimore's recommendations of Protestant ministers for Maryland, see *Maryland Archives*, 5:461, and Nelson Waite Rightmyer, *Maryland's Established Church* (Baltimore, 1956), 19–20.

63. *Maryland Archives*, 5:133.

64. Ibid., 5:267–68, 130.

65. Ibid., 5:301, 88, 316; Lovejoy, *Glorious Revolution*, 84–87.

66. *Maryland Archives*, 5:300–301, 353.

67. For an account of the rumors of the Indian-Catholic conspiracy, see Bernard C. Steiner, "The Protestant Revolution in Maryland," *Annual Report of the American Historical Association for the Year 1897* (Washington, D.C., 1898), 291–98; Carr and Jordan, *Maryland's Revolution*, 46–83; Lovejoy, *Glorious Revolution*, 260–70.

68. *Maryland Archives*, 8:101–8; Carr and Jordan, *Maryland's Revolution*, 102; *Maryland Citizens. The Address of the Representatives of Their Majesty's Protestant Subjects* (St. Mary's, 1689).

69. Carr and Jordan, *Maryland's Revolution*, 63–64, 190, 194, 200; Steiner, "Protestant Revolution," 300–353.

70. Carr and Jordan, *Maryland's Revolution*, 189, provides a chart giving the attitudes of ex-Assembly members toward the revolution. *Maryland Archives*, 8:133–51 contain County petitions for and against the revolution that were sent to England.

71. Leonard Woods Labaree, ed., *Royal Instructions to British Colonial Governors, 1670–1776*, 2 vols. (New York, 1935), 2:482–94.

72. Carr and Jordan, *Maryland's Revolution*, 34. See also Evarts B. Greene, "The Anglican Outlook on the American Colonies in the Early Eighteenth Century," *AHR* 20 (1914): 64–65; Philip S. Haffenden, "The Anglican Church in Restoration Colonial Policy," in James M. Smith, ed., *Seventeenth-Century America* (New York, 1972), 166–91. For the disallowed acts and discussion surrounding them, see *Maryland Archives*, 13:425–30, 123; 19:426, 390, 393, 395–98; Kammen, "The Causes of the Maryland Revolution of 1689," 300, for the disputes over the extension of English law to the colony; William Stevens Perry, ed., *Papers Relating to the History of the Church in Maryland, 1694–1775* (privately printed, 1878), 29.

73. *Maryland Archives*, 24:91.

74. Perry, *Papers Relating to Maryland*, 39; *Maryland Archives*, 25:91–92.

75. Perry, *Papers Relating to Maryland*, 49–50.

76. *Maryland Archives*, 24:265, 273, and 13:425–30.

77. Ibid., 25:583.

78. Ibid., 22:380; 19:35, 24:420; Spencer Ervin, "The Established Church of Colonial Maryland," *HMPEC* 24 (1955): 243.

79. Perry, *Papers Relating to Maryland*, 8–13.

80. For united Catholic and Quaker opposition to the establishment, see Perry, *Papers Relating to Maryland*, 11–12, 32; *Maryland Archives*, 25:582, 93, 55; Albert W. Werline, *Problems of Church and State in Maryland During the Seventeenth and Eighteenth Century* (South Lancaster, Mass., 1948), 67. David W. Jordan, "Sidelights. A

Plea for Maryland Catholics," *Maryland Historical Magazine* 67 (1972): 429–35, prints the Catholic petition.

81. Kenneth L. Carroll, "Quaker Opposition to the Establishment of a State Church in Maryland," *Maryland Historical Magazine* 65 (1970): 157, and "Maryland Quakers in the Seventeenth Century," *Maryland Historical Magazine* 47 (1952): 312.

82. Carroll, "Quaker Opposition," 157, 163–70; Bernard C. Steiner, ed., *Rev. Thomas Bray, His Life and Selected Works*, Fund Publication No. 37 (Baltimore, 1901), 184 and 230–33 for Quaker influence in the Maryland Assembly.

83. *Maryland Archives*, 8:215; Beverly McAnear, ed., "Mariland's Grevances Wiy They Have Taken Op Arms," *Journal of Southern History* 8 (1942): 392–95.

84. Perry, *Papers Relating to Maryland*, 11–12.

85. Denis, M. Moran, "Anti-Catholicism in Early Maryland Politics: The Protestant Revolution," *Records of the American Catholic Historical Society* 61 (1950): 139–54. An Act To Prevent the Growth of Popery is in *Maryland Archives*, 8:107, 20, 144, 448, and 24:340–41. Private Catholic worship allowed is in *Maryland Archives*, 26:380, 381, 431, 543–44; W. L. Grant and James Munro, eds., *Acts of the Privy Council, Colonial Series*, 6 vols. (London, 1908–12), 2:498; *Maryland Archives*, 26:630–31, 27:146–48, 24:262.

86. McIlwaine and Kennedy, eds., *Journals of the House of Burgesses*, 3:99; H. R. McIlwaine, ed., *Legislative Journals of the Council of Colonial Virginia*, 3 vols. (Richmond, 1918), 1:469; Seiler, "Established Church," 504; Brydon, *Virginia's Mother Church*, 1:280–86.

87. H. R. McIlwaine and W. L. Hall, eds., *Executive Journals of the Council of Colonial Virginia, 1680–1715*, 6 vols. (Richmond, 1925–45), 1:427, 214, 160; Hening, ed., *Statutes*, 3:170–73; Brydon, *Virginia's Mother Church*, 1:249; Seiler, "Church of England," 496–97.

88. Cotton Mather, *Magnalia Christi Americana*, 2 vols. (Hartford, 1853), 2:520; Samuel Green Arnold, *History of the State of Rhode Island and Providence Plantations*, 2 vols. (New York, 1859), 1:490.

89. *Maryland Archives*, 8:362; McAnear, ed., "Mariland's Grevances," 392–409.

3. *Church and State in the Restoration Colonies*

1. J. P. Kenyon, *The Stuart Constitution 1603–1688 Documents and Commentary* (Cambridge, 1966). M. Green, *The Re-Establishment of the Church of England 1660–1663* (Oxford, 1978); A. A. Seaton, *The Theory of Toleration under the Later Stuarts* (Cambridge, 1911; reprint ed., New York, 1972), 84–236; Richard Burgess Barlow, *Citizenship and Conscience—A Study in the Theory and Practice of Religious Toleration in England During the Eighteenth Century* (Philadelphia, 1962), 15–56.

2. Barlow, *Citizenship and Conscience*, 57–97. For Act of Toleration, see E. N. Williams, ed., *The Eighteenth-Century Constitution, 1688–1715* (Cambridge, 1960), 42–46.

3. "The Anglican Church in Restoration Colonial Policy," in James Morton Smith, ed., *Seventeenth-Century America—Essays in Colonial History* (New York, 1959), 166–91. For surveys concerning religion in the colonies, see William Hand Browne, *Archives of Maryland*, 72 vols. (Baltimore, 1883-), 2:129–30, 253, 261–62. Arthur Lyon Cross, *The Anglican Episcopate and the American Colonies* (Cambridge, Mass., 1902; reprint ed., Hamden, Conn., 1964), 33, gives figures on Anglican ministers.

4. The quotation from the Carolina planter is found in Theodore Stephens, "An Account of the Attempts at Establishing a Religious Hegemony in Colonial North Carolina" (Ph.D. dissertation, University of Pittsburgh, 1955), 59. The quotation from Archdale is found in Alexander J. Salley, ed., *Narratives of Early Carolina, 1650–1708* (New York, 1911), 305.

5. For a brief overview of the origins of the Restoration colonies, see Wesley Frank Craven, *The Colonies in Transition 1660–1713* (New York, 1968), 68–103, 175–211. On the beginnings of North and South Carolina, see Charles M. Andrews, *The Colonial Period in American History*, 4 vols. (New Haven, 1937), 1:182–277; Hugh T. Lefler and William G. Powell, *Colonial North Carolina—A History* (New York 1973), 29–55; M. Eugene Sirmans, *Colonial South Carolina—A Political History 1663–1763* (Chapel Hill, 1966), 3–18.

6. Craven, *Colonies in Transition*, 43, 55, 88, 98–103, 243–79; Andrews, *Colonial Period*, 1:262–63.

7. Mattie Erma Parker, ed., *North Carolina Charters and Constitutions 1578–1698* (Raleigh, 1963), 77, 88, 103, 114; William L. Saunders, ed., *The Colonial Records of North Carolina*, 10 vols. (Raleigh, 1886–90), 1:54, 45. Stephen Beauregard Weeks, *The Religious Development in the Province of North Carolina* (Baltimore, 1892), 14–15; Robert Horne, *A Brief Description of the Province of Carolina* (London, 1666), and Salley, ed., *Narratives*, 71. For comments by travel writers, see Gloria Beth Baker, "Dissenters in Colonial North Carolina" (Ph.D. dissertation, University of North Carolina at Chapel Hill, 1970), 37–38.

8. Saunders, ed., *North Carolina Colonial Records*, 1:571, 227.

9. Rufus M. Jones et al., *The Quakers in the American Colonies* (London, 1923), 285–92, 339–44; Weeks, *Religious Development in North Carolina*, 23–34; Saunders, ed., *North Carolina Colonial Records*, 1:184, 334, 391; Baker, "Dissenters in North Carolina," 89–90.

10. Saunders, ed., *North Carolina Colonial Records*, 1:601–2. Spencer Ervin, "The Anglican Church in North Carolina," *HMPEC* 25 (1956): 105–6. Jones et al., *Quakers in the American Colonies*, xvi, estimated that in 1700 there were 5000 Quakers in all of Carolina, most of whom lived in the northern part.

11. Sirmans, *Colonial South Carolina*, 19–54, 60–61; John P. Thomas, "The Barbadians in Early South Carolina," *South Carolina Historical Magazine* 31 (1930): 88.

12. Sirmans, *Colonial South Carolina*, 61–67, 76; Alexander S. Salley, ed., *Journal of the Commons House of Assembly, 1692–1735*, 21 vols. (Columbia, S.C., 1907–46), Journal for the House for 1698, 24 28. For accounts of religion in seventeenth-century South Carolina, see Quenten Begley Keen, "Alexander Garden, Commissary for the Carolinas" (Ph.D. dissertation, University of California at Los Angeles, 1961), 10–30; Sidney Charles Bolton, "The Anglican Church of Colonial South Carolina, 1705–1754: A Study in Americanization" (Ph.D. dissertation, University of Wisconsin, 1973), 8–35. On the affinity of French Huguenots for the Anglican Church elsewhere in the colonies, see George McLaren Brydon, *Virginia's Mother Church*, 2 vols. (Richmond, 1945), 1:262–65; Hugh Hastings and Edward L. Corwin, comps., *Ecclesiastical Records of the State of New York*, 7 vols. (Albany, 1901–16), 3:1750; Robert M. Kingdon, "Why Did the Huguenot Refugees in the American Colonies Become Episcopalians?," *HMPEC* 49 (1980): 317–35.

13. For English attempts at greater political and commercial control over the colonies, see Michael G. Hall, *Edward Randolph and the American Colonies*

1673–1703 (Chapel Hill, 1960), 154–77. For Anglican expansionism, see Carl Bridenbaugh, *Mitre and Sceptre—Transatlantic Faith, Ideas, Personalities, and Politics 1689–1775* (New York, 1962), 54–55; Cross, *Anglican Episcopate*, 28–34; Evarts B. Green, "The Anglican Outlook on the American Colonies in the Early Eighteenth Century," *AHR* 20 (1914): 65. Samuel Clyde McCulloch, "The Foundation and Early Work of the Society for the Propagation of the Gospel in Foreign Parts," *HMPEC* 20 (1951): 121–35; David Humphreys, *An Historical Account of the Incorporated Society for the Propagation of the Gospel in Foreign Parts* (London, 1730; reprint ed., New York, 1919); C. F. Pascoe, *Two Hundred Years of the S.P.G.—An Historical Account of the Society for the Propagation of the Gospel in Foreign Parts* (London, 1901), 1–9.

14. Thomas Cooper and D. J. McCord, eds., *Statutes at Large of South Carolina*, 10 vols. (Columbia, 1836–41), 2:232, 236–48.

15. Their arguments are found in John Archdale, *A New Description of that Fertile and Pleasant Province of Carolina* (London, 1707), in Salley, ed., *Narratives*; Daniel Defoe, *Party-Tyranny* (London, 1705); *The Case of the Protestant Dissenters in Carolina* (London, 1706); Joseph Boone, "Petition of Joseph Boone," in Leo Francis Stock, ed., *Proceedings and Debates of the British Parliament Respecting North America*, 5 vols. (Washington, 1930), 3:115–18.

16. Boone, "Petition," in Stock, ed., *Proceedings*, 3:115–18; Salley, ed., *Narratives*, 249, 256, 260, 295, 303–5, 307, 309.

17. Cooper and McCord, eds., *Statutes*, 2:286–96.

18. Ibid., 2:137, 339.

19. Bolton, "Anglican Church," 99.

20. Babette M. Levy, "Puritanism in the Southern Colonies," *American Antiquarian Society Proceedings* 70 (1960): 269.

21. Bolton, "Anglican Church," 195; Frederick L. Weis, *The Colonial Clergy of the Middle Colonies* (Lancaster, Mass., 1956).

22. Cooper and McCord, eds., *Statutes*, 2:646; Francis X. Curran, *Catholics in Colonial Law* (Chicago, 1963), 91.

23. Sirmans, *Colonial South Carolina*, 141–42. For a discussion of the adaptation of the Church of England to the needs of South Carolina, see Bolton, "Anglican Church."

24. Saunders, ed., *North Carolina Colonial Records*, 1:572, 544, 558, 601, 604.

25. The evidence for the law of 1705 rests on a letter written by the Reverend William Gordon to the Society for the Propagation of the Gospel in 1709 and contained in Saunders, ed., *North Carolina Colonial Records*, 1:709. Gordon noted that the act provided £30 maintenance, the same amount given by the disallowed law of 1701, which raises the possibility that he was referring to that law. For further discussion, see Weeks, *Religious Development in North Carolina*, 45–51, and Baker, "Dissenters in Colonial North Carolina," 100–101.

26. Saunders, ed., *North Carolina Colonial Records*, 1:780, 787. Again, no copy of the act establishing the Church of England remains, and our knowledge of it depends on a letter sent to the Society for the Propagation of the Gospel in 1713 by the Anglican missionary John Urmstone, in Saunders, ed., *North Carolina Colonial Records*, 2:77.

27. Jones et al., *Quakers in the American Colonies*, 353; Baker, "Dissenters in Colonial North Carolina," 118–19.

28. Saunders, ed., *North Carolina Colonial Records*, 2:207–13, 884, 876.

29. Baker, "Dissenters in Colonial North Carolina," 47, 49, 45; Saunders, ed., *North Carolina Colonial Records*, 1:709. Pascoe, *Two Hundred Years of the S.P.G.*, 850, provides a list of thirty-three Anglican ministers who served in colonial North Carolina. More than half of them served one year or less.

30. Saunders, ed., *North Carolina Colonial Records*, 2:188, 374; Sandra Tyler Wood, "The Reverend John Urmstone: A Portrait of North Carolina," *HMPEC* 41 (1972): 263–85.

31. Saunders, ed., *North Carolina Colonial Records*, 1:765, 769–70.

32. Ibid., 1:601, 688, 710, 720, 774, 765; 2:293, 331; see also *North Carolina State Records*, 22:733 (1703).

33. Saunders, ed., *North Carolina Colonial Records*, 1:709–10, 2:37.

34. Edmund B. O'Callaghan, ed., *The Documentary History of the State of New York*, 4 vols. (Albany, 1849–51), 1:145; E. Clowes Chorley, "The Beginnings of the Church in the Province of New York," *HMPEC* 13 (1944): 5–25; E. T. Corwin, ed., *Ecclesiastical Records of the State of New York*, 7 vols. (Albany, 1901–16), 2:879.

35. Michael Kammen, *Colonial New York: A History* (New York, 1975), 71–72.

36. Fredrick J. Zwierlein, *Religion in New Netherland 1623–1664* (Rochester, N.Y., 1910; reprint ed., New York, 1971), 136–265; John Webb Pratt, *Religion, Politics and Diversity—The Church-State Theme in New York History* (Ithaca, 1967), 3–25; Thomas F. O'Connor, "Religious Toleration in New York," *New York State Historical Association* 34 (1936): 391–410; George L. Smith, *Religion and Trade in New Netherland: Dutch Origins and American Development* (Ithaca, 1973), 179–249.

37. *Ecclesiastical Records*, 1:649, 571, 600, 618.

38. Ibid., 2:864–65, 192, 828.

39. Ibid., 2:880, and (for ministers' difficulties in collecting their salaries) 1:711; 2:844, 812, 879, 929, 960.

40. O'Callaghan, ed., *Documentary History*; Cotton Mather, *Memorable Providences Relating to Witchcraft and Possession* (Boston, 1689), Appendix 1–14; Jones, *Quakers in the American Colonies*, 231–32, 237, 247. Instances of Quaker disruption of services are in *Ecclesiastical Records*, 1:691, 2:906, 957. For Ranterism, see Leonard W. Levy, *Treason Against God. A History of the Offense of Blasphemy* (New York, 1981), 234–57; A. L. Morton, *The World of the Ranters: Religious Radicalism in the English Reformation* (London, 1970).

41. *Ecclesiastical Records*, 1:723, 744; 2:956, 958.

42. David S. Lovejoy, *The Glorious Revolution in America* (New York, 1972), 98–121, 251–57; Kammen, *Colonial New York*, 120–21.

43. For Leisler's contacts with other colonies, see O'Callaghan, ed., *Documentary History*, 2:19–25. For the Leislerian influence in later politics, see Alison Gilbert Olson, "Governor Robert Hunter and the Anglican Church in New York," in Anne Whiteman et al., eds., *Statesmen, Scholars and Merchants: Essays in Eighteenth-Century History Presented to Dame Lucy Sutherland* (Oxford, 1973), 44–64; Michael G. Hall et al., eds., *The Glorious Revolution in America: Documents on the Colonial Crisis of 1689* (Chapel Hill, 1964), 83–139.

44. *Ecclesiastical Records*, 2:1012–16; Pratt, *Religion*, 38–39; Kenneth B. West, "Quakers and the State: The Controversy over Oaths in the Colony of New York," *The Michigan Academician* 2 (1970): 100.

45. *Ecclesiastical Records*, 2:1088, 1073–79; *An Act Passed . . . 1693* (New York, 1693).

46. Sanford H. Cobb, *The Rise of Religious Liberty in America* (New York, 1902), 341–42, agreed with New York dissenters that the act had not established the Church

of England; Bridenbaugh, *Mitre and Sceptre*, 118–19, agreed with the eighteenth-century Lewis Morris that the governor had "finessed the assemblymen"; Elizabeth H. Davidson, *The Establishment of the English Church in the Continental American Colonies* (Durham, 1936), 41, held that the law could not have been interpreted as an establishment of the Church of England, and R. Townsend Henshaw, "The New York Ministry Act of 1693," *HMPEC* 2 (1933): 199, held that the Assembly had been hoodwinked.

47. "Col. Morris to the secretary of the Society for the Propagation of the Gospel," in O'Callaghan, ed., *Documentary History*, 3:244.

48. *Ecclesiastical Records*, 2:1299, 1037, 1079.

49. Ibid., 2:1054.

50. Jean Paul Jordan, "The Anglican Establishment in Colonial New York" (Ph.D. dissertation, Columbia University, 1971), 74, wrote that the legislators "hedged their bets."

51. *Ecclesiastical Records*, 2:1114; 1:570.

52. Pratt, *Religion*, 44–45. For Trinity charter, see *Ecclesiastical Records*, 2:1136–65, and (for assertions by Anglicans that their church was established) 2:1178, 1213, 1220, 1478, 1486, 1595; Nelson R. Burr, "The Episcopal Church and the Dutch in Colonial New York and New Jersey, 1664–1784," *HMPEC* 19 (1950): 90–111.

53. Dixon Ryan Fox, *Caleb Heathcote, Gentleman Colonist* (New York, 1926), 228. O'Callaghan, ed., *Documentary History*, provides population estimates. Vesey's report is found in William Stevens Perry, *The History of the American Episcopal Church, 1587–1833*, 2 vols. (Boston, 1885), 1:174.

54. *Ecclesiastical Records*, 2:1302, 1392; "Earl of Bellomont to the Lords of Trade," in *Documents Relative to the Colonial History of the State of New York*, 15 vols. (Albany, 1856–87), 4:536.

55. William Smith, Jr., *The History of the Province of New York*, Michael Kammen, ed., 2 vols. (Cambridge, Mass., 1972), 1:117.

56. *Ecclesiastical Records*, 3:1503–7, 1620.

57. Ibid., 3:1615–19, 1660, 1667, 1679.

58. *Ecclesiastical Records*, 3:1430, 1716, 1718, 1859, 1856, for advice from Amsterdam Classis.

59. Ibid., 3:2207.

60. The records of the controversy are found in Louis Rou, *A Collection of Papers Concerning Mr. Louis Rou's Affair* (New York, 1725); *The True State of Mr. Rou's Case* (New York, 1726); *Ecclesiastical Records*, 3:2238–40, 2241, 2292, 2293. Missing are two Memorials, the first one probably never published, by Rou and a long defense by his opponents.

61. "The answer of Mr. Moulinars and the rest of the French Consistory," in Rou, *Collection*, 56, 9–13, 116, and *Ecclesiastical Records*, 3:2235–38.

62. Rou, *Collection*, 13–24; *Ecclesiastical Records*, 3:2294–2303.

63. The information that he took his case to the Court of Chancery rests on a note to Rou's *The True State of Mr. Rou's Case*, 23. Weis, *The Colonial Clergy of the Middle Colonies*.

64. *Ecclesiastical Records*, 3:1, 2187–8.

65. "A Narrative of a New and Unusual American Imprisonment of two Presbyterian Ministers and Prosecution of Mr. Francis Makemie One of them, for Preaching one Sermon at the City of New York," in Peter Force, ed., *Tracts and Other Papers*, 4 vols. (Washington, 1847; reprint, ed., Gloucester, Mass., 1963), 4:9, 31, 40, 44;

Boyd S. Schlenther, ed., *The Life and Writings of Francis Makemie*, (Philadelphia, 1971), 21–25; "Lord Cornbury to the Lords of Trade," in *Documents Relating to the Colonial History of the State of New York*, 4:1186–87.

66. "Narrative," in Force, ed., *Tracts*, 4:44, 40, 51–52, 5.

67. Josephine C. Frost, ed., *Records of the Town of Jamaica, Long Island, New York, 1656–1751*, 3 vols. (Brooklyn, 1914), 1:13, 14, 21, 25, 39, 49, 113, 160; *Ecclesiastical Records*, 1:646, 2:921, 960, 1021, 1463; Pratt, *Religion*, 54, 61–62.

68. The controversy can be followed in Frost, ed., *Records of Jamaica*, 2:264, 314–74, 376; 3:411–13, 423, 425–26; and especially in O'Callaghan, ed., *Documentary History*, 3:120–340. See also Jordan, "Anglican Establishment," 103–32.

69. O'Callaghan, ed., *Documentary History*, 3:244–49.

70. *Ecclesiastical Records*, 3:1865. For Jews in colonial New York, see Jacob R. Marcus, *The Colonial American Jew, 1492–1776*, 3 vols. (Detroit, 1970), 1:306–10, 402, 409.

71. West, "Quakers," 102–3.

72. Curran, *Catholics in Colonial Law*, 76–78; John Tracy Ellis, *Catholicism in Colonial America* (Baltimore, 1963), 363–76.

73. Pratt, *Religion*, 47; Leonard W. Levy, "No Establishment of Religion: The Original Understanding," in Leonard W. Levy, *Judgments. Essays on American Constitutional History (Chicago, 1972)*, 194.

74. O'Callaghan, ed., *Documentary History*, 3:278.

75. *Ecclesiastical Records*, 2:1619; 3:2173, 2239.

76. On early New Jersey, see John E. Pomfret, *Colonial New Jersey: A History* (New York, 1973), 1–48, and *The Province of West New Jersey, 1609–1702* (Princeton, 1956) and *The Province of East New Jersey, 1609–1702* (Princeton, 1962); Julian P. Boyd, ed., *Fundamental Laws and Constitutions of New Jersey 1664–1694* (Princeton, 1964), 54. The early public documents of New Jersey are found in Aaron Leaming and Jacob Spicer, *New Jersey—Grants, Concessions and Original Constitutions of the Province of New Jersey 1664–1682* (Philadelphia, 1752) and Francis Newton Thorpe, *The Federal and State Constitutions*, 7 vols. (Washington, 1909), 5:2533–84.

77. Boyd, ed., *Fundamental Laws*, 120; Pomfret, *East New Jersey*, 371–81. "Colonel Robert Quarry to the Lords of Trade," in W. A. Whitehead et al., eds., *Archives of the State of New Jersey, 1631–1800*, 30 vols. (Newark, 1880–1906), 2:18. For the defeat of the attempt by the legislature of East Jersey to provide a public maintenance see "The Memorial of Colonel Morris Concerning the State of Religion in the Jerseys, 1700," in *Proceedings of the New Jersey Historical Society* 4 (1849): 118–20; Nelson R. Burr, *The Anglican Church in New Jersey* (Philadelphia, 1954), 10.

78. "The Memorial of Colonel Lewis Morris," 118–20. For the exclusion of Catholics, see Leaming and Spicer, eds., *Grants*, 372.

79. Boyd, ed., *Fundamental Laws*, 141–42; Pomfret, *Colonial New Jersey*, 77–91; Samuel Allison, ed., *Acts of the General Assembly of the Province of New Jersey 1702–1776* (Burlington, 1776), 62–66; Curran, *Catholics*, 98–99. For Catholic worship, see Nelson R. Burr, "The Religious History of New Jersey," *Proceeding of the New Jersey Historical Society* 56 (1938): 255.

80. For Cornbury's complaints and proposals that they should not hold office, see Whitehead et al., eds., *Archives of New Jersey*, 3:66, 70.

81. Deborah Logan and Edward Armstrong, eds., *William Penn and James Logan Correspondence*, 2 vols. (Philadelphia, 1870–72), 1:373.

82. William S. Perry, *Papers Relating to the Church in Pennsylvania* (privately printed, 1871), 205.

83. William Penn, *The Great Case of Liberty of Conscience* (1671), in *The Select Works of William Penn*, 3 vols. (London, 1825), 2:128–64; Seaton, *Theory of Toleration*, 172–77; See also Sally Schwartz, "William Penn and Toleration: Foundations of Colonial Pennsylvania," *Pennsylvania History* 50 (1983): 284–312.

84. Penn stressed the pragmatic reasons for liberty of conscience in *England's Present Interest Considered* (1675), in *Works*, 2:299–319, and *Persuasive to Moderation* (1686), in *Pamphlets on Religion and Democracy* (San Francisco, 1940), 221–71. See also Hugh Barbour, "William Penn, a Model of Protestant Liberalism," *Church History* 48 (1979): 163–67.

85. Andrews, *Colonial Period*, 3:279–81. For accusations of Catholicism against Penn, see the forgery François D'Aix La Chaise, *Letter from Father La Chaise* (Philadelphia, 1686), and Joseph J. Casino, "Anti Popery in Colonial Pennsylvania," *PMHB* 105 (1981): 285.

86. For Pennsylvania charter, see Thorpe, *Constitutions*, 5:3036–44; Andrews, *Colonial Period*, 3:281–85; Joseph E. Illick, *Colonial Pennsylvania* (New York, 1967), 12.

87. Thorpe, *Constitutions*, 5:3036.

88. Perry, *Papers Relating to Pennsylvania*, 2–4, 69–70, 101, 136; W. L. Grant and James Monro, eds., *Acts of the Privy Council. Colonial Series*, 6 vols. (London, 1908–12), 2:645, 668, 420, 851; *A Conference Between a Parish Priest and a Quaker* (Philadelphia, 1725); Charles J. Stille, "Religious Tests in Provincial Pennsylvania," *PMHB* 9 (1885): 365–406; Samuel Hazard, ed., *Pennsylvania Provincial Council . . . Minutes of 1683–1790*, 16 vols. (Philadelphia, 1852–53), Vol. 2 passim; William T. Root, *The Relations of Pennsylvania with the British Government, 1696–1756* (New York, 1912), 233–55; *Act for the Advancement of Justice* (Philadelphia, 1718).

89. William Penn, *Primitive Christianity Revived* (London, 1696), quoted in H. Sheldon Smith, Robert L. Handy, Lefferts A. Loetscher, eds., *American Christianity. An Historical Interpretation with Representative Documents*, 2 vols. (New York, 1960), 1:245.

90. Thorpe, *Constitutions*, 5:3036–44; Perry, *Papers Relating to Pennsylvania*, 5, 38, 16.

91. Thomas Chalkley, *Forcing Maintenance* (Philadelphia, 1714), 4–12, 28–46.

92. Thomas Gordon and John Trenchard, *The Independent Whig* (Philadelphia, 1724); Thomas Wollston, *A Free Gift to the Clergy . . .* (Philadelphia, 1724); *Antient Testimony of Quakers* (Philadelphia, 1723); Jacob Taylor, *Almanack* (Philadelphia, 1726); *Two Treatises . . . Why the People Called Quakers do not pay Tithes . . .* (Philadephia, 1771).

93. Thorpe, *Constitutions*, 1:558; Robert W. Johannsen, "Conflict Between the Three Lower Counties on the Delaware and the Province of Pennsylvania 1682–1704," *Delaware History* 5 (1952): 96.

94. For an estimate of Pennsylvania's population, see Illick, *Colonial Pennsylvania*, 63, 113. Falckner's comment is found in *PMHB*, 101 (1977): 151. Ellis, *Catholics*, 373–75.

4. *Liberty of Conscience in Eighteenth-Century Colonial America*

1. Stephen Hopkins, "An Account of the Planting and Growth of Providence," *Collections of the Massachusetts Historical Society* 19 (1832): 184.

2. Moses Dickinson, *A Sermon* (New London, 1775), 35.

3. "An Act Exempting their Majestys Protestant Subjects, dissenting from the Church of England from the Penalties of Certain Laws," 1 William & Mary C 8.

Statutes of the Realm, 11 vols. (London, 1810–28), 6:74–77; "A Letter Concerning Toleration," in *The Works of John Locke*, 10 vols. (London, 1823; reprint ed., Germany, 1968), 6:250; A. A. Seaton, *The Theory of Toleration Under the Later Stuarts* (Cambridge, 1911; reprint ed., New York, 1972), 237–74.

4. Francis Newton Thorpe, ed., *The Federal and State Constitutions, Colonial Charters, and Other Organic Laws*, 7 vols. (Washington, D.C., 1909); Leonard Woods Labaree, ed., *Royal Instructions to British Colonial Governors, 1670–1776*, 2 vols. (New York, 1935).

5. *Connecticut Acts and Laws* (Boston, 1702), 48. W. L. Grant and James Munro, eds., *Acts of the Privy Council, Colonial Series*, 6 vols. (London, 1908–11), 2:832–33, gives the disallowance, and J. H. Trumbull and C. J. Hoadly, eds., *Public Records of the Colony of Connecticut, 1636–1776*, 15 vols. (Hartford, 1850–90), 4:546, 5:87, gives the repealing law and the toleration allowed in 1708. The English authorities regarded all non-Anglican Protestants in England and the colonies as "Dissenters"; however, although regarded as Dissenters by England, dominant New England Congregationalists made provisions for their own "dissenters."

6. Richard Burgess Barlow, *Citizenship and Conscience, A Study in the Theory and Practice of Religious Toleration in England during the Eighteenth Century* (Philadelphia, 1962), 57–76.

7. "An Act for the Abrogating of the Oathes of Supremacy & Allegiance and Appointing other Oathes," 1 William & Mary C 8, *Statutes of the Realm*, 6:57–60, substituted oaths acceptable to Dissenters, but not to Catholics, because the subscriber was required to renounce all foreign powers, both temporal and spiritual. Other religious tests, however, still prevented English Dissenters from holding office.

8. John Tracy Ellis, *Catholics in Colonial America* (Baltimore, 1965), 346–59. Mary Augustina Ray, *American Opinion of Roman Catholicism in the Eighteenth Century* (New York, 1936).

9. Thorpe, ed., *Federal and State Constitutions*, 5:3063; Ray, *American Opinion*, 70; Samuel Hazard et al., *Minutes of the Pennsylvania Provincial Council, 1638–1790*, 16 vols. (Philadephia, 1852–1949), 3:546; Ellis, *Catholics in Colonial America*, 370–80.

10. Frank Hayden Miller, "Legal Qualifications for Office in America," *Annual Report of the American Historical Association for the Year 1899*, 2 vols. (Washington, D.C., 1900), 1:89–153; Samuel Allison, ed., *Acts of the General Assembly of the Province of New Jersey 1702–1772* (Burlington, 1776), 62; Francis X. Curran, ed., *Catholics in Colonial Law* (Chicago, 1963).

11. Jacob R. Marcus, *The Colonial American Jew, 1492–1776*, 3 vols. (Detroit, 1970), 1:507–15; *Evening Service for Roshashanah* (New York, 1761); *The Form of Prayer* (New York, 1760); *Prayers for Shabbath* (New York, 1765); *A Manual of Catholic Prayers* (Philadelphia, 1774).

12. *The Antient Testimony of the People Called Quakers* (Philadelphia, 1723), 22–25. William Addison Blakely, *American State Papers Bearing on Sunday Legislation* (Washington, D.C., 1911; reprint ed., New York, 1970), 33–78; "Appendix 1 to Opinion of Mr. Justice Frankfurter. Principal Colonial Sunday Statutes and Their Continuation Until the End of the Eighteenth Century," 366 *U.S. Reports*, 543–50 (1961); David H. Flaherty, "Law Enforcement of Morals in Early America," *Perspectives in American History* 5 (1971): 203–53.

13. On Quaker opposition to war, see Samuel Hazard et al., eds., *Pennsylvania Archives, 1664* (Philadelphia, 1852–1949), 4th Series, 1:759; John Smith, *The*

Doctrine of Christianity (Philadelphia, 1748); *An Apology for Quakers* (Philadelphia, 1757). *The Christian Duty, To Render to Caesar* (Philadelphia, 1756) argued that Quakers should pay taxes for war. Guy F. Hershberger, "Pacifism and the State in Colonial Pennsylvania," *Church History* 8 (1939): 54–74.

14. Winfred T. Root, *The Relations of Pennsylvania with the British Government, 1696–1775* (New York, 1912), 222–55; George Stoughton et al., eds., *Charter to William Penn and Laws of the Province* (Harrisburg, 1879), 182, 199, 224, 295, 393, 593; J. R. Bartlett, ed., *Records of the Colony of Rhode Island and Providence Plantations in New England, 1636–1792* (Providence, 1856–65), 2:498; 3:339; *Rhode Island Session Laws* (Newport, 1737), 117; Rufus M. Jones, *The Quakers in the American Colonies* (London, 1923), 171–212, 192, 198, 298–300; W. A. Whitehead et al., eds., *Archives of the State of New Jersey*, 30 vols. (Newark, 1880–1906), 2:407; Grant and Munro, eds., *Acts of the Privy Council*, 2:654, 738, 848; *New Jersey Acts and Laws* (New York, 1717), 45; *New Jersey Session Laws* (Burlington, 1728), 27; *New Jersey Session Laws* (Philadelphia, 1732), 214, 216; W. L. Saunders, ed., *Colonial Records of North Carolina, 1662–1772*, 10 vols. (Raleigh, 1886–90), 2:884, 4:885; Walter Clark, ed., *State Records of North Carolina 1777–1790*, 16 vols. (Winston & Goldboro, 1886–1914), 1:577; Nicholas Trott, ed., *Laws of the Province of South Carolina before 1734*, 2 vols. (Charleston, 1736), 2:231; *New York Session Laws* (New York, 1734), 418–19; Kenneth B. West, "Quakers and the State: The Controversy over Oaths in the Colony of New York," *The Michigan Academician* 2 (1970): 95–105; W. W. Hening, ed., *The Statutes at Large, Being a Collection of all Laws of Virginia 1619–1792*, 13 vols. (Richmond, 1809–23), 3:172; *Massachusetts Acts and Resolves, Public and Private, of the Province of Massachusetts Bay 1692–1835*, 21 vols. (Boston, 1869–1922), 3:123; *Laws of New Hampshire 1679–1835*, 10 vols. (Manchester, 1902–22), 2:263, 530; William H. Browne, *Archives of Maryland*, 72 vols. (Baltimore, 1883-), 24:273.

15. The continuing hostility to Quakers can be seen in Andrew Jones, *The Black Book of Conscience* (Boston, 1742), 6; *An Address to the Freeholders of Massachusetts* (Boston, 1751), 7; "Samuel Seabury to the Society for the Propagation of the Gospel," in E. B. O'Callaghan, ed., *Documentary History of the State of New York*, 4 vols. (Albany, 1856–87), 3:196–98; John Shelbeare, *A Letter from Batista Angeloni* (Philadelphia, 1764). Quaker reminders of Puritan persecution appeared in John Jerman, *Almanack* (Philadelphia, 1723); William Sewall, *The History of the Rise, Increase, and Progress of the . . . Quakers* (Philadelphia, 1728), 157–59; Peter Folger, *A Looking Glass for the Times, 1724, 1763*, 13.

16. Whitehead et al., eds., *Archives of the State of New Jersey*, 3:413. See also William G. McLoughlin, *New England Dissent 1630–1833. The Baptists and the Separation of Church and State*, 2 vols. (Cambridge, Mass., 1971), 1:190–91, 233, 236, 253; Evarts B. Greene, "The Anglican Outlook on the American Colonies in the Early Eighteenth Century," *AHR* 20 (1914): 77; Frederick Tolles, "The Transatlantic Quaker Community in the Seventeenth Century," *Huntington Library Quarterly* 14 (1951): 239–58; Henry J. Cadbury, "Intercolonial Solidarity of American Quakerism," *PMHB* 60 (1936): 362–74. *Epistle to the Society of Friends* (Philadelphia, 1734) and William Douglass, *A Summary, Historical and Political* (Boston, 1749), 463, indicate the increasing respectability of Quakers.

17. For references to New England Congregationalists as "Dissenters," see William Stevens Perry, *Papers Relating to the History of the Church in Massachusetts* (privately printed, 1878), 366–67 and passim. On Anglicanism, see Arthur Lyon Cross, *The Anglican Episcopate and the American Colonies* (Cambridge, Mass., 1902), 1–50. Carl

Bridenbaugh, *Mitre and Sceptre: Transatlantic Faiths, Ideas, Personalities, and Politics, 1689–1775* (New York, 1962), 171–313.

18. McLoughlin, *New England Dissent*, 2:833–40; Charles B. Kinney, Jr., *Church and State: The Struggle for Separation in New Hampshire 1639–1900* (New York, 1955), 8–82.

19. For the Massachusetts ecclesiastical system after 1691, see Susan Martha Reed, *Church and State in Massachusetts, 1691–1740* (Urbana, Ill., 1914), 18–34.

20. McLoughlin, *New England Dissent*, 1:248; Williston Walker, ed., *Creeds and Platforms of Congregationalism* (New York, 1893; reprint ed., Philadelphia, 1960), 495–523; M. Louise Green, *The Development of Religious Liberty in Connecticut* (Boston, 1905), 133–58; Benjamin Trumbull, *A Complete History of Connecticut Civil and Ecclesiastical*, 2 vols. (New London, 1898), 2:1–18.

21. Cotton Mather, *Optanda* (Boston, 1692), 44; Perry Miller, *The New England Mind: From Colony to Province* (Cambridge, Mass., 1953), 167.

22. Walker, *Creeds and Platforms*, 389.

23. Thomas Hutchinson, ed., *Collection of Original Papers*, 2 vols. (Boston, 1865; reprint ed., New York, 1967), 2:132; Increase Mather, *The Danger of Apostacie* (Cambridge, Mass., 1679), 76.

24. Mather, *Optanda*, 45; Jonathan Russell, *A Plea for the Righteousness of God* (Boston, 1704), 19.

25. For references to rulers as "Nursing Fathers," see Gurdon Saltonstall, *A Sermon Preached Before the Assembly* (Boston, 1697), 50; Cotton Mather, *The Bostonian Ebenezer* (Boston, 1698), 23; Solomon Stoddard, *The Way for a People To Live Long in the Land* (Boston, 1703), 1; John Woodward, *Civil Rulers Are God's Ministers* (Boston, 1712), 18; John Hancock, *Rulers Should be Benefactors* (Boston, 1728), 14. For assertions that the magistrate was the custodian of "Both Tables," see Stoddard, *Way for People to Live*, 11; Nicholas Noyes, *New Englands Duty and Interest* (Boston, 1698), 82; Joseph Moss, *Election Sermon* (Hartford, 1715), 9; Joseph Sewall, *Rulers Must Be Just* (Boston, 1724), 36; Azariah Mather, *Good Rulers a Choice Blessing* (Boston, 1725), 4–5. For references to Old Testament figures as models for New England's rulers, see Jonathan Marsh, *An Essay, to Prove the Thorough Reformation* (New London, 1721), 32; Benjamin Wadsworth, *Public Worship a Christian Duty* (Boston, 1704), 20; Joseph Moss, *The Discourse Sheweth*, 14; Thomas Prince, *Civil Rulers Raised Up* (Boston, 1728), 19.

26. Increase Mather, *The Great Blessing* (Boston, 1693), 10; Samuel Willard, *The Character of a Good Ruler* (Boston, 1694), 12; Cotton Mather, *Things for a Distres't People* (Boston, 1696), 43; Joseph Belcher, *The Singular Happiness* (Boston, 1701), 21, 31; John Rogers, *A Sermon Preached Before His Excellency* (Boston, 1706), 36–37; Samuel Cheever, *Gods Sovereign Government* (Boston, 1712), 45; Samuel Woodbridge, *Obedience to Divine Law* (New London, 1724), 10. For ministers' assertions that the magistrate was to be the protector of prosperity and civil happiness, see L. H. Breen, *The Character of a Good Ruler: A Study of Puritan and Political Ideas in New England 1630–1720* (New Haven, 1970), 180–202.

27. Mather, *Optanda*, 46; Noyes, *New Englands Duty*, 79; Rogers, *A Sermon*, 41.

28. Saltonstall, *Sermon Before the Assembly*, 81; Stoddard, *The Way for a People To Live*, 11; Samuel Estabrook, *A Sermon Showing that Peace and Quietness* (New London, 1718), 12–13; Stephen Hosmer, *A People's Living in Appearance* (New London, 1720), 10; Marsh, *An Essay*, 41.

29. Hancock, *Rulers Should Be Benefactors*, 22; Benjamin Colman, *The Piety and Duty of Rulers* (Boston, 1708), 6–8.

30. Samuel Whitman, *A Practical Godliness* (New London, 1714), 33; Estabrook, *Sermon*, 12; Sewall, *Rulers Must Be Just*, 36.

31. Mather, *Optanda*, 46. For comments on maintenance, see Samuel Willard, *Israels True Safety* (Boston, 1704), 26; Benjamin Colman, *The Piety and Duty of Rulers*, 10; Ebenezer Pemberton, *The Divine Origin and Dignity of Government* (Boston, 1710), 102; John Bulkley, *The Necessity of Religion* (New London, 1713), 4, 30–32; Benjamin Wadsworth, *Rulers Feeding and guiding their people* (Boston, 1716), 18; Benjamin Colman, *The Religious Regard We Owe to Our Country* (Boston, 1718), 34–35; Joseph Sewall, *Rulers Must Be Just*, 52; Jabez Fitch, *A Plea for Ministers of New England* (Boston, 1724), 1; Eliphalet Adams, *Ministers Must Take Heed* (New London, 1726), 45; Jeremiah Wise, *Rulers the Ministers of God* (Boston, 1729), 27; John Bulkley, *An Impartial Account* (New London, 1729), 126; Jabez Fitch, *Gospel Ministers* (Boston, 1732), 17; John Barnard, *The Throne Established* (Boston, 1734), 41; Jonathan Ashley, *The United Endeavours* (Boston, 1742), 11; Benjamin Lord, *Religion and Government Subsisting Together* (New London, 1752), 36; James Cogswell, *The Necessity of Piety* (New Haven, 1757), 20; Philemon Robbins, *A Sermon* (Boston, 1760), 30; Edward Dorr, *The Duty of Civil Rulers* (Hartford, 1765), 1, 26.

32. Willard, *The Character of a Good Ruler*, 26; Belcher, *The Singular Happiness*; Wadsworth, *Public Worship a Christian Duty*, 20; Pemberton, *The Divine Origin and Dignity of Government*, 100; Whitman, *Practical Godliness*, 36; William Williams, *A Plea for God* (Boston, 1719); Prince, *Civil Rulers Raised Up*, 19; Wise, *Rulers the Ministers of God*, 74.

33. Increase Mather, *The Great Blessing*, 17; Samuel Torrey, *Man's Extremity* (Boston, 1695), 18; Noyes, *New Englands Duty and Interest*, 45; Increase Mather, *The Excellence of a Public Spirit* (Boston, 1702), 15; Woodbridge, *Obedience to Divine Law*, 21; Thomas Prince, *The People of New England* (Boston, 1730), 25, all recall the original religious purpose of New England.

34. Azariah Mather, *Good Rulers a Choice Blessing*, 30. On the desire in Massachusetts for uniformity and consensus, see Miller, *The New England Mind*, 395–416, and Michael Zuckerman, *Peaceable Kingdoms: New England Towns in the Eighteenth Century* (New York, 1970).

35. For pleas for the college, see Increase Mather, *The Surest Way* (Boston, 1699), 41; Cotton Mather, *A Pillar of Gratitude* (Boston, 1700), 23; Colman, *Piety and Duty of Rulers*, 21.

36. Colman, *Religious Regard We Owe*, 32.

37. Cotton Mather, *Little Flocks* (Boston, 1691), 103, and *Optanda*, 44–45, and *Johannes in Eremo* (Boston, 1695), 29.

38. Benjamin Colman, *A Brief Enquiry* (Boston, 1716), 22, 24–25.

39. Mather, *Optanda*, 42; Increase Mather, *Excellence of a Public Spirit*, 16; Colman, *Piety and Duty of Rulers*, 6.

40. Increase Mather, *Great Blessing*, 1; Noyes, *New Englands Duty and Interest*, 79; Rogers, *Sermon before His Excellency*, 36; Benjamin Colman, *Davids Dying Charge* (Boston, 1723), 23.

41. Thomas Maule, *Truth Held Forth* (New York, 1695), 175–77; A. C. Goodell, "A Biographical Sketch of Thomas Maule, of Salem . . .," *Historical Collections of the Essex Institute* 3 (1861): 250; Thomas Maule, *New England Persecutors Mauled* (New York, 1697), 1–18, 53, 62; Leonard W. Levy, *Freedom of Speech and Press in Early American History—Legacy of Suppression* (New York, 1963), 32. Thomas Maule, *An*

Abstract of a Letter (New York, 1701), 6–7, and *Tribute to Caesar* (Philadelphia, 1712), 6–16, relied on history to prove the lack of civil power in the Church.

42. Edmund F. Slafter, *John Checkley, or the Evolution of Religious Tolerance in Massachusetts Bay*, 2 vols. (Boston, 1897; reprint ed., New York, 1967), 1:33–40, 55–57. The publications were Charles Leslie, *The Religion of Jesus Christ the only True Religion, or a Short and Easie Method with the Deists* (Boston, 1719) and John Checkley, *Choice Dialogues* (Boston, 1720). For the reaction of the Massachusetts authorities, see *Massachusetts Acts and Resolves*, 2:153, and Perry, *Papers Relating to the History of the Church in Massachusetts*, 157, 146, 201, 247. Thomas C. Reeves, "John Checkley and the Emergence of the Episcopal Church in New England," *HMPEC* 34 (1965): 349–60; Levy, *Freedom of Speech and Press*, 34–35; Miller, *The New England Mind*, 468–73.

43. McLoughlin, *New England Dissent*, gives a complete account of the disputes in New England regarding ministerial maintenance. Broader than its title suggests, this monumental work is in fact a complete study of Church-State relations in New England from its beginnings until the early nineteenth century.

44. *Massachusetts Acts and Resolves*, 1:305, 2:494–95.

45. John Callendar, *An Historical Discourse* (Boston, 1739), 58.

46. Samuel Arnold, *History of the State of Rhode Island*, 2 vols. (New York, 1860), 2:490–94, provides the best commentary on the law excluding Catholics, which he termed an "interpolation" and dated to 1699. He reasoned that at that time, the colony felt the need to conform to the more accepted standards of the other colonies and Britain, in order to protect the charter. Sanford H. Cobb, *The Rise of Religious Liberty in America* (New York, 1902), 437–38, stressed that the law was never passed by the people. Cobb relied on George Bancroft's *History of the United States*, 10 vols., 15th ed. (Boston, 1852), 2:65, which cited the 1744 version as the earliest printed edition of Rhode Island's laws. Arnold, however, cited versions for 1719 and 1730 and found a manuscript collection of 1707 containing the law excluding Catholics. Sidney S. Rider, *An Inquiry Concerning the Origin of the Clause in the Laws of Rhode Island from 1719 to 1783 Disenfranchising Catholics* (Providence, 1889), 27, held that the law was an error printed in the Collection of 1719 and retained thereafter. On the scarcity of Catholics, see "Answer of Rhode Island to the Inquiries of the Board of Trade (1680)," in Arnold, *History*, 1:490; Cotton Mather, *Magnalia Christi Americana*, 2 vols. (Hartford, 1853), 2:520–21. For the law against "Popish Recusants," see *Rhode Island Laws, Statutes* (Newport, 1769), 7.

47. Jacob Marcus, *Colonial American Jew*, 3 vols. (Detroit, 1970), 1:314–20, 427–38.

48. For unfavorable references to Rhode Island, see Joshua Scottow, *A Narrative of the Planting* (Boston, 1694), 19; Mather, *Magnalia*, 2:520–21; Whitman, *Practical Godliness*, 38; Solomon Stoddard, *An Answer to Some Cases of Conscience* (Boston, 1722), 11; Perry, *Papers Relating to the Church in Massachusetts*, 225; Thomas Paine, *Gospel Light* (Boston, 1731), 27; Noah Hobart, *A Second Address to the Church of England* (Boston, 1751), 145; Douglass, *A Summary*, 2:76.

49. William G. McLoughlin, ed., *The Diary of Isaac Backus*, 3 vols. (Providence, 1979), 2:868, documents Backus's discovery of Williams. For Williams's lack of influence during the eighteenth century, see LeRoy Moore, Jr., "Religious Liberty: Roger Williams and the Revolutionary Era," *Church History* 34 (1965): 57–75, and William G. McLoughlin, "Isaac Backus and the Separation of Church and State in America," *AHR* 73 (1968): 1392. References by New Yorkers to Rhode Island are found in "A Narrative of a New and Unusual American Imprisonment of Two

Presbyterian Ministers . . .," in Peter Force, ed., *Tracts and Other Papers*, 4 vols. (Washington, D.C., 1867; reprint ed., Gloucester, Mass., 1963), 4:31; William Smith, Jr., *The History of the Province of New York*, 2 vols., Michael Kammen, ed., (Cambridge Mass., 1972), 1:243.

50. J. Franklin Jameson, ed., *Johnson's Wonder-Working Providence 1628–1651* (New York, 1937), 254. Other comments on toleration are found in "Petition to Governor," in Saunders, ed., *Colonial Records of North Carolina*, 2:910, 916–23; John Archdale, *A New Description of that Fertile and Pleasant Province of Carolina* (London, 1707), in Alexander J. Salley, Jr., ed., *Narratives of Early Carolina, 1650–1708* (New York, 1911), 110, 112, 305; Francis Makemie, "A Narrative of a New and Unusual American Imprisonment," in Force, *Tracts and Other Papers*, 4:35; Babette M. Levy, "Early Puritanism in the Southern and Island Colonies,'" *American Antiquarian Society Proceedings* 70 (1960): 69; Daniel Leeds, *The American Almanack* (New York, 1712); Titan Leeds, *The American Almanack* (Philadelphia, 1715); McLoughlin, *New England Dissent*, 1:113–64; Miller, *The New England Mind*, 464–678; Eric Tobias Biorck, *A Little Olive Leaf Put in the Mouth* (New York, 1704).

51. Cotton Mather, *Letter to Ungospellised Plantations* (Boston, 1702), 12.

52. Leonard J. Trinterud, *The Forming of an American Tradition: A Re-examination of Colonial Presbyterianism* (Philadelphia, 1948), 38–52.

53. Hugh Fisher, *A Preservation from Damnable Error* (Boston, 1730), 23, 39, 45, 63, 77; For Fisher, see William B. Sprague, *Annals of the American Pulpit*, 9 vols. (New York, 1857–69), 1:351. See also Henry May, *The Enlightenment in America* (New York, 1976), 1–88; Hugh Fisher, *The Divine Right of Private Judgment. A Reply* (Boston, 1731), 23, 56, 73, 81; Josiah Smith, *The Right of Private Judgment Vindicated* (Boston, 1730), 23, 30, 38, 8, 26. For Smith's denial that he wavered from Calvinistic doctrine, see *No New Thing to be Slandered* (Boston, 1730). For biographical information on Smith, see John L. Sibley and Clifford K. Shipton, *Biographical Sketches of Those Who Attended Harvard College*, 14 vols. (1873–1968), 7:569–85.

54. Jonathan Dickinson, *A Sermon Preached at the Opening of the Synod* (Boston, 1723), 23; the principal opposing viewpoint is found in John Thompson, *An Overture to the Synod* (Philadelphia, 1729). Dickinson responded with *Remarks upon a Discourse Intitled, An Overture* (New York, 1729). See also Bryan F. LeBeau, "The Subscription Controversy and Jonathan Dickinson," *Journal of Presbyterian History* 54 (1976): 317–35; Trinterud, *Formation of an American Tradition*, 38–52. For a brief summary of illustration of Dickinson's religious reasons against subscription, see the extract from his *Remarks upon a Pamphlet* in Sheldon Smith, Robert T. Handy, Lefferts A. Loetscher, *American Christianity. An Historical Interpretation with Representative Documents*, 2 vols. (New York, 1960), 1:262–68; Leonard W. Labaree et al., *The Papers of Benjamin Franklin*, 21 vols. (New Haven, 1959-), 2:27 and passim; Merton A. Christensen, "Franklin on the Hemphill Trial: Deism Versus Presbyterian Orthodoxy," *WMQ* 10 (1953):422–40; Jonathan Dickinson, *Remarks upon a Pamphlet* (Philadelphia, 1735), 3, 5, 7, 12, 17–28.

55. *American Mercury*, Feb. 3, 1730; *The Independent Whig* (Philadelphia, 1724).

56. Trinterud, *Forming of an American Tradition*, 53–108; Martin E. Lodge, "The Crisis of the Churches in the Middle Colonies, 1720–1750," *PMHB* 95 (1971): 195–212.

57. Eugene White, "Decline of the Great Awakening in New England, 1741–1746," *New England Quarterly* 24 (1951): 44–45; Edwin Scott Gaustad, *The Great*

Awakening in New England (New York, 1957), 61–79; Leonard W. Labaree, "The Conservative Attitude Towards the Great Awakening," *WMQ* 1 (1944): 331–52. The principal attacks at the time came from Charles Chauncy, in *Enthusiasm Described* (Boston, 1742) and *Seasonable Thoughts* (Boston, 1743).

58. *Connecticut Acts and Laws* (New London, 1742). For Williams, see Shipton, ed., *Sibley's Harvard Graduates*, 5:588–98; Trumbull, *History of Connecticut*, 2:251–52; Richard L. Bushman, *From Puritan to Yankee. Character and the Social Order in Connecticut, 1690–1765* (Cambridge, Mass., 1967), 227–30, 236–37.

59. Elisha Williams, *The essential Rights and Liberties of Protestants. A seasonable Plea for the Liberty of Conscience, and The Right of private Judgment in Matters of Religion without any Control from Human Authority. Being A Letter, from a Gentleman in the Massachusetts-Bay to his Friend in Connecticut* (Boston, 1744); Locke, *Works*, 6:45.

60. Nathaniel Eells, *The Wise Ruler* (New London, 1748), 26–27, 32; For Old Light comments, see William Worthington, *The Duty of Rulers* (New London, 1744), 11, 10; Samuel Hall, *The Legislatures Rights* (New London, 1746), 20; Jonathan Todd, *Civil Rulers the Ministers of God* (New London, 1749), 3, 14, 18, 42–47. See also Bushman, *From Puritan to Yankee*, 238–39; *Connecticut Acts and Laws* (New London, 1750); Morgan, *The Gentle Puritan. A Life of Ezra Stiles 1727–1795* (New Haven, 1962), 197–202; Trumbull, *History of Connecticut*, 2:408–49; Louis Leonard Tucker, *Puritan Protagonist. President Thomas Clap of Yale* (Chapel Hill, 1962), 215–22.

61. Gewehr, *The Great Awakening in Virginia 1740–1790* (Durham, 1930), 25–26, 40–105; Brydon, *Virginia's Mother Church and the Political Conditions under Which It Grew*, 2 vols. (Richmond, 1947), 2:154–72; George William Pilcher, "Samuel Davies and Religious Toleration in Virginia," *Historian* 48 (1965): 48–71; William S. Perry, *Historical Collection of the Protestant Episcopal Church of Virginia* (privately printed, 1870), 381, 372–74, 379–80, 389; Henry R. McIlwaine, *The Struggle of Protestant Dissenters for Religious Toleration in Virginia* (Baltimore, 1894), 12:40–64.

62. Perry, *Historical Collection*, 380.

63. Samuel Davies, *The State of Religion* (Boston, 1751), 42; Maurice W. Armstrong, "The English Dissenting Deputies and the American Colonies," *Journal of Presbyterian History* 40 (1962): 80; Pilcher, *Samuel Davies*, 65–71.

64. Charles W. Akers, *Called unto Liberty. A Life of Jonathan Mayhew, 1720–1766* (Cambridge, Mass., 1964), 60–97; May, *Enlightenment in America*, 55–61; Conrad Wright, *The Beginnings of Unitarianism in America* (Boston, 1955).

65. Jonathan Mayhew, *Seven Sermons* (Boston, 1749), 20–40, 37, 57–59, 70; "Jonathan Mayhew's Memorandum," Appendix to Bernard Bailyn, "Religion and Revolution," in *Perspective in American History* 4 (1970): 140–43.

66. Jonathan Mayhew, *A Sermon Preach'd* (Boston, 1754), in A. W. Plumstead, ed., *The Wall and the Garden. Selected Massachusetts Election Sermons 1670–1775* (Minneapolis, 1968), 304; Akers, *Called unto Liberty*, 104; Heimert, *Religion and the American Mind*, 47–48, 169–70, 292–93.

67. For Mayhew's views on Catholicism, see *A Sermon Preach'd*, 310–11, and *Popish Idolatry* (Boston, 1765). George Berkeley, *A Word to the Wise* (Boston, 1750), 15.

68. Bernard Bailyn, ed., *Pamphlets of the American Revolution* (Cambridge, Mass., 1965), 1:210.

69. Brydon, *Virginia's Mother Church*, 2:178–91; Rhys Isaac, "Evangelical Revolt: The

Nature of the Baptist Challenge to the Traditional Order in Virginia, 1756–1775," *WMQ* 31 (1974): 345–68.

70. William Douglass, *A Summary*, 2:128; Charles Chauncy, *A Reply to Dr. Chandler's "Appeal Defended"* (Boston, 1770), 145.

71. Paul Conkin, "The Church Establishment in North Carolina, 1765–1776," *North Carolina Historical Review* 30 (1955): 18; Saunders, ed., *Colonial Records of North Carolina 1667–1776*, 8:322, 334, 352, 372, 451, 466, 469; Clark, ed., *State Records of North Carolina, 1777–1790*, 1:826; David T. Morgan, Jr., "The Great Awakening in North Carolina, 1740–1775," *North Carolina Historical Review* 45 (1968): 264–83, and "The Great Awakening in South Carolina, 1740–1775," *South Atlantic Quarterly* 70 (1971): 595–606.

72. Benjamin Colman, *Religious Regard*, 34–35. For comments by various New England ministers on the role of the magistrate, see Charles Chauncy, *Civil Magistrates* (Boston, 1747), 36; William Cooper, *The Honours of Christ* (Boston, 1740), 22; Chauncy, *Civil Rulers*, 37; Ebenezer Devotion, *The Civil Ruler* (New London, 1753), 23, 51; Edward Dorr, *The Duty of Civil Rulers* (Hartford, 1765), 1–10; Noah Hobart, *Civil Government* (New London, 1751), 24–26; Moses Dickinson, *A Sermon Preached before the General Assembly*, 15, 31; Stephen Johnson, *Integrity and Piety* (New London, 1770), 25; Charles Turner, *A Sermon Preached before His Excellency* (Boston, 1773), 13.

73. Thomas Barton, *Unanimity and Public Spirit* (Philadelphia, 1755), Preface by William Smith, 1–11; Barnabas Binney, *An Oration* (Boston, 1774), 24.

74. Benjamin Gale, *A Reply to a Pamphlet* (New London, 1755).

75. Herman Husbands, *An Impartial Relation* (n.p., 1770), 99. For the view that political practice forged ahead of theory, see Bernard Bailyn, "Political Experience and Enlightenment Ideas in Eighteenth Century America," *AHR* 67 (1962): 345–46.

5. *Establishment of Religion in Colonial America*

1. Thomas Bradbury Chandler, *The Appeal Farther Defended* (New York, 1771), 226–27.

2. R. W. G. Vail, "A Check List of New England Election Sermons," *American Antiquarian Society Proceedings* 45 (1935): 233. For church disputes in New Hampshire, see George G. Kirsh, "Clerical Dismissals in Colonial and Revolutionary New Hampshire," *Church History* 49 (1980): 166–69; Charles B. McKinney, *Church and State in New Hampshire* (New York, 1955).

3. *Connecticut Acts and Laws* (New London, 1702), 30; J. H. Trumbull and C. J. Hoadly, eds., *Public Records of Connecticut (1636–1776)*, 15 vols. (Hartford, 1850–90), 5:50; Williston Walker, *The Creeds and Platforms of Congregationalism* (Boston, 1960), 507; *Connecticut Acts and Laws* (New London, 1715), 134.

4. Phineas Fiske, *The Good Subject's Wish* (New London, 1726), 31–32; John Bulkley, *An Impartial Account* (New London, 1729), 132, 141. For the Anglican petition, see Francis L. Hawks and William Stevens Perry, eds., *Documentary History of the Protestant Episcopal Church in Connecticut 1704–1789* (Hartford, 1959).

5. Susan Martha Reed, *Church and State in Massachusetts 1691–1740* (Urbana, Ill., 1914), 24–32; Samuel Willard, *The Character of a Good Ruler* (Boston, 1694), 12; Benjamin Colman, *The Piety and Duty of Rulers* (Boston, 1708), 6.

6. Cotton Mather, *Brethren Dwelling* (Boston, 1718), 40; Benjamin Colman, *David's Dying Charge* (Boston, 1723), 23; Cotton Mather, *Ratio Disciplinae* (Boston, 1726), 21; William G. McLoughlin, *New England Dissent, Baptists and the Separation of Church and State 1630–1833*, 2 vols. (Cambridge, Mass., 1971), 1:217–18. For Colman quotations, see Ebenezer Turell, *The Life and Character of . . . Benjamin Colman* (Boston, 1749), 138–39.

7. Hawks and Perry, eds., *Documentary History*, 47; William Stevens Perry, *Papers Relating to the History of the Church in Massachusetts* (privately printed, 1873), 96, 116, 127. For Checkley, see Edmund F. Slafter, ed., *John Checkley, or the Evolution of Religious Tolerance in Massachusetts Bay*, 2 vols. (Boston, 1897; reprint ed., New York, 1967), 2:27–28; Perry Miller, *The New England Mind: From Colony to Province* (Cambridge, Mass., 1953), 468–75; Edgar Lee Pennington, *The Reverend John Checkley* (Hartford, 1935); Thomas C. Reeves, "John Checkley and the Emergence of the Episcopal Church in New England," *HMPEC* 34 (1965): 349–63; Henry Wilder Foote, *Annals of King's Chapel*, 3 vols. (Boston, 1882), 1:285–325.

8. Thomas Walter, *An Essay upon that Paradox* (Boston, 1724), 30.

9. Perry, *Papers Relating to the Church in Massachusetts*, 170–73, 181; McLoughlin, *New England Dissent*, 1:214–18.

10. Perry, *Papers Relating to the Church in Massachusetts*, 188, 153, 189–90, 198–99.

11. *Connecticut Acts and Laws* (New London, 1727), 340.

12. *Massachusetts Acts and Resolves*, 1:459; Trumbull and Hoadly, eds., *Public Records of Connecticut*, 7:106. For the difference between the two laws, see McLoughlin, *New England Dissent*, 1:269.

13. McLoughlin, *New England Dissent*, 1:218.

14. Perry, *Papers Relating to the Church in Massachusetts*, 286–87.

15. Foote, *Annals of King's Chapel*, 1:465.

16. Perry, *Papers Relating to the Church in Massachusetts*, 225; Foote, *Annals of King's Chapel*, 1:466–67; Maurice W. Armstrong, "The English Dissenting Deputies and the American Colonies," *Journal of Presbyterian History* 20 (1963): 25–26; Carl Bridenbaugh, *Mitre and Sceptre. Transatlantic Faiths, Ideas, Personalities, and Politics* (New York, 1962), 44–45.

17. An incomplete bibliography of pamphlets issued in the debates between Anglicans and Congregationalists can be found in Slafter, ed., *John Checkley*, 2:229–98. James Wetmore, *A Letter from a Minister of the Church of England to his Dissenting Parishioners* (New York, 1730), 19; James Honeyman, *A Sermon Preached at King's Chapel* (Boston, 1733), 11; Samuel Johnson, *A Letter from a Minister* (New York, 1733) and *A Second Letter* (Boston, 1734) and *A Third Letter* (Boston, 1737); Arthur Browne, *The Scripture Bishop* (n.p., 1733).

18. Jonathan Dickinson, *The Scripture-Bishop Vindicated* (Boston, 1733), 29, 30. For Dickinson's controversial works, see Slafter, ed., *John Checkley*, 2:233–67; John Graham, *Some Remarks upon a Late Pamphlet* (Boston, 1733), 2, 15, and *Some Remarks upon a Second Letter* (Boston, 1736), 23–25; Samuel Mather, *Apology for the liberty of the Churches* (Boston, 1737), Dedication.

19. Noah Hobart, *A Serious Address* (Boston, 1748), 43. For Hobart's part in the controversy, see Arthur Lyon Cross, *The Anglican Episcopate and the American Colonies* (Cambridge, Mass., 1902; reprint ed., Hamden, Ct., 1964), 140–43; Bridenbaugh, *Mitre and Sceptre*, 87–90; Foote, *Annals of King's Chapel*, 2:50–51.

20. Noah Hobart, *A Second Address* (Boston, 1751), 28, 30–34. This pamphlet was in response to John Beach, *A Calm and Dispassionate Vindication* (Boston, 1749). Noah

Hobart, *Civil Government* (London, 1751), 26, 41, and *The Principles of the Congregational Churches* (New London, 1759), 4.

21. William Douglass, *A Summary, Historical and Political*, 2 vols. (Boston, 1749, 1753), 1:443 and 2:121, 144, 336.

22. Perry, *Papers Relating to the Church in Massachusetts*, 449.

23. Hawks and Perry, eds., *Documentary History*, 150, 166, 299; Samuel Johnson, *A Second Letter*, 4; Perry, *Papers Relating to the Church in Massachusetts*, 504, 479; James McSparran, "America Dissected," in William Updike, *History of the Episcopal Church in Narragansett, Rhode Island* (New York, 1847), 510; William Stevens Perry, *Papers Relating to the History of the Church in Pennsylvania* (privately printed, 1876), 136, 156, 245, 260. See also *A True Copy of a Genuine Letter sent to the Archbishop of Canterbury by Eighteen Presbyterian Ministers* (New York, 1761), 12–13.

24. Samuel Mather, *Apology*, 7. On the use of the terms "Articles of Faith" and/or "Modes of Worship" to denote a kind of establishment disapproved of by New England writers, see John Barnard, *The Throne Established* (Boston, 1734), 41; Peter Clark, *The Rulers Highest Dignity* (Boston, 1739), 18; William Cooper, *The Honours of Christ* (Boston, 1740), 22; Thomas Barnard, *Tyranny and Slavery . . .* (Boston, 1743), 12; Charles Chauncy, *Civil Magistrates* (Boston, 1747), 36; Elihu Hall, *The Present Way* (New London, 1749), 52; William Welsteed, *The Dignity & Duty* (Boston, 1751), 17.

25. Cotton Mather, *Brethren Dwelling* (Boston, 1718), 37; Benjamin Colman, *The Religious Regards* (Boston, 1718), 35.

26. On Arminianism and subscription, see J. William L. Young, Jr., *God's Messengers. Religious Leadership in Colonial New England* (Baltimore, 1976), 80–88; Conrad Wright, *The Beginnings of Unitarianism in America* (Boston, 1955), 9–27; "Robert Breck" and "Benjamin Kent," in John L. Sibley and Clifford K. Shipton, eds., *Biographical Sketches of Those Who Attended Harvard College*, 14 vols. (Cambridge, Mass., 1873–1968), 8:661–80, 220–30; John Swift, *A Sermon Preach'd at Boston* (Boston, 1732), 20; Barnard, *The Throne Established*, 41; Clark, *The Rulers Highest Dignity*, 18; Cooper, *The Honours of Christ*, 12; William Rand, *Minister's Duty* (Boston, 1739), 27.

27. See pages 97–98 above.

28. Elisha Williams, *The essential Rights and Liberties of Protestants* (Boston, 1744), 13, 18–19, 92, 19–20, 50, 39; Richard L. Bushman, *From Puritan to Yankee—Character and the Social Order in Connecticut, 1690–1765* (Cambridge, Mass., 1967), 227–30.

29. For Old Light comments, see William Worthington, *The Duty of Rulers* (New London, 1744), 11; Samuel Hall, *The Legislatures Right* (New London, 1746), 26; Jonathan Todd, *A Defense* (New London, 1748), 104, and *Civil Rulers* (New London, 1749), 16, 47.

30. Bushman, *Puritan to Yankee*, 239; Noah Hobart, *Civil Government*, 32, 34, 41; Moses Dickinson, *A Sermon Preached Before the General Assembly* (New London, 1755), 31–33; Benjamin Gale, *The Present State* (New London, 1755), II, and *A Reply* (New London, 1755), xi–xii.

31. Ashbel Woodbridge, *A Sermon* (New London, 1753), 32.

32. Chauncy, *Civil Magistrates*, 37; Welsteed, *The Dignity and Duty*, 18–19; Benjamin Stevens, *A Sermon* (Boston, 1761), 11.

33. Ezra Stiles, *A Discourse on the Christian Union* (Boston, 1761), 80–83, 98–99; on Stiles, see Morgan, *The Gentle Puritan. The Life of Ezra Stiles 1727–1795* (New Haven, 1962). On the *Discourse* see Bridenbaugh, *Mitre and Sceptre*, 3–21. For

contemporary comments that Rhode Island had no establishment, see Ebenezer Frothingham, *A Key To Unlock the Door* (New Haven, 1767), 172; James McSparran, "America Dissected," in Updike, *History of the Episcopal Church in Narragansett, Rhode Island*, 510; John Callendar, *An Historical Discourse* (Boston, 1739), 103.

34. Benjamin Franklin, *A Catalogue of Choice and Valuable Books* (Philadelphia, 1744); *Philadelphia Library Company* (Philadelphia, 1757); Society of Friends, *Philadelphia Yearly Meeting* (Philadelphia, 1737), 2; Perry, *Papers Relating to the Church in Pennsylvania*, 312.

35. William Smith, *A General Idea of the College of Mirania* (New York, 1753), 84. On the controversy surrounding the founding of King's College, see John Webb Pratt, *Religion, Politics and Diversity—The Church-State Theme in New York History* (Ithaca, 1967), 67–74; Milton Klein, ed., *The Independent Reflector* (Cambridge, Mass., 1963), 1–50, and "Church, State, and Education in Colonial New York," *New York History* 45 (1964): 290–303; Beverly McAnear, "American Imprints Concerning King's College," *The Papers of the Bibliographical Society of America*, 44 (1950): 301–39; Bridenbaugh, *Mitre and Sceptre*, 144–67.

36. Thomas Jones, *History of New York During the Revolutionary War*, quoted in Klein, ed., *The Independent Reflector*, 37. Thomas Gordon, *The Craftsman. A Sermon from the Independent Whig* (New York, 1753).

37. E. T. Corwin ed., *Ecclesiastical Records Of the State of New York*, 7 vols. (Albany, 1901–16), 5:3457–58, 3388, 3503, 3611; "Thomas Sherlock, Bishop of London, to Samuel Johnson," in Herbert and Carol Schneider, eds., *Samuel Johnson, President of King's College. His Career and Writings*, 4 vols. (New York, 1929), 4:23–24.

38. William Livingston, *Address to Sir Charles Hardy* (New York, 1755), vii–viii; Klein, ed., *Independent Reflector*, 171–78, 369; *The Preface to the Independent Reflector* (New York, 1754), 13, 23; Theodorus Frelinghuysen, *A Remonstrance* (New York, 1754), 5. For the argument that the colonists carried the Church of England establishment to America, see *New York Mercury* 51 (July 30, 1753). Livingston's and his associates' answers to this and other arguments are found in Klein, ed., *Independent Reflector*, 367–77. William Smith, Jr., *The History of the Province of New York* (Albany, 1814), 334–50.

39. *The Occasional Reverberator* 4 (Oct. 5, 1752), 15; Klein, ed., *Independent Reflector*, 181–83; *Ecclesiastical Records*, 5:3339–41.

40. Klein, ed., *Independent Reflector*, 201–2, 242–48.

41. Ibid., 368, 442; Livingston, *Address to Sir Charles Hardy*, viii; "The Watchtower," in *New York Mercury* 26 (May 19, 1755).

42. Klein, ed., *Independent Reflector*, 375; Smith, Jr., *History of New York*, 335, 338.

43. Smith, Jr., *History of New York*, 335, 338.

44. For Anglican correspondence that did not assume an establishment throughout the colonies, see Herbert and Carol Schneider, eds., *Samuel Johnson*, 4:201, 23–24; Perry, *Papers Relating to the Church in Massachusetts*, 495; *Ecclesiastical Records*, 5:3716.

45. Jonathan Mayhew, *Observations on the Society for the Propagation of the Gospel* (Boston, 1763), 22, 108, 42. For the Mayhew controversy, see Bridenbaugh, *Mitre and Sceptre*, 266; Cross, *Anglican Episcopate*, 146–60; Foote, *Annals of King's Chapel*, 2:258–74; Richard James Hooker, "The Mayhew Controversy," *Church History* 5 (1936): 239–55.

46. Henry Carver, *A Candid Examination* (Boston, 1763), 27–39; Arthur Browne,

Remarks (Portsmouth, 1763), 15; John Aplin, *Verses on Dr. Mayhew's Book* (Providence, 1763); Jonathan Mayhew, *A Defense of the Observations* (Boston, 1763), 50–51, 57–58, 59–65.

47. Perry, *Papers Relating to the Church in Massachusetts*, 519; Foote, *Annals of King's Chapel*, 2:267; Charles Francis Adams, ed., *The Works of John Adams*, 10 vols. (Boston, 1850), 10:187–88.

48. John Ewer, *A Sermon Preached before the Incorporated Society* (New York, 1768), 12; Bridenbaugh, *Mitre and Sceptre*, 293–96; Cross, *Anglican Episcopate*, 161–63; Edgar Legare Pennington, "The S.P.G. Anniversary Sermons 1702–1783," *HMPEC* 20 (1951): 33–35. For a list of other publications concerning the Anglican-Congregationalist dispute, see Foote, *Annals of King's Chapel*, 2:274–76.

49. Thomas Bradbury Chandler, *An Appeal to the Public* (New York, 1767), 77, 79, 103–7.

50. Thomas Bradbury Chandler, *The Appeal Defended* (New York, 1769) and *The Appeal Farther Defended* (New York, 1771); Charles Chauncy, *The Appeal to the Public Answered* (Boston, 1768) and *A Reply to Dr. Chandler's "Appeal Defended"* (Boston, 1770). John Holt, a New York printer, gathered the newspaper articles about the controversy printed in New York and Pennsylvania and issued them in two volumes: *A Collection of Tracts from the Late Newspapers* (New York, 1768) and *A Collection of Tracts from the Late Newspapers Vol. II* (New York, 1769). The combined volumes exceeded 800 pages. For an analysis of the complete controversy, see Cross, *Anglican Episcopate*, 164–214.

51. Chauncy, *The Appeal Answered*, 120, 152, 179, 200; Chandler, *The Appeal Farther Defended*, 178–179.

52. Anthony Lincoln, *Some Political and Social Ideas of English Dissent 1763–1800* (Cambridge, 1938; reprint ed., New York, 1971); *An Interesting Appendix to Sir William Blackstone's Commentaries* (Philadelphia, 1772).

53. George McLaren Brydon, *Virginia's Mother Church*, 2 vols. (Philadelphia, 1952), 2:343–59.

54. Bridenbaugh, *Mitre and Sceptre*, 322; Cross, *Anglican Episcopate*, 256.

55. Sarah McCulloch Lemmon, "The Genesis of the Protestant Episcopal Diocese of North Carolina, 1701–1823," *North Carolina Historical Review* 28 (1951): 426–53; Paul Conkin, "The Church Establishment in North Carolina, 1765–1776," *North Carolina Historical Review* 32 (1955): 1–30.

56. Charles A. Barker, *The Background of the Revolution in Maryland* (New Haven, 1940), 359–67; Albert W. Werline, *Problems of Church and State in Maryland* (South Lancaster, Mass., 1948), 158; Frederick V. Mills, *Bishops by Ballot. An Eighteenth-Century Ecclesiastical Revolution* (New York, 1978), 91–92.

57. *Reasons for the Present Glorious Combination of Dissenters in this City, against the farther encroachments and strategems of the episcopaleans* (New York, 1769); *A Letter from a Gentleman in New York to His Friend in the Country* (New York, 1772); *Truth Triumphant* (New York, 1769), 19; E. B. O'Callaghan, ed., *Documentary History of the State of New York*, 4 vols. (Albany, 1849–51), 3:330–31, 336–37.

58. Andrew Eliot, *A Sermon* (Boston, 1765), 10; Noah Hobart, *An Attempt To Illustrate* (New Haven, 1765), Introduction, 44; Edward Dorr, *The Duty of Civil Rulers* (Hartford, 1765), 12, 24–25, 26; Noah Welles, *A Vindication of Presbyterian Ordination* (New Haven, 1767), 21; Thomas Clap, *The Annals of Yale* (New Haven, 1766), 13; Ebenezer Bridge, *A Sermon Preached before His Excellency* (Boston, 1767), 22, 41; Andrew Croswell, *Observations on Several Passages* (Boston, 1768), 14; Amos

Adams, *Religious Liberty* (Boston, 1768), 29; Mark Leavenworth, *Charity Illustrated* (New London, 1772), 37.

59. Izrahiah Wetmore, *A Sermon Preached before the General Assembly* (New London, 1773), 12, 29, 21, 36–39, Appendix.

60. Franklin B. Dexter, ed., *The Literary Diary of Ezra Stiles*, 3 vols. (New York, 1901), 2:473; Charles Francis Adams, ed., *Works of John Adams*, 2:399, William G. McLoughlin, ed., *The Diary of Isaac Backus*, 3 vols. (Providence, 1979), 2:916. For Backus, the New England Baptists, and the Warren Association, see William G. McLoughlin, *Isaac Backus and the American Pietistic Tradition* (Boston, 1967), 110–35; William G. McLoughlin, ed., *Isaac Backus on Church, State, and Calvinism. Pamphlets, 1754–1789* (Cambridge, Mass., 1968), 1–60, 303–44; McLoughlin, *New England Dissent*, 1:529–30.

61. Dexter, ed., *Literary Diary of Ezra Stiles*, 2:475.

62. McLoughlin, ed., *Diary of Isaac Backus*, 2:917. Adams in his diary (*Works* 2:399) recorded the sentiment as, "I knew they might as well turn the heavenly bodies out of their annual and diurnal courses, as the people of Massachusetts at the present day from their meeting house and Sunday laws." Isaac Backus, "An Appeal to the Public," in McLoughlin, ed., *Isaac Backus on Church, State*, 324; *Warren Association Minutes of the Proceedings 1773* (Boston, 1773), 6.

63. McLoughlin, ed., *Isaac Backus on Church, State*, 319.

64. For the Quebec Act, see Samuel E. Morison, ed., *Sources and Documents Illustrating the American Revolution 1764–1788*, 2nd ed. (New York, 1929), 104.

6. *Religion and Government in Revolutionary America—Part I*

1. David Thomas, *The Virginian Baptist* (Baltimore, 1774); Wesley M. Gewehr, *The Great Awakening in Virginia, 1740–1790* (Durham, N.C., 1930), 106–37; Charles F. James, *Documentary History of the Struggle for Religious Liberty in Virginia* (Lynchburg, 1900; reprint ed., New York, 1971), 29–48; George M. Brydon, *Virginia's Mother Church*, 2 vols. (Philadelphia, 1952), 1:181–85; L. F. Greene, ed., *The Writings of John Leland* (New York, 1845; reprint ed., New York 1969), 104–7; H. J. Eckenrode, *Separation of Church and State in Virginia* (Richmond, 1910; reprint ed., New York, 1971), 37–39; William T. Thom, *The Struggle for Religious Liberty in Virginia: The Baptists* (Balitmore, 1900); Sandra Rennie, "Virginia's Baptist Persecution, 1765–1778," *Journal of Religious History* 12 (1982): 48–61.

2. For proposed and final wordings of the item on religion and Madison's part in their formulation, see William T. Hutchinson, William M. E. Rachal, and Robert A. Rutland, eds., *The Papers of James Madison*, 14 vols. to date (Chicago and Chartlottesville, 1962-), 1:170–79.

3. Julian P. Boyd, ed., *The Papers of Thomas Jefferson*, 21 vols. (Princeton, 1950–83), 1:344.

4. Hutchinson et al., eds., *Madison Papers*, 1:171; "Edmund Randolph's Essay on the Revolutionary History of Virginia 1774–1782," *VMHB* 44 (1936): 47.

5. On the revolutionary period in Virginia, see especially Thomas E. Buckley, *Church and State in Revolutionary Virginia, 1776–1787* (Charlottesville, 1977).

6. Buckley, *Church and State*, 35, 45, 48, 62; *Virginia Session Laws, 1776* (Williamsburg, 1776), 9; William Walter Hening, ed., *The Statutes at Large. Being a Collection of All Laws of Virginia 1619–1792*, 13 vols. (Richmond, 1809–28), 9:164–67. For

discussion of difficulties caused for Anglicans by release of dissenters, see Boyd, ed., *Jefferson Papers*, 1:534, note 6.

7. *Session Laws, 1776*, 9.
8. James, *Documentary History*, 76–77, 86–87; Buckley, *Church and State*, 24–29. *Religious Petitions Presented to the General Assembly of Virginia, 1774–1802*, Oct. 28, 1786 (Virginia State Library: Microfilm, 2 vols.), pages 1–42, gives a Calendar of Religious Petitions. *Virginia House Journals* 63; *Religious Petitions*, Nov. 8, 1776. *Virginia Gazette*, Nov. 1, 1776.
9. "Virginia Legislative Papers," *VMHB* 18 (1910): 268–70, 141–42, 148–50, 259, 265, 257, prints selected petitions sent to the legislature; *Religious Petitions*, Oct. 1776.
10. James, *Documentary History*, 69; *Religious Petitions*, Oct. 1776.
11. *Religious Petitions*, Aug. 1775; James, *Documentary History*, 73.
12. Paul L. Ford, ed., Jefferson "Autobiography," in *The Works of Thomas Jefferson*, 12 vols. (New York, 1904–05), 1:63. Because of their centralized religious system, Connecticut Congregationalists often referred to themselves as Presbyterians.
13. "Hanover Presbytery Petition 1777," in James, *Documentary History*, 226; Fred J. Hood, "Revolution and Religious Liberty. The Conservation of the Theocratic Concept," *Church History* 40 (1971): 175.
14. *Religious Petitions*, Petition from Cumberland and King William counties, 1778.
15. Boyd, ed., *Jefferson Papers*, 1:660–61.
16. "Declaration of Virginia Baptists 1776" and "Jefferson's Third Draft 1776," in Boyd, ed., *Jefferson Papers*, 1:661, 363.
17. James, *Documentary History*, 90; *Religious Petitions*, May 1777.
18. For texts of the two bills, see Buckley, *Church and State*, 40–61 and 185–88, 190–91.
19. *Virginia Gazette*, Sept. 18 and Nov. 6, 1779.
20. James, *Documentary History*, 120, 125.
21. Paul F. Boller, Jr., "George Washington on Religious Liberty," *WMQ* 17 (1960): 490.
22. Hutchinson et al., eds., *Madison Papers*, 8:149.
23. Hening, ed., *Statutes at Large*, 11:503–5.
24. For text of the bill, see Buckley, *Church and State*, 188–89.
25. Hutchinson et al., eds., *Madison Papers*, 8:229; Boller, "Washington on Religious Liberty," 490.
26. James, *Documentary History*, 229–31.
27. Ibid., 234–35.
28. For a discussion of Presbyterian motives, see Hood, "Revolution and Religious Liberty," 174–81.
29. "Jefferson's Outline of Argument," in Boyd, ed., *Jefferson Papers*, 1:537–39. For summary of formula used by opponents of assessment, see Buckley, *Church and State*, 147–51.
30. Hutchinson et al., eds., *Madison Papers*, 8:197.
31. Thomas Jefferson, *Notes on the State of Virginia* (New York, 1964), 152.
32. Hutchinson et al., eds., *Madison Papers*, 8:197–99.
33. Buckley, *Church and State*, 147.
34. "A Memorial and Remonstrance" is found in Hutchinson et al., eds., *Madison Papers*, 8:298–306, and James, *Documentary History*, 256–62.
35. *Religious Petitions*, Prince George County, Nov. 1785. For an analysis of this

petition, see Buckley, *Church and State*, 148–50. Although the term "religious establishment" strictly interpreted denotes a church or religious institution, many petitioners, including James Madison, used the term interchangeably with "establishment of religion."

36. *Religious Petitions*, Oct., Nov. 1785.
37. Hutchinson et al., eds., *Madison Papers*, 8:137, 261.
38. *Religious Petitions*, Calendar of Religious Petitions, 20–21.
39. *Religious Petitions*, Surrey County, Dec. 1784, Essex County, Nov. 1785, and Acconac County, Oct. 1785.
40. *Religious Petitions*, Amherst County, Nov. 1779, and Mecklenburg County, Nov. 1785.
41. *Religious Petitions*, Chesterfield County, Nov. 1785.
42. *Religious Petitions*, Botetourt County, Nov. 1785.
43. *Religious Petitions*, Amherst County, Dec. 1785.
44. Jefferson's bill for religious liberty is found in Boyd, ed., *Jefferson Papers*, 2:545–53.
45. Hening, ed., *Statutes at Large*, 9:165.
46. James, *Documentary History*, 224–25; "Virginia Legislative Papers," 141, 256, 260, 265, and 147, for clergy petition; *The Freeman's Remonstrance Against an Ecclesiastical Establishment* (Williamsburg, 1777).
47. F. B. Dexter, ed., *The Literary Diary of Ezra Stiles* (New York, 1901), 2:447.
48. *Religious Petitions*, Culpeper County, Oct. 1779; James, *Documentary History*, 92–94; *Religious Petitions*, Essex County, Oct. 1779.
49. Eckenrode, *Separation of Church and State*, 99; *Religious Petitions*, Dinwiddie County, Dec. 1784; Surrey County, Nov. 1785; Southhampton County, Dec. 1785.
50. Hutchinson et al., eds., *Madison Papers*, 8:306, 301, 197, 137, 209. For the "Memorial and Remonstrance," see James, *Documentary History*, 256–60.
51. *Religious Petitions*, Caroline County, Oct. 1785; Pittsylvania County, Oct. 1785; Chesterfield County, Nov. 1785; Orange County, Nov. 1785.
52. *Religious Petitions*, Amherst County, Oct. 1785.
53. Hening, ed., *Statutes at Large*, 11:504.
54. Boyd, ed., *Jefferson Papers*, 2:556.
55. For brief comment on the Quebec Act, see Gordon Wood, *The Creation of the American Republic, 1776–1787* (New York, 1969), 42. See also Charles H. Metzger, *The Quebec Act. A Primary Cause of the American Revolution* (New York, 1936).
56. *Minutes of Charleston Association of Baptists of South Carolina* (Charleston, 1777), 3. See also Edward McCrady, *The History of South Carolina in the Revolution 1775–1780* (New York, 1902), 206–13, 235–36; John Wesley Brinsfield, *Religion and Politics in Colonial South Carolina* (Easley, S.C., 1983), 105–28.
57. Newton B. Jones, ed., "Writings of the Reverend William Tennent," *South Carolina Historical Magazine* 61 (1960): 195.
58. Ibid., 202–3.
59. Francis Newton Thorpe, *The Federal and State Constitutions* ..., 7 vols. (Washington, D.C., 1909), 6:3251–53, 3255–56.
60. "Richard Hutson to Isaac Hayne, Jan. 18th 1777," in McCrady, *History of South Carolina*, 212–13.
61. For South Carolina constitution of 1790, see Thorpe, *Constitutions*, 6:3264.
62. *Minutes of Charleston Association of Baptists of South Carolina* (Charleston, 1778), 4.

South Carolina Laws (Charleston, 1785), 8; (Charleston, 1786), 43; (Charleston, 1787), 48; (Charleston, 1790), 11–12.

63. Thomas Reese, *An Essay on the Influence of Religion* (Charleston, 1788), 79–81.

64. Thorpe, *Constitutions*, 6:3664. *South Carolina Laws* (Charleston, 1791), 74.

65. Gary Freeze, "Like a House Built on Sand: The Anglican Church and Establishment in North Carolina, 1765–1776," *HMPEC* 48 (1979): 430. For comments on the lack of religion in North Carolina, see A. Roger Ekirch, *"Poor Carolina" Politics and Society in Colonial North Carolina 1729–1776* (Chapel Hill, 1981), 30; Charles Chauncy, *Reply to Chandler* (Boston, 1770), 145. On the Anglican Church in North Carolina, see also Paul Conkin, "The Church Establishment in North Carolina, 1765–1776," *North Carolina Historical Review* 32 (1955): 1–30; Sarah McCulloch Lemmon, "The Genesis of the Protestant Episcopal Diocese of North Carolina 1701–1823," *North Carolina Historical Review* 28 (1951): 426–62; Spencer Ervin, "The Anglican Church in North Carolina," *HMPEC* 25 (1956): 102–59. For Quaker complaints, see Stephen B. Weeks, *Church and State in North Carolina* (Baltimore, 1893), 51.

66. Walter Clark, ed., *State Records of North Carolina, 1777–1790*, 16 vols. (Winston and Goldsboro, 1886–1914), 23:997.

67. W. L. Saunders, ed., *Colonial Records of North Carolina, 1662–1776*, 10 vols. (Raleigh, 1886–90), 10:1004, 1011, 241, 820d, 810g, 870f.

68. Thorpe, *Constitutions*, 5:2788, 2793. Weeks, *Church and State in North Carolina*, 61–63; Robert M. Calhoun, *Religion and the American Revolution in North Carolina* (Raleigh, 1976), 69–73; Anson Phelps Stokes, *Church and State in the United States*, 3 vols. (New York, 1950), 1:403.

69. *United Baptist Association* (Newbern, 1791), 6.

70. Reba Carolyn Strickland, *Religion and the State in Georgia in the Eighteenth Century* (New York, 1939), 14, 34, 37–45, 113; For act establishing the Church of England, see A. D. Chandler, ed., *Colonial Records of the State of Georgia 1732–1782*, 26 vols. (Atlanta, 1904–16), 18:258–72; Elizabeth H. Davidson, *The Establishment of the English Church in Continental American Colonies* (Durham, N.C., 1936), 67–72.

71. A. D. Chandler, ed., *Revolutionary Records of Georgia 1769–1784*, 3 vols. (Atlanta, 1908), 1:241, 243, 265.

72. Thorpe, *Constitutions*, 2:779, 784.

73. Strickland, *Religion in Georgia*, 164; Chandler, ed., *Colonial Records*, Vol. 19, Part 2: 395–98, and *Revolutionary Records*, 3:141.

74. Thorpe, *Constitutions*, 2:789, 800–801. On lack of implementation of the law of 1785, see Strickland, *Religion in Georgia*, 167.

75. Charles Albro Barker, *The Background of the Revolution in Maryland* (New Haven, 1940), 359–65.

76. *The Declaration and Charter of Rights . . .* (Baltimore, 1776); Thorpe, *Constitutions*, 3:1689–90; John C. Rainbolt, "The Struggle To Define 'Religious Liberty' in Maryland, 1776–1785," *Journal of Church and State* 17 (1975): 445, and "A Note on the Maryland Declaration of Rights and Constitution of 1776," *Maryland Historical Magazine* 66 (1971): 421–25.

77. *Laws of Maryland* (Annapolis, 1787), chap. 9; Spencer Ervin, "The Established Church of Colonial Maryland," *HMPEC* 24 (1955): 282–83.

78. *Maryland Session Laws* (Annapolis, 1799), chap. 24.

79. Albert W. Werline, *Problems of Church and State in Maryland During the Seventeenth and Eighteenth Centuries* (South Lancaster, Mass., 1948), 171; Ervin, "Established

Church in Maryland," 276; Walter Herbert Stone, "The State or Diocesan Conventions of the War and Post-War Periods," *HMPEC* 8 (1939): 226–27.

80. Werline, *Problems of Church and State*, 173; Ervin, "Established Church in Maryland," 275.

81. *Maryland Gazette or the Baltimore Advertiser*, Sept. 12, 1783.

82. Patrick Allison, *Candid Animadversions* (Baltimore, 1793), 29. For newspaper writers supporting Allison, see *Maryland Gazette or the Baltimore Advertiser*, Oct. 10, 1783. William Smith defended the Episcopalians in the same newspaper on Sept. 19, 1783. See also Werline, *Problems of Church and State*, 173, 183.

83. Ervin, "Established Church in Maryland," 273; Werline, *Problems of Church and State*, 171; Stone, "State or Diocesan Conventions," 227.

84. *Notes and Proceedings of the Senate* (Annapolis, 1784), 53; Werline, *Problems of Church and State*, 172, 175.

85. *Maryland Gazette or the Baltimore Advertiser*, Feb. 18, 1785. For Speaker's claim, see *Maryland Gazette*, Jan. 25, 1785. Rainbolt, "Struggle To Define 'Religious Liberty'," notes that numerous petitions arrived. For the Episcopalian request, see *Protestant Episcopal Church. An Address* (Baltimore, 1784), 3.

86. For the division in the House, see Rainbolt, "Struggle To Define 'Religious Liberty'," 448; *Maryland Gazette or the Baltimore Advertiser*, March 18, 1785; *Votes and Proceedings of the House of Delegates* (Annapolis, 1785), 88, 103. For the act and House recommendations, see *Maryland Gazette*, Jan. 20, 1785, and *An Act To Lay a General Tax* (Annapolis, 1785).

87. *Maryland Gazette*, Jan. 20, 1785.

88. Ibid., for the Assembly's prediction; *Maryland Gazette or the Baltimore Advertiser*, Jan. 28, Feb. 11, Feb. 18, March 11, March 18, March 25, 1785; Rainbolt, "Struggle To Define 'Religious Liberty'," 457.

89. *Maryland Gazette or the Baltimore Advertiser*, March 25, 1785.

90. Werline, *Problems of Church and State*, 174; Rainbolt, "Struggle To Define 'Religious Liberty'," 451; Allison, *Candid Animadversions*, v.

91. Thomas O'Brien Hanley, *The John Carroll Papers*, 3 vols. (Notre Dame, Ind., 1976), 1:168, and *The American Revolution and Religion in Maryland 1770–1800* (Washington, D.C., 1971), 66–67; William Duke, *Observations on the Present State of Religion* (Baltimore, 1795), 36–37.

92. William Kilty, *History of a Session of the General Assembly* (Annapolis, 1786), 10–11. For references to the petitions sent to the legislature, see *Maryland House Journals* (Annapolis, 1786), 7.

93. Ervin, "Established Church in Maryland," 271; Thorpe, *Constitutions*, 3:1705. For a subsequent call for an assessment, see John Bisset, *A Sermon* (Philadelphia, 1791), Appendix 4.

94. Alexander DeConte, "William Vans Murray on Freedom of Religion in the United States, 1787," *Maryland Historical Magazine* 50 (1955): 287.

95. Werline, *Problems of Church and State*, 173; *Baltimore Advertiser*, Aug. 15, 1783.

96. Quoted in J. Moss Ives, *The Ark and the Dove. The Beginnings of Civil & Religious Liberty in America* (New York, 1936, 1939), 399.

97. Hanley, ed., *Carroll Papers*, 1:53, 164, 329.

98. Benjamin H. Hartogensis, "Unequal Religious Rights in Maryland since 1776," *American Jewish Historical Society Publications* 25 (1917): 93–107; E. Milton Altfield, *The Jews' Struggle for Religious and Civil Liberty in Maryland* (Baltimore, 1924).

7. *Religion and Government in Revolutionary America—Part II*

1. Francis Newton Thorpe, *The Federal and State Constitutions . . .*, 7 vols. (Washington, D.C., 1909): 1:558–61, 567–68.
2. For the Delaware Declaration of Rights, see *Delaware Convention Proceedings* (Wilmington, 1776), 14, and *Delaware Convention* (Wilmington, 1776), 2. For the states' constitutions, see Thorpe, *Constitutions*, 1:567–68; 5:2597–98.
3. Thorpe, *Constitutions*, 1:568.
4. For such a reading, see Chester James Antieau, Arthur L. Downey, Edward C. Roberts, *Freedom from Federal Establishment. Formation and Early History of the First Amendment Religion Clauses* (Milwaukee, 1964), 134.
5. Joseph J. Casino, "Anti-Popery in Colonial Pennsylvania," *PMHB* 105 (1981): 279–309; Charles H. Metzger, *The Quebec Act. A Primary Cause of the American Revolution* (New York, 1936), 50–51.
6. Thorpe, *Constitutions*, 5:3082, 3085.
7. *Pennsylvania Evening Post*, Sept. 26, 1776. For Franklin's comments on religion in the constitution, see J. Paul Selsam, *The Pennsylvania Constitution of 1776* (Philadelphia, 1936; reprint ed., New York, 1971), 216–21. See also "Abstract of a Letter of Rev. Henry Muhlenberg . . .," *PMHB* 22 (1908): 129–31.
8. For Jewish protest, see *Journal of the Council of Censors, December 23, 1783* (Philadelphia, 1783); Thorpe, *Constitutions*, 5:3100.
9. Thorpe, *Constitutions*, 5:2636. John Webb Pratt, *Religion, Politics, and Diversity. The Church-State Theme in New York History* (Ithaca, 1967), 90–91; C. Z. Lincoln, *Constitutional History of New York*, 5 vols. (Rochester, 1906), 1:540.
10. Pratt, *Religion, Politics, and Diversity*, 100–103.
11. For scarcity of Catholics in New York, see Charles H. Metzger, *Catholics and the American Revolution* (Chicago, 1962), 150–54.
12. Thorpe, *Constitutions*, 5:2636–38; Pratt, *Religion, Politics, and Diversity*, 86–89, 107.
13. *New York Session Laws* (New York, 1784), 21.
14. J. R. Bartlett, ed., *Colonial Records of Rhode Island* (Providence, 1780–83), 1:674.
15. For the Massachusetts Baptists, the Ashfield case, and their appeal to Congress, see McLoughlin, *New England Dissent, 1630–1833. The Baptists and the Separation of Church and State*, 2 vols. (Cambridge, Mass., 1971), 1:454–88, 572–87, 531–60, 598–99, 640–42; Isaac Backus, *A History of New England with Particular Reference to the Baptists*, 2 vols. David Weston, ed. (Newton Mass., 1871; reprint ed., New York, 1969), 2:149–66, 197–205.
16. Oscar and Mary Handlin, eds., *The Popular Sources of Political Authority. Documents on the Massachusetts Constitution of 1780* (Cambridge, Mass., 1966), 190, 201, 202, 251, 268, 326, 374, 385, 402, 434–36. Samuel E. Morison, "The Struggle over the Adoption of the Constitution of Massachusetts, 1780," *Massachusetts Historical Society Proceedings* 50 (1917); Robert J. Taylor, "Construction of the Massachusetts Constitution," *American Antiquarian Society Proceedings* 90 (1980): 325–46.
17. Oscar and Mary Handlin, eds., *Popular Sources*, 442–43; Thorpe, *Constitutions*, 3:1889–1890.
18. Oscar and Mary Handlin, eds., *Popular Sources*, 467–468.
19. See, for instance, John Tucker, *Remarks on a Discourse* (Boston, 1774), 12.
20. William G. McLoughlin, ed., *Isaac Backus on Church, State, and Calvinism. Pamphlets, 1754–1789* (Cambridge, Mass., 1968), 324.

21. Daniel Foster, *A Sermon Preached before his Excellency* (Boston, 1790), 11.
22. Tucker, *Remarks on a Discourse*, 5, 10–12; Henry Cummings, *A Sermon* (Boston, 1763), 46. See the following Election Sermons: Samuel West, *A Sermon* (Boston, 1776), 43; Phillips Payson, *A Sermon* (Boston, 1778), 19; Simeon Howard, *A Sermon* (Boson, 1780), 23–24; Samuel Williams, *The Influence of Christianity* [Ordination Sermon] (Boston, 1780), 20; Jonas Clark, *A Sermon* (Boston, 1781), 34; Moses Hemmenway, *A Sermon* (Boston, 1784), 34, 38, 39–40; William Symmes, *A Sermon* (Boston, 1785), 15; David Parsons, *A Sermon* (Boston, 1788), 12–13; Josiah Bridge, *A Sermon* (Boston, 1789), 45; Foster, *A Sermon*, 11; David Tappan, *A Sermon* (Boston, 1792), 23.
23. *Massachusetts Session Laws* (Boston, 1774), 519.
24. *Independent Ledger*, May 8, 1780, quoted in McLoughlin, *New England Dissent*, 1:621; Hemmenway, *A Sermon*, 38; Parsons, *A Sermon*, 13.
25. *Continental Journal*, March 9, 1780. See McLoughlin, *New England Dissent*, 1:624.
26. *Massachusetts Session Laws* (Boston, 1789), 730.
27. Morison, "Constitution of Massachusetts, 1780," 381, 411; Oscar and Mary Handlin, eds., *Popular Sources*; McLoughlin, *New England Dissent*, 1:630–31.
28. McLoughlin, *New England Dissent*, 1:502–11, 529–30. For difficulty of correlating Baptists and opposition to Article III in towns, see Oscar and Mary Handlin, eds., *Popular Sources*, 933. Morison, "Constitution of Massachusetts, 1780," 392, includes a map of Baptist churches and areas' responses to Article III. For a list of Baptist churches in Massachusetts, see Backus, *History*, 2:306–8.
29. For Baptist theology, see Backus, *History*, 2:232, 238, 330, and also the Warren Association's "Broadside," in Morison, "Constitution of Massachusetts, 1780," 377.
30. William G. McLoughlin, ed., *The Diary of Isaac Backus*, 3 vols. (Providence, 1979), 2:1033, 1086. For a letter from the Baptists of Charleston, South Carolina, offering to do anything they could to help their suffering brethren in Massachusetts, see *Proceedings of the Warren Association 1775* (Norwich, 1775), 5. See also William G. McLoughlin, "The Balkcom Case and the Pietistic Theory of Separation of Church and State," *WMQ* 24 (1967): 275.
31. *Boston Gazette*, March 8, 1779, Dec. 14, 1778. For Backus's reaction to criticism, see Backus, *History*, 2:157, 231, 146–47, 222–24. Backus, "Truth is Great . . . ," in McLoughlin, ed., *Pamphlets*, 406.
32. The responses of towns objecting to Article III are found in Oscar and Mary Handlin, eds., *Popular Sources*.
33. Ibid., 634.
34. Moses Hemmenway, *A Sermon*, 33–34; Backus, *History*, 2:294, 228.
35. Samuel Stillman, *A Sermon* (Boston, 1779), 28–30.
36. McLoughlin, ed., *Pamphlets*, 433. See also McLoughlin, *New England Dissent*, 1:606.
37. Oscar and Mary Handlin, eds., *Popular Sources*, 693–94. This interpretation disagrees with that of McLoughlin, *New England Dissent*, 1:629, which sees the response from Middleborough as a defeat for the Baptists.
38. McLoughlin, ed., *Pamphlets*, 422. For an excellent description of the Baptist world view, see generally McLoughlin, "Isaac Backus and the Separation of Church and State," *AHR* 73 (1968): 1398. On Universalists' difficulties with Massachusetts, see John D. Cushing, "Notes on Disestablishment in Massachusetts, 1780–1833," *WMQ* 26 (1969): 175–77.

39. Oscar and Mary Handlin, eds., *Popular Sources*, 741–42, 747.

40. For towns that rejected Article III but wanted officeholding limited to Protestants, see ibid., 507, 549, 550, 554, 595, 597, 603, 614, 618, 658, 682, 703, 741, 782, 819.

41. Ibid., 641.

42. *Independent Chronicle*, March 2, 1780, April 6, 1780, April 13, 1780, March 23, 1780, March 16, 1780; *Continental Journal*, April 6, 1780; *Boston Gazette*, Aug. 21, 1780. For "Philanthropos," see McLoughlin, *New England Dissent*, 1:608–9, 618. For the towns influenced by "Philanthropos," see Morison, "Constitution of Massachusetts, 1780," 379.

43. See "Irenaeus," in *Continental Journal*, March 9, 1780.

44. McLoughlin, ed., *Pamphlets*, 393.

45. *Independent Chronicle*, Dec. 2, 1779; *Boston Gazette*, Nov. 2, 1778.

46. McLoughlin, "The Balkcom Case," 266–83; McLoughlin, *New England Dissent*, 1:636–59; Cushing, "Notes on Disestablishment," 169–90. For Baptist hopes following the Balkcom case, see Isaac Backus, "A Door Opened for Equal Christian Liberty," in McLoughlin, ed., *Pamphlets*, 428–38.

47. *Boston Gazette*, March 8, 1779.

48. Ibid., Nov. 2, 1778, Dec. 28, 1778.

49. Ibid., March 8, 1779; *Independent Chronicle*, Nov. 19, 1778, Dec. 17, 1778, Jan. 14, 1779; *Independent Gazette*, Feb. 5, 1779.

50. *Boston Gazette*, Jan. 18, 1779.

51. *Independent Chronicle*, Dec. 17, 1778, and Feb. 25, 1779.

52. *Boston Gazette*, Nov. 2, 1778; Dec. 29, 1778; Jan. 18, 1779.

53. *Independent Chronicle*, Feb. 25, 1779; McLoughlin, ed., *Pamphlets*, 381.

54. *Boston Gazette*, March 8, 1779.

55. McLoughlin, ed., *Pamphlets*, 361.

56. For the provisions for Harvard, see Oscar and Mary Handlin, eds., *Popular Sources*, 466. Backus pointed out the preference for Congregationalists at Harvard in *History*, 2:346.

57. Samuel Baldwin, *A Sermon Preached at Plymouth* (Boston, 1775), 24, and Joseph Perry, *A Sermon* (Hartford, 1775), 8, referred to the "establishment" of the Roman Catholic religion in Quebec.

58. West, *A Sermon*, 44; Symmes, *A Sermon*, 45–46; Chandler Robbins, *A Sermon* (Boston, 1791), 37; David Tappan, *A Sermon* 23.

59. Oscar and Mary Handlin, eds., *Popular Sources*, 251. Boothbay made no response to the constitution of 1780.

60. Cushing, "Disestablishment in Massachusetts," 180.

61. Backus, *History*, 2:342, 346.

62. For subsequent developments of Church and State in Massachusetts, see McLoughlin, *New England Dissent*, 2:1189–1261. For the Unitarian-Trinitarian controversy, see Leonard W. Levy, *The Law of the Commonwealth and Chief Justice Shaw. The Evolution of American Law* (New York, 1967), 29–58, 41. See also Cushing, "Disestablishment in Massachusetts," 190.

63. McLoughlin, ed., *Backus Diary*, 2:917.

64. McLoughlin, ed., *Pamphlets*, 405. For a later critique of the ministers for constantly complaining about their salaries, see James Sullivan, *Strictures upon the Rev. Mr. Tachers Pamphlet* (Boston, 1784).

65. Cushing, "Disestablishment in Massachusetts," 184.

66. L. F. Greene, ed., *The Writings of Elder John Leland* (New York, 1845; reprint ed.,

New York, 1969), 19–29; L. H. Butterfield, "Elder John Leland, Jeffersonian Itinerant," *American Antiquarian Society Proceedings* 62 (1952): 155–242.

67. Greene, ed., *Writings of Elder John Leland*, 52, 75, 107, 118, 119, 224, 226, 229, 254, 444, 490, 539, 561.

68. Isaac Backus, *The Liberal Support of Gospel Ministers* (Boston, 1790), 34; Hanley, ed., *The John Carroll Papers*, 3 vols. (Notre Dame, 1976), 1:355.

69. Samuel West believed that Article II gave "ample Liberty of Conscience . . . to Deists, Mahometans, Jews, and Christians." See McLoughlin, *New England Dissent*, 1:623. In 1775 an Anglican minister wrote that Massachusetts did not allow Anglicans to celebrate Christmas Day or walk or ride on the Sabbath. See *An Englishman's Answer* (Rivington, N.Y., 1775), 21. For a brief comparison of Church and State in Massachusetts and Virginia, see McLoughlin, *New England Dissent*, 1:592.

70. Elizur Goodrich, *The Principles of Civil Union* (Hartford, 1787), 26; Samuel Lockwood, *A Sermon* (Hartford, 1774), 18; Joseph Perry, *A Sermon* (Hartford, 1775), 8; Judah Champion, *Christian and Civil Liberty* (Hartford, 1776), 10; John Devotion, *The Duty and Interest* (Hartford, 1777), 30; Chauncey Whittelsey, *Importance of Religion* (Hartford, 1778), 9; James Dana, *A Sermon* (Hartford, 1779), 14; Nathan Williams, *A Sermon* (Hartford, 1780), 13; Josiah Huntington, *A Sermon* (Hartford, 1784), 25; Josiah Whitney, *The Essential Requisites* (Hartford, 1788), 24; Nathan Strong, *A Sermon* (Hartford, 1790), 7; Timothy Dwight, *A Sermon* (Hartford, 1791); Timothy Stone, *A Sermon* (Hartford, 1792), 22.

71. In *The Description of a Good Character* (Hartford, 1786), 23, Levi Hart preached to the legislature that the "boundaries between the rights of conscience, and the magistrate, may be difficult, in some cases . . . the most important and practical principles, on this subject, are extremely plain; and are admitted by the most enlightened, of every denomination, as essential to good order and happiness in society."

72. Champion, *Christian and Civil Liberty*, 10–11; Strong, *A Sermon*, 7, 9, 15–16, 20. For reference to the "Fathers," see Joseph Bean, *A Sermon Delivered at Wrentham* (Boston, 1774); Huntington, *A Sermon*, 24; Whitney, *The Essential Requisites*, 31.

73. Champion, *Christian and Civil Liberty*, 10–11.

74. C. C. Goen, *Revivalism and Separatism in New England, 1740–1800: Strict Congregationalists and Separate Baptists in the Great Awakening* (New Haven, 1962), 302–27 lists all the towns and their churches in Connecticut. On the growth of the Baptists after 1784, see Richard J. Purcell, *Connecticut in Transition* (Washington, D.C., 1918), 47. On the same subject and the lack of importance of the Quakers in Connecticut, see McLoughlin, *New England Dissent*, 2:919 and 1:447, 277.

75. Israel Holly, *An Appeal* (Norwich, 1778), 3.

76. On the Separates' views, see McLoughlin, *New England Dissent*, 1:388–417. For attacks on the Saybrook Platform around the time of the Revolution, see David Judson, *Sermons on Church Government* (New Haven, 1774) and Isaac Foster, *A Defense of Religious Liberty* (Worcester, 1780).

77. The "Memorial" is printed in Holly's *An Appeal*, 5–8.

78. Ibid., 3.

79. C. J. Hoadly and L. W. Labaree, eds., *Public Records of the State of Connecticut 1776–1792*, 7 vols. (Hartford, 1894–1948), 1:232.

80. Holly, *An Appeal*, 2, 14. For Separates' reaction to the exemption law of 1777, see McLoughlin, *New England Dissent*, 2:922.

81. *Acts and Laws of the State of Connecticut* (New London, 1784), 21–22. Backus, *History*, 2:316–17, prints the text of the law.
82. *Connecticut Courant*, Sept. 4, 1786, and Sept. 11, 1786; M. Louise Greene, *The Development of Religious Liberty in Connecticut* (Boston, 1905), 352–53; McLoughlin, *New England Dissent*, 2:924–25.
83. Hoadly and Labaree, eds., *State Records*, 7:357. For an account of the dispute at New Salem, see McLoughlin, *New England Dissent*, 2:952–57.
84. Hoadly and Labaree, eds., *State Records*, 7:256; McLoughlin, *New England Dissent*, 2:926–27.
85. Greene, ed., *Writings of John Leland*, 183, 187, 182, 188.
86. *Connecticut Courant*, May 23, 1791. For other protests, see May 23, 1791, and Sept. 12, 1791; *Connecticut Gazette*, Sept. 22, 1791.
87. *Connecticut Gazette*, Sept. 1, 1791; *Connecticut Courant*, May 30, 1791, and Oct. 20, 1791.
88. *Connecticut Courant*, Nov. 17, 1791. For certificate law, see Hoadly and Labaree, eds., *State Records*, 7:311 and McLoughlin, *New England Dissent*, 2:937.
89. Perry, *A Sermon*, 8; Devotion, *The Duty and Interest*, 31.
90. *American Mercury*, Feb. 7, 1785; *Connecticut Journal*, Feb. 16, 1785; *Connecticut Courant*, Feb. 22, 1785. For Price, see Anthony Lincoln, *Some Political & Social Ideas of English Dissent, 1763–1800* (Cambridge, 1938; reprint ed., New York, 1971), 101–50.
91. Zephaniah Swift, *A System of the Laws of Connecticut*, 2 vols. (Windham, 1796), 1:139–46.
92. Backus, *History*, 2:534.
93. *Laws of New Hampshire*, 10 vols. (Manchester, 1902–22), 1:560–61; Charles B. Kinney, Jr., *Church and State. The Struggle for Separation in New Hampshire 1630–1690* (New York, 1955), 36–37. For a review of the Church-State legislation in New Hampshire, see McLoughlin, *New England Dissent*, 2:834–38.
94. McLoughlin, *New England Dissent*, 2:839; Kinney, Jr., *Church and State*, 59–60.
95. *Laws of New Hampshire*, 4:368–70. See also Kinney, Jr., *Church and State*, 57, 64, 86–88, 191.
96. McLoughlin, *New England Dissent*, 2:842–43; Kinney, Jr., *Church and State*, 72–74, 83; *New Hampshire—Provincial and State Papers*, 23 vols. (Concord, 1867–91), 13:53–54, 60–67; Backus, *History*, 2:534, 539; Robert F. Lawrence, *The New Hampshire Churches* (Claremont, N.H., 1856), 284.
97. For the Plan of Government, the rejected constitution of 1779, and the constitution of 1783, see *Provincial Papers*, 11: Appendix A and 10:71. McLoughlin, *New England Dissent*, 2:843–44.
98. Thorpe, *Constitutions*, 4:2454.
99. Mcloughlin, *New England Dissent*, 2:847–49; Lynn W. Turner, *William Plumer of New Hampshire 1759–1850* (Chapel Hill, 1962), 10–11.
100. McLoughlin, *New England Dissent*, 2:861; Kinney, Jr., *Church and State*, 86.
101. "Petition of Inhabitants . . . 1782" is in *Provincial Papers*, 11:83.
102. Ibid., 11:454–56, 13:206.
103. Kinney, Jr., *Church and State*, 87–88; McLoughlin, *New England Dissent*, 2:858.
104. Backus, *History*, 2:538, 542; McLoughlin, *New England Dissent*, 2:859–60.
105. For letter to Isaac Backus, see McLoughlin, *New England Dissent*, 2:858, 859. For continued struggles for exemption from taxes, see Kinney, Jr., *Church and State*, 86, 89–90; Lawrence, *New Hampshire Churches*, 137.
106. Gershon Clark Lyman, *A Sermon* (Windsor, 1784), 12–13; Samuel MacClintock,

A Sermon (Portsmouth, 1784), 33; Samuel Haven, *An Election Sermon* (Portsmouth, 1786), 4, 10, 16; John Cosens Ogden, *A Sermon* (Concord, 1790), 13, 17, 23.

107. McLoughlin, *New England Dissent*, 2:853–54; *Provincial Papers*, 10:41–42, 46, 114–15, 121, 141–42, 153, 156.
108. McLoughlin, *New England Dissent*, 2:794.
109. Thorpe, *Constitutions*, 6:3740, 3743.
110. William Slade, ed., *Vermont State Papers 1779–1786* (Middlebury, 1823), 472–73. Also in *Vermont Acts and Laws . . .* (Windsor, 1784), 3–4.
111. McLoughlin, *New England Dissent*, 2:800; Thorpe, *Constitutions*, 6:3752; *Vermont Acts and Laws . . . .*
112. Backus, *History*, 2:548–49.
113. McLoughlin, *New England Dissent*, 2:864.
114. Caleb Blood, *A Sermon* (Rutland, 1792), 27, 34.
115. Quoted in McLoughlin, *New England Dissent*, 2:801–2.
116. Kinney, Jr., *Church and State*, 96.
117. Blood, *A Sermon*, 34; Slade, ed., *Vermont State Papers*, 355.
118. Pratt, *Religion, Politics, and Diversity*, 115.
119. Hanley, ed., *Carroll Papers*, 1:329, 365–69, 348.

8. "*Congress shall make no law . . .*"

1. Richard Henry Lee, "Letters from the Federal Farmer," in Herbert J. Storing, ed., *The Complete Anti-Federalist*, 7 vols. (Chicago, 1981), 2:249.
2. Leonard W. Levy, "No Establishment of Religion: The Original Understanding," in Leonard W. Levy, *Judgments. Essays on American Constitutional History* (Chicago, 1972), 173. Although written in 1958, this essay remains both the best survey of the events surrounding the passage of the First Amendment and summary of the sources for these events. Several multivolume works of primary source materials dealing with the period of the passage and ratification of the First Amendment have recently been published. Although these works do not add any significant new evidence on the meaning of the First Amendment, they do illustrate the relatively small role that Church-State relations played in contemporary discussion. The works are: Storing, ed., *Complete Anti-Federalist*; Merrill Jensen et al., eds., *The Documentary History of the Ratification of the Constitution*, 4 vols. to date (Madison, Wisc., 1976-); Linda Grant DePauw, ed., *Documentary History of the First Federal Congress of the United States of America*, 3 vols. to date (Baltimore, 1977-); Merrill Jensen, ed., *Documentary History of the First Federal Elections*, 3 vols. to date (Madison, Wisc., 1976-).
3. Max Farrand, *Records of the Federal Convention of 1787*, 4 vols. (New Haven, 1911–37), 2:587–88.
4. Jonathan Elliot, ed., *The Debates in the Several State Conventions on the Adoption of the Federal Constitution*, 5 vols. (Washington, D.C., 1836; reprint ed., New York, n.d.), 2:151.
5. Robert A. Rutland et al., eds., *The Papers of James Madison*, 14 vols. to date (Chicago and Charlottesville, 1962-), 11:297; *The Federalist #84* (New York, 1969), 513.
6. Storing, ed., *Complete Anti-Federalist*, 5:240.
7. Rutland et al., eds., *Madison Papers*, 12:368, 347, 21, 453; 11:23.

8. Storing, ed., *Complete Anti-Federalist*, 2:249; Edward Dumbauld, *The Bill of Rights and What It Means Today* (Norman, Okla., 1957), 8–12; "Thomas Jefferson to James Madison July 1788," in Rutland et al., eds., *Madison Papers*, 11:213. For the letter from Madison, Sr., see Gaillard Hunt, ed., *The Writings of James Madison*, 9 vols. (New York, 1900–1910), 5:105; L. H. Butterfield, "Elder John Leland, Jeffersonian Itinerant," *American Antiquarian Society Proceedings* 62 (1952): 188. See also the reply of Washington to the Virginia Baptists in May 1789, quoted in Anson Phelps Stokes, *Church and State in the United States*, 3 vols. (New York, 1950), 1:495.

9. Jackson Turner Main, *The Antifederalists: Critics of the Constitution, 1781–1788* (Chapel Hill, 1961), 159.

10. Storing, ed., *Complete Anti-Federalist*, 4:232, 248.

11. Ibid., 2:75.

12. Elliot, ed., *Debates*, 3:204, 330, 469; 4:192, 208; Levy, *Judgments*, 172.

13. Elliot, ed., *Debates*, 2:120. On the common attitudes on Church-State relations shared by Federalists and Anti-Federalists, see Morton Borden, "Federalists, Antifederalists, and Religious Freedom," *Journal of Church and State* 21 (1978): 470–82. On Massachusetts, see pp. 170–71 above.

14. Storing, ed., *Complete Anti-Federalist*, 2:152, 6:119; Jensen, ed., *Ratification*, 2:623.

15. Jensen, ed., *Ratification*, 13:535–36, 2:386, 392, 399, 400; Storing, ed., *Complete Anti-Federalist*, 3:36–37, 179 and 6:124; Elliot, ed., *Debates*, 200.

16. Elliot, ed., *Debates*, 3:330, 204, 659.

17. *City Gazette or Daily Advertiser of Charleston*, May 26, 1788, cited in Chester James Antieau, Arthur L. Downey, and Edward C. Roberts, *Freedom from Federal Establishment. Formation and Early History of the First Amendment Religion Clauses* (Milwaukee, 1964), 106.

18. Elliot, ed., *Debates*, 4:191, 199, 200, 208.

19. *Candidates To Represent the State. Friends to Amendments* (Baltimore, 1788).

20. Storing, ed., *Complete Anti-Federalist*, 3:37; Jensen, ed., *Ratification*, 2:592.

21. Elliot, ed., *Debates*, 2:328. See also "A Countryman," in Storing, ed., *Complete Anti-Federalist*, 6:87; Levy, *Judgments*, 176–77. For further comments by New Yorkers on an establishment of religion, see Elliot, ed., *Debates*, 2:399, and Storing, ed., *Complete Anti-Federalist*, 6:87.

22. Elliot, ed., *Debates*, 2:202. For Ellsworth's statement, see Jensen, ed., *Ratification*, 3:498.

23. Joseph Gales, ed., *The Debates and Proceedings of the Congress of the United States [Annals of Congress]* (Washington, D.C., 1834) gives the debates in the First Congress compiled from newspapers. The sections dealing with the Bill of Rights can be found in Bernard Schwartz, *The Bill of Rights: A Documentary History*, 2 vols. (New York, 1971), Vol. 2. For the nature of the reports on the debates in the House and Senate, see Levy, *Judgments*, 215–16.

24. Rutland et al., eds., *Madison Papers*, 11:23, 382–83, 302–3.

25. Ibid., 11:130, 404, 405, 408, 424, 442; Butterfield, "Elder John Leland," 185–87; *Annals of Congress*, 1:441, 444, 448, 459, 733, for Madison's concern that his constituents be aware of his diligence in seeking amendments.

26. *Annals of Congress*, 1:441–50, 459–68, 730–44, 745–57, 761–78.

27. Ibid., 1:456, 454, 451–52.

28. Ibid., 1:468, 685; Schwartz, ed., *Bill of Rights*, 2:1057–61; DePauw, ed., *First Federal Congress*, 3:117. North Carolina and Rhode Island had not yet ratified the Constitution.

29. *Annals of Congress*, 1:757–59.

30. See page 133 above.

31. *Annals of Congress*, 1:460.

32. *Annals of Congress*, 1:758–59; Griffith J. McRee, *Life and Correspondence of James Iredell*, 2 vols. (New York, 1857–58), 2:265.

33. *Annals of Congress*, 1:783–84.

34. Leonard W. Levy, "The Fourteenth Amendment and the Bill of Rights," in *Judgments*, 64–78.

35. Rutland et al., eds., *Madison Papers*, 11:382; 12:257, 272, 250; *Annals of Congress*, 1:725.

36. Rutland et al., eds., *Madison Papers*, 12:21; *Annals of Congress*, 1:454–55, 458, 805.

37. *Annals of Congress*, 1:796, 808; DePauw, ed., *First Federal Congress*, 3:165–66.

38. DePauw, ed., *First Federal Congress*, 1:137–38.

39. Ibid., 1:151, 166.

40. Ibid., 3:218; 1:181–82; Schwartz, ed., *Bill of Rights*, 2:1162.

41. DePauw, ed., *First Federal Congress*, 1:182; 3:228; 1:186, 189, 192.

42. *Everson v. Board of Education* 330 U.S. 15 (1947).

43. For opposing positions and a review of the debate, see Levy, *Judgments*, 169–224, and Michael Malbin, *Religion and Politics: The Intentions of the Authors of the First Amendment* (Washington, D.C.: American Enterprise Institute, 1978).

44. Robert L. Cord, *Separation of Church and State* (New York, 1982), 8; Antieau et al., *Freedom from Federal Establishment*, 127; John Courtney Murray, "Law or Prepossessions?" in *Law and Contemporary Problems* 14 (1949): 42, all argue that Madison advanced a "narrow" interpretation.

45. Irving Brant, "Madison: On the Separation of Church and State," *WMQ* 8 (1951): 13.

46. See above pp. 181–82.

47. Thomas Jefferson, *Notes on the State of Virginia* (New York: Harper & Row, 1961), 152–54.

48. *Acts and Laws of His Majesty's Colony of Rhode Island* (Newport, 1745), 60; Isaac Backus, *A History of New England with Particular Reference to the Baptists*, ed., David Weston, 2 vols. (Newton, Mass., 1871; reprint ed., New York, 1969), 2:8.

49. Isaac Hunt, *A Looking Glass for Presbyterians* (Philadelphia, 1764), 1.

50. William G. McLoughlin, ed., *Isaac Backus on Church, State, and Calvinism. Pamphlets, 1754–1789* (Cambridge, Mass., 1968), 333. See also Backus, *History*, 2:178.

51. Julian P. Boyd, ed., *The Papers of Thomas Jefferson*, 19 vols. (Princeton, N.J., 1950-), 1:530; *Religious Petitions Presented to the General Assembly of Virginia, 1774–1802*, Oct. 28, 1786 (Virginia State Library: microfilm, 2 vols.), Nov. 18, 1784.

52. See page 149 above.

53. *Maryland Gazette and the Baltimore Advertizer*, Oct. 10, 1783.

54. Oscar and Mary Handlin, eds., *The Popular Sources of Political Authority. Documents on the Massachusetts Constitution of 1780* (Cambridge, Mass., 1966), 855; see also in the same work 618, 674, 728, 785, 819, 773.

55. Robert C. Cotner, ed., *Theodore Foster's Minutes of the Convention Held at South Kingston, Rhode Island, in March, 1790* (Freeport, N.Y., 1929), 93.

56. L. F. Greene, ed., *The Writings of John Leland* (New York, 1845; reprint ed., New York, 1969), 229.

57. James Madison, *Memorial and Remonstrance*, in Charles F. James, ed., *Documentary History of the Struggle for Religious Liberty in Virginia* (Lynchburg, Va., 1900; reprint ed., New York, 1971), 260.

58. Jensen, ed., *Ratification*, 2:711.

59. William G. McLoughlin, *New England Dissent. Baptists and the Separation of Church and State, 1630–1833*, 2 vols. (Cambridge, Mass., 1971), 2:784–85.

60. Seth Ames, ed., *Works of Fisher Ames with a Selection from His Speeches and Correspondence*, 2 vols. (Boston, 1854), 1:65.

61. Levy, *Judgments*, 187–90; Schwartz, ed., *Bill of Rights*, 2:1171–1203; Matteson, *Organization of the Government*, 175–88; Robert A. Rutland, *The Birth of the Bill of Rights 1776–1791* (Chapel Hill, 1955), 215–18.

62. Levy, *Judgments*, 187; David M. Matteson, *Organization of the Government under the Constitution* (New York, 1970), 185–88; C. J. Hoadly and L. W. Labaree, eds., *Public Records of the State of Connecticut 1776–1792*, 7 vols. (Hartford, 1857–58), 7:ix–xi; Schwartz, ed., *Bill of Rights*, 2:1172.

63. Schwartz, ed., *Bill of Rights*, 2:1186.

64. Ibid., 2:1187, 1191–93; DePauw, ed., *First Federal Congress*, 1:158–65; "Madison to Washington, January 4, 1790," in Rutland et al., eds., *Madison Papers*, 12:467.

65. *Journal of the Senate of Virginia*, quoted in Levy, *Judgments*, 188.

66. "Madison to Washington January 4, 1790," in Rutland et al., eds., *Madison Papers*, 12:467, "Jefferson to William Short, December 14, 1789," in Jefferson, *Works*, 16:26.

67. Rutland et al., eds., *Madison Papers*, 11:442–43; 12:453.

68. Mark DeWolfe Howe, *The Garden and the Wilderness. Religion and Government in American Constitutional History* (Chicago, 1956). For Court decisions, see Robert T. Miller and Ronald B. Flowers, eds., *Toward Benevolent Neutrality: Church, State, and the Supreme Court* (Waco, Texas, 1982).

69. Stokes, *Church and State*, 1:448, 482. See also Leo Pfeffer, *Church, State and Freedom*, rev. ed. (Boston, 1967), 119–21.

70. *Annals of Congress*, 1:914–15. For Senate and House Resolutions, see DePauw, ed., *First Federal Congress*, 1:197, 3:237.

71. *Minutes of the Warren Association* (Boston, 1790), 6; McLoughlin, *New England Dissent*, 2:711; Isaac Backus, *The Liberal Support of Gospel Ministers* (Boston, 1790), 32, and *History*, 2:346.

72. DePauw, ed., *First Federal Congress*, 3:114, 137; Henry Steele Commager, *Documents of American History*, 9th ed., 2 vols. (Englewood Cliffs, N.J., 1973), 1:131.

73. For the attitude of Catholics, see above pp. 177, 191; For the Jewish petitioner, see Farrand, *Records*, 3:78–79, and Antieau et al., *Freedom from Federal Establishment*, 96.

74. Jensen, ed., *Ratification*, 3:500.

75. Greene, ed., *Writings of John Leland*, 75, 107, 119, 224, 254, 444, 490, 539; Butterfield, "Elder John Leland," 210. On Madison and Jefferson and religion, see Brant, "Madison: On Separation," 2–24; Elizabeth Fleet, ed., "Madison's 'Detached Memoranda'," *WMQ* 3 (1946): 534–62; Marvin Meyers, ed., *The Mind of the Founder* (Indianapolis, 1973), 6–16; Leonard W. Levy, *Jefferson and Civil Liberties. The Darker Side* (New York, 1973), 3–15, and *Judgments*, 203–14; Stokes, *Church and State*, 1:333–49; Jefferson, *Notes on the State of Virginia*, 150–56.

76. W. C. Ford, ed., *Journals of the Continental Congress, 1774–1789*, 34 vols. (Washington, D.C., 1904–37), 12:1001. For examples of similar statements from diverse states, see Antieau et al., *Freedom from Federal Establishment*, 89.

77. Hunt, ed., *Madison Writings*, 2:143; Ford, ed., *Continental Congress*, 28:292–96, 225; 32:276. See also Butts, *The American Tradition in Religion and Education* (Boston, 1950), 69–71; Ronald A. Smith, "Freedom of Religion and the Land Ordinance of 1785," *Journal of Church and State* 24 (1982): 589–602.

78. Vermont, Rhode Island, New Hampshire, New York, New Jersey, Pennsylvania, Delaware, Maryland, Virginia, North Carolina, and South Carolina ratified.
80. On the assumptions of late eighteenth-century Americans about religion, see Borden, "Federalists, Antifederalists, and Religious Freedom," 469–82.
81. "Address by Denatus to the Virginia Federal Convention," in Storing, ed., *Complete Anti-Federalist*, 5:264. For studies on non-denominational Protestantism in nineteenth-century America, see Robert T. Handy, *A Christian America: Protestant Hopes and Historical Realities*, 2nd ed. (New York, 1984); Martin E. Marty, "Living with Establishment and Disestablishment in Nineteenth-Century Anglo-America," *Journal of Church and State* 18 (1976): 61–77, and *Righteous Empire, The Protestant Experience in America* (New York, 1970).
82. Thorpe, *Constitutions*, 3:1690.
83. Borden, "Federalists, Antifederalists, and Religious Freedom," 481. For the influence of the federal Constitution on Georgia's abandonment of a test, see *Annals of Congress*, 1:444.

Index